M000288506

PLATO AND THE HERO

Plato's thinking on courage, manliness and heroism is both profound and central to his work, but these areas of his thought remain under-explored. This book examines his developing critique of both the notions and embodiments of manliness prevalent in his culture (particularly those in Homer), and his attempt to redefine them in accordance with his own ethical, psychological and metaphysical principles. It further seeks to locate the discussion within the framework of his general approach to ethics, an approach which focuses chiefly on concepts of flourishing and virtue. The question of why courage is necessary in the flourishing life in its turn leads to Plato's bid to unify the noble and the beneficial, and the tensions this unification creates between human and divine ideals. The issue of manliness also raises problems of gender: does Plato conceive of the ethical subject as human or male?

ANGELA HOBBS is Lecturer in Philosophy at the University of Warwick.

PLATO AND THE HERO

Courage, Manliness and the Impersonal Good

ANGELA HOBBS

University of Warwick

CAMBRIDGE
UNIVERSITY PRESS

CAMBRIDGE UNIVERSITY PRESS
Cambridge, New York, Melbourne, Madrid, Cape Town, Singapore, São Paulo

Cambridge University Press
The Edinburgh Building, Cambridge CB2 2RU, UK

Published in the United States of America by Cambridge University Press, New York

www.cambridge.org
Information on this title: www.cambridge.org/9780521417334

© Cambridge University Press 2000

This publication is in copyright. Subject to statutory exception
and to the provisions of relevant collective licensing agreements,
no reproduction of any part may take place without
the written permission of Cambridge University Press.

First published 2000
This digitally printed first paperback version 2006

A catalogue record for this publication is available from the British Library

Library of Congress Cataloguing in Publication data
Hobbs, Angela.
Plato and the hero : courage, manliness, and the impersonal good / Angela Hobbs.
p. cm.
Includes bibliographical references and index.
ISBN 0 521 41733 3 (hardback)
1. Plato – Contributions in concept of courage. 2. Plato – Contributions in concept of
masculinity. 3. Courage – History. 4. Masculinity – History. I. Title.
B398.C69 H63 2000
179′.6′092 – dc21   99-050142

ISBN-13 978-0-521-41733-4 hardback
ISBN-10 0-521-41733-3 hardback

ISBN-13 978-0-521-02897-4 paperback
ISBN-10 0-521-02897-3 paperback

For my mother, and in memory of my father

Contents

Acknowledgements

During the writing of this book I have benefited from the generosity of many. Work on it began whilst I was a Research Fellow at Christ's College, Cambridge, and was completed in the Philosophy Department at Warwick University, and I am grateful to my colleagues at both institutions for their friendship and support – and of course for providing me with the opportunity to write anything at all. And as some of the ideas and research have their roots in my Ph.D. thesis, I should also like to express my thanks to the Fellows of New Hall, Cambridge, and to the members of the Cambridge Classics Faculty for their assistance throughout.

My intellectual debts to individuals are manifold, though no one but myself should be held responsible for – or indeed assumed necessarily to endorse – a single sentence of what follows. My interest in ancient philosophy was first aroused, and then nourished, by the teaching and work of M. M. McCabe; I am profoundly grateful both for that early guidance, and for her continued advice and support. Geoffrey Lloyd, Malcolm Schofield and David Sedley are also teachers to whom I owe much. All of them have helped me (whether knowingly or not) with certain issues in the present work, and I have also received invaluable assistance on a number of points from Christine Battersby, Frank Beetham, Paul Cartledge, Christopher Gill, Michael Hobbs, T. I. Irwin, Mary-Hannah Jones, Penelope Murray, Peter Poellner, Christopher Rowe, Dominic Scott, Robert Sharples, C. C. W. Taylor, Martin Warner, Simon Williams and Michael Whitby. I should also like to take this opportunity to thank the Feminist Philosophy Society at Warwick University for many stimulating discussions, and all my students over many years for their often penetrating questions and robust scepticism about my suggested answers; both groups have made me look at several topics in a fresh light.

My greatest intellectual debt, however, is to my former supervisor, Myles Burnyeat, from whose intellectual acuity and breadth of vision I have received immeasurable benefit. He has been generous with his time and knowledge far beyond the call of duty, and he has my deep gratitude and respect.

It is a pleasure, too, to record various other forms of help. My long-suffering editor, Pauline Hire, has displayed great patience over a project that took far longer to complete than intended; I have further profited from the painstaking care and useful suggestions of my copy-editor, Linda Woodward. Cliff Robinson produced a wonderful cover illustration at very short notice. Profound thanks are also due to my mother and late father for their constant support, good humour and relaxed encouragement – as well as for refusing to let me give up Latin when I was twelve, despite my urgent pleadings. I owe them more than I can say. And David Gibbins has provided strength, succour and wise advice during many periods of the book's production – particularly in the final stages which have coincided with the birth of our beautiful daughter, Molly. For his patience and presence, he has my thanks and love.

Preface

This book arose initially from my fascination with certain of the Platonic Socrates' interlocutors, and in particular with Callicles and Alcibiades. Why was Plato so ready to give room to the views of such unSocratic and charismatic opponents? The answer, I believed, had largely to do with his abiding interest in different conceptions of manliness and courage (*andreia*), and hence also with different conditions of the spirited element of the *Republic*'s tripartite *psuchē* (the *thumos*), with which *andreia* is especially connected. At this juncture I came across Allan Bloom's interpretative essay on the *Republic*, in which he highlights the central role played by Achilles in Books 2 and 3, and it became evident that Plato's concern with Achilles throughout the early and middle dialogues was also part of this interest in notions of *andreia*. In short, it seemed to me that there was a book to be written on *andreia* and *thumos* in early and middle Plato, focusing not only on the theoretical discussions of the *Laches* and *Protagoras*, but also on these three characters (who were quickly joined by Thrasymachus).

Such a study necessarily touches on many overlapping aspects of Plato's thought. The introduction of Achilles inevitably raises the issue of Plato's complex attitude to Homer, and his ambivalent deployment of other Homeric heroes, most notably Odysseus. Such topics in their turn prompt questions concerning role models and education in general, and relations between individual and community. And these questions can only properly be understood when viewed in the context of Plato's overall approach to ethics, which takes the fundamental ethical concerns to be 'how should one live?' and 'what sort of person should one be?' – in brief, an ethics chiefly of flourishing and virtue, rather than one of, say, consequences or duties. But if flourishing is so important, then we may well wonder where this leaves courage: does courage not require that one be prepared to forgo personal wellbeing for the noble and fine? In Plato, such difficulties will rapidly lead to a consideration not simply of the relation between fine and beneficial particulars, but between the Forms of the Beautiful and the Good themselves. Furthermore, the concentration on *andreia* also brings to the surface the question of gender: does Plato conceive of the ethical subject as human or male? What form does *andreia* take in the female Auxiliaries and the Philosopher-Queens?

The chapters that follow are supposed to form a continuous argument, and I have accordingly provided a fairly large number of cross-references to enable the reader to keep the whole in mind. I also hope that such references will help those who only have the time, or inclination, to pursue a particular topic. Constraints of space have meant that only the material most directly relevant to *andreia* in the early and middle dialogues could be included; consideration of *andreia* in the *Politicus* and *Laws*, therefore, is confined to a brief epilogue. Nor is there any exploration of *thumos* in the *Phaedrus* or *Timaeus*, dialogues in which *andreia* is not a central theme. I am sadder that I have had to restrict myself to examining Plato's use of (arguably) 'masculine' imagery, although much could be said of his deployment of images concerned with pregnancy, midwifery and weaving. Such discussions must wait for another occasion.

Some words of explanation are needed on the practices I have adopted regarding certain controversial issues. 'Socrates' refers to the character who appears in the Platonic dialogues, a character I distinguish from the 'historical Socrates'. 'Plato' refers to the author of the dialogues, who may or may not endorse the views and arguments put into Socrates' mouth. Another vexed question for any modern classicist (particularly one who thinks of herself as a feminist) is whether to employ 'he' or 'she'. After much thought I have used 'he' when paraphrasing ancient arguments, unless the context makes it absolutely clear that women are – or at least could be – the subject. My reasons for this will, I hope, become clear in the course of this book: very briefly, it is one of my main contentions that, despite the radical proposals of the *Meno* and *Republic* 5, Plato still usually writes both about and for males, even when it seems at first glance that an ungendered 'human' subject is in play.

Further decisions are required regarding the respective use of such terms as 'subject', 'person' and 'self'. When discussing 'how should I live?' questions, I have tended to employ 'person' and 'subject' (or 'ethical subject') interchangeably: for the purposes of this book, it is persons and subjects who live certain kinds of life. When discussing 'who am I?' questions, I have generally talked of the 'self'; it should be stressed that such talk is not supposed to imply any Cartesian theory of self-transparency, though it may well include capacities for various forms of second-order reasoning or feeling. Since Plato suggests a number of answers to 'who am I?' questions, he correspondingly operates with a number of different senses of what I have termed 'self'. Sometimes 'I' am viewed as my *psuchē*-plus-body; sometimes as my embodied *psuchē* or personality; and sometimes as a particular part or aspect of my *psuchē*, the part which survives bodily death and which is perceived as somehow 'truly' me, essential and not contingent on embodiment. There is thus a distinction in some passages between what we might loosely call the 'self' and the 'true self' (though again we should be careful not to read such a distinction in the light of any particular modern metaphysics, such as that of Kant).

In respect of whether to use translation, transliteration or the original Greek, my aim has been to make the main text accessible to the Greekless reader, whilst providing enough evidence for the classicist to test my claims. In the main text, therefore, passages of Greek are translated, while single terms are either translated or transliterated (see the Glossary); original Greek only appears in the notes, though even here I have employed translation and transliteration of single words. Unless otherwise stated, all translations are my own. The two exceptions are the translations used of the *Republic* and the *Iliad*, where I have usually employed Lee and Lattimore respectively. Where I have adapted their translations (or, in the case of the *Republic*, provided my own), I have specified this in the notes.

Finally, an apology to Christopher Gill. Some readers may well be surprised that Gill's absorbing and important study of personality in Greek literature (Gill: 1996) is not discussed in either the main text or the notes. The reason for this is simple. *Plato and the Hero* has been through a number of drafts, and when Gill's work appeared I had just begun what I (correctly) hoped was the final version. In consequence, I took the difficult decision not to read his book until my own text was finished: I knew that our interests overlap at a number of points, and I was concerned that if I took the time to reflect on and respond to his ideas, the completion of my task would be delayed still further. As I express in the Acknowledgements and Bibliography, however, in writing the present study I have profited greatly from other work of Professor Gill, as well as from a number of stimulating discussions with him.

Glossary

The following transliterations occur most frequently in the text. All are accompanied by a translation on at least their first appearance; after that, however, they generally appear on their own. In several cases the question of how best to translate the term, both in general and specific contexts, is a matter of dispute, and some of these words are discussed in the text; in particular, the issues surrounding the translation of *thumos* and *andreia* are absolutely central to the book. It should also be noted that many of the terms can be translated in far more ways than those indicated here. This glossary, therefore, should be taken as a rough guide only.

agathon (s.)/*agatha* (pl.)	good, beneficial (thing/s)
aischron/*aischra*	foul, shameful, ugly (thing/s)
andreia	manliness, courage
andreios/*a*/*on* (s.)	manly, courageous
andreĩa (pl.)	manly, courageous (deeds)
aretē	excellence, virtue
doxa	opinion, belief
epistēmē	knowledge
epithumētikon	the appetitive part of the *psuchē* (hence 'epithumeitic': pertaining to the *epithumētikon*)
epitēdeuma/*ata*	practice, habit
erōs	erotic love
eudaimonia	flourishing, happiness
harmonia	mode (in music), harmony
hēdonē	pleasure
hēdu	pleasant, pleasurable
kakon/*kaka*	bad, harmful (thing/s)
kala erga	fine and noble deeds

xvi

kalon/kala	fine, noble, praiseworthy, beautiful (thing/s)
kalos k'agathos	gentleman
logistikon	the reasoning part of the *psuchē*
logos	reason, argument
megalopsuchia	greatness of soul
mousikē	literary, artistic and musical culture
nomos	law, convention
phronēsis	practical wisdom
phusis	nature
psuchē	psyche, soul, personality
sōphrosunē	temperance, self-control
sōma	body
technē	skill, craft
thumos	life-force, mettle, the spirited part of the *psuchē* (hence 'thumoeidic': pertaining to the *thumos*)
timē	honour, respect

CHAPTER I

The puzzle of Plato's thumos

THE LIFE OF REASON AND THE LIFE OF DESIRE

In Plato's early dialogue the *Gorgias*, Socrates and his interlocutor Callicles debate what Socrates says is the most important question of all: how one should live.[1] Socrates argues for the philosophic life, in which one's desires are ordered by reason; Callicles advocates the life of the forceful man of affairs, who as far as possible acts as he pleases both in public and private. Underlying their differences lies an implicit disagreement about the nature of the self.[2] While both appear to believe that the human personality consists of two main aspects, reason and the desires,[3] Socrates seems to identify himself with the former, whereas Callicles identifies himself with the latter. Thus for Socrates freedom and happiness depend on the desires' obedience to reason, while for Callicles freedom and happiness depend on reason's obedience to the desires. Callicles is adamant that it is his view of human nature that is correct: the philosopher is a pathetic creature who is entirely ignorant of human pleasures and desires and the characters of men.[4] When Socrates asks whether Callicles agrees that those who need nothing are happy, Callicles scathingly replies that if that were true then

---

[1] 500c; see also 492d and 487a and pp. 50–1 below.

[2] Although Socrates' and Callicles' dispute is not explicitly framed in such terms, their different conceptions of freedom, slavery and happiness are most naturally read as implying different conceptions of a 'true self' (for my use of the terms 'self', 'true self', 'person' and 'subject' see Preface pp. xiii–xiv; for a similar dispute see *Resp.* 589c). The interchange between Socrates and Callicles is discussed in detail in ch. 5.

[3] See for example 491d–494a, especially 492a. From 491–4 reason and the desires both appear to be located in the *psuchē* (e.g. at 493a). In 505a–b, however, a distinction is made between the desires of the *psuchē* and the desires of the body; whether the latter group are still located in the *psuchē* in some way is unclear. In order to make sure of covering both reason and all the desires, therefore, it is safer to speak of 'personality' rather than '*psuchē*' in this context.

[4] 484d.

stones and corpses would be happiest of all. *Impasse* appears to have been reached. Although Callicles later formally capitulates to Socrates, he also claims that he is only agreeing with him so that the discussion may be brought to a speedy conclusion.[5] One may well feel that the dialogue concludes without the potential for conflict between reason and the desires being properly addressed.

The *Phaedo*, too, portrays reason and at least the majority of desires as naturally tending in different directions,[6] and maps this division on to an alleged division between *psuchē* and *sōma*. The *psuchē* is said to consist of reason alone and its desire for truth (66a); all other desires and fears are connected with the body (66c) and both deceive and hinder the *psuchē* in its search for knowledge. Yet it is in this search for knowledge that true happiness, salvation and virtue lie. The virtuous person, therefore, must as far as possible cut himself off from the body and its distractions and try to become pure disembodied reason. The practice of philosophy and virtue thus becomes a practice for death (66a; 67e).

Two problems immediately present themselves. Firstly, it is far from clear in the *Phaedo* how such an austere and remote ideal is to be achieved. How can the desire for truth win out on its own against all the myriad and powerful desires of the body, which here comprise not only the desires for food, drink and sex, but *all* other desires, including the love of honour (68c2)? It does not seem a particularly likely prospect. Even if such transcendence were possible, however, it is improbable that many would wish to attain it. To the uninitiated such an ideal could seem repugnant: Callicles' apprehensions about the life of reason being that of a stone or corpse appear to be justified. Yet no one is born an initiate of philosophy; the rational ideal needs to be attractive. As in the *Gorgias*, Plato's psychology in the *Phaedo* presents considerable difficulties.

In the *Republic*, however, the picture of the human personality becomes considerably more complex. All the desires, including the physical appetites, are now firmly located in the *psuchē* rather than the body. Even more importantly, the *psuchē* is now divided into three elements: reason, the appetites and the *thumos* or *thumoeides*.[7]

---

[5] E.g. 501c; 505c.   [6] See especially 61b–69e.
[7] The relation between the two terms is discussed pp. 6–7 below.

Each element is analogous to one of the three classes in the ideally just state: reason to the Rulers, the *thumos* to the Auxiliaries and the appetites to the Producers. Although *thumos* is normally translated 'spirit' or 'spiritedness', the exact meaning of the term in the *Republic*, and its function within the work, have generally been regarded as highly problematic. I believe that the *thumos* plays a vital role within the dialogue and is used by Plato as the focal point for a number of key issues; while some of these issues are new to the *Republic*, most have been raised in earlier works such as the *Gorgias* but left unresolved. It is in consequence the *thumos* which forms the axis for this book.

THE PUZZLE OF THE *THUMOS*

At first sight the *thumos* of the *Republic* seems one of the more bizarre creations of an already bizarrely creative period in Plato's life. At different points it is connected with a very wide range of characteristics, not all of which obviously cohere: anger, aggression and courage; self-disgust and shame; a sense of justice, indignation and the desire for revenge; obedience to the political authorities though not necessarily to one's father; a longing for honour, glory and worldly success; some interest in the arts but a fear of intellectualism; a preference for war over peace and increasing meanness over money. It is perhaps not surprising that the majority of critics, even amongst Plato's most sympathetic commentators, have been sceptical or puzzled in their treatment of the *thumos*. In the comparison at 588b–d of the tripartite soul to a composite mythical beast, it might initially appear that the *thumos* has as much in common with the 'complex and many-headed monster' supposed to represent the appetites, as it does with its own symbol of the lion.

It is more difficult to understand why so few have been concerned to see whether its various features form an intelligible and important motivational set. Hardie and Penner, for example, hold that Plato never really provides justification for anything more than a bipartite division of the *psuchē* into rational and irrational faculties, and Penner in particular is uncompromising in his belief that the *thumos* is only created in Book 4 for *ad hoc* political and moral purposes, chief of which is the completion of the analogy between soul and state.[8] Plato's true view is to be found in the traditional rational/irrational distinction of Book 10.[9] Robinson finds the *thumos* 'ambiguous' and 'amphibian', and the epithets Plato uses to describe it 'confused'. Like Penner, he thinks its main function is purely *ad hoc*: 'But for the political analogy, one's first reaction would be to place it among the "desires", or "crude impulses" which go to form the "desiderative element" ...' 'On the face of it Plato stands open to the charge of a mild self-contradiction here, and one probably does him most justice by letting it stand as such.' The status of the *thumos* remains irredeemably 'obscure'.[10] Nussbaum admits that the relation of the *thumos* to reason is 'more complex' than that of the basic bodily desires, but nevertheless holds that Plato's account of it is 'cryptic' and 'not consistently invoked'. In general she judges it best simply to couple it with the appetitive element as forming the 'non-intellectual elements'.[11]

Even critics who do think the *thumos* represents some important aspects of our motivation pay it surprisingly scant attention, and few have considered whether these aspects form a coherent set. Those that have made the attempt have generally replied in the negative. Annas, for instance, distinguishes a tendency to aggression and violence and a delight in victory and honours, but says that it is 'hard ... to characterize this part in a way bringing out its character as a single source of motivation ... Plato seems to be talking about two very different kinds of thing'.[12] In this vein we also find Guthrie, who in a very brief reference holds that the *thumos* covers fighting spirit and remorse, but does not suggest any particular link between these characteristics.[13] Crombie, too, although favourable to Plato's account, simply groups the complex manifestations of the *thumos* under the vague headings of 'non-rational response' or 'capacity to feel', which scarcely serves to distinguish the activities of the *thumos* from those of the appetitive part.[14]

---

[8] Hardie 1936: 141–3; Penner 1971: 111–13.
[9] For a discussion of the bipartite division of the *psuchē* in *Resp.* 10, see pp. 36–7 below.
[10] Robinson 1995: 44–5.
[11] Nussbaum 1986: 272 and note; the *thumos* is coupled with the appetitive element on p. 214.
[12] Annas 1981: 126–8.
[13] Guthrie 1975: 474.
[14] Crombie 1962: 344–5.

Not all the verdicts on the *thumos*, however, are negative or cursory. Cornford makes some suggestive comparisons between the Platonic *thumos* and the psychological theories of his day, and there is a suitably spirited defence in Cross and Woozley.[15] Most illuminating of all are the discussions in Gosling and in Cairns.[16] There is no question, however, that in bestowing such careful attention on the *thumos* they are in a minority.

Nevertheless, such positive reactions to the *thumos* provide the most rewarding approach to the subject for a very good reason: they do justice to Plato's own remarks on the importance of the *Republic*'s tripartite *psuchē* for understanding the dialogue as a whole. The fundamental question of the *Republic* is whether a 'better life is provided for the unjust man than for the just by both gods and men' (362c), and Plato is adamant that this question can only be resolved through an understanding of human psychology. At 580d, during the detailed attempt to show that the necessarily just philosopher has the happiest type of life, we are told that

Since we divided the mind of the individual into three elements (*eidē*), corresponding to the three classes of the state, this makes a further proof possible.

This is because each of the three elements has its own set of pleasures and desires, distinguished by three different types of desired object: reason desires truth and reality, the appetites desire food, drink and sex and the money needed to acquire them, and the *thumos* desires glory and worldly success. Furthermore, each type of desire, if allowed to predominate, gives rise to a whole way of life. The choice offered to us in the *Gorgias* has thus become more complicated: there are now three kinds of life between which we must choose. Which kind will make us happiest will depend on which of the three aspects of our *psuchē* has the superior pleasures and goals.

It is this dependence of ethics on psychology which accounts for the emphatic exchange between Socrates and Adeimantus at 504a. Socrates asks whether Adeimantus remembers how they distinguished three elements of the *psuchē*, and accordingly went on to analyse the four cardinal virtues of courage, wisdom, self-control

---

[15] Cornford 1930: 206–19; contrast his earlier dismissal of the *thumos* in Cornford 1912: 246–65. Cross and Woozley 1964: 120–3.
[16] Gosling 1973: 41–51. Cairns 1993: 383–92.

and justice. Adeimantus replies that, 'If I did not remember that, I should not have any claim to hear the rest of the argument.'

Plato, if not the majority of his modern critics, certainly believes his tripartite – not bipartite – division of the *psuchē* to be fundamental. This does not of course mean that he is necessarily right, but it does mean that we should at least give the *thumos* serious consideration and try to understand why Plato places the significance on it that he does.

THUMOS OR THUMOEIDES?

The first question that we need to face is a methodological one: when referring to the *Republic*, should one speak of '*thumos*', 'the *thumos*' or 'the *thumoeides*'? I believe that the real question here is whether the passage is primarily viewing *thumos* informally as a quality or emotion (or a cluster of qualities and/or emotions), or formally as the set of qualities and emotions which makes up one part of the tripartite *psuchē*.[17] When Plato's chief concern is with a quality or emotion *simpliciter*, as in Book 2, he employs *(ho) thumos* and *(to) thumoeides* interchangeably. However, when he is considering the set of such qualities and emotions as a formal part in relation to a general anatomy of the *psuchē*, he usually, though not invariably,[18] employs *to thumoeides*. For the sake of clarity, I have used '*thumos*' on its own, without the definite article, for a quality or emotion (or cluster of qualities and emotions) viewed *simpliciter*. When discussing such qualities or emotions as a distinct part of the tripartite *psuchē*, I have generally used 'the *thumos*', and occasionally 'the *thumoeides*'. The reason I have modified Plato's own practice and employed 'the *thumos*' more often than 'the *thumoeides*' when referring to the part is purely stylistic: repeated use of 'the *thumoeides*' can daunt the eye. What matters is not which term is used to render the Greek, but whether one feels it should be prefaced in English by a definite article.

This, however, is not always so easy to decide. Given Plato's relatively relaxed terminology, it is sometimes difficult to know

---

[17] Similarily, we may talk of 'reason' and 'appetite', or 'the reasoning element' and 'the appetitive element'. The latter phrase explicitly relates reason and appetite to a general anatomy or theory of the *psuchē*; the former does not (though it does not preclude it).

[18] E.g. 439e.

whether *thumos* or *thumoeides* is to be viewed primarily as a formal part or not. The trickiest passages come in Book 3: although the *psuchē* has not yet been formally divided, a number of comparisons are made between its thumoeidic and philosophic elements. I have generally found it more natural to speak of 'the *thumos*' here.

One might also wonder how much really depends even on the use of the English definite article. Is there any significant difference in reference between '*thumos*' or 'the *thumos*', or is it simply a matter of the context in which *thumos* is viewed? The answer will naturally depend on how one interprets Plato's language concerning parts of the soul. When talking of a part is he speaking of a distinct *source* of a motivational set, or simply of the motivational set itself? And what, if anything, hangs in practice on even this distinction? These are complicated issues, and will be discussed in more detail below.[19] The main point to bear in mind here is that any distinction between '*thumos*' and 'the *thumos*'/'the *thumoeides*' is by no means watertight.

A similar problem occurs when attempting to translate '*thumos*' in earlier authors. Although Plato is the first to treat the *thumos* as a separate part of the *psuchē*, there is still an ambivalence in earlier writers between viewing it as a passion (or set of passions) or as the physical embodiment or source of the passion. Again, in the former case it usually seems more natural to speak of '*thumos*' alone, in the latter to speak of 'the *thumos*'. But here too it would be unwise to make any very sharp distinctions.

THUMOS IN HOMER

Plato does not discuss the relation between Homeric[20] *thumos* and his own use of the term, but the simple fact that the *psuchē* in Homer is not presented as tripartite shows that the *thumos* of the *Republic* cannot be precisely the same conception. Nevertheless, when searching for a name for the third part of the *psuchē*, Plato deliberately chose a word with strong Homeric connotations. Before looking at *thumos* in the *Republic*, therefore, we should first consider what those connotations might have been.

[19] Pp. 33–7.
[20] This is not the place to debate whether the *Iliad* and the *Odyssey* are principally the work of one, two or more individuals. For the purposes of this book, 'Homer' is simply a term employed to refer to the authorship and contents of both poems.

In the *Iliad* and *Odyssey*, *thumos* is a general term for both the seat of feeling and thought and for the passions themselves, particularly anger. Amongst a wide range of meanings, Liddell and Scott offer 'soul', 'the principle of life, feeling and thought'; 'breath'; 'heart'; 'desire'; 'mind, temper, will'; 'spirit, courage'; 'anger'. They also endorse Plato's derivation of the word from *thuō*, 'rage', 'seethe'.[21] In an illuminating discussion, Onians refines Liddell and Scott's loose identification of *thumos* with both breath and heart and argues that the *thumos* in Homer is the breath, which in turn is the moist, warm vapour arising from the blood concentrated in both heart and lungs.[22] It is a physical thing with spiritual dimensions, the stuff of consciousness, passions and thought. It is perhaps best viewed as the life force, and from it stem fierceness and energy (*menos*), boldness and courage (*tharsos*) and anger (*cholos*). This connection between *thumos*, fierceness and courage continues with the tragic poets; of particular significance from the point of view of the *Republic* is Aeschylus' *Seven Against Thebes*, where it is said of warriors before a battle that, 'Their iron-lunged *thumos*, blazing with valour, Breathed out as if from lions glaring with the war-god's might.'[23] The word rendered 'valour' is *andreia*, and literally means 'manliness'. We shall see shortly just how difficult this word is to translate.

THUMOS IN THE REPUBLIC

Book 2

While we clearly cannot know whether Plato interpreted Homer as Onians does on this issue, Onians' reading does help us to make sense of the first mention of *thumos* in the *Republic*, at 375a–376c. In Book 1 the sophist Thrasymachus has forcefully presented the case for injustice, arguing that the unjust man leads a better life than the just,[24] and Socrates has been challenged by Glaucon and Adeimantus to defend the intrinsic benefits of justice, irrespective

---

[21] *Cratylus* 419e. *Thumos* is said to possess its name ἀπὸ τῆς θύσεως καὶ ζέσεως τῆς ψυχῆς, 'from the raging and boiling of the soul'.

[22] Onians 1951: 22–5; 44–57.

[23] *Sept.* 52–3. The translation is adapted from the version of Ewans (1996).

[24] Thrasymachus is discussed in ch. 5 pp. 164–74.

of consequences. At 369a Socrates replies that before considering justice in the individual, it will be easier to examine it first on the broader canvas of an imaginary and ideally organized state; the purpose of the search (implied in 369 and made explicit at 420b–c) is to see whether the effects of justice are advantageous or otherwise to the state as a whole. Once this is decided, they are then to consider whether their findings about justice in the state can be transferred to the individual person.

Socrates therefore begins to construct a picture of an ideally just community based on economic exchange and the principle that each person should perform only one job: specialization both accords with the natural distribution of skills and allows the citizens to concentrate on perfecting their particular task. Initially this community consists of just one class: everyone is both a producer and a consumer of goods and services. Glaucon scornfully complains that such a life would be fit only for pigs, and in response Socrates allows the introduction of more sophisticated activities and pursuits. As the community expands, however, it comes into conflict with its neighbours, and an army is required. On the principle that no one should perform more than one job, this army will form a separate class, termed Guardians (374d).

The Guardians will need to be endowed with certain natural qualities: speed, strength and courage (*andreia*). *Andreia*, however, requires *thumos*: it is *thumos* which makes both men and animals fearless and indomitable. The problem is how to ensure that this necessary aggressiveness is directed towards the enemy alone, and does not turn against its own side. Those chosen as Guardians must possess characters which combine *thumos* with its natural opposite, gentleness; further, they must be naturally inclined to display this gentleness to those they know, reserving *thumos* for strangers.

The fact that *thumos* is now said to be crucial for the exercise of *andreia* is a major development in Plato's thinking. In the *Laches*, *andreia* is at one point defined solely as 'knowledge of what is to be feared and what dared', and in the *Protagoras* Socrates defines it as 'knowledge of what is and is not to be feared'.[25] At this stage in the *Republic* we do not know what the relation is between *andreia*

---

[25] *Laches* 194e12–195a1; *Protagoras* 360d4–5. These definitions are discussed on pp. 99–112 and 130–5 below.

and knowledge; but we do know that knowledge alone will not be enough. At the very least there must also be emotional commitment and drive. This may in general seem more plausible than the earlier definitions, but we may also wonder exactly what *kind* of emotional drive is required. Is it really necessary to become so worked up that one risks being aggressive to one's friends? Does the virtue of courage always require to be driven by such a volatile force? The reference to *thumos* making its possessor 'fearless' is also striking. In what sense do courageous people need to be fearless? Might one not argue that on the contrary the courageous are those who do feel fear, but still take risks for what they perceive as the greater good? Is it not rather the insensible and the stupid who feel no fear?

Before considering any definitions of *andreia*, however, we need to consider precisely how the term should be translated. The context of the Book 2 passage makes it clear that the virtue of courage is being discussed, but we also need to ask whether the word here retains its original meaning of 'manliness'. *Thumos* is certainly necessary for courage; is it also being claimed that courage is a male preserve? If so, does this mean that *thumos* is itself a male preserve? If it is, then serious problems will arise when we come to the tripartite psychology of Book 4, in which the *thumos* is part of the make-up of every human, male and female. Difficulties will also occur when we consider the female Guardians of Book 5, who are said to possess the same virtues as their male counterparts, including *andreia*, and consequently are to go to war. These are complex issues, and we will see in the next chapter just why it is so particularly difficult to translate *andreia* in any Platonic dialogue; in the course of the book some suggestions will be made about how Plato wanted the term to be read.

Whatever the precise meaning of *andreia* here, it is clear that both it and *thumos* are at this stage of the dialogue perceived as being of use primarily in war. This prompts the question of whether *thumos* and *andreia* – and indeed the military class in general – have a role to play in peacetime. It also helps explain why *thumos* is seen as such an ambivalent force, with the capacity both to save the state and to cause it great harm: what is to become of all that adrenalin when it is not needed on the battlefield? Can it just be switched off? It will plainly have to be handled with extreme care.

Primary education (Books 2 and 3)

We see the form that this careful handling should take in the account of the future Guardians' primary education which follows. Although this education is directed at the *psuchē* in general,[26] it is significant that the question of education is raised immediately after the introduction of the need for *thumos*, and the claim that it is also potentially dangerous. It is also significant that we have just been told (375e10) that the future Guardians will require the disposition of a watchdog: the *thumos* is explicitly compared to a sheepdog at 440d2. The summing-up of the proposals for early education from 410b–412a further clarifies that the *thumos* is a principal target: the primary education of the future Guardians should aim to achieve the correct balance between stimulating the *thumos* and civilizing it. If the *thumos* is stimulated by physical training to the correct degree then, as in 375a, its possessor will be courageous (*andreios*: 410d; 411c), but if it is overstrained its possessor will be wild, hard and harsh (410d). His life will be one of ignorance and awkwardness, without rhythm or grace (411e). This danger can be avoided if physical training is combined with literary and musical studies (simply termed *mousikē* in the Greek) which make the *thumos* softer and more workable, as iron is softened by the furnace (411a–b). It can then exist in harmony with the gentler 'philosophic' element of the *psuchē*, which if appropriately nurtured by the same studies in *mousikē* makes its possessor civilized and orderly (410e). However, if *mousikē* is emphasized at the expense of athletic pursuits, then the balance will be upset and the *thumos* will become too soft: it will 'melt and run'. In consequence the 'sinews of the soul' will be cut out and the boy will end up a poor fighter. If he does not contain much *thumos* anyway, then he will just be feeble and passive; but if he is naturally thumoeidic (*thumoeidēs* 411b7), then his unused *thumos* will make him irritable and unstable.

This accent on *thumos* should not be surprising. Socrates makes it clear at 429e7–430a1 that the first stage of education is specifically directed towards the young Guardians *qua* future soldiers, the *thumos*' equivalent in the analogy between state and soul. Even

---

[26] 410c. At 441a, however, Glaucon says that reason does not develop until after early childhood (he does not say precisely when).

though some of the soldiers will later be selected for further math-
ematical and philosophic training, this is not Socrates' present
concern.

Several points immediately strike us. Firstly, the *thumos* is susceptible not only to physical training but also to poetry and music.
This is made even clearer at 442a, where it is reaffirmed that the
programme for primary education 'tones down and soothes the
spirited element by mode (*harmonia*)[27] and rhythm'. Furthermore,
if we regard the *thumos* as being a principal target throughout the
whole section from 376c–412a, then it seems plain that *mousikē*
is not only able to soften the *thumos*, but to stir it up as well. At
399a–c the Dorian mode in music is said to represent the brave
man on military service, and Socrates is emphatic that representations stimulate imitative behaviour in both the players and the
audience. Though the *thumos* is not explicitly mentioned it would
be perverse to exclude it from a context which mentions courage
and fighting. The young Guardians are also prone to imitate literary representations of warrior heroes (388a; 388d), and Socrates
is consequently concerned that epic and tragic heroes should be
portrayed as calmly courageous and resilient.[28] Again, though the
thumos is not explicitly mentioned, the talk of courage and endurance makes it clear that it will be directly affected by the kind of
heroes portrayed. The *thumos*, therefore, is emerging as a more
complex phenomenon than it originally appeared. It is not simply
a raw drive, but is responsive to rhythm, mode and beauty. It is
also highly susceptible to – indeed partly formed by – social and
cultural influences, particularly its society's heroes. We are not yet
in a position to understand exactly why the *thumos* both responds
to sensible beauty and searches out role models, but it is vital to
note that it does. It is not just Homeric 'mettle'.

The portrayal of *andreia* in this section helps us to appreciate
just why *thumos* needs to be as precisely attuned as it does. *Andreia* is
not represented as wild risk-taking or a lust for killing, but as calm,
controlled endurance (e.g. 399a–e). Control requires balance. A
more puzzling feature is Socrates' insistence that the *andreios* does
not fear death, or only to a very slight degree (386a–387c): again,

---

[27] See n. 31 p. 62 below.
[28] For a detailed discussion of Socrates' exploration of role models in the *Republic*, see chs.
7 and 8.

one might initially suppose that such fearlessness would be more likely to be linked with ill-attuned recklessness.[29]

The association between *thumos* and *andreia* also returns us to the question of gender. We saw when considering 375–6 that it was unclear whether the *thumos'* link to *andreia* was to be regarded simply as a link to courage or also as a link to manliness, and we noted the problems a connection with manliness would present for the tripartite psychology of Book 4 and, in particular, for the courageous female Guardians of Book 5. This ambiguity is also apparent in 376–412. However, although the word '*andreia*' is itself inconclusive, it seems clear that at this stage of the dialogue Socrates is only concerned with the education of males: there is absolutely no suggestion as yet that any of the Guardians are to be women, and a number of explicit references to the 'young men' (*neoi*) to whom this early education is directed.[30] In consequence Socrates concentrates solely on role models who are both male and for men; the young male Guardians are not to be allowed to imitate women at all:

Since we care for our Guardians and say that they must become good men, we will not allow them, being men, to imitate a woman, whether young or old.[31] (395d5–7)

At this stage of the *Republic*, then, *andreia* as 'manliness' seems very much to the fore. It would therefore seem that the *thumos* which is required for *andreia* is also associated with the notion of manliness at this juncture. Whether these links are essential or contingent is one of the questions that this book will address.

One final point. There is just one reference to *andreia* which might seem to contradict this link. At 381a Socrates maintains that the most courageous (*andreiotatēn*) and wisest type of *psuchē* is that which is least liable to be altered by external influences. This might appear unexceptionable, except that here Socrates is talking primarily about the nature of god. In what sense, if any, can god

---

[29] The general depiction of *andreia* in *Resp.* 2 and 3 will be discussed in more detail in chapter 8. The complex relation between courage and fear is discussed further pp. 22, 99–102, 130–2 and 235–6 below.

[30] E.g. 388d2; 390a4; 391d6; 392a1; 401c6; 404d5. And notice that the discussion in 402d–403c of the relation between early education and later sexual relations concentrates solely on male homosexuality.

[31] Οὐ δὴ ἐπιτρέψομεν ... ὧν φαμὲν κήδεσθαι καὶ δεῖν αὐτοὺς ἄνδρας ἀγαθοὺς γενέσθαι, γυναῖκα μιμεῖσθαι ἄνδρας ὄντας, ἢ νέαν ἢ πρεσβυτέραν.

be said to be 'manly'? Or is 'courageous' here supposed to transcend gender?

Book 4

The central discussion of the *thumos* comes in 434d–444e, in the
analysis of the different elements in the *psuchē* which account for
mental conflict. To see how it operates, however, we first need to
return to Socrates' search for justice on the broader canvas of the
ideally organized state.

In 412b ff., after the account of the Guardians' early education,
Socrates proceeds to divide the Guardian class into two: the military class are now called Auxiliaries (414b), and are to assist an
elite group of Rulers, whose task is to plan and care for the
state as a whole. Socrates then proceeds to locate the virtues of
the state in the functions performed by its three classes and in the
relations between them. It is owing to the wisdom of its Rulers
that the state as a whole will be wise (428d), and owing to the
courage (*andreia*) of its Auxiliaries that the state as a whole is courageous (429b). Moderation or self-control (*sōphrosunē*) in the state
results when all three classes agree about who ought to rule (431d–
e), and the desires of the majority of the citizens are controlled by
the (rational) desires and wisdom of the Rulers (431c–d); it is thus
a kind of harmony or concord and, unlike wisdom or courage, belongs to all three classes. Finally, justice is the condition which
makes all the other virtues possible: the condition that each individual perform his or her own job and not interfere with anyone
else (433d). And if each person is performing his or her job, then,
even more critically, each class will also be performing its proper
function. It is this maintenance of the proper divisions between
classes that can strictly be termed justice in the state (434b–c).

Justice, therefore, appears on this account to be in Socrates'
eyes unquestionably beneficial to the state: it makes for peace and
security, wise ruling and concord between the classes. Without it,
the state would simply fall apart (434b).[32] Thrasymachus' challenge, however, was directed at justice in the individual. If Soc-

---

[32] What seems unquestionably beneficial to Socrates has not, of course, seemed so to all
readers of the *Republic*. This is not the place to discuss the vigorous and continuing debate over such issues as personal freedom and propaganda, but see Popper (1966) and
Bambrough (1967).

rates is to prove that, *pace* Thrasymachus, justice in fact benefits its possessor, then he must show that justice in the individual operates in a similar way. To do this, however, he must in turn show that the individual's *psuchē* is also in some way divided into three parts.

In 435e Socrates claims that three basic character traits exist in humanity at large: love of learning (here said to be exemplified by the Athenians); a thumoeidic or spirited element (exemplified by the Thracians and Scythians);[33] and a money-loving element (exemplified by the Phoenicians and Egyptians). Immediately below, the money-loving element is further associated with the physical appetites. Even if one ignores the racism, such a claim is problematic in a number of ways.[34] For our present purposes, Socrates needs to show that all three characteristics exist in each individual. He also needs to show that the individual does not display them in the same part of him or herself, but that the three traits are evidence for three divisions in the human *psuchē*.

The first requirement is not addressed by Socrates; he seems unaware of it. He is, however, keenly aware of the second obligation and from 436b–441b seeks to demonstrate the complexity of the *psuchē*. He does this by appealing to the evident phenomenon of psychic conflict.[35] According to Socrates,

> One and the same thing cannot act or be affected in opposite ways at the same time in the same part of itself and in relation to the same object; so if we find these contradictions, we shall know we are dealing with more than one object. (436b)

Such contradictions are, however, observable in the human mind: we may simultaneously have an impulse towards and an aversion to the same thing. These contradictory desires, Socrates argues, must therefore arise in different parts of the *psuchē*. The first case he takes is that of a man simultaneously desiring and rejecting a drink; this can be explained, Socrates suggests, if we assume an internal conflict between the man's reasoning and appetitive elements. The text here requires some elaboration, but let us assume

---

[33] The thumoeidic element is said to be that by which we θυμούμεθα, which is normally translated 'feel anger'. I feel that to attempt a specific translation at this stage is begging the question.

[34] For an incisive analysis of the main difficulties see Williams (1973) 'The analogy of city and soul in Plato's *Republic*'.

[35] This is a significant development from the *Protagoras*, where the existence of almost all mental conflict is denied. See pp. 126–7 below.

that the man has some illness such as dropsy, and that his doctor has forbidden him to drink, for the good of his overall health.[36] One of the symptoms of dropsy, however, is raging thirst; the man's physical appetites, which do not care about his overall good (437d–438a), crave liquid. His reason, on the other hand, *is* concerned with his general wellbeing, and urges that the physical craving be denied.

Such a conflict seems straightforward enough, though in what sense it is correct to talk of 'parts' of the *psuchē* will be discussed below.[37] What, however, of *thumos* and (if such a distinction is valid) that by which we feel it? Does it constitute a genuine third element in the *psuchē*, or is it somehow part of, or attached to, reason or appetite (439e)? Is there a *bonafide* counterpart in the *psuchē* to the Auxiliary class in the state?

Glaucon's first reaction is to say that *thumos* is the same as appetite. In response, Socrates relates a strange story concerning a certain Leontius. As Leontius walked past a pile of corpses and their executioner, he simultaneously felt a pressing desire to go back and look at them and a strong revulsion with himself for feeling such a desire. After a fierce internal struggle, during which he covered up his eyes, the desire finally overwhelmed him and he ran back to the corpses. As he looked, he spoke to his eyes in disgust, savagely telling them to 'get their fill of the beautiful (*kalon*) sight'. The story shows, says Socrates, that anger (*orgē*) is different from desire and sometimes opposes it.[38]

What are we to make of this curious offering? *Thumos* is again closely linked to anger,[39] but this time the anger is directed not towards an enemy but towards oneself.[40] There is also the strong suggestion that Leontius views his moral failure not simply as an isolated incident but in relation to an ideal of how he would like himself to be. In his mind he cherishes an image of himself, and his lapse over the corpses makes him painfully aware that that image is false. He is ashamed.

---

[36] Cf. *Gorgias* 505a6–9.

[37] Pp. 33–7.

[38] Leontius' desire may be sexual. See Adam (1963) ad. loc., citing an emendation suggested by Kock (1880–8) 1.739.

[39] 440a5–6 could even be read as identifying *thumos* and anger, but it is also possible to interpret it as saying that anger is one of the *thumos*' manifestations.

[40] Irwin (1995: 212) makes the point that the *thumos* is here not merely opposed to the appetite, but to the indulgence that allows one to *act* on the appetite.

What is the source of this shame? Why does Leontius' self-image preclude an act that would not do any obvious harm?[41] The presence of the executioner may be relevant here. Leontius wants to think well of himself, but perhaps thinking well of himself at least partly depends on being thought well of by his society, and idling round corpse piles would be unlikely to earn the approval of his fellow Athenians; whether consciously or not, Leontius is responding to a received social code. Even if he has so internalized that code that he is no longer aware of its external origins, those origins remain. Nevertheless, while this seems a plausible account of Leontius' motivation, we are still left with the question of how the aggressive drive of Book 2 can be so responsive to accepted social practice.

In Leontius' case, the form of this social responsiveness is a sensitivity to what is or is not perceived as *kalon*. '*Kalon*' in Greek is used of both the morally noble and fine and also of sensible beauty, and its ironical use here probably carries both connotations: Leontius is angry with himself because looking at the corpses is both physically distasteful and morally shameful. Furthermore, the physical and moral ugliness of the act are closely intertwined. We may remember that in Book 3 the *thumos* was said to be softened by *kala* works of art and respond to their rhythm and grace. There too it seemed that both senses of *kalon* were in play: the works of art were both beautiful and morally uplifting, and the two qualities were interconnected. But if it is difficult to see how an aggressive drive can respond to social values, it is even more puzzling to see how it can respond to sensible beauty. In order to understand how this might be possible, we shall need to know more not only about the *thumos*, but also about the Greek concept of the *kalon*, and why sensible beauty and moral nobility are covered by the same term.[42]

Leontius feels fierce indignation towards his desires, and *thumos* is portrayed chiefly as indignation throughout the Book 4 discussion: a man can be indignant with his own desires if he feels they are forcing him to do something against reason (440a–b), or in-

---

[41] If Leontius' desire is sexual (see n. 38), then it is important that his self-disgust is aroused simply by an act of looking. Consummated necrophilia clearly poses a serious danger to the physical health of the agent (to say nothing of his mental and moral state), and perhaps also to the physical health of his society.

[42] See pp. 61–3 and 227–30 below.

dignant with someone else if he feels he is being wronged (440c).
Indignation, therefore, necessarily involves an evaluative belief,
and is thus the natural ally and auxiliary of reason in its struggle
with the appetites – a struggle which would otherwise be heavily
weighted in the appetites' favour, since they are insatiable, while
reason is relatively weak.[43] Indeed, at first we are told that the
thumos never takes the side of the desires against reason (440b),
though this is soon qualified by the proviso 'unless corrupted by
bad upbringing' (441a). In 440e the *thumos* is simply 'much more
likely' to take up arms for reason.

Does this mean that *thumos* is simply a 'kind' of reason (*logistikou
ti eidos* 440e8)? Socrates denies this: conflicts between *thumos* and
reason can sometimes occur, showing that the two must comprise
separate parts of the *psuchē*.[44] As an example, he cites the anger of
Odysseus when he returns in disguise to his palace in Ithaca to
discover that his servant girls have been sleeping with his wife's
unwelcome suitors. Odysseus' immediate response is a furious desire to kill the disloyal servants; however, if he gives in to his anger
he will ruin his disguise and thus reduce his chances of achieving
his main purpose, which is to kill the suitors themselves. With
this in view, 'striking himself on the chest he called his heart to
order'.[45] According to Socrates, this internal dispute reflects a
distinction between unreasoning *thumos* and 'the power to reflect
about the better and the worse'.

If we consider all the conflicts involving *thumos*, we can begin to
see why reason and *thumos* can be at odds. It is one of the main
tenets of the *Republic* that reason always desires to know the truth
(581b) and does not assume that the appearances are necessarily a
reliable guide. The *thumos*, however, does not question the appearances: at 440c it is said to fight simply for 'what seems to be
just'.[46] Linked to this is the fact that it is also distinguishable from
reason in the scope of its evaluations. It responds to certain acts as

---

[43] 442a5–7; 442c5.

[44] To say that the *thumos* is reason's natural auxiliary only means that it is likely to side with
reason in a conflict between reason and appetite; it does not preclude struggles between
thumos and reason in which the appetites are not involved. See Irwin 1995: 212.

[45] *Od.* 20.17. It is clear from 20.5–10 that Homer here views the heart (*kardiē*) as the seat of
thumos.

[46] τῷ δοκοῦντι δικαίῳ. This unquestioning acceptance of appearances is of course different from the concern for appearances *as* appearances that we will find attributed to the
thumos in Book 9 and to the timocratic state and man in Book 8.

fine or shameful, just or unjust, but it is not directly concerned with the special provenance of reason, the overall good of state or soul.[47] Its responses are immediate, unreflective and above all *partial*: they are concerned with moral issues only in so far as those issues relate directly to the agent's self-image. It is notable, for instance, that there is no mention of an agent's *thumos* becoming indignant if someone else is being wronged.

At this point some may think a difficulty arises. To describe the *thumos'* responses as partial may be thought to beg the vexed question of whether Plato regards the parts of the soul as homunculi, as agents within agents. A proper consideration of this issue would clearly require another book; here I shall simply state that I do not believe that the homunculus question is a genuine problem for Plato. I agree with Annas (1981: 142–6) that homunculi only present a logical problem if they replicate *all* the features of the whole which they are introduced to explain, and that Plato's parts do not do this. I also agree with Price (1989: 260) that if the mind is partly its own construct, homunculi are thus legitimate in that they reflect this self-construction. My present point is simply that in 440c–441b Plato distinguishes two kinds of beliefs (though they will ideally coincide in practice): beliefs which give rise to indignation and anger and involve a partial viewpoint and fully rational beliefs based on reasoning about the overall good.

If one grants these differences between *thumos* and reason, it is easy enough to appreciate how *thumos* on its own can get things wrong. Firstly, given that it responds to the mere appearance of an offence, it can flare up in a situation where anger is simply uncalled for: no offence has in fact been committed. Secondly, even if an offence has occurred, *thumos* can still overreact: it has a tendency to 'boil over' (440c7) in a way which may either be inappropriate to the scale of the offence or unhelpful to the agent's long-term goals. In such cases, *thumos* must be quieted; reason must 'call it back to heel and calm it, as a shepherd calls his dog' (440c–d), a metaphor which deliberately calls to mind the image of the Auxiliary as a watchdog at 375a–376e.[48] Nevertheless, although these instances show that *thumos* is not rational in the full

---

[47] 428c–d; 442c.
[48] See also *Resp.* 404a; 416a; 422d and 451c. Odysseus' *thumos* and heart are also likened to a growling dog at *Od.* 20.9–16.

sense, the very fact that it can heed to reason at all shows again that it is more than simply a brute force. Indeed, as we have seen, the overall emphasis in Book 4 is on its propensity to obey reason, although we need to remember that for the most part we are here dealing with an ideal *thumos*, the counterpart of the Auxiliaries in the ideally just state (441d1–3).

A distinction between ideal and unideal versions of the *thumos* may help us at least partly to understand what some commentators have seen as an anomaly in the Book 4 account.[49] At 441a–b Glaucon claims that one argument for thinking that *thumos* is different from reason is that *thumos* is observable in small children, in whom reason has not yet developed; Socrates agrees, and adds that *thumos* also exists in animals (in whom reason in the *Republic*'s sense presumably never develops at all).[50] We seem to be back to the raw drive of Book 2, and it is initially difficult to see how this drive is compatible with the obedient *thumos* of 440b–e. However, to say that small children cannot reason for themselves is not to say that they cannot be guided – whether directly or indirectly – by the reason of an adult, except perhaps when extremely young. If the *thumos* of children could not be so guided, then the primary education system outlined in Books 2 and 3 would be entirely misconceived. It is stated clearly in 401c–402a that the purpose of this stage of education is to train the moral and aesthetic responses of the pre-rational child in such a way that 'when reason comes he will recognize and welcome it as a familiar friend because of his upbringing'.[51] Such a training can plainly only be devised and implemented by fully rational adults who understand the connections between sensible and moral beauty and reason, and it is no surprise to learn at 540e–541a that education in the ideal state is to be the responsibility of the Philosopher-Rulers. A properly trained *thumos* is thus a very different entity from an untrained one.

However, though this reading reduces the difficulties of 441a–b, it does not make them completely disappear. We are not yet in a position to understand precisely *how* the *thumos* can be guided, even unwittingly, by the reason of another, and as we have seen

---

[49] E.g. Annas 1981: 127.
[50] Sorabji (1993: 9–12) argues that, in contrast to Aristotle, Plato does generally grant animals not only beliefs but also a reasoning part of the soul. He does, however, admit that *Resp.* 441a–b is one of the exceptions.
[51] The translation is based on Lee. This passage is discussed in detail on pp. 228–9 below.

there may still be a very early stage in the child's life when he or she cannot respond to reason at all, even indirectly.

This latter possibility is clearly even more acute when we consider the notion of *thumos* in animals. What, for instance, is the nature of the watchdog's response to the command of its master? It is at least a moot point whether its *thumos* can be said to involve an evaluative belief:[52] it may simply (though still problematically) be responding to habituation. Most animals, however, cannot be domesticated even to this extent, a point we shall have to consider when we come to the comparison between the *thumos* and the lion in Book 9. In most animals, *thumos* does after all appear to be very close to a raw drive which is not only untrained but untrainable. Is Plato simply being inconsistent, or is there a connection between this drive and the *thumos* which is 'reason's natural auxiliary' (441a2–3)?[53]

These problems aside, by 441c Socrates believes he has established that there are 'the same three elements in the individual as there are in the state'. He accordingly proceeds to analyse the virtues of the individual along the same lines. It is owing to his reason that the individual is wise, and owing to his *thumos* that he is brave; simply possessing reason and *thumos*, however, will not be enough: they must also be performing their proper functions. Reason must be in control of the *psuchē* as a whole, and *thumos* must be supporting reason's orders. Similarily, the individual will be self-disciplined when all three parts of his *psuchē* are in 'friendly and harmonious agreement' about which part ought to rule, and there is no civil war amongst them.[54] And justice in the individual will again be the condition which makes such harmonious agreement possible, namely the condition that each part perform its own proper function and not try to usurp the function of any other part. As justice in the state brought about peace, security and concord, so justice in the individual allows him to keep 'all three elements of himself in tune, like the notes of a scale'. He can live at peace with himself, and channel all his energies into achieving his overall goals, because he has 'genuinely become one instead of many'. Injustice, on the other hand, is a 'kind of civil

---

[52] For a detailed examination of whether animals can possess beliefs, see Sorabji 1993.
[53] For further discussion of this issue, see pp. 25–7 and 103–4 below.
[54] 442c10–d1.

war' which occurs when the elements of the mind are 'confused and displaced'.[55]

Justice is therefore, Socrates claims, unquestionably to the benefit of the individual as well as the state: it is 'a kind of psychic health' (444d–e),[56] and we all want mental health at least as much as we want bodily health. In dismissing the value of justice, Thrasymachus simply got it wrong.

The treatment of *andreia* in this passage is interesting. At 442b11–c3 the individual is said to be courageous when his *thumos* 'holds fast to the orders of reason about what he ought or ought not to fear, in spite of pleasure and pain', a definition which recalls the definition of courage in the state at 430b as 'the ability to retain safely in all circumstances a judgement about what is to be feared, which is correct and in accordance with law'. These definitions mark a significant change in the *Republic's* conception of the relation between courage and fear. At 375 and 386–7 we saw *andreia* being linked to the absence of fear;[57] we are now told that the courageous man will after all fear certain things, though we are not told which. All we learn is that the *andreios* will ignore pain, which may imply that he is still supposed to be fearless in the face of physical hardship or risk. Yet if this is true, then the same question arises as before: why is it not permissible for the *andreios* to fear such things, providing he does not actually shrink from them? Why cannot courageous people be precisely those who do feel fear in dangerous circumstances, but risk their lives anyway?[58]

On a more positive note, what does clearly emerge from 442 is that courage involves both emotional commitment and evaluative belief, an intellectual and emotional appreciation of what things are worth taking risks for, and in what circumstances. Neither the emotive nor the belief component will be enough on its own. This should not surprise us when we consider Plato's claim in the *Republic* that courage requires *thumos*: the examples of Leontius and the person who feels he has been wronged have made it very clear that the *thumos'* emotions – in adult humans, at any rate – involve

---

[55] 443d–444b; the translation is based on that of Lee. This passage is explored further on p. 230 below.
[56] Taking 'excellence' (*aretē*) here to be synonymous with 'justice'.
[57] See pp. 9–10 and 12–13 above.
[58] For further examinations of the relation between courage and fear in the *Republic*, see the references on p. 13 n. 29 above.

an intrinsic belief-component. Less clear, however, is the precise relation between the belief-component or evaluative appreciation of the *thumos* and the knowledge supplied by reason on which the *thumos'* appreciation is ideally based.

It is also still unclear whether *andreia* here is supposed to retain any of its root meaning of 'manliness'. On the one hand, the tripartite psychology is plainly meant to apply to all humans, and it would be strange if women possessed *thumos* but either did not possess the specific virtue for which *thumos* is responsible, or were able to possess it only by abrogating their femininity. On the other hand, *thumos* is the counterpart in the *psuchē* of the Auxiliaries in the state, and as we have seen there is no indication as yet that any of the Auxiliaries are to be female; on the contrary, all the evidence to date suggests that Plato is only thinking of males for this role.[59] It is also notable how many military images are used to describe the *thumos'* activities: it is reason's 'ally' and 'more likely to take up arms for reason' when there is a conflict between reason and the desires, since it 'fights on behalf of what seems to be just'.[60] Until Plato reveals in Book 5 that in his ideal state women are to go to war along with the men, such metaphors will inevitably have 'masculine' associations in the minds of his readers. Indeed, such associations may remain, and be intended to remain, even after the introduction of female Auxiliaries. It may be that Plato is ambivalent about whether he wants *thumos* and *andreia* to be entirely divested of their masculine associations, whatever he says in Book 5.[61]

Books 8 and 9

The *thumos* is not explicitly mentioned again until Books 8 and 9; for reasons of clarity, I shall consider the Book 9 references first. At 580d, in the course of his final examination of the lives of the just and the unjust person, Socrates refers back to the tripartite division of the *psuchē* of Book 4. There, in order to establish that reason, *thumos* and the appetites arose in (or constituted)[62] different parts of the soul, Socrates had considered conflicting attitudes in

---

[59] As well as 395d and the other references given on p. 13 n. 30, see also 416d8.
[60] 440b3–4; 440e5–6; 440c8. Leontius' *thumos* is also said to 'fight' his desires at 439e10.
[61] This issue is discussed further on pp. 96–8 and 244–8 below.
[62] See pp. 33–7 below.

an individual towards a *single* object, such as a drink. The examples chosen to illustrate such mental conflicts, however, had seemed noticeably abstruse, and we now learn the reason why. For Socrates now tells us that in fact reason, *thumos* and the appetitive element each has its own natural objects of desire: its own pleasures, desires and governing principles. Reason desires truth and knowledge, the appetites desire food, drink, sex and material wealth, and *thumos* desires worldly success and reputation. Its motives are therefore ambition and love of honour. In each human *psuchē* one of these three sets of motives predominates; there are thus three basic types of humanity and three corresponding ways of life, each with its own particular set of pleasures.[63] Each type of person naturally prefers their own way of life and despises the pleasures of the other types. The man who loves honour, for instance, considers 'the pleasures of money-making rather vulgar, and those of learning, unless they bring him prestige, mere vapour and nonsense' (581d).

There follow a series of arguments which seek to demonstrate that the philosophic life is superior to the other two. Although each type of person thinks their own way of life is preferable, the superior experience, intelligence and reasoning ability of the philosopher give his[64] preferences authority (582e7–583a5). His pleasures are more real, pure and stable than those of the lover of honour or gain because of the superior – indeed complete – reality, purity and stability of their objects, the Forms (583b–585e).[65] The thumoeidic life is to be ranked second, and the appetitive life last. However, this does not mean that the philosophic life is to be entirely devoid of the pleasures of honour or material satisfaction; on the contrary, the philosopher requires experience of such pleasures in order to be in a position to compare them with the pleasures of knowledge. The point is rather that his *thumos* and appetitive element are to be guided by reason, and thus achieve the best and truest pleasures of which they are capable (586d–587a). He will ensure that he possesses enough money to satisfy those physical desires which are necessary for life, but he will not

---

[63] See also 435e–436a (p. 15 above).
[64] The reference to '*androin*' in 588a1 makes it clear that Socrates is still thinking of philosophers as male, despite the inclusion of Philosopher-Queens in Books 5 and 7.
[65] All these arguments are problematic, but the problems need not concern us here. For a balanced discussion see Gosling and Taylor 1982, ch. 6.

own so much wealth that the balance of his *psuchē* is upset.[66] He will also allow himself to accept and enjoy public or private honours, if he thinks they will make him a better man; but if he thinks they will destroy his internal harmony, then he will shun them (591e–592a).[67]

In the course of this crucial section a number of key points are made concerning the *thumos*. At 582e *andreia* again emerges as the primary virtue of the thumoeidic life, and at 583a the ambitious man is termed 'soldierly'; the Auxiliaries of Book 4 are plainly in view. Here, however, a puzzle presents itself. As we have seen, in Book 4 the Auxiliaries were to assist the Rulers as their faithful watchdogs, and *thumos* was portrayed as the natural supporter and watchdog of reason. At 586c–d, however, Socrates talks of the thumoeidic life being a life devoted to 'honour or success or ambition without reason or sense',[68] and he stresses how 'in the achievement of satisfaction the desires for honour and success lead to envy and violence, ambition to discontent'. Furthermore, at 588d the *thumos* is compared not to a watchdog but to a lion – an undeniably powerful and majestic animal, but scarcely the most reliable. Left to itself, the leonine *thumos* will attack the many-headed monster of the appetites and the two will 'snarl and wrangle and devour each other'; the internal struggle seems even fiercer than it was for the wretched Leontius. It is no accident that the lion is a favourite epithet in Homer for the proudly egoistic and volatile warrior.[69]

A partial and superficial answer is straightforward enough. In Book 4 the *thumos* was only said to be reason's natural auxiliary if properly educated; clearly the *thumos* of the ambitious man of 586c–d, who is brought to envy, discontent and violence, has not been so educated, and the same goes for the snarling lion. The real problem, however, is that it is hard to see how education can make any difference. At 589b Socrates says blithely that reason (here represented by a man) must 'make an ally of the lion', and enlist its support in the struggle to tame the many-headed mon-

---

[66] In the ideal state, of course, the Philosopher-Rulers will possess no wealth at all, as all their physical requirements will be supplied by the Producers.

[67] How any honours could make the philosopher a better person is not immediately clear. We shall be returning to this question on pp. 240–1.

[68] 'Ambition' translates *thumos*.

[69] E.g. *Il.* 11.383; 18.318; 20.164–75; 24.41–3.

ster. One wonders how many lion-tamers Socrates knew. To make matters worse, at 590b the *thumos* is further compared to a dragon or serpent. While Plato can respond that to take such metaphors literally is pedestrian in the extreme, the images still raise the central issue of how the social and 'raw drive' aspects of the *thumos* are supposed to interrelate.[70] Precisely *how* is a snarling lion supposed to be transformed into an obedient watchdog? If the Auxiliaries are the equivalent in the state to the *thumos* in the soul, they must presumably be motivated by thumoeidic desires. So how is it that the thumoeidic life of the Auxiliaries can be supportive of the rational decrees issued by the Rulers, whereas the thumoeidic life of 586 is inimical to sense and reason?

Some help is provided by 590c–d, where we are reminded that people of a naturally 'animal'[71] nature are to be subjected to the highest type of being, the class of philosophers. Plato wants us to appreciate that there are two ways in which someone may be naturally thumoeidic or appetitive and lead a thumoeidic or appetitive life. On the one hand are the Auxiliaries and Producers who are *characterized* by thumoeidic or appetitive impulses, but still ruled by the reason of the Rulers, and on the other are those who are in a position to let their thumoeidic or appetitive impulses take complete control: they are entirely *dominated* by them. It is true that this distinction still fails to explain what it is about the *thumos* which allows it to take both these forms. We may, however, find that it provides the seeds for such an explanation: the graphic depiction in Books 8 and 9 of how a person may become dominated by their non-rational desires suggests that there is an important distinction between the raw drive of small children and the raw drive of mostly untameable animals. It may be more accurate to say that *thumos* in humans is not born as a lion, but rather that it can in certain unfavourable circumstances develop into one.[72] In other words, the *thumos* of humans is not born uneducable, though it may become so.

Such distinctions, I believe, help us begin to resolve the apparent inconsistencies between Book 4 and Books 8 and 9. Yet they also raise a troubling question of their own, the question of

---

[70] See p. 21 above.
[71] τῶν ἐν αὑτῷ θρεμμάτων (590c4–5).
[72] Contrast Callicles' paean to nature's 'young lions' at *Gorgias* 483e (discussed in ch. 5).

whether the untamed Homeric lion might not be a better fighter than a tamed Auxiliary. What guarantee is there that a domesticated *thumos* will have sufficient edge when it comes to a crisis such as war?[73]

Despite such problems, Socrates' recommendations concerning the thumoeidic lion are suggestive. In a passage reminiscent of 410–12 we are warned at 590a–b that obstinacy and bad temper will over-develop the lion's strength, while if it is subordinated to the many-headed monster then it will cravenly put up with insults and turn into an ape. Particularly revealing is the statement that 'luxury and softness' will make it grow slack and cowardly. 'Softness' (*malthakia*) is sometimes associated with effeminacy;[74] again one may wonder whether Plato intends the *thumos'* virtue of *andreia* to carry overtones of its root meaning of 'manliness'.[75]

The timocratic state and man

A vivid picture of what can happen when thumoeidic desires take over unchecked is given to us in the portraits of the timocratic state and man (545c–550c). Timocracy is ranked second in the hierarchy of types of state and *psuchē*, preferable to oligarchy, democracy and tyranny. At 544c the timocratic state is said to be currently exemplified by the 'much admired' states of Sparta and Crete, and its keynote features, shared by the corresponding individual, are a love of success and a love of honour (545a2–3). The ideal state degenerates into a timocracy as a result of eugenic mistakes and the consequent decline in the system of education. In a timocracy, the citizens are educated by force rather than persuasion and physical training is overemphasized to the detriment of *mousikē*, in contrast to the ideal balance between the two recommended in 410–12. The result is a state which, due to its thumoeidic element (548c6), values success, honours and military conquest; it fears intellectuals, feeling more comfortable with 'simple' (*haploi*), thumoeidic types who prefer war to peace. However, because it lies halfway between the ideal state and oligarchy, it will

---

[73] See p. 207 below.

[74] E.g. *Phaedr.* 239c, where the *malthakos* is specifically said to be unmanly (*anandros*).

[75] A slack *thumos* is also said to make a man *malthakos* at *Resp.* 411b4.

also share some features of each. From the former it will inherit a respect for authority and the seclusion of the soldier-class from agriculture and business; with the latter it will share a love of money, though this passion must be cherished in secret.

The corresponding timocratic man is competitive, self-willed, ambitious for political office and possessed of a good military record. He has some interest in the arts, but is inarticulate; he is more interested in physical exertion and hunting. A stickler for traditional hierarchies, he is obedient to the political authorities, but harsh to slaves. As he grows older, he also becomes increasingly avaricious, as he lacks the stabilizing harmony of reason and *mousikē* which can only be produced by the education of the ideal state.

Particularly telling is the account of the social forces which create such a character. A man of philosophic bent finds himself in a society which does not value the disinterested search for truth, but applauds instead the self-assertive scramble for political office and honours, and the protection of one's self-image through constant litigation. In such an environment the philosophic man is marginalized and, an Athenian Mr Bennet, he retreats into his study, and lets the world say of him what it will. His wife, however, is annoyed at the family's consequent lack of social status and wealth, and complains to their son that his father is not a 'real man'.[76] The servants repeat her complaints:

If they see the father failing to prosecute someone who owes him money or who has done him some wrong, they tell the son that when he grows up he must avenge all things of this kind and be more of a man than his father.[77]

The boy also hears the same kind of disparagement of his father from society at large, and he sees how those who keep quietly to themselves are thought foolish (*ēlithioi*), whereas self-assertion and retaliation win praise and honour. On the other hand, he also hears his father's point of view and recommendation of the philosophic way of life. Torn between his father's values and the thumoeidic and appetitive values of the rest of society, he opts for the middle course and 'resigns control of himself to the middle ele-

---

[76] *Anandros* 549d6.
[77] 549e5–550a1. 'Be more of a man': ἀνὴρ μᾶλλον ἔσται τοῦ πατρός.

ment, which is competitive and thumoeidic, and so becomes an arrogant and ambitious man'.

The story demonstrates skilfully how thumoeidic impulses, without the guidance of reason, differ from their ideal manifestation in the Auxiliaries: glory and recognition seem to be sought simply for their own sake, rather than as confirmation of one's ability to respond to the fine and noble.[78] The desire for honour is also shown sliding towards materialism. The wife desires wealth because wealth symbolizes status, and this desire may have led her into valuing wealth for its own sake. The text is unclear on this point, but it would nicely illustrate the accusation of acquisitiveness directed against the timocratic society at 548a.[79] Most notable of all is the change in the relation between the *thumos* and manly ideals. In Book 4, the special virtue of the *thumos* is *andreia* in the form of military courage; as we saw, however, it is unclear to what extent *andreia* is here supposed to carry overtones of its root meaning of 'manliness'. In Book 8 the problem is reversed. Here there is no ambiguity about whether notions of manliness are in play: the son is explicitly exhorted to be a 'real man' and 'more of a man' than his father. The difficulty now is in deciding how much 'being a real man' entails the exhibition of courage, military or otherwise: the passage itself does not directly mention *andreia* but simply refers to self-assertion and a willingness to take state-sanctioned revenge. Whether such bald assertiveness can be termed 'courageous' is, I believe, precisely the question Plato wishes us to ask. It certainly appears that this is what notions of courage and manliness can be reduced to in the society which derides the philosophic man.

Equally important in this passage is the implication that one becomes a 'real man' by imitating socially approved role models. The son of the philosophic man painfully comes to see that his father cannot be such a model, as he is not regarded as 'manly' by his society. This takes us back to Socrates' critique in Books 2 and 3 of the traditional role models on offer in Greek literature. There, however, the models are the semi-divine heroes of the *Iliad*

---

[78] For the intricate relation between the desire for glory and responsiveness to the claims of the *kalon*, see pp. 38–9 and 191 below.

[79] Though in 548 the citizens are not allowed to acquire wealth openly. The philosophic man's household seems to be situated in a society closer to contemporary Athens.

and *Odyssey*; whereas we are now being asked to think about suitable exemplars in contemporary society. These discussions prompt some difficult questions. Are role models necessary, or even helpful, to moral development at all? If they are useful, should they be fictional or historical? Mortal, semi-divine or divine? There is also the issue of whether Plato intends such discussions to be relevant to young women as well as young men: we shall see in chapter 8 that it is not easy to decide who (or what) are supposed to serve as models for the young female Auxiliaries and Philosopher-Queens.

A careful consideration of the *thumos* in the *Republic* thus suggests that it would be highly unwise to dismiss it out-of-hand: Plato's treatment of it is extremely rich and a focal point for a large number of important issues. It also undeniably presents us with some tough questions concerning the possibility of education and the precise connotations of *andreia*. We would be ill-advised, however, to assume unthinkingly that these are necessarily problems for Plato; they may well be problems set up by Plato for us to solve.

THE *THUMOS* AS A COHERENT WHOLE

It will be helpful at this point to construct a rough working sketch of the *thumos* in the *Republic*, indicating how its various features may be connected.

I wish to claim that the essence of the human *thumos* is the need to believe that one counts for something, and that central to this need will be a tendency to form an ideal image of oneself in accordance with one's conception of the fine and noble. If one's behaviour reveals this cherished image of oneself to be a sham, then anger, self-disgust and shame are likely to be the result. This ideal of oneself also needs to be confirmed by social recognition: others must treat one in accordance with one's self-image. Indeed, this recognition can be seen as forming a vital part of the image itself. The obtaining of this recognition will require self-assertion and perhaps aggression; and any offence committed to one's self-image by others will prompt anger and a desire to retaliate. This violent aspect of the human *thumos* certainly has connections with the assertive drive (also termed *thumos*) of some animals, but one should not look for any exact parallels: in humans, *thumos* will always be a more complex phenomenon, more responsive to reason and social expectations.

Society is also needed to provide the general content of one's self-ideal through its values, and particularly through the embodiment of these values in its heroes. The *thumos* will thus lead to a tendency to take some hero as a role model, to be emulated either generally or in detail: if one wishes for social recognition then it makes sense to conform to those models which already receive it. In Plato's Athens, with its sharp segregation between the sexes, men are likely to focus only on male heroes: their self-ideal will take the form of 'being a real man'. Hence the association between *thumos* and ideals of manliness, *andreia* in its root meaning. *Andreia* as courage will also usually be involved given that ideals of manliness in Plato's day generally implied some notion of courage.[80]

The above describes, I believe, Plato's view of how the *thumos* operates in contemporary Athens. Whether he wants its ideals to be gendered in the ideal state is considerably less clear. Indeed, it is not yet apparent how women are supposed to fit into this picture at all, either in Athens or utopia.

THE *THUMOS* AND PLATO'S GENERAL PSYCHOLOGY

We also now have sufficient material to return to the issue of Plato's psychology as a whole.[81] Two questions in particular need to be addressed. If the *thumos* is a part of the tripartite *psuchē*, then what is meant by *psuchē* here and what is meant by 'part'?

The meaning of psuchē

The former question is perhaps the easier to answer. In the *Republic* 608c–611a Socrates argues for the immortality of the *psuchē*, on the grounds that its own particular evil, moral wickedness, cannot destroy it, and if not even its own specific evil can do this, then nothing else will be able to do so either. However, at 611a–612a he also suggests that when he uses *psuchē* in this sense, the sense of that in us which is divine and immortal, he does not think it likely

---

[80] Though see Socrates' depiction in *Resp.* 549c–550b of how 'manly' ideals may be corrupted (discussed above pp. 28–9). All these issues are discussed in more detail in ch. 2.
[81] See p. 16 above.

to include the *thumos* and the appetites, but only our strictly rational element, the *logistikon*:

> Our argument will not allow us [to believe] that in its essential[82] nature the *psuchē* is such as to be full of much diversity and dissimilarity and internal conflict.
> Why do you say that?
> It is not easy for a synthesis composed of many parts to be everlasting, especially when the synthesis is not mixed in the finest possible way – as appeared to us to be the case just now with the *psuchē*.[83]

The synthesis which constitutes our incarnate *psuchē* is simply not of sufficient quality to be everlasting (or eternal).[84] Socrates does not commit himself entirely on whether the *psuchē* is essentially composite or incomposite (cf. 612a3–5), but he does say that in our search to discover the *psuchē's* true and immortal nature we should look to its 'love of philosophy' (611e1), not to those characteristics which arise only through its incarnation, and which encrust and obscure its pure essence as barnacles encrusted the fisherman Glaucus when he was transformed into a sea-god. In other words, the tripartite division of Books 4, 8 and 9 is a division not of the immortal soul but of the incarnate *personality* of mortal man. Of this tripartite personality, it seems that only reason is immortal; the *thumos* and the appetites are just temporary barnacles, things 'earthy and wild' (612a1–2), which encrust reason and make it appear like a beast (611d5). They belong to an account of the experiences and elements of the *psuchē* 'in its mortal life'.[85]

The same doctrine is found in the *Timaeus*. Here too the *psuchē* of the living person is tripartite, but the only immortal element of this is reason alone (41c–d; 73c–d); the desires of the *thumos* and the appetites arise simply as a result of the *psuchē's* placement in a body (69c–d). They are the 'mortal part of the soul'.[86] The *Phaedo* too, while not propounding any tripartite division, holds that our immortal soul essentially consists of pure reason alone,[87] and that

---

[82] ἀληθεστάτῃ.
[83] My translation.
[84] The perfect, indissoluble synthesis may well be possible in another, less compromised world. Compare *Phdr.* 245c5–246b4 and 253c7–255a1, where, in the realm of the Forms, the *psuchē* does appear to be composite. See Ferrari 1987: 125–32 and notes.
[85] ἐν τῷ ἀνθρωπίνῳ βίῳ, 612a5.
[86] *Tim.* 61c7–8; 69c5–6; 73d3.
[87] *Phd.* 79d–80b; 83a–84b.

all the other desires and passions of the living person are the result of its association with the body (81c), though if these desires are strong during life they will survive death and drag the immortal soul back to earth again, to flit around tombs and seek another incarnation. The distinction between the embodied and the disembodied *psuchē* is therefore critical. It is only to the embodied *psuchē* that thumoeidic passions and physical appetites accrue, and when the body dies, they also vanish. The soul that is reason is immortal, but the tripartite personality is not.[88]

This distinction, however, would seem to give rise to a profound dilemma for Plato. Should one concentrate on harmonizing the three parts of one's embodied personality, or focus instead on trying to disentangle one's immortal soul from its earthly trappings? The *Phaedo* urges us to the latter task; Book 4 of the *Republic* exhorts us to the former. Other passages in the *Republic*, however, are more ambivalent. 608c–612a, cited above, is a case in point: at 611e1–5 Socrates presses Glaucon to look to the *psuchē*'s love of wisdom, and to

think how, being akin to the divine and the immortal and the everlasting, it longs to associate with them and apprehend them; think what it might become if it followed this impulse wholeheartedly and was lifted by it out of the sea in which it is now submerged.

This dilemma seems to me to be connected to the problem raised earlier about what kind of role model is appropriate for a mortal: another mortal, a semi-divine hero or something fully divine?[89] As we shall see in chapter 8, the problems will converge in the question of what it means for a human to try to shape their character and life according to the pattern of the divine Forms. Does being human require one to try to transcend what is usually meant by humanity?

The meaning of 'part'

The *thumos*, then, together with the appetites, is a part of the living personality, not of the immortal soul. But what precisely is meant

---

[88] This may explain the reference to the 'mortal *psuchē*' (as opposed to mortal part of the *psuchē*) at *Laws* 691c6. Reason is later identified with the immortal part of the *psuchē* at 713e8–714a2.

[89] P. 30 above.

by 'part' here? The diction Plato employs is varied to say the least. The normal Greek term for 'part', *meros*, is sometimes used, but not until relatively late in the Book 4 argument.[90] More frequently employed are *eidos* (kind), *genos* (class, sort), phrases with the dative and phrases with *kata* (in relation to) plus the accusative.[91] It is true that Plato warns us at 435c–d not to expect precision at this stage, a reservation repeated at 504b; yet if we are properly to understand what questions he intends the *thumos* to address, the diverse terminology is not something we can gloss. What are we to say?

Since Stocks (1915), a number of scholars have held that any talk of 'parts' (*merē*) is purely metaphorical; Plato's only concern is with a three-fold classification of psychic phenomena.[92] Woods (1987) has I believe disproved this interpretation, effectively demonstrating that Plato's argument for the division of the soul, based on what Woods terms the Principle of Opposites of 436b8–c1, requires that the notion of part be taken seriously: there is a logical need for three distinct sources of action.[93] I would, however, concur with Stocks *et al.* that what really *interests* Plato is the notion of a part *qua* set of motivations and behavioural characteristics. As our examination of the *thumos* has shown, Plato deploys his psychology to explore the *Republic*'s central questions concerning how one should live and what sort of person one should be. As well as 435e and 580d,[94] it is also significant that a motivational triumvirate of desires is introduced as early as 347b, long before the official psychology of the *Republic* is even mentioned. It will be difficult, says Socrates, to persuade wise men to rule because they do not want money and are not ambitious; the only inducement will be the thought that anyone else would inevitably do the job badly. Thus when we do come to the tripartite *psuchē* of Book 4 we are already disposed to view its divisions principally in terms of different kinds of behaviour, arising from different goals.

---

[90] 442b11; 442c5.
[91] *Eidos*: 439e2; 440e8; 504a4; 580d3. *Genos*: 441c6; 441d9; 442b2; 443d3; 444b5. Phrases with the dative: 436a8–10; 439b5; 439d5–6; 441d1. Phrases with *kata* plus the accusative: 436b8; 436c5; 436d8; 436e9–437a1.
[92] See Crombie 1962: 355; Cross and Woozley 1964: 128; Cooper 1984.
[93] Whether the parts are supposed also to be topographically distinct is a highly complex and interesting issue, but not germane to my central thesis. For a sensible discussion see Price 1990: 259–61.
[94] See pp. 15 and 23–4 above.

The linguistic evidence for the main emphasis being on motivational sets is also strong. At 435e2 *eidos* is also one of the terms used (together with *ēthos*, disposition) to describe the different characteristics and traits of individuals which account for the different kinds of states,[95] and it is in keeping with this non-technical usage that at 435e4 we meet *to thumoeides* standing not for any specific part of the *psuchē*, but for the spiritedness of the Thracians in general. Furthermore, while Plato speaks of *meros* in 442b–c, it is *genos* that he uses in the important summing-up at 443c–e, where the truly just man is said to bind the three elements of his *psuchē* together into a harmonious whole and live at peace with himself. Clearly *meros* (or *morion*) would not sufficiently suggest the required sense of diverse and potentially conflicting kinds of behaviour which need to be harmonized: after all, we know from the *Protagoras* 329d that, as with gold, there may be no difference at all between the parts (*moria*) of a thing other than location, and thus no danger of conflict. *Genos*, however, does permit the necessary notion of different kinds of behaviour, as well as allowing for different sources.[96]

Further evidence of Plato's real interests is suggested by the fact that similar triumvirates of desire appear in dialogues which make no clear reference to a correspondingly tripartite *psuchē*:[97] on this reading, the *Republic* is attempting to give a scientific explanation of this phenomenon, but it is the phenomenon with which Plato is chiefly concerned. The Pythagorean apologue may also be relevant here. This tale makes an appearance in many ancient texts, the fullest accounts being those of Diogenes Laertius and Cicero. According to the story, Leon the tyrant of Phlius asked Pythagoras what he was and Pythagoras answered '*philosophos*'; this term was new to Leon and he asked Pythagoras what it meant. In reply,

he compared life to the Great Games, which some attend as competitors, some as merchants, and the best as spectators. Similarly in life, he said,

---

[95] See Crombie 1962: 341.

[96] Ancient support for Plato's subtle deployment of *eidos* and *meros* can be found in Galen *De Placitis Hippocratis at Platonis* 6.2 = De Lacy 1980: 368 and 372.

[97] *Phd.* 68b–c; 82c; *Symp.* 205d; *Laws* 632d. Of these, the *Phaedo* is definitely not operating with a tripartite *psuchē*, and the *Symposium* and *Laws* make no explicit reference to such a division, though it is possible that such a division is assumed. (For the *Symposium*, see pp. 250–1 below.)

the slavish are hunters after fame and profit, but the philosophers are hunters of truth.[98]

The existence of this story, which is plainly concerned with moral psychology rather than psychology *simpliciter*, throws light on how Plato should be interpreted irrespective of whether it pre- or post-dates the *Republic*. If it is a genuine part of early Pythagorean folklore,[99] then it is highly likely that it is the origin of Plato's interest in comparing the lives of wisdom, honour and material gain, and this would increase the probability of his interest in psychology being primarily ethical. If, on the other hand, its source lies in the *Republic* itself,[100] then this is a further indication (though clearly not proof) that Plato's tripartite division is to be read chiefly in ethical terms.

This emphasis on the parts of the *psuchē* as motivational sets may also help us to solve a problem raised earlier,[101] namely why Plato apparently abandons his tripartite division in Book 10 602c–605c, and opts for a bipartite division instead. It is true that in 604d–e Plato talks of the 'wise' element in the *psuchē* which opposes the 'irrational' element in the assessment of misfortune. However, the explicit conflict here is between judgements rather than motives: our irrational element misjudges the size and importance of human misfortunes in the same way that it misjudges the position of a stick under water. While motivations may play a role in accounting for these conflicting judgements, the immediately relevant distinction is simply between the rational and the irrational. The passage should thus not be read as a denial of the three-way motivational distinctions of Books 4, 8 and 9: there is nothing to prevent our irrational element being subdivided into two. Plato may be working towards Aristotle's claim in the *De*

---

[98] Diogenes Laertius *Lives of the Philosophers* 8.8. See also Cicero *Tusculan Disputations* 5.3; Iamblichus *Vita Pyth.* 12.58 and *Protrepticus* c.9; Diodorus 10.10.1. Isocrates *Busiris* 28 accepts that Pythagoras was the first 'philosopher' and may thus indicate knowledge of the story. Delatte 1922: 109 lists many later references up to the sixteenth century.

[99] In favour of a pre-Platonic source are Cameron 1938: 29; Morrison 1958; Guthrie 1962: 165; Burnet 1930: 98; Joly 1956: 21–40.

[100] Suggested by Festugière 1971: 117–56 and Jaeger 1948: 432 and *Scrip. Min.* 1.356. Diogenes says that his direct source is Sosicrates, but he mentions in 1.12 that Sosicrates is using Heraclides of Pontus; Cicero just mentions Heraclides. Heraclides, however, was a student of Plato (Cic. *Tusc. Dis.* 5.3); hence the possibility that the apologue is an oblique tribute from pupil to master. For a balanced discussion of the controversy see Gottschalk 1980: 23–36.

[101] Pp. 3–4 above.

Anima that the *psuchē* can be divided up according to a number of different principles.[102]

The *thumos*, then, is best regarded as one of three sets of characteristics which together make up the personality of a living human being. To appreciate more fully why Plato is so concerned with the motivations and behavioural traits that it comprises we shall need to step back and place it in a more general philosophical and historical context. Before we do this, however, it will helpful to look at some other thinkers, both ancient and modern, who have valued characteristics which bring Plato's *thumos* to mind.

ARISTOTLE

The above interpretation of Plato's primary concern in *Republic* 4 is strengthened when we turn to Aristotle, and consider his differing assessments of Plato's psychology in the *De Anima* and the *Nicomachean Ethics*. In the *De Anima* passage referred to above (432a), his view of Plato's tripartite *psuchē* is at best equivocal: he agrees that there are three types of desire (*orexis*) in the *psuchē*, and that these can be termed *boulēsis*, *epithumia* and *thumos*, but thinks that beyond this any attempt to divide up the *psuchē* on the lines of Plato's *logistikon*, *epithumētikon* and *thumikon* would be artificial, there being so many other natural principles of division which could apply just as well: what, for instance, of the nutritive, sensitive and imaginative parts? In the *Nicomachean Ethics*, however, Aristotle is quite happy to accept the idea that there are three basic kinds of life, the hedonistic, the political and the contemplative, directed to the three basic goals of pleasure, honour and knowledge.[103] A similar tripartition of goals and lives is made in the *Eudemian Ethics*.[104] The inference is plain: as pure psychology, Aristotle finds Plato's divisions unconvincing; but as an account of our fundamental sources of motivation, he thinks that Plato's three elements are on the right lines.

---

[102] Aristotle *De An.* 432a15–b7. See Plato *Resp.* 603d5–7.
[103] *E.N.* 1095b14–1096a6. That knowledge is the goal of the contemplative life is made explicit at 1177a20–1.
[104] 1214a30–1215a35. The three goals here are said to be wisdom, pleasure and virtue (*aretē*); it is clear, however, from *E.N.* 1095b26–30 that Aristotle believes the goals of honour and virtue to be intimately connected. See the discussion on pp. 38–9 below.

Providing we bear this in mind, we can see that Aristotle gives considerable support for 'thumoeidic' motivations. The account at *E.N.* 1149a24–b3 of the man who lets his *thumos* run away with him is of particular interest because it is so clearly indebted to Plato: while Aristotle does not mean by *thumos* anything more technical than a certain emotional response (anger or indignation), there is no doubt about the passage's source in the description of the over-hasty watchdog at *Republic* 440d.[105] Incontinence of anger (*thumos*) is, Aristotle says, less shameful than incontinence of appetite because,

> It appears that anger does to some extent hear reason, but that it hears it wrongly; just as hasty servants hurry out of the room before they have heard the whole of what you are saying, and so mistake your order, and as watchdogs bark at a mere knock at the door, without waiting to see if it is a friend. Similarily anger, owing to the heat and swiftness of its nature, hears, but does not hear the order given, and rushes off to take vengeance. When reason or imagination suggests that an insult or slight has been received, anger flares up at once, but after reasoning as it were that you ought to make war on anyone who insults you. Desire on the other hand, at a mere hint from the senses[106] that a thing is pleasant, rushes off to enjoy it. Hence anger follows reason in a manner, but desire does not.[107]

As in the Platonic original, *thumos* reacts to uncorroborated appearances and has a tendency to go over the top in its responses; it has no internal checks, but requires the outside assistance of reason to calm it. And here too, the angry man is angry because he feels he has been *wronged*; honour must be upheld.

Republic 4 also made it clear, however, that the concept of honour is closely bound up with a sense of the *kalon*, the noble or fine: to obtain honour one must do what one's society regards as the noble thing. It is, of course, entirely possible to perform outwardly fine acts in a cynical spirit, solely for the purpose of achieving regard and with no love for the fine as such. In other cases, however, the person who desires honour will want to be applauded specifically for the noble characteristics and acts which they genuinely believe they possess and have performed: 'people seek honour in order to convince themselves of their own goodness'.[108] In other

---

[105] See p. 19 above.
[106] I agree with Rackham (1926) that ὁ λόγος ἢ at 1149a35 are an interpolation.
[107] Trans. Thomson (1976).
[108] *E.N.* 1095b26–8. *Vide* also 1159a22–4.

words, a love of honour may be intimately linked to a love of the noble itself, albeit in a personal context.[109] Anger arises if such people feel that their fine qualities and acts have been slighted by others, or if – as in Leontius' case – they become painfully aware that their noble self-image is false. This nexus of ideas is supported by Aristotle's accounts of the good and bad dispositions with regard to *timē* and anger. In *Nicomachean Ethics* 4.4, the honour-loving man is blamed if he seeks honour too much or from the wrong source, but he is also sometimes praised as 'manly and a lover of the noble' (*andrōdēs kai philokalos*);[110] no explanation is given, but presumably 'manly' here indicates a 'masculine' ability to stand up for oneself and defend one's honour, which in turn depends on one's sense of the *kalon*. Real men assert their finer selves. Similarly, in 4.5 Aristotle not only claims that there is a praiseworthy mean with regard to anger; he also acknowledges that there are times when we commend those who display anger in excess of this mean, calling them manly (*andrōdeis*) and fitted to command (1126b1–2).[111] Conversely, it is also possible to be deficient in anger; such men are blamed on the grounds that if a man is never angry, he will never stand up for himself, and 'it is considered servile to put up with an insult to oneself or to allow one's friends to be insulted.' (1126a3–8)

Equally telling is Aristotle's delicately tongue-in-cheek account of the exemplar of the traditional Athenian gentleman, the *megalopsuchos* or great-souled man, who combines a proper attitude to honour with genuine worth.[112] The *megalopsuchos* 'thinks himself deserving of great things and does indeed deserve them'; and what he thinks himself worthy *of* is honour because 'worth' is spoken of in relation to external goods and honour is 'the greatest external good of all'. To win honour, however, will again require a commitment to what is fine and noble, for honour is 'the prize awarded for the noblest (*kallista*) deeds'. He is also drawn towards

---

[109] In this section, 'honour' translates *timē*. The ambiguities inherent in the notion of *timē* are if anything even more marked in the English term: consider 'love of honour', 'defend one's honour', 'honourable' and – most ambivalent of all – 'sense of honour'. This last perfectly encapsulates the complex interweaving of moral integrity and personal pride that the concept of honour suggests.

[110] *E.N.* 1125b8–25. Aristotle is also sympathetic to honour and shame as motivating forces at 1115a12–13; 1127b11–12; 1147b29–31.

[111] See also *E.N.* 1109b17–18.

[112] *E.N.* 1123a34–1125a17. It is significant that Aristotle appears to assume that greatness of soul, and love of honour in general, are distinctively *male* characteristics.

the *kalon* in its other guise of sensible beauty: in a key passage, it is said that he

> prefers to own beautiful (*kala*) and unprofitable things rather than prof-
> itable and useful ones. For the former are a sign of his independence.
> (1125a11–12)[113]

Partly as a result of this indifference to normal material comforts, he can appear haughty (*huperoptēs* 1124a19), though his contempt is also said to be always just (1124b5).

Most illuminating of all is the description in the *Art of Rhetoric* 2.12 of the character of young men, who appear to be almost ex- act embodiments of Plato's conception of the – or a – thumoeidic type; they are also portrayed as a younger and untamed version of the more statesmanlike *megalopsuchos* of the *Ethics*. The passage is worth quoting at some length:

> They are passionate (*thumikoi*), keen-tempered, carried away by anger[114]
> and unable to control their *thumos*. For owing to their love of honour
> they cannot bear to be slighted, but become indignant if they think they
> are being wronged. However, though they love honour, they love victory
> even more: for youth longs for superiority, and victory is a kind of supe-
> riority ... And they are more courageous (*andreioteroi*), for they are full of
> *thumos* and hope, and the former quality prevents them from feeling fear,
> while the latter gives them confidence[115] ... And they are great-souled
> (*megalopsuchoi*), for they have not yet been humbled by life, but are untried
> by necessity; and thinking oneself worthy of great things is the mark of
> *megalopsuchia* ... And they would rather perform noble (*kala*) actions than
> useful ones: for they live according to their habitual character rather
> than calculation, and calculation aims at the useful, while virtue aims
> at the noble ... And all their errors are the result of excess and over-
> zealousness, ignoring the maxim of Chilon.[116] For they do everything to
> excess: they love to excess, and they hate to excess, and everything else in
> the same way ... They do wrong as a result of arrogance and over-
> reaching (*hubris*) rather than wickedness.[117]

These passages show that Aristotle regards the characteristics which Plato groups under the *thumos* as naturally tending to occur together, albeit in different proportions, to form a small number

---

[113] For the significance of this potential split between the *kalon* and the useful see especially
ch. 7; Plato's attempt to resolve it is discussed in ch. 8.

[114] Reading ὀργῇ (anger) rather than ὁρμῇ (impulse). It makes little difference to the overall sense.

[115] The courageous are also said to be *thumoeideis* at *E.N.* 1116b25–7.

[116] μηδὲν ἄγαν, 'nothing too much'.

[117] 1389a3–b13.

of related character types. They also show that Aristotle thinks that this group of characteristics *matters*: young men and the *megalopsuchos* are significant actors in the life of the state, particularly in its defence.[118] It is also significant that although Aristotle rejects the claims of honour as a candidate for the human good in *Nicomachean Ethics* 1.5, he still believes it to be an important goal: this is because, as we have seen, he takes the desire for honour to be essentially a desire for confirmation of our excellence (*aretē*). The life of pleasure, on the other hand, is curtly dismissed as bovine.

NIETZSCHE

This concern with what we may term 'thumoeidic' motivations and behavioural characteristics has continued until the present century, though the connections with Plato's *thumos* have gone strangely unremarked.[119] The three most influential modern thinkers to address such issues have been Nietzsche, Adler and Freud, and with respect to their interest in 'manliness' it is perhaps no accident that all three were born into related Germanic and Middle European cultures still heavily imbued with the Romantic heroes and ideals of Goethe and Schiller and their English counterparts: Nietzsche, for instance, came to revere Goethe as a precursor of the Superman, and as a young man he was also overwhelmed by Shelley's *Prometheus Unbound*.[120] I would certainly not wish to claim any exact parallels; but I do believe that a brief sketch of certain preoccupations in these thinkers will support my contention that in the *thumos* Plato has hit upon psychological traits of real importance.

Nietzsche is of particular interest in this context because he was a direct and acknowledged influence on Adler and, to a lesser extent, Freud.[121] It might at first sight seem odd to suggest any points

---

[118] *Ars Rhet.* 1389a11–13 and 25; *E.N.* 1124b8–9.

[119] An exception is Cornford (1930). A number of writers have fruitfully explored more general connections between Plato and Freud, but they say little about the *thumos'* relation to the superego. See Santas 1988 and Price 1989.

[120] For references to Goethe see *The Will to Power* 95; 104; 380; 396; 747. *Prometheus Unbound* is discussed by Nietzsche in a letter to Erwin Rohde, August 28 1877.

[121] Adler acknowledges Nietzsche in many works, especially in *On the Neurotic Constitution* (1912), where he emphasizes that his own concept of striving for superiority derives from Nietzsche's will to power (see p. 45 below). For Freud, see *Introductory Lectures in Psychoanalysis* (1933) where Freud says that, following Nietzsche, from now on the unconscious will be called '*das Es*'. Cf. also *Towards a Psychopathology of Everyday Life* (1910).

of contact between Plato and a philosopher who explicitly attacks him, denies any absolute notions of being or self, and thinks instead in terms of a discontinuous becoming which fluctuates according to historical and psychological contingencies. However, despite the vast differences, the motivations and values which Plato locates in the *thumos* are still notably similar to some of Nietzsche's chief concerns. Throughout his works, from the early *Thoughts Out of Season* of 1873–6 to the final *Ecce Homo* (published posthumously in 1908), Nietzsche emphasizes the supreme importance of the all-embracing will to power:

This world is the will to power – and nothing besides! And you yourselves are also this will to power – and nothing besides!122

It is of course true that the will to power covers far more than the timocratic man's desire for victory and success; it is also true that Nietzsche would arguably despise the *thumos*' need for conventional forms of social validation (it would presumably depend on the kind of society in question). Yet this does not alter the fact that the *thumos* and the will to power both comprise a combined desire, need and imperative for self-assertion and self-enhancement, even if Nietzsche's concept of 'self' differs considerably from that of Plato.123 Furthermore, the main quality required in Nietzsche's ethic of strenuousness will be the *thumos*' particular excellence of courage: it is courage, claims Nietzsche, in which we must have faith, even above dialectics and reason.124 Such an injunction, however, should also strike a warning note: is it really true that courage need not require reason? In *Republic* 4, Plato is emphatic that courage and clear thinking can never be separated.125

Another significant point of contact with the *thumos* is the basic form which Nietzsche believes the will to power takes in humans. Its fundamental expression is self-achievement, having the courage to become what you are. In *The Gay Science* 270 we hear the impassioned cry: 'What does your conscience say? – "You should become him you are" '126 – an ethic confirmed by the subtitle of *Ecce*

---

122 *The Will to Power* 1067 trans. Kaufmann and Hollingdale.

123 Such self-enhancement does not necessarily include physical self-preservation, either for Nietzsche or, as we shall see in ch. 6, for the *thumos*. In some circumstances self-assertion can be compatible with self-sacrifice.

124 In a letter of 1887 to his Danish editor Georg Brandes.

125 Pp. 22–3 above. We shall also find courage being dependent on reason in the *Laches* and *Protagoras*.

126 Trans. Kaufmann.

Homo: 'How one becomes what one is.' In a philosophy of becoming, however, the self that one should become is not something static and final; it is, rather, the dynamic expression of the will to power itself. The will to power is both the striving for self-achievement and the self that must be achieved. This 'self', however, that is the creation and manifestation of power lies far above what we normally take it to be:

Your true nature does not lie hidden within you, but immensely high above you, or at least above that which you usually regard as 'I'. (*Thoughts Out of Season* 3.1)

Such passages call to mind the *thumos*' tendency to create an ideal self-image and strive to live up to it, and will be worth remembering when we come to examine some of the embodiments of heroism emulated by the *thumos*, and whether such emulation is appropriate. Also notable is Nietzsche's insistence that only a very few come even close to achieving their potential selves. Indeed, for full self-achievement we may have to wait for the arrival of the superman, whose coming is so eloquently anticipated by Zarathustra. In our discussion of the *Gorgias*, we shall find that this conception of the superman not only has very probable roots in the ideal promoted by Callicles, but also derives, perhaps unknown to Nietzsche, from the Platonic *thumos*.[127]

Equally illuminating, however, is the fact that although the will to power is certainly reminiscent of the Platonic *thumos* in some respects, it is perhaps even more reminiscent of *thumos* in Homer, *thumos* as the life-force itself.[128] For Plato, thumoeidic motivations are part of what drives us; for Nietzsche, the will to power is the fundamental force of nature:

'Where I found a living creature, there also I found will to power' ... 'And life itself told me this secret; "Behold," it said, "I am that *which must overcome itself again and again*." '[129]

The Gay Science 349 puts the point even more forcefully:

The struggle, great and small, everywhere turns on ascendancy, on growth and extension, on power, in accordance with the will to power, which is precisely the will of life.[130]

---

[127] P. 151.
[128] See p. 8 above.
[129] *Thus Spake Zarathustra* 2.12: 'Of Self-Overcoming'. Trans. Hollingdale.
[130] Trans. Kaufmann.

These Homeric echoes remind us of a critical but often overlooked fact: in creating his concept of the *thumos*, Plato has attempted to harness and limit a drive which in its Homeric origin is essentially limitless. This will be important when we try to understand in chapters 7 and 9 why the Platonic *thumos* is so difficult to tame.

It is in keeping with these Homeric echoes that Nietzsche portrays the Homeric hero as one of the most vital manifestations of the will to power.[131] Even more importantly from our point of view, he explicitly contrasts 'Homeric' values with what he sees as the enfeebled, life-denying, rational values of Plato:

Plato *against* Homer: that is the whole, authentic antagonism – on that side the deliberate transcendentalist, the great slanderer of life; on this side, the instinctive panegyrist, the *golden* nature.[132]

An explanation of Plato's hostility to Homer is offered in the *Will to Power* 427:

Gradually everything genuinely Hellenic is made responsible for the state of decay (and Plato is just as ungrateful to Pericles, Homer, tragedy, rhetoric, as the prophets were to David and Saul). The decline of Greece is understood as an objection to the foundations of Hellenic culture: basic error of philosophers – Conclusion: the Greek world perishes. Cause: Homer, myth, the ancient morality etc!

The clash that Nietzsche perceives between Plato and the Homeric or tragic hero will be exemplified by Plato's treatment of Achilles.[133] As we shall see, Plato's *thumos* does not just have its roots in Homer; it is to some extent the living repository of Homeric values.

ADLER[134]

Any connections between Plato's psychological theories and those of Adler and Freud are illuminating, in that the work of Adler and Freud is the result of extensive clinical practice, a resource which Plato obviously did not have at his disposal, and apparently felt no

---

[131] This is, however, a highly complex issue: Nietzsche's philosophy of becoming necessarily entails that the Homeric hero cannot be straightforwardly recreated.

[132] *On the Genealogy of Morals* 3.25 (trans. Kaufmann and Hollingdale).

[133] Plato's complex and shifting stance towards Achilles is explored in chs. 6, 7 and 8.

[134] Unless otherwise stated, all page references for Adler refer to *The Individual Psychology of Alfred Adler* eds. H. and R. Ansbacher (1956). This should be distinguished from Adler's own work entitled *Individual Psychology* of 1930. To indicate that the page numbers do not refer to the original texts, I have placed them in brackets.

need to invent. The particular relevance of Adler to an investigation of the *thumos* is the central role Adler gave in his psychology to what he terms 'the striving for self-enhancement'. The notion is a direct inheritance from Nietzsche, as Adler freely states in *On the Neurotic Character*: 'Much of our view of the enhancement of the self-esteem ... is included in Nietzsche's 'will to power' and 'will to seem'.[135]

A brief survey of the origin and development of this impulse provides a fruitful comparison with Plato's *thumos*. It is significant that it first emerges in Adler's thought as a straightforward aggression drive;[136] it is soon developed, however, into a striving after a final goal, a 'fictional abstract ideal' which takes the form of an ideal self.[137] This ideal self gives the personality its unity and is an attempt by the individual to 'raise himself to the full height of the self-esteem, toward complete manliness, toward the idea of being above' (pp. 109–10). The emphasis on 'manliness' is particularly interesting: in some of his writings Adler explores contemporary feminism, but when writing of the formation of personal ideals he finds it natural to speak of specifically masculine models; there is no suggestion that there are supposed to be ideals of womanliness.[138] As with the connections between the *thumos* and manliness, one needs to consider whether the association is meant to be essential or contingent, or even whether it is simply assumed without thought.

Further links between Adler and Plato reveal themselves in Adler's view that this self-ideal of true manliness is perceived as 'victory over men, over difficult enterprises',[139] and that its specific form is often based on some popular hero: 'the greater and the stronger men and their size are made into the fictional final goal'.[140] Moreover, basing one's ideal on a cultural hero will clearly mean that one's values will be largely conditioned by the society, or sub-section of society, in which one lives, or with which

---

[135] (P. 111). See also *On the Origin of the Striving for Superiority and the Sense of Community* (pp. 257–63).

[136] *The Aggression Drive* (pp. 34–8).

[137] *On the Neurotic Character* (p. 94).

[138] See also Adler's extensive exploration of notions of masculinity and what he calls the 'masculine protest' in *Individual-Psychological Treatment of Neuroses* and *Understanding Human Nature*.

[139] *Individual Psychology* (p. 95).

[140] *On the Neurotic Character* (p. 110).

one mentally associates oneself. This in turn will lead to a desire for social acceptance and recognition.[141] Similarly, the tendency to emulate a social ideal can also be educated and modified by society: hence the possibility of psychiatry. Such malleability recalls the *thumos'* susceptibility to *mousikē* in *Republic* 2 and 3.

Psychiatry requires patients. It is notable that although Adler thinks the impulse to strive after an ideal self-image is generally for the good, he also holds that it can be taken too far. If we set our ideals too high, then this will carry with it a 'dark side' which,

brings a hostile, belligerent tendency into our life, robs us of the simplicity of our sensations, and continuously attempts to alienate us from reality by tempting us to violate it. Furthermore, anyone who forms this goal of godlikeness as real and personal, who takes it literally, is soon forced to flee from real life – since it is a compromise – and to seek a life apart from real life, at best in art, but usually in pietism, neurosis and crime.[142]

The aggressive origins of the idealizing impulse are never far below the surface; it is an aspect of the human mind to be handled with extreme care. We shall have cause to remember this when we examine Plato's treatment of Achilles as a role model in chapters 6 and 7. We shall also have reason to remember Adler's doubts about forming a 'goal of godlikeness': is such a goal appropriate for humans, or should they follow Pindar and restrict themselves to mortal thoughts?[143]

FREUD

Freud's analyses of the different aspects of human motivation are also illuminating, particularly when we recall his deep admiration for Plato, and considerable, if fragmentary, knowledge of a number of his works.[144] For present purposes, the best starting-point is

---

[141] See the preface to *Individual and Community* (1926) no. 1: 9–11.

[142] *Individual-Psychology, its Assumptions and Results* (p. 97). The warning is repeated in *Melancholia* (p. 319) and *Problems of Neurosis* (p. 314).

[143] Pindar *Isth.* 5. 14–16. See pp. 29–30 above and 189–90 and 249 below.

[144] In *Three Essays on Sexuality* (1905), Freud speaks of the 'divine Plato'. He was particularly well acquainted with the *Symposium*, and with certain passages from the *Republic* and the *Phaedrus*. (*Symposium: Jokes and their Relation to the Unconscious* (1906); *Beyond the Pleasure-Principle* (1920); *Republic: Introductory Lectures on Psychoanalysis* (1920), lectures 20 and 22; *Civilization and its Discontents* (1930) ch. 4; *Phaedrus: The Question of Layanalysis* (1926) section 3; *The Ego and the Id* (1923) ch. 2. See Santas 1988 and Price 1989.

On Narcissism (1914). Freud notes four main types of narcissistic love and one of these is, again, for an ideal self, 'what one would like to be' (p. 84).[145] This ego-ideal is associated with a sense of indignation at anything felt to be unworthy of it, and a tendency to repress it:

Repression ... proceeds from the same self-respect of the ego. The same impressions, experiences, impulses and desires that one man indulges or at least works over consciously, will be rejected with the utmost indignation by another, or even stifled before they enter consciousness ... We can say that one man has set up an ideal in himself by which he measures his actual ego, while the other has formed no such ideal. (pp. 87–8)

The comparison with Leontius' self-disgust is clear. Another point of contact is Freud's belief that this creation of an ideal self is the special function of a particular faculty in the psyche:

It would not surprise us if we were to find a special psychical agency (*Instanz*) which performs the task of seeing that narcissistic satisfaction from the ego-ideal is ensured, and which, with this end in view, constantly watches the actual ego and measures it by the ideal. (p. 89)

Such a faculty is conscience. As with Adler, the content of the ideal ego that conscience creates will be largely influenced by the values and norms of one's society: parents, teachers, public opinion (p. 90). The repressive function of conscience itself, however, 'proceeds from the self-respect of the ego' (p. 87). Freud highlights this complex of social and self-regarding factors in his summing-up:

The ego ideal opens up an important avenue for the understanding of group psychology. In addition to its individual side, this ideal has a social side: it is also the common ideal of a family, a class or a nation. (p. 96)

Lastly, and again in agreement with Adler, this tendency to try to live according to a self-created but socially conditioned ideal can have both good and bad consequences. Generally, fulfilment of the requirements of this ideal is considered to be happiness (p. 95). If the ideal is set too high, however, or pursued obsessively, the damage to one's mental health can take the form of neuroses

---

[145] Page numbers refer to the Penguin Freud Library vol. 11: *On Metaphysics*. With minor corrections, the translation employed by the Penguin Freud Library is that of the Standard Edition edited by James Strachey.

or even total paranoia (p. 91). Here again, though Plato concentrates as much on the external as on the internal harm that can be caused by a misguided *thumos*, the resemblances between the *thumos* and Freud's conscience and ego-ideal are striking.

The resemblances continue when we look at Freud's later works. In *The Ego and the Id* the ego-ideal and the conscience of *On Narcissism* combine in a single term, a third agency in the mind which Freud calls the superego. He is reasonably confident that this tripartite division is supported by clinical justification (p. 383), though he is equally clear that one should be wary of giving this division any topographical location (p. 376).[146] The question is rather one of the functioning of the mind than of its 'parts' as such. Although there is again no exact parallel with the *thumos*, the similarities are nevertheless sufficient to be revealing. While it is plainly a self-regarding agency, the content of the superego's ideal is largely taken from the culture in which it develops; as in *On Narcissism*, Freud lays great emphasis on the role of authorities:

As a child grows up, the role of father is carried on by teachers and others in authority; their injunctions and prohibitions remain powerful in the ego ideal. (pp. 376-7)

Particularly important is Freud's claim that the superego displays responses and aspects which are aesthetic as well as moral: one of the most intriguing aspects of our survey of the *thumos* was its ability to respond to the *kalon* as both moral nobility and sensible beauty.[147] Furthermore, its moral–aesthetic nature 'manifests itself in the form of a categorical imperative' (p. 374) which, if denied or not properly carried out, leads to feelings of deep guilt.[148] It is, of course, vigorously debated whether the Greeks possessed a concept of guilt,[149] but the story of Leontius certainly shows how closely the *thumos* is associated with shame – an association which will be reinforced when we come to consider Plato's depiction of Achilles and Alcibiades.

Finally, there is again the danger that the superego can take over

---

[146] Though see Price 1989.
[147] See p. 12 above. We shall be exploring this link between the moral and the aesthetic further in chs. 2 and 8.
[148] In *Civilization and its Discontents* chs. 7 and 8, Freud undertakes a profound analysis of the superego which links it with feelings of guilt, remorse and the need for punishment.
[149] See Cairns 1993 for some thoughtful discussions of the issue.

the whole personality and give rise to calamitous consequences. If it pursues objects which,

take control and become too numerous, over-powerful and incompatible with one another, then a pathological outcome will be not far off. (p. 370).

Such detrimental outcomes include obsessional neurosis, hysteria, paranoia and pathological states of mourning.[150] Again, we shall find ourselves considering the last of these in particular when we examine Plato's attack on Achilles in chapter 7.

It should be emphasized once more that these points of contact between Plato and Nietzsche, Adler and Freud need to be viewed with clear eyes; there are certainly no exact parallels. In Nietzsche and Adler, for example, the tendency to strive after a self-ideal does not belong to a distinct agency within the mind, but is portrayed as the governing principle of the whole personality. My point is simply that in his description and analysis of the *thumos*, Plato highlights motivations and ideals similar to some of those which three major modern thinkers have, in different ways, regarded as central. There is even the same area of ambiguity: it is as uncertain in Nietzsche and Adler as it is in Plato whether the concern with male subjects and models is supposed to be essential or is merely contingent.

It is now time to consider in more depth quite why Plato is so interested in self-ideals, role models, courage and manliness. This will require us to outline the general framework of his approach to ethics, and to place this framework in a wider philosophical and historical context. Details of the design must wait for the textual exegeses that follow, but it is important that we first gain some sense of the overall structure of the main issues.

---

[150] See also *Mourning and Melancholia* (1917).

CHAPTER 2

Thumos, andreia *and the ethics of flourishing*

PLATO'S ETHICAL FRAMEWORK

Let us return to the passage with which this book opened. At *Gorgias* 500c, in response to Callicles' trenchant attack on philosophers as unmanly wimps, Socrates issues a challenge of his own:

> So you see how our discussion concerns that which should be of the greatest importance to any person, even if he has only a modicum of sense – that is to say, how one should live.[1]

An almost identical claim is made in *Republic* 1. At 352d Socrates says that they must study Thrasymachus' attack on conventional justice with great care: 'For our discussion is not about some trivial question, but about how one should live.'[2]

This question of how best to live is, I would suggest, Plato's fundamental ethical starting-point. As we have seen, the question of which way of life is best runs throughout the *Republic*, and we shall find that it provides the basic structure of all the dialogues we shall consider. In the *Gorgias*, for instance, Socrates stresses again at 487a that he and Callicles are concerned with 'how to live correctly', and at the end of the dialogue he concludes that they now have some evidence that 'the philosophic way of life is best'.[3] Underlying the debates concerning virtue in the *Protagoras* is the issue of how to 'live well' (351b), and in the *Laches* Nicias tells us that Socrates always compels his interlocutor to 'give an account

---

[1] ὁρᾷς γὰρ ὅτι περὶ τούτου εἰσὶν ἡμῖν οἱ λόγοι, οὗ τί ἂν μᾶλλον σπουδάσειέ τις καὶ σμικρὸν νοῦν ἔχων ἄνθρωπος, ἢ τοῦτο, ὅντινα χρὴ τρόπον ζῆν.

[2] οὐ γὰρ περὶ τοῦ ἐπιτυχόντος ὁ λόγος, ἀλλὰ περὶ τοῦ ὅντινα τρόπον χρὴ ζῆν. The fact that the formulation for 'how one should live' is almost exactly the same as *Grg.* 500c (and indeed *Laches* 187e–188a: see below) suggests that it may have been the formulation of the historical Socrates.

[3] 527e3.

of himself, of the way in which he currently lives, and of the kind
of life he has lived until now'.[4]

The *Laches'* passage is particularly telling, because it shows
clearly how for Plato questions concerning how to live are naturally associated with questions concerning what sort of person one
should be. *Gorgias* 487e–488a also makes this plain, as Socrates expands on his theme of how best to live by continuing that,

> For the most noble inquiry of all, Callicles, concerns those very issues
> with which you yourself reproached me – what sort of man one should
> be, and what one should practise, and up to what point.

And at *Republic* 365a–b Adeimantus says that young men, in
weighing up the pros and cons of justice and the mere appearance
of justice, consider

> the implications of what they hear for their own lives and how best to
> lead them, the sort of person they ought to be and the sorts of ends they
> ought to pursue.

The assumption is that a person is a discrete and continuous entity, living a discrete and continuous life, and that the type of life
lived reveals the type of person living it. By 'discrete', I do not
mean that Plato denies that a person is a part of various family,
social and political networks; I simply mean that Plato assumes
that a person can be viewed as a whole in his or her own right, as
well as a part of other wholes.[5] It is nevertheless a significant assumption, because it shows that Plato's approach to ethics requires
the support of a relatively stable ontology. At this point, however,
a problem arises. Although early dialogues such as the *Laches* and
Gorgias do not seem aware of the metaphysical implications of
their ethical assumptions, there is nothing to suggest that their implied metaphysical framework would not meet the ethical requirements. Yet by the time we reach the *Republic*, the sensible world is
portrayed as perspectival, transient and shifting:[6] this is the reason
that it cannot be an object of knowledge, but only of opinion. The
critical question, of course, is whether it is so unstable that it
cannot contain discrete and continuous ethical subjects, living
discrete and continuous lives. For in the post-*Republic Theaetetus*,

---

[4] *Laches* 187e10–188a2.
[5] The difficulties of distinguishing 'self' from 'other' in Greek thought are discussed on
pp. 150–1 below.
[6] See, for example, *Resp.* 479a–b; 508d.

Socrates discusses an alternative metaphysical conception, attributed to followers of Heraclitus, in which 'nothing *is* anything in itself, but all things, of all kinds whatsoever, are coming to be through association with each other, as the result of motion ... nothing exists as one thing itself by itself, but everything is always coming to be in relation to something, and "being" should be completely abolished'.[7] Proper names, for example, are misleading labels for a stream of transient 'perceivers' who only come into being in conjunction with a stream of ever-changing perceptions: in a world of radical flux, Socrates argues, discrete identities could never form, and we may infer that there could be no coherent notion of a whole person living a whole life. It seems to me that unless we are to accuse Plato of extreme incoherence, the kind of flux attributed to the phenomenal world in the *Republic* must be considerably less radical than that discussed in the *Theaetetus*; it must be the kind of flux which allows the ethical subject to remain intact (though probably often bewildered).[8]

The issues of how to live and what sort of person to be also assume, in Plato's hands, an intricate and indissoluble relation between a person and his or her beliefs. It is significant that in both the *Gorgias* and the *Republic* these fundamental ethical questions are prompted by the overt challenges to the conventionally just life posed by Callicles and Thrasymachus, and that these challenges are not just posed by what they say but also by who they are. By means of the dialogue form, Plato articulates the debates through a clash of personalities and ways of life. The beliefs, he suggests, are both the natural products and the natural producers of such personalities and types of life.

HAPPINESS AND VIRTUE

The first thing to note is that Plato does not assume that the answers to the basic questions need necessarily be 'moral' in any

---

[7] *Tht.* 156e8–157a3; 157a8–b1; the translation is adapted from that of Levett (in Burnyeat 1990). For the general theory, see 156a–157c; 179c–183b. I am neither suggesting nor denying that Socrates' depiction of Heraclitus' followers is accurate.

[8] At *Met.* 987a32–4 Aristotle says that when Plato was a young man he became acquainted with Heraclitus' student Cratylus and Heraclitean beliefs concerning flux; Aristotle also states that Plato continued to hold that the sensible world was in a state of flux 'in his later years'. This is doubtless true, but flux exists on a sliding scale and can consequently take an infinite variety of – presumably fluctuating – forms. There is nothing in the *Republic* to suggest that Plato believes the sensible world to be in a state of really radical flux.

conventional sense of just and fair treatment of others. Callicles and Thrasymachus are certainly not advocates of virtue so conceived, but they are quite happy to frame their positions in terms of how best to live. On the contrary, Plato believes that a virtuous way of life is one for which he must argue with all the forces he can muster. What he does hold, however, is that all human beings, Socrates and his most aggressive opponents alike, will naturally answer such questions in terms of *eudaimonia*, happiness or – more accurately – flourishing. At *Republic* 361d Glaucon restates Thrasymachus' challenge and says that their task is to discover whether the just or the unjust person is happier, *eudaimonesteros*, irrespective of consequences;[9] and it is in terms of pleasure and *eudaimonia* that the final comparison between the just philosopher and the unjust tyrant is conducted.[10] Similarily at *Gorgias* 472c Socrates tells Polus that,

> the issues over which we disagree are certainly not trivial – one might even say that they are matters concerning which it is most honourable to have knowledge and most shameful to lack it. For in short they involve our knowing or not knowing who is happy and who is not.[11]

It is, for Plato, simply a self-evident fact that *eudaimonia* is what we want, as *Symposium* 205a makes clear: the happy are happy through their acquisition of good things and, 'we no longer need to ask why the man who wants to be happy wants to be happy; the answer seems to be final.'[12]

Plato, in short, seems to take it as axiomatic that the best way of life will be the most flourishing life, and for this reason his ethical approach has often been termed eudaimonist. However, though *eudaimonia* is his starting-point, this does not mean that he prioritizes *eudaimonia* over *aretē* in his conclusions; indeed, as we saw in chapter 1, he argues forcefully in *Republic* 4 for an identification of the two.[13] He is equally a proponent of both an ethics of virtue and an ethics of flourishing; flourishing receives priority in his methodology simply because he assumes that it will be an uncontroversial base from which to argue for a controversial conclusion. The best way of persuading an immoralist to become moral, he

---

[9] See also 364a7; 365d1–2.
[10] 576b11 ff. *Eudaimonia* is mentioned specifically at 576d7, 576e5 and 577b3.
[11] See also e.g. 492e, 494d and 527c.
[12] And see *Euthyd.* 278e (we all wish to fare well) and *Meno* 78a (there is no one who wishes to be unhappy).
[13] *Resp.* 443–4.

believes, is to convince him that his immorality will make him miserable.

Whether one speaks of an ethics of virtue or an ethics of flourishing, the salient point is that Plato's approach is centred on the internal state of the soul rather than the act. What is less easy to decide is whether this emphasis on the agent is simply a matter of focus and concern, or whether it also implies logical and epistemological priority. Plato appears to support the latter option: at *Republic* 443e–444a Socrates states that actions are to be termed just if they contribute to or maintain the harmony of the just soul, and unjust if they destroy this harmony. I believe that Plato is mistaken in this ascription of logical priority to the just soul: I am not yet persuaded that the notion of a good soul (or good person) can be defined independently of the notion of a good act. Fortunately, this does not affect Plato's main claim, or perhaps assumption, which is that the internal state of the soul rather than the act should be the principal focus of our ethical concern.

This, then, is the general shape of Plato's ethics in the *Republic*. What are its implications? Clearly, if one begins with Plato's two basic questions, then an immediate issue will be the status and location of the questioner. The urgency of this task may be masked by the impersonal formulation, but it is plain that although Plato believes such questions to be generally applicable, he also wants them to be individually applied.[14] Each of Socrates' interlocutors, and each reader or hearer of the dialogues, is meant to ask of himself: 'how should *I* live?'; 'what sort of person should *I* be?' What we need to understand is the underlying psychology that makes such self-reflective questions possible. Who (or what) is the 'I' that is asking the question, and who is the 'I' being asked about? If we understand something of the structure of the self involved in such a complex thought process, then we shall understand better what sorts of factors will influence the answers. In particular, we shall be able to appreciate better what sort of

---

[14] See Nicias' comment at *Laches* 187e10–188a2, cited above.

choice is available to the questioner, or even whether it is appropriate to speak of the kind of life lived as a 'choice' at all. The
questioning 'I' is not speaking from nowhere, but from a locatable
position in time and space, and this position may already have determined the response. Indeed, it may even have determined the
possibility of such questions being asked in the first place. The
concepts of choice and determinism, of course, have been defined
in a number of ways, and these ways are not necessarily incompatible;[15] nevertheless, both questions and answers concerning
what sort of life to live inevitably require one to consider issues of
determinism and choice, and such consideration is impossible
without an analysis of the structure of practical reasoning, which
will in turn require an analysis of the self. We also need such
analyses if we are to appreciate the potentiality for ethical development: is there a time limit beyond which ethical change becomes
impossible?

It might seem that in the *Republic* it is reason that asks such
questions, and that it asks them about the tripartite *psuchē* as a
whole. After all, we know from 441e and 586d–e that it is reason
that is able to see the complete picture and act for the whole *psuchē*.
This, however, is to ignore the *thumos* and its tendency to emulate
cultural heroes in a bid to satisfy its desire for glory. It may be true
that 'how should I live?' and 'what sort of person should I be?' are
formally framed by reason, but the *thumos* will surely play a key
part in prompting them.

In either event, both the condition and the actual – as opposed
to ideal – functioning of all three parts of the *psuchē* will be critical
to the way such questions are answered, or whether they are even
asked. If reason has been able to develop to its full potential and
assume its rightful place as ruler in the *psuchē*, then, through its
kinship with the divine, it will be able to pose and reflect on such
fundamental ethical questions in comparative freedom, and see
beyond immediate cultural influences. This will be true even if the
thumos has played a part in suggesting the questions in the first
place. If, however, either *thumos* or the appetitive part is in control,
and reason is weak and undeveloped, smothered by the barnacles
of its temporary incarnation, then the questions will either not
be asked at all, or will be answered according to thumoeidic or
appetitive objectives. And given that the precise nature of these

---

[15] See Watson (1982).

objectives is formed by the immediate cultural and physical environment, the answers of the enslaved reason will be similarly confined. In *Republic* 8 and 9 Plato gives us some vivid and depressing portraits of reason stunted by its environment; he leaves us in no doubt that, when embodied, the 'divine' *logistikon* is very much at the mercy of the material world. If he is to ensure that appropriate answers are given to his basic ethical questions, then he must provide the right social and political setting.

THE NORMS OF NATURE

Moral psychology also has a normative part to play in how we answer Plato's basic questions. If I am reflecting on how to live, then, unless I am an extreme Kantian, I will need to consider what needs and desires I have, and whether they are essential or contingent. Plato certainly views such issues as fundamental to ethics: as we have seen, in the *Republic* he usually accounts for both well-being and moral goodness in terms of the harmony of the three parts of the *psuchē*. This could not be achieved by ignoring the needs of any element. Adeimantus' claim at *Republic* 504a that the analysis of the tripartite *psuchē* is absolutely pivotal to the entire work seems justified.

However, to say that no part of the *psuchē* should be ignored is not to say that every desire of each part should be satisfied in practice. Plato firmly believes that reason should only seek to satisfy our 'best and truest' desires (586e–587a); having analysed what my desires are, reason must decide what weight and space, if any, to allocate to each in my life as a whole. It is certainly not going to be a cosy matter of simply accepting my current wishes and trying, in Humean fashion, to work out how to gratify them. Plato's notion of human flourishing is an objective one, and reason will in consequence need to consider whether the satisfaction of a particular desire is likely to help or hinder the objective overall goal. As the coupling of 'best and truest' indicates, this task is metaphysical as well as evaluative: what it is to be a good human and what it is to be truly human are, for Plato, the same question.[16]

---

[16] Concerns over whether Plato commits the Naturalistic Fallacy at this point are thus misguided: Plato cannot make illegitimate moves from fact to value because he conceives the facts to be value-laden from the start. Whether this conception is persuasive is, of course, another question. For a thoughtful discussion of similar issues in Aristotle, see Nussbaum (1995).

Two issues immediately arise. Firstly, such an ambitious ideal of reason's function is clearly one that can be realised more or less well: the degree to which reason can take an objective overview will again plainly depend on whether it is in control of *thumos* and the appetites, and this, as we have seen, will in turn depend on the social and political climate. The post-Freudian will also hold that even if reason is in control in Plato's sense, it will still be unable to take account of our unconscious desires in its attempts to give shape to our lives; to this extent its influence must always be limited. This, however, is not a point that Plato makes, and he plainly lacks the terminology to do so. He does speak at 571b–d of 'violent and unnecessary' desires which arise while we sleep, but his claim here is rather that in a life guided by reason such desires will diminish or even wither away altogether. In other words, in so far as he possesses a concept of the unconscious, he seems to believe that reason does still have influence over it, albeit indirectly.

Secondly, we need to return to the problematic question of what norm of humanity is to serve as the criterion by which desires are to be judged better or worse. 586–7 may talk of satisfying the best and truest desires of each part of the *psuchē*, but, as we have seen,[17] at 611–12 Socrates says that if we wish to discover the *psuchē*'s 'true and immortal nature' we should look to its love of philosophy alone, and its longing to associate with the divine Forms. We are also exhorted to think what the *psuchē* might become if it followed its philosophic impulse wholeheartedly. This exhortation, also voiced in other dialogues, makes us wonder whether Plato really is so intent on harmonizing the three parts of the *psuchē*, or whether he in fact perceives the human task to be the transcendence of what humanity is normally taken to be. As we shall see, this dilemma is also central to Plato's exploration of role models, and consequently of the *thumos* as well. We shall be returning to it in chapters 5–8.

FIRST- AND SECOND-ORDER DESIRES

Whichever model of humanity is at issue, however, there remains the question of what precisely is involved in reason's selection of certain desires for fulfilment. Such discrimination is only possible

---

[17] Pp. 31–2 above.

in practice, I would suggest, in that all three parts of the *psuchē*, but particularly reason and *thumos*, have *evaluative attitudes* towards the feelings and desires of the other elements: Leontius' *thumos* is revolted by the first-order desire of his appetites to look at the corpses.[18] Such attitudes usually consist of both a belief and an emotional response – the balance will presumably differ depending on which part is in question – and are very similar to modern second-order desires.[19] In chapter 1 we considered the importance of the early training of first-order emotional responses as the best preparation for rational development;[20] we can now see that the cultivation of 'right feeling' is central to Plato's ethics of flourishing at a second-order level as well. Without second-order attitudes, the plans of reason concerning which desires should be satisfied would have no practical force. It thus becomes critical to consider also how these second-order attitudes are formed. More generally, it is clear that Plato is certainly no subscriber to the idea that the desire to perform an action, or the desire to have such a desire, somehow prevents either the action or the agent from being pure and good. Correct ethical choice, at both the first and the second-order levels, will be at least partly a matter of taking pleasure in the right things, of possessing good taste.

The focus on 'right feeling' has implications beyond the straightforwardly ethical, narrowly conceived. As we have already begun to see, it is one of the main reasons why Plato makes so much use of rhetoric in his methodology, despite his avowed hostility to the current practice of rhetoric and its practitioners. For his ethical programme to have any chance of success, he must convince our emotions as well as our reasoning minds. Furthermore, in trying to persuade our emotions, he will in the first instance need to pay particular attention to those of the *thumos*. The fact that the *thumos* is present before reason has fully developed makes it a key player

---

[18] Although *Resp.* 4 gives the impression that the appetites simply focus on their own objects of desire, Books 8 and 9 show that this cannot be the case. See for example 581c10–d3.

[19] The classic discussion of second-order desires is Frankfurt 'Freedom of the will and the concept of a person' (1971). Also highly influential are Watson 'Free agency' (1975) and C. Taylor 'Responsibility for self' (1976), which are in part responses to Frankfurt. Watson's paper is particularly illuminating in that it explicitly draws on central Platonic tenets.

[20] See the discussion of *Resp.* 376–412 (particularly 401d–402a) on pp. 11–12 above; *Resp.* 400–3 is explored in more depth on pp. 228–30 below.

in early emotional training, while its sensitivity to *kala* and receptivity to the reason of others make such training possible. Its responsiveness to *kala* is crucial here: if Plato's approach to ethics requires the early cultivation of good taste, then it is to the *thumos* that he must first turn.[21] It is only in this way that he can ensure that the basic ethical questions will be correctly answered, when reason has developed sufficiently to ask them.

Similarly, the *thumos*' concern with self-image and self-esteem makes it particularly likely to form second-order desires. Leontius simply does not want to be the kind of man who wants to look at corpses. Again, these second-order responses will require careful training.

ROLE MODELS

This tendency to develop second-order desires will in turn lead us to another central and closely related aspect of Plato's ethics of flourishing, the *thumos*' readiness to look for role models.[22] In thinking about what kind of person we want to be, and which desires we want to cultivate or discourage, we will naturally be led to consider the range of lives and role models currently on offer in our society, either in the citizen body itself, whether past or present, or in our society's art and mythology. Here again we can see how Plato's basic ethical questions lead us swiftly to issues of environment and community, and here too the part played by the *thumos* is critical. Though a concern with role models would form part of any ethics based on questions of how to live,[23] it will clearly have a special prominence in Plato's version, given the *thumos*' desires for social recognition and success.

I believe that this emphasis on role models is both extremely important and strangely overlooked in contemporary ethical philosophy, even by supporters of modern virtue ethics.[24] By 'role

---

[21] Although the *epithumētikon* will often be attracted to people and things which happen to be *kala*, it will not be attracted to them because they are *kala*, but because it finds them pleasurable.

[22] See pp. 12–13 and 29–31 above. The *Republic*'s exploration of role models will be discussed in detail in ch. 7.

[23] Even if the concern is to try to dissuade us from emulating any kind of model. This is the line that Nietzsche sometimes takes, though he is not consistent.

[24] Though as we saw in ch. 1, role models have received attention from some modern psychologists, Adler in particular.

model' I do not wish to imply that our lives and personalities are simply a composite of social and familial 'roles';[25] all I intend by the phrase is its usual untechnical sense of a character, whether historical or fictional, who serves as a model to be emulated to a greater or lesser extent. In some cases, perhaps, 'life model' would be a more accurate term, though I shall continue to employ 'role model' as it is in more general use. If these points are granted, then it seems to me an empirical fact that though few people try to copy another person in all particulars, many of us do emulate someone else in more limited ways, whether consciously or not. Even more commonly, we may employ someone else's image for general inspiration and motivation, or turn to it as a guide when faced with a difficult situation, asking 'what would x do?' If 'role model' is allowed to cover all these gradations, then I would suggest that Plato is absolutely right to give role models the central place in his ethics that he does; I would also argue that the importance of role models in turn lends support to his use of 'how should I live?' and 'what sort of person should I be?' as the fundamental ethical starting-points.

What particular functions do role models perform? They perhaps have special appeal to our non-rational elements, and thus have a critical part to play in early emotional training, before reason has fully developed. This is certainly one of the main uses to which they are put in the *Republic*, where as we shall see they form the major component in the early education of the *thumos*. In this respect, Plato is simply making explicit and developing a common feature of Greek culture and educational practice: as early as the *Odyssey*, we find Athena and Nestor encouraging the youthful and unformed Telemachus to take Orestes as a role model.[26] It also appears that Plato's attempt to exploit this tradition of fostering emulation was anticipated by Protagoras. At any rate, the character of Protagoras says in his Great Speech that children are made

---

[25] As, for example, Goffman has sometimes been thought to imply in such works as *The Presentation of Self in Everyday Life*, *Interaction Ritual* and *Strategic Interaction* (though his notion of 'role distance' seems to suggest a tension between the presented self and the self as performer).

[26] *Od.* 1.296–302 and 3.195–200. Several of the Homeric heroes have heroes of their own: even Achilles looks up to Heracles (*Il.* 18.117), and is discovered singing of the 'illustrious deeds of men' by the embassy at 9.189.

to learn the works of 'good poets' off by heart, since in these writings exist,

> many admonitions, but also many descriptions and praises and encomia of good men in times past, so that the boy may, through envy, imitate them and long to become such as they. (*Prt.* 326a)[27]

The diction is arresting: the young boy is portrayed as being in a state of real yearning to emulate the heroes of old. Society may need such heroes to fulfil a vital pedagogic function, but the reason that they can be so employed is because they answer a deep need in the individual as well.

So much is straightforward enough. More contentiously, it may be held that the emulation of appropriate role models can give a life shape and structure. Such a view will clearly not be attractive to Heracliteans ancient and modern, who believe that the notion of a life simply refers to an unstructured stream, or disjointed series, of experiences. It is, however, a view firmly held by Plato. He believes that our lives can and should possess an overall shape, and furthermore that the judicious employment of role models can help us to achieve this. As we have seen, his basic approach to ethics is simply not designed to accommodate more fragmentary or unstructured conceptions of a life,[28] though his discussion of Heracliteanism in the *Theaetetus* shows that he is perfectly aware of such conceptions.

Substantiation for such large assertions can only be provided by the textual exegeses contained in the following chapters. However, although we are not yet in a position to comment on Plato's practice, we can make some preliminary observations about his theory. At *Republic* 377a–c, Socrates says that it is vital to 'shape' the *psu-*

---

[27] For the Great Speech being based on Protagoras' *On the Original State of Things*, see Heinimann (1945: 115); Guthrie (1971: 63–4); Kerferd (1981: 125); Taylor (1991: 78). If this is correct, then the Great Speech suggests that Plato was substantially indebted to Protagoras as an educational theorist. Indeed, Diogenes Laertius reports (3.37 and 57) that, according to Aristoxenus (fourth century BC), most of the *Republic* is lifted from Protagoras' *Antilogika*. While the charge as it stands appears utterly fantastic (surely Aristotle would have known?), it is still much disputed whether the *Republic* nevertheless owes some debt to the *Antilogika*. The continued absence of the latter makes the question impossible to decide, but it seems to me that if the Great Speech has authentic origins then this alone is sufficient to show Plato's obligation to Protagoras in, at least, *Republic* 2 and 3.

[28] A possible exception is the *Symposium*. See Price's challenging interpretation of *Symp.* 207–12 in *Love and Friendship in Plato and Aristotle*, ch. 2.

chai of the young while they are still soft and malleable; the verb, *plattein*, is that used of a sculptor moulding clay or wax.[29] And the best way to effect this sculpting of character, we quickly learn, is to tell the children appropriate stories, thereby presenting them with suitable models to imitate.[30] Children are natural copiers, but imitating any and everything will not only flout the 'one person one job' principle, but also result in a chaotically dissolute personality; a true education in *mousikē*, based on discriminate mimesis of sound characters to appropriate musical accompaniment, allows rhythm and mode (*harmonia*)[31] to penetrate deeply into the *psuchē* and make what lies within 'shapely' (*euschēmos* 401d).

It is true that these passages talk of moulding characters rather than lives. We have, however, already seen that for Plato the characteristics of a person are necessarily expressed in their way of life: if a person's *psuchē* is 'ordered and beautiful' (403a), then this implies that their way of life will be too. In this respect he again appears to be influenced by the educational theory of the historical Protagoras. Shortly after the passage on role models from the Great Speech cited above, Protagoras claims that music teachers,

> insist on familiarizing the children's *psuchai* with the rhythms and modes, that they may become more gentle, and by gaining in rhythmic and harmonic grace may become effective in both speech and action. For the whole of a human life requires the graces of rhythm and harmony.[32]

For Protagoras, modern distinctions between ethics and aesthetics would make little sense, a point we shall be returning to shortly. And, as in Plato's *Republic*, it is clear that Protagoras' appeal for suitable music is connected to his earlier appeal for suitable poetic heroes to emulate. It would seem that the reason rhythym and mode can penetrate a receptive young *psuchē* is because the child is somehow able to imitate abstract patterns of music as well as

---

[29] Plato can also use *plattein* in a more literal sense: at *Laws* 789e the Athenian Stranger prescribes exercise for pregnant women, in order that they may 'mould the developing child like wax' (τὸ γενόμενον δὲ πλάττειν τε οἷον κήρινον).

[30] Mimesis is first mentioned explicitly at 388a.

[31] *Harmonia* covers a broad range of meanings and is often a difficult word to translate. When applied solely to music (as opposed to the broader concept of *mousikē*), it means 'mode' rather then 'harmony'; however, when Plato metaphorically applies the musical term to the *psuchē*, or even to other art forms, 'harmony' is usually the best translation. When I wish to convey both of these two senses, I have the left the term untranslated.

[32] *Prt.* 326b. The translation is adapted from Lamb 1924.

historical or fictional characters; after all, it is stated clearly at
326c7–8 that the child should be compelled to live according to
his community's laws and customs '*kathaper paradeigma*', 'as if after
a pattern'. The scope of mimesis may turn out to be wider than
normally thought.

The connection between a harmonious *psuchē* and a harmonious
way of life is also made explicit in Book 7 of the *Laws*, where Plato
returns to the question of early education in *mousikē*. At 803a–b
the Athenian Stranger claims that,

Just as a shipwright at the commencement of his building outlines the
shape of his vessel by laying down her keel, so I appear to myself to be
doing just the same – trying to frame, that is, the shapes of lives[33] according to the ways[34] of their *psuchai*, and thus literally laying down
their keels, by correctly considering by what means and by what ways of
living we shall best navigate our barque of life through this voyage of
existence.[35]

While there are significant differences between the education systems of the *Laws* and the *Republic*, this does not detract from the
basic conception of an educator's task as the shaping of a person
and a life. And the *Laws* is in agreement with the *Republic* that a
crucial element of such shaping is the judicious employment of
suitable role models.[36] There is thus strong evidence not only that
Plato thinks our lives can and should possess shape, but also that
role models can help instil the appropriate shape, at least when we
are young and pliable.

At this juncture, however, a difficult question arises. The two
functions of role models just outlined are employed by Plato in
early education, before reason is fully formed. Does this mean that
once reason has developed, role models are no longer of help to
the moral educator, that they can only assist a stage in our moral
training? Such assumptions are often made, but I believe that role
models can continue to be of use after the development of reason,
and, further, that they are employed in this way by Plato (whose
dialogues are after all directed to an audience at least capable of
rational thought). Firstly, just because reason comes along does
not mean that emotional training suddenly becomes redundant, or

---

[33] τὰ τῶν βίων ... σχήματα.
[34] 'Ways' translates *tropous*; a *tropos* can also mean a mode in music.
[35] The translation is adapted from that of Bury 1926.
[36] E.g. *Laws* 659b; 798d–e.

that it can only be conducted by strictly ratiocinative argument. Secondly, it is my contention that role models do not work on our emotions alone; I believe that they can also appeal to our intellects, and that this appeal can play an important part in our adult ethical life. I also believe that Plato recognizes and makes use of this intellectual aspect of role models, though he remains ambivalent about whether they still need ultimately to be transcended.

Let us consider first the general claim, before seeing whether it applies to Plato in particular. The above quotes from the *Republic* and the *Laws* show how role models can be employed to impart structure to a life; the person consciously employing them in this way, however, is the adult educator, not the imitative child. There is no suggestion that the children themselves view their lives as potentially possessing shape, or regard role models as a good way of achieving this. It is my belief that role models can also be consciously employed by the rational adult (or nearly adult) imitator, both to import structure and to perceive emerging structures more clearly. The argument runs as follows. If we need to feel that our lives have meaning, then one way of achieving this would be to feel that they possess shape as a whole; the question 'how should life be lived?' also seems to lead in this direction. It is, however, usually very difficult to discern any kind of structure and shape from inside the stream of one's own experiences: the messy onward rush of everyday life can all too easily strike us as just one damned thing after another. It is often easier to discern some sort of shape in the lives of others, particularly if those lives are in some sense complete – either because the people are dead, or because they are fictional. Reflection on the overall structure of these whole lives then makes two further moves possible. Firstly, through comparison and contrast one may come to perceive some sort of structure emerging in one's own life. Secondly, through emulation one may be able consciously to *impart* some kind of structure to one's life.

A weaker version of the thesis may even disarm the Heracliteans who deny that life can possess a structured shape at all: perhaps all that role models do is to help one create a *sense* of pattern, which may be all that is needed. To be successful, however, such a manoeuvre will usually rely on the subject's ignorance of it,[37] and

---

[37] It seems at least possible that in some cases a person could be aware that the imported sense of pattern was artificial, and yet still find that sense of pattern comforting.

in any case it is not as we have seen the line that Plato takes. What is rather more difficult to discern is whether Plato thinks that role models can be consciously emulated by adults for the reasons I have suggested. Evidence, if it exists, will depend on Plato's use of role models for rhetorical purposes, beyond the strict confines of early education programmes in utopian states. I believe that we shall find clear examples of such proof, most notably in the way he sets up Socrates as a new exemplar, albeit a complex one.[38]

Whatever the truth of such suggestions, there is no doubt that the central place that Plato allocates to role models has important implications for his ethics as a whole. Firstly, it shows that an ethics based on the notions of flourishing and virtue need not be so lacking in substantive content and practical guidance as some modern commentators have claimed,[39] though we should admittedly not expect detailed precision. If it is true that the question 'how should I live?' positively invites one to consider possible role models, then it would seem that any ethics based on such a question strongly encourages one to fill in a picture – or pictures – of what human flourishing might be. It is in this pragmatic light, I believe, that we should read the many discussions in the dialogues of the traditional Greek heroes of myth and legend: would we really want to live the life of – for example – Achilles, even if we could? And in choosing the dialogue form, Plato also allows us to see a wide range of potential or actual role models in action, whether they are self-proclaimed authorities and guides such as Protagoras and Hippias, *ancien régime* officers such as Nicias and Laches, or charismatic mavericks such as Callicles and Alcibiades. Furthermore, we shall find that through the skilful use of forward-shadowing we are enabled to glimpse not only what their lives are currently like, but what they will shortly become. Far from tossing us vague injunctions, Plato wishes to ensure that our choices are as concrete as possible.

A further consequence is that the particular selection of role model (or models) will again bring into sharp focus the question of whether we want to aim at a human or divine ideal. This will especially be the case in a culture such as that of ancient Greece

---

[38] Socrates' status as a role model is discussed in detail in chs. 5, 6 and 8. The issue of whether all role models, including Socrates, must ultimately be transcended is also discussed in ch. 8.

[39] See Louden 1984: 'On some vices of virtue ethics'.

which possesses a mythology and literature in which gods and semi-divine heroes figure so prominently.[40] Is it appropriate for an ordinary mortal to seek to emulate a divine or semi-divine being, even if only in a limited respect?

More tentatively, I would also like to suggest that the emphasis on role models can be added to the growing body of evidence that what we distinguish as ethics and aesthetics are, for Plato, at the very least extremely closely linked. Such a link is, of course, inherent in the term *kalon* itself, embracing as it does both sensible beauty and moral nobility;[41] yet while the general connection has been frequently observed, surprisingly little attention has been paid to precisely how it operates in Plato's thought. When discussing the early training of the *thumos* outlined in *Republic* 3, we saw how correct ethical choice was portrayed in part as the exercise of good taste;[42] we are now, I believe, in a position to make some sense of this suggestive but nebulous claim. At the beginning of this chapter I argued that Plato's approach to ethics requires a certain conception of a person as a discrete, continuous whole, living a discrete, continuous life; we also saw that this whole can simultaneously be viewed as a part of the greater wholes of family or state. The focus on role models suggests that this basic notion needs to be expanded: the ethical subject may now appear as a character both constructing and participating in a *narrative* whole,[43] particularly if the role model emulated is from fiction, legend or myth. Furthermore, the idea that role models can help us both to perceive and to create structure in our lives can clearly also be used to reinforce this conception of life as a narrative, capable of aesthetic evaluation. Plainly, we need to be careful here. When MacIntyre, for example, employs the metaphor of narrative structure in relation to a person's life, he seems to be interested mainly in the metaphor's capacity to render that life morally intelligible.[44] Nevertheless, such metaphors certainly invite one to view and evaluate the subject and his or her life in similar terms to

---

[40] Kirk (1970: 179) writes that 'The Greeks are a special case. In the mythology of most other peoples, heroes ... are either inconspicuous or altogether absent.'

[41] See p. 17 above.

[42] Pp. 58–9 above. See also pp. 11–12 and 17.

[43] Again, the individual narrative will also form part of the larger narratives of family, race or political community.

[44] MacIntyre 1985; see particularly 204–25.

those sometimes used for viewing and evaluating works of art: they encourage us to consider a person's character and life in terms of the relations between parts, and between parts and whole, and such considerations will centrally depend on notions of proportion and harmony. Structure, after all, can impart not only intelligibility but grace.

ROLE MODELS AND SOCIETY

These suggested links between ethics and aesthetics will be explored in more depth below, particularly in chapter 8;[45] less tendentious, perhaps, are the political and sociological implications of Plato's approach to ethics. If role models are normally supplied by our culture (or some sub-section of it), then relations between individual and community will clearly be important in any ethics of virtue and flourishing. And even more generally, if there is an objective account to be given of human excellence and wellbeing, we may wonder what social and political conditions are necessary for its achievement. In Plato, however, individual/community relations will be particularly critical, given his belief that, in the shape of the *thumos*, there is a part of our *psuchē* which will naturally tend to absorb cultural influences in its bid for social recognition and success. On this psychological model more than most it will – initially at any rate – be society which largely forms both our first- and second-order desires: our social and cultural environment not only helps explain what we are, but also offers possibilities for what we might become.

The emphasis on role models also draws attention to the possibility that an individual may in turn influence his or her community, by wittingly or unwittingly serving as a current or future ideal. As *Republic* 8 and 9 make clear, the dynamic between individual and community is, on the surface at any rate, by no means one-way. If one analyses this mutual influence a little more deeply, however, the picture takes on a more disturbing aspect. For, given the *thumos'* goals, the person who is taken as a role model by his society is likely to be someone who epitomizes that society's current values; individual models may well be able to influence their environment, but their effect is more likely to be one of reinforce-

---

[45] See especially pp. 227–9.

ment than revolution. Role model cultures, in short, would seem to have an intrinsic tendency to reproduce themselves.

Plato's approach to ethics, then, leads inevitably and swiftly to issues of politics and education, and equally swiftly it runs into a serious practical difficulty. In order to secure what he considers to be the right role models, Plato is acutely aware that he must first engineer the right society, educated in the appropriate *mousikē*. Despite his powerful idealist tendencies, he is far from dismissive of the influence of contemporary social conditions and the strength of historical forces, as again *Republic* 8 and 9 make clear. The problem is how to set about this restructuring, given the conservative tendencies of the *thumos*' desire to emulate recognized local heroes. Plato wishes to utilize what would appear to be a resistant force.

In order to appreciate the strength of this force, we need to consider the ideals and role models most likely to appeal to a young Athenian of the fourth century BC. Given the segregation of the sexes and the general lack of interest in female education, this will in practice mean considering the ideals of young Athenian males. First, however, we need to remind ourselves of the principal views on the relation between virtue and gender available to Plato's generation.

MALE AND FEMALE VIRTUE

The traditional view, voiced throughout Homer and the generally conservative choruses of Greek tragedy, is that some virtues are specifically 'male' and others 'female', and that a virtuous man will necessarily display different characteristics from those displayed by a virtuous woman. A good example of this assumption is given at *Meno* 71e, where the aristocratic young Meno is asked by Socrates to define *aretē*:

But there is no difficulty, Socrates, in saying what it is. First of all, if it is the virtue of a man[46] that you are after, it is easy to see that a man's virtue consists in managing the city's affairs capably, and in such a way that he will help his friends and injure his enemies, while taking care to come to no harm himself. Or if you want a woman's virtue, that is not difficult

---

[46] ἀνδρὸς ἀρετή.

to describe either – she must run the house well, look after the indoor property and be obedient to her husband.

In this traditional scheme of gendered virtues, the supremely male virtue is of course *andreia*, 'manliness', the behaviour or qualities most proper to a man. In chapter 1 we saw how difficult *andreia* is to translate, and some of the problems this raises in the *Republic*.[47] We now need to consider the nature of its ambiguity in more depth.

In the Archaic period, the quality most proper to a man was felt to be effectiveness in fighting, which in turn might involve a number of factors: physical strength and speed, technical skill, and courage. Of these, courage is perhaps the most critical, and in practice *andreia* almost always at least partly implies courage or resolution; indeed, in much of its usage the notions of 'manliness' and 'courage' can appear to be inextricably intertwined. The word almost seems to denote praise of an *event*, the event of a man performing courageous acts, paradigmatically on a battlefield.[48] It appears that generally users of the word did not stop to consider whether they were praising the act simply because it was courageous or because it was also perceived as quintessentially male, and linguistic constraints clearly made it difficult even to formulate the question. One of the main tasks of this book is to ask whether what we perceive as the separate connotations of *andreia* were ever fully disentangled in Greek thought. Was it ever open to an ancient author to use *andreia* to mean 'courage' alone, with no appeals to notions of manliness?

In order to understand the difficulties involved, we need first to ask why courage should have been viewed as such a male preserve at all. The criterion cannot simply have been the risk of pain or death, or women would also have been regarded as having a strong claim to the virtue, given that the risks of childbirth were extremely high: witness Medea's heartfelt plea that she would prefer to stand three times in the front line of battle rather than give birth once.[49] Whatever the relative statistics, something more must

---

[47] See pp. 8, 10, 23, 27 and 29.

[48] The neuter plural of the adjective, τὰ ἀνδρεῖα, always refers to brave and manly deeds.

[49] Euripides *Medea* 248. It is true that at *Il.* 11.267–72, Agamemnon's wounded arm is said to cause him pains as piercing as those of a woman in labour, but there is still no suggestion that the labouring woman displays any kind of *aretē*.

be at stake than one's own comfort and life. The answer is surely provided by Aristotle in the *Nicomachean Ethics*, where *andreia* proper is defined as risking one's life in the noblest (*kallista*) circumstances – and this, Aristotle adds, 'describes death in warfare, where the danger is greatest and most noble'.[50] This superior nobility presumably results from the fact that the male warrior is perceived as saving an entire community, rather than simply adding to its numbers; there may also be a feeling that courage in battle is to some extent a matter of choice, whereas a woman in labour has no option but to go through with it.

Be this as it may, once the association between manliness and courage is embedded in the language, some tough problems follow. Firstly, even if the agents are male, it is as we have seen usually very hard to know the extent to which their maleness is an issue. Sometimes it appears that both connotations are in play: in his account of how the civil war in Corcyra subverted the application of moral terms, Thucydides complains in 3.82.4 that:

Foolish daring was now regarded as the courage (*andreia*) one would expect to find in a party member; prudent delay was a specious cloak for cowardice (*deilia*), moderation a screen for unmanliness (*anandros*); and to be wise in all matters was to get nothing done.

Here, *andreia* is clearly contrasted with both cowardice and unmanliness. Yet one still cannot be entirely sure whether Thucydides is aware of what the double opposition implies about the meaning of *andreia*; it is just possible, if unlikely, that he drew the double opposition unthinkingly. And in the vast majority of cases it is even more ambiguous whether the author is consciously appealing to notions of maleness, or whether they are thinking primarily of the virtue of courage – or even just effectiveness in action – and simply taking the masculine connotations of the word for granted.

Even more problematic is the question of courageous women. Given that Greek mythology contained a number of women who were prepared to endure hardship or sacrifice their lives for the sake of some perceived *kalon*, how was their behaviour to be described? It seems unlikely that an author could ascribe *andreia* to a female without being conscious of the word's root meaning, and

---

[50] *E.N.* 1115a6–b6.

arguably impossible that he could write of female *andreia* without making some kind of statement, whether intentional or not, on the proper connection between the virtues and gender. Even in cases where the author seems to approve of a woman displaying *andreia* and daring, her behaviour is always treated as unusual: see, for example, Herodotus' ascription of *andreia* to Xerxes' ally Artemisia in 7.99, and Thucydides' account of women joining in the fray *tolmērōs*, 'boldly', in support of the democratic party in the Corcyran civil war (3.74). Thucydides adds that the Corcyran women endured the din and confusion in a way that was *para phusin*, 'beyond their nature'. Such apparent endorsement, however, is rare: in general male responses to the notion of female courage are far more ambivalent. Amongst the more conservative views, Aristotle holds in the *Politics* that *andreia* can be attributed to a woman, but not in the same way that it is attributed to a man:

> The *sōphrosunē* and *andreia* of a man and a woman are different. For a man would appear a coward if he only possessed the *andreia* of a woman, and a woman would appear a gossip if she were only as discreet as a good man.[51]

A reason is given at 1260a: the temperance, *andreia* and justice of a man are the virtues of a ruler, whereas these qualities in a woman are those of a servant. And in the *Poetics* he takes an even tougher line. While not precisely denying that women can display *andreia*, he nevertheless maintains that it is 'not fitting' for a poet to ascribe it (or cleverness) to a female character.[52] For Aristotle, good men and good women are not good in the same way.

An extreme instance of this view is provided by Chrysothemis in Sophocles' *Electra*, where the poet clearly exploits the ambiguities of *andreia* to raise questions about the nature of women who perform *andreia* acts. In trying to persuade Chrysothemis to help her kill Aegisthus, Electra claims that if they uphold the honour of their house everyone will praise them for their *andreia* (983), though quite what she intends by the term is debatable. There is no way of telling whether she simply means 'courage', or whether she is consciously and willingly embracing a specifically masculine ideal. In either case, Chrysothemis is certainly conscious of the word's root meaning when she replies curtly that Electra should

---

[51] *Pol.* 1277b20–3.   [52] *Poet.* 1454a23.

remember that she was born a woman, not a man: it is not appropriate for a woman to take up arms. The chorus also take this
view; there could be no plainer indication of the entrenched opinions Plato must overcome if he is to persuade his readers to accept
the *andreia* and martial practices of the female Auxiliaries and
Philosopher-Queens of *Republic* 5.[53]

In the traditional picture, therefore, what is praised as virtuous
behaviour in a man is by no means necessarily praised in a
woman,[54] and the converse also holds. The traditional picture,
however, is not the only one that Plato possessed. Also available to
him was the Socratic inheritance, and there is persuasive evidence
that the historical Socrates did not believe that virtue was gendered. This is certainly what Aristotle claims in *Politics* 1.13, where
he criticizes Socrates for holding that the temperance and courage
and justice of a man and a woman are the same,[55] and a similar
belief is attributed to Socrates in Xenophon *Symposium* 2.9, though
here there is the proviso that women are still lacking in judgement
and strength.[56] It is also the view of the Socrates of the *Meno*, and
I take the traditional line that the Socrates of the early and early–
middle dialogues bears a fairly close resemblance to the historical
character. At *Meno* 73a–c Socrates replies to Meno's view of the
division between male and female virtues cited above:

– Didn't you say that a man's virtue lay in directing the city's affairs
well, and a woman's in directing her household well?

---

[53] Female Guardians are discussed on pp. 245–8 below.
[54] Intelligence in a woman can also be singled out as specifically 'masculine', and the tone
of the speaker in these cases is often ambivalent to say the least: *vide* the watchman's
equivocal description of Clytemnestra as 'ἀνδρόβουλος', 'of masculine wits', at Aeschylus *Ag.* 11.
[55] *Pol.* 1260a20–4.
[56] This may also be the implication of Xenophon *Symposium* 2.12, where Socrates tells
Antisthenes that a sword-dancer has learnt *andreia* even though she is a woman. There is
certainly irony in the 'καίπερ γυνή', but it seems to me that this is directed at Antisthenes' conservative expectations of female capabilities, and does not indicate that Socrates himself is surprised. An apparent anomaly is Socrates' patronizing ascription of an
'ἀνδρικὴν ... διάνοιαν', a 'masculine intelligence', to Ischomachus' wife at Xenophon
Oec. 10.1, but this may simply indicate Xenophon's own (probably unconscious) ambivalence on the issue of women's abilities. At a more general level, the fact that Xenophon
portrays Socrates as perfectly happy to debate with women presumably counts for something, as does the claim of Plato's Socrates at *Apology* 41c that he is greatly looking forward to examining the great and the good in Hades, 'both men and women', to see who
is wise and who is not.

– Yes.
– And is it possible to direct either a city or a household or anything else well, if you do not direct it temperately and justly?
– Certainly not.
– ... Then both women and men require the same qualities, justice and temperance, if they are going to be good.
– So it seems.
– ... So all humans are good in the same way, since they become good by acquiring the same qualities.

Discussion of the virtuous male or female is to be replaced by discussion of the virtuous human (*anthrōpos*): gender is simply not relevant to considerations of the ethical subject.[57]

Socrates, then, is I believe the first Greek on record to ask explicitly what it is, for example, about a man fighting in a battle that deserves praise. He is certainly the first Greek on record explicitly to claim that what we are praising is simply the man's courage, and furthermore that this courage could in theory be displayed just as well by a woman, even if she has fewer opportunities in practice. The fact that courage is termed 'manliness', in other words, is simply the result of historical contingency.

These are the overt positions on the relation between virtue and gender that Plato must consider. There is, however, also a more equivocal way in which the issue might be treated by a post-Socratic thinker: the writer may discuss a virtue ostensibly as if it were gender-neutral, while still investing it, whether consciously or not, with undertones of masculinity. An example may be the discussion of *andreia* in *Nicomachean Ethics* 3.6 that we considered above, in which the paradigm case of *andreia* is said to be risking one's life in warfare, where the danger is greatest and most noble.[58] In this passage Aristotle appears to be defining what we would term courage rather than manliness, and he certainly does not say outright in the *Ethics*, as he does in the *Politics*, that *andreia* properly belongs to males. However, given his belief that the noblest ends are those of the battlefield, and his assumption that the battlefield is male territory, it is not difficult to see why he writes else-

[57] Though the spheres in which men and women operate may still be different; Socrates does not commit himself. For Plato's more radical approach, see pp. 245–7. A stimulating examination of these issues can be found in Ward Scaltsas 1992.
[58] P. 70.

where as if *andreia* were chiefly a masculine preserve. The *Politics* passages suggest that even in the *Ethics*, though nothing is explicitly said, Aristotle is unconsciously assuming that his 'human' subject is in fact male. If this is the case, then it seems clear that in these unconscious assumptions he is influenced by the word's root meaning. A modern instance might be the apparently casual use of a phrase such as 'virile' language: the user may think that they just mean something like muscular, and not intend any gender-specificity, but what they think they are doing may not be the whole story.

Alternatively, a writer could quite consciously exploit the ambiguities of *andreia* to play a double game. It was suggested in chapter 1 that Plato sometimes appears reluctant in the *Republic* to divest *andreia* of all its masculine associations, despite the apparent gender-neutrality of the virtues in Book 5.[59] Whether this is true, and what the nature of the game might be, is an issue to which we shall return.[60] One thing, however, is not in doubt. If the meaning of *andreia* in the *Republic* is ambivalent, then these ambivalences will presumably also apply to the *thumos*, of which *andreia* is the particular virtue. This might help explain how the *thumos*' connections with courage in Book 4 can degenerate into the timocratic man's obsession with manliness in Book 8.[61] The hybrid appearance of the *thumos* is starting to seem more explicable.

THE COMPLEXITY OF COURAGE

Quite apart from the issue of gender, however, the virtue of *andreia* raises plenty of questions, as our review of *thumos* in the *Republic* made clear. What is the relation between courage and anger, violence and aggressive self-promotion? What is the relation between courage, risk and fear? Does courage require a particular knowledge- or belief-component, or a particular kind of reasoning? And does it manifest itself primarily in war, or can it also exist in peacetime? We may also wonder how it can be reconciled to the *Republic*'s central claim that the life of virtue brings happiness to its practitioner: surely courage, of all the virtues, requires that the agent suffer, whether the suffering be in the form of risk or actual hardship? In terms of the debate over role models, perhaps cour-

[59] P. 23.   [60] See particularly pp. 96–8 and 244–8 below.   [61] P. 29.

age should be viewed simply as the personal ideal of a heroic few, to be admired but not necessarily emulated by the rest of us.

Before returning to the *Republic*, however, we need to step back some way and consider Plato's treatment of *andreia*, male role models and the proper education of young men in a number of earlier dialogues. Our aim in so doing will be two-fold. Firstly, Plato's early explorations of these themes are of the utmost interest in their own right, and show how the issues later associated with the *thumos* were always of central importance to him. Secondly, it is only by considering these earlier discussions that we can fully appreciate the kinds of problems that the *Republic* is trying to solve. We shall in particular need to ask whether any of the difficulties raised in the pre-*Republic* works require the assistance of the tripartite *psuchē* in general and the *thumos* in particular.

CHAPTER 3

Arms and the man: andreia *in the* Laches

As we saw in chapter 2, the *Laches* is one of the clearest examples of Plato's belief that ethical enquiry should begin from questions of how to live and what sort of person to be. Two worthy but undistinguished Athenian gentlemen, Lysimachus and Melesias, are worried about the best way to educate their sons: their own education was neglected by their famous fathers, and they do not want to repeat the mistake. In particular, they cannot decide whether the boys should be taught the controversial new technique of fighting in armour, and they have invited two Athenian generals, Laches and Nicias, to watch a display with them and give their advice. Lysimachus and Melesias wish their sons to become *aristoi*, excellent and successful men: will learning to fight in armour promote this?

Before considering Nicias' and Laches' answers, it is worth noting a further way in which the opening scene accords with the suggested framework of an ethics of virtue and flourishing. This concerns general pedagogic method. All four characters take it for granted that becoming an *aristos* depends on the cultivation of the right studies and practices:[1] it is the result of years of careful training. To be fully effective, however, such studies should not be viewed in isolation, but should be seen as forming part of an entire character and way of life. For the natural way to learn good practices is to reflect on and associate with those who already embody them. Lysimachus and Melesias thus relate to their sons the 'many noble deeds' of the boys' grandfathers, and Nicias has recently employed the illustrious Damon to instruct his own son in *mousikē*, claiming that Damon is not only a skilled musician, but 'in every

---

[1] The importance of ἐπιτηδεύματα is stressed in 179d and 180a.

other respect a worthy companion for young men of that age'
(180d).[2] Though mimesis is not explicitly mentioned, it is clearly
hoped that the boys will be inspired by such examples, and adopt
their characters and ways of life as models for their own.

It is with this in mind that Laches recommends that they also
ask the advice of Socrates, who is standing nearby. Socrates has
not only devoted himself to the study of which practices young
men should pursue, but is himself of excellent character, having
acquitted himself with honour in the retreat from Delium. Later
in the dialogue, in another telling instance of the close ties between virtue ethics and aesthetics, Laches says he only respects the
arguments of the man whose life and speech are in harmony; such
a man is the true *mousikos*.[3] Laches admits he has not yet heard
Socrates' arguments, but his experience of Socrates' courage at
Delium inclines him towards them. His counsel is worth having
because his life legitimizes his words.

Again, though it is not explicitly stated, the clear implication is
that Socrates would be a worthy role model for his young male
companions: far from corrupting the youth, his example can enable them to develop into *aristoi*. At this point, however, a question
presents itself. The focus of the *Laches* is not education in general,
but very specifically the education of young males and what pursuits are suitable for them.[4] Does this mean that Socrates is being
recommended by Laches as a specifically male role model? If so,
then we need to ask whether Socrates would be happy about this,
given his commitment in Aristotle, Xenophon and the *Meno* to an
ungendered notion of human excellence, and his forthright rejection of specific male and female virtues.[5]

The difficulty here is in distinguishing the essential from the historically contingent. After all, the starting-point for the *Laches* is the

---

[2] In terms of the formation of Plato's ethical views, Damon is a shadowy but important
figure. It is plain from *Resp.* 400b and 424c that he devoted much study to the moral and
social effects of different musical modes and rhythms, and was particularly interested in
their ability to reflect and shape different ways of life. His work offers the clearest possible
example of how ethics and aesthetics were blended in Greek thought. For further references to Damon, see Guthrie 1971: 35 n.1.

[3] 'Such a man seems to me the genuine *mousikos*. He has created the finest harmony – not
on the lyre or other instrument of entertainment, but by making his own life a symphony
between his words and his deeds in the true Dorian mode – not the Ionian nor the Phry-
gian nor the Lydian, but in the true Hellenic harmony' (188d2–8).

[4] E.g. 179e1–2; 180a4; 180c3–4; 181d8–e1.

[5] See pp. 72–3 above.

particular question of how to educate Lysimachus' and Melesias' sons: we are not told whether they even had any daughters. Even if they did, it is undeniable that at this time the education of males was of far more political and social significance than the education of females. Indeed, Socrates himself says at 185e1–2 that their real topic of discussion is the *psuchai* of young men, and that if sons turn out badly then it can ruin the whole family,[6] a point with which Lysimachus concurs. The issue is whether current social conditions are simply a matter of contingency, or whether they reflect an essential difference in the way the virtues are structured in men and women. If there is no such difference, then Socrates can coherently acknowledge contemporary social conditions while still allowing for the possibility of their transformation. It may, for instance, be significant that at 186d1 Socrates employs gender-neutral terminology when he says that he is sure Laches and Nicias are able to educate an *anthrōpos* (person). In contrast, Laches always employs the specifically male term '*anēr*'; indeed at 188c8 he speaks of the *mousikos* who harmonizes his words and actions as '*hōs alēthōs ontos andros*', a 'real man'. Nicias also talks of 'any self-respecting male' at 200a8, though his position is a more ambivalent one, as we shall see.

The question of the extent to which maleness is essential or contingent to the different speakers in the *Laches* does not only have implications for Socrates' status as a guide and role model. It is, of course, absolutely central to the dialogue's main theme, the attempt to define *andreia*. While the context makes it clear that courage is always at least part of what is being discussed, we shall find that it is far more difficult to decide whether a particular speaker is also concerned with manliness. It is not, however, a problem that can be ducked: as I hope to show, it seems to me that one of Plato's main purposes in writing the dialogue is to try to disentangle the two main threads intertwined in current usage of the term, and to see how they relate. By attributing to Laches fairly conventional views on *andreia*, he gives himself the opportunity to explore the deep tensions that lie within it.

Conventional beliefs about moral excellence are also evident in Lysimachus' conception of what it is to be *aristos*: for Lysimachus, the touchstone of *aretē* is renown in general and the approval of

---

[6] 186b5–8. See also 187a.

the already renowned in particular. His anxiety over his and Melesias' sons, for instance, takes the form of a concern that they will win no fame and be unworthy of the illustrious names of their grandfathers (179d4–5); and when Socrates is introduced to him as a suitable adviser he is reassured to hear that Socrates has a good reputation amongst those whose opinion is 'worth trusting' (181b6). This traditional view of moral worth also comes under scrutiny later in the dialogue. At 189a–b, for example, we find Laches asserting that the harmony between Socrates' words and actions is sufficient guarantee of his educational credentials: he is, he claims, completely indifferent to whether or not Socrates has acquired a fine reputation.

FIGHTING IN ARMOUR: NICIAS' DEFENCE (181d–182d)

Having placed the debate in context, Plato now returns us to the dialogue's opening question: is the new technique of fighting in armour a suitable accomplishment for a young man to learn? Nicias claims that it is both useful and noble, one of the skills which are worthwhile for any man to acquire and practise. It will improve physical fitness and be extremely helpful in war, giving its practitioner a formidable appearance and making him a more skilful soldier both when fighting in line and when involved in Homeric-style one-to-one combat, with its swooping attacks and quick retreats. It will also increase his desire to acquire other military skills, such as troop-management and generalship. And above all, it will make him *tharraleōteron kai andreioteron* (182c6), bolder and more *andreios*. In all these respects it is a fitting accomplishment for a free man.

This defence of military technique seems straightforward enough until we reach the claim that the skill of fighting in armour will make one bolder and more *andreios*. The first question to decide is whether the two terms are supposed to be synonymous. The answer is probably that they are not: at 197b Nicias will be at pains to distinguish *andreia* proper from mere *tolmē*, boldness or rashness, and there is no reason to suppose that that distinction does not hold good here. This, however, does not mean that Nicias' precise reasons for distinguishing boldness and *andreia* in the later passage necessarily apply at this early stage: by 197 his thinking has received the benefit of Socratic questioning. We still need to ask how *tharros* (boldness) and *andreia* are to be interpreted in 182, before we can speculate on why a technical skill should be thought to promote them.

At first sight the claims about *tharros* may seem unproblematic. If it means something like 'a willingness to take risks', then the ability to fight in armour could give one the confidence to take risks more readily. Deeper reflection, however, reveals a number of serious puzzles stemming from this simple reading. Surely technical expertise alone will not be sufficient to make one prepared to risk injury or death: some kind of psychological or behavioural trait must also be required. Without such a trait, there is always the possibility that accurate knowledge of one's capabilities might actually make one more cautious on occasion, fearing to tread where fools rush in. Again, even if the confidence arising from technical expertise does make one more inclined to take risks in the first place, it will also decrease the gravity of those risks. If boldness is to be correlated not just with risk-taking, but with the severity of the risk, then perhaps it is the person who enters danger without the support of technical accomplishments who is the bolder.[7] There is also the tricky question of whether the risks need to be actual risks, or only perceived ones. And what of the high-spirited fighter who is so carried away by the heat of the moment that he temporarily ceases to be aware of the risks at all? It would seem that even with boldness the relation between the property and different kinds of knowledge and belief is highly complex. Technical expertise alone can never be the whole story, and sometimes may not even be part of it.

The claim that fighting in armour makes one more *andreios* presents even more intricate problems. Once more, our first question must be to ask what *andreia* means here: to what extent is masculinity an issue, and is the main emphasis on success in warfare or on the virtue of courage? These issues will have considerable bearing on the plausibility of Nicias' claim. If *andreia* here denotes a specifically masculine ideal, and war is seen as male terrain (whether essentially or contingently), then learning a new martial skill could be seen as enhancing one's masculinity. Again, if the term principally connotes being a successful fighter, then the acquisition of a new military technique may well help promote this.

---

[7] Laches will make this point re. *andreia* at 193a–c. See pp. 91–2 below.

If the accent is chiefly on courage however, then, even more than with boldness, we need to ask why possession of a technical skill should be thought to promote it. Here too, such a question cannot be answered until we have made a working attempt to say what courage is. If it is to be distinct from boldness, then it cannot simply amount to risk-taking; yet if it involves (or can involve) taking risks, then precisely the same issues arise as arose in the case of *tharros*. We may also want to consider the possibility that some cases of courage do not involve taking risks at all. What, for instance, about endurance of present hardships? And, crucially, what about the ultimate goals which the risk-taking or endurance are supposed to achieve? As with boldness, it would appear that technical military knowledge is at most only an element of *andreia*, and will sometimes play no part at all.

Nicias' position here is extremely difficult to interpret. Taken as a whole his speech suggests that, whatever his later position in the dialogue, his initial concern is with the traditional ideal of the successful male warrior. His interest in success is particularly revealed by his reference to current fighting practices: if *andreia* implies success, then the precise form that it takes in any age will depend on being able to master contemporary fighting styles. As these styles change, so will the way *andreia* is manifested. However, being a good and successful fighter can never result solely from technical proficiency; as we have seen, courage too will almost always be required. So even if Nicias is using *andreia* in its pre-Socratic sense at this stage of the proceedings, he still needs to face the questions outlined above about the relations between courage, confidence and risk.

Nicias' defence of military expertise, then, raises many of the dialogue's central issues, and we shall be discussing them in more detail when we consider Laches' claim at 193a–c that it is on the contrary the man without technical proficiency who is the more *andreios*. We shall also need to reconsider Nicias' support for technical skill when we examine his definition of *andreia* as knowledge of what is to be feared and what dared. Is such end-related knowledge supposed to supplant the technical knowledge praised earlier, or is it meant somehow to incorporate it? The question is of fundamental importance not just for the *Laches*, but for all the occasions in which Plato and Xenophon portray Socrates comparing virtue to a craft.

FIGHTING IN ARMOUR: LACHES' CRITIQUE (182d–184c)

Laches' opinion of the new skill is as sceptical as Nicias' is favourable. If it is so useful in war, he asks, then why have the war-obsessed Lacedaimonians not shown an interest in it? Even more tellingly, why is it that none of the self-professed experts at fighting in armour has ever distinguished himself in battle? They have just been watching Stesilaus, and hearing the grandiose claims he makes for his so-called art; yet when he attempted to put some of his strange techniques and equipment to use in a real-life skirmish, he made a complete fool of himself. All of which shows that this new-fangled fashion is not worth bothering about:

> For it seems to me that if some *deilos* believed that he had learnt this skill (*epistēmē*), he would become more foolhardy as a result and thus make his true nature the more conspicuous. Whereas in the case of an *andreios*, he would be scrutinized by everybody to see if he made some tiny mistake, and he would be fiercely criticized. For laying claim to such a skill provokes jealousy, so that unless the claimant is remarkably superior to everyone else in excellence (*aretē*), there is no way that he can escape becoming a laughing-stock, through alleging that he possesses a skill of this kind. (184b3–c4)

This passage has been found puzzling for a number of reasons, most of which again arise from the difficulty of translating *andreios* and *deilos*.[8] Do they mean simply courageous and cowardly, or good and bad at fighting in general? If *deilos*, for instance, means simply bad at fighting in general, then the point of 184b3–6 will be that the poor fighter is lured by his overreaching confidence into situations which he is in fact ill-equipped to handle, thus exposing his woeful lack of prowess. Whereas if the term is limited solely to cowardice, then the implication must be that when the *deilos* realises how dangerous the situation actually is, he reveals his weakness by running away. At first glance one may feel that the distinction hardly matters: courage, after all, will always be part of military excellence; on either interpretation the fighter's courage or lack of it is at least a factor. Yet I believe the ambiguity is significant, for it suggests that Laches has not clearly distinguished the different threads of *andreia* in his own mind: he has probably never thought about the issue at all.

A further ambiguity results from Laches' switch from *andreia* to

---

[8] See the discussion in Stokes 1986: 44–9.

aretē at 184c2. Is *aretē* supposed to be a straight replacement for *andreia*? Or is it that *andreia* is a part of *aretē* in such a way that to be superior in *andreia* implies that one is necessarily superior in excellence as a whole? At 190d Laches is quite happy to concur with Socrates' (possibly ironical)[9] characterization of *andreia* as only a part of *aretē*, and such a view is in keeping with his conventional moral outlook. Yet the most natural reading of 184c is that *andreia* and *aretē* are here being used interchangeably in a casual and unreflective way. It is this very unreflectiveness which is revealing: Laches' unconscious ambivalence in his treatment of the relation between *andreia* and *aretē* again exposes a profound ambivalence in conventional moral thought. On the one hand, most Greeks were happy to regard *andreia* as just one of the cardinal virtues, along with justice, temperance, wisdom and piety; such a view follows naturally if *andreia* is seen principally as courage. On the other hand, if *andreia* is conceived both more generally and more specifically as manliness, the attributes required to be a 'real man', then what need does a man have of any other quality in order to count as fully virtuous? We have only to consider the Homeric poems where, in the absence of the term *andreia*, *aretē* is frequently employed in this sense.

Despite such significant unclarities, we can, however, draw some positive conclusions from Laches' rejection of fighting in armour. His scornful dismissal of its teachers because they have shown themselves inadequate in actual combat is a good illustration of his later requirement that one's words should harmonize with one's deeds (188c–d); if they do not, then they carry no weight. As for his conception of *andreia* itself, though we do not yet know exactly what it is, we do know something about what it is not. The technical skill of fighting in armour is irrelevant to its possession, and there may be the implication that technical skill in general is either irrelevant or insignificant. Certainly when asked later to define *andreia* as part of overall moral excellence, Laches initially answers only in terms of a psychological or behavioural attribute. He is also clear in 184 that *andreia* is to be distinguished from mere rashness or daring (*thrasos*), a point which will be important when we come to examine the complexities of his and Socrates' discussion of courage and risk in 193.[10]

The plainest fact of all, however, is that whatever the precise

---

[9] See pp. 85–6 below.   [10] Pp. 91–5.

nuances of Laches' position, his view of the value of fighting in armour is diametrically opposed to that of Nicias. If the impasse is to be broken, a third voice is needed. It is fortunate that Socrates is standing by.

MATTER AND METHOD: 184c–190d

Socrates' opening move is to seek clarification on the subject of their discussion. Nicias is puzzled: is it not fighting in armour? Socrates disagrees. Their real concern is the *psuchai* of young men,[11] and how *aretē* may be joined to them.[12] Fighting in armour is at most only a means to this general goal; to discover whether it would be an effective means, they must first consider the therapy of the soul.

This redefinition of the terms of the discussion is critical. It is the first time in the dialogue that an explicit distinction is made between means and ends, a distinction which will prove central to the later debate on which kinds of knowledge are involved in *andreia*. Whether the difference will remain so clear-cut, however, is another matter, and one that we shall have to examine closely. Equally important is Socrates' characterization of the end as '*aretē* of the soul'. At first glance this may look like a simple restatement of Lysimachus' desire that his and Melesias' sons become *aristoi* (179b2), but the appearance is deceptive. Lysimachus' other re-marks make it clear that by *aristoi* he means those who have honourably achieved social success and status; it is not that he disregards excellence of character, but rather that he does not discriminate between outward reputation and inner excellence. If pressed, he might say that worldly acclaim is the proper criterion of nobility of soul. As we have seen, this assumption that *aretē* implies social success is also present in Nicias' opening speech; he further adds physical strength to the list of qualities that an *aristos* should display. Socrates' innovation is in conceiving *aretē solely* in terms of intellectual and moral qualities. Witness too his ironical regret that he was unable to pay for tuition under the sophists, 'who were the only people who claimed to be able to make me a gentleman' (*kalos k'agathos* – another term with well-established class connotations), and contrast his invitation to Laches and Nicias

[11] 185e1–2.   [12] 190b 3–5.

to indicate which 'Athenians or strangers, either slaves or freemen' owe their goodness to them.

With *aretē* thus divorced from social status, Socrates asks if any of them is equipped to teach it to boys. It is at this point that Nicias remarks that he knew all along that the discussion would turn out to be principally about themselves,[13] and that Laches gives his support to Socrates because his courageous behaviour at Delium lends authority to his words. Lysimachus then asks Socrates to question Laches and Nicias on his behalf, a request which considerably complicates any attempt to interpret what follows. From now on, does Socrates say what he himself believes, or what he thinks Lysimachus would hold?

A key instance of this interpretative difficulty occurs straightaway. Socrates says that if the task is to join *aretē* to the souls of young men, then they first need to define *aretē*. Such a task may be too huge for the present occasion, however, so perhaps they should begin simply by trying to define that part of *aretē* which is arguably fostered by fighting in armour, namely *andreia*. The problem, of course, is how we are to understand Socrates' apparently casual reference to *andreia* as a 'part' of *aretē*, given the well-attested adherence of both the historical and the dramatic figure to some form of the Unity of Virtue (or the Virtues),[14] a thesis which most scholars have taken the final argument in the *Laches* to support. One possibility, which has won considerable backing,[15] is that Socrates is simply employing Lysimachus as a useful cover at this point: by appearing to accept the traditional view that virtue consists of different parts, he lulls us into a false sense of security which will heighten the impact when the traditional view is exploded. This is not, however, the only option: it is also possible that Socrates' stance on the unity or otherwise of virtue may be more ambivalent in the *Laches* than has generally been thought. It may be that, as well as speaking on Lysimachus' behalf, Socrates himself finds it natural to speak of *andreia* as a part of *aretē*; if we may anticipate a little, this would suggest that the final argument of the dialogue is more aporetic than is usually supposed. Socrates may be genuinely perplexed at how such an apparently natural

---

[13] See pp. 50–1 above.

[14] As well as evidence from Plato, see also Xenophon *Mem.* 3.9.5. The thesis is discussed briefly on pp. 108–10 below (and *vide* also p. 133 n. 41).

[15] See, for example, Stokes 1986: 68–9.

and intuitive conception of virtue – that it is comprised of parts – can be reconciled with the thesis that virtue is knowledge. A third possibility is that even if the character of Socrates is not perplexed, Plato is. We shall be returning to these issues when we review the purpose of the dialogue as a whole, but in the meantime we should, I submit, beware of assuming that Nicias speaks for Plato in the final section, or even entirely for Socrates.

Whatever the correct reading of 'part' here, Socrates goes on to say that once they have defined *andreia*, they will then be able to consider how it can accrue to young men, 'in so far as it can accrue by means of pursuits and studies'. Here too Socrates' tone is difficult to register. It may seem that the phrase is wholly ironic, and that Socrates is in fact indicating that such studies as learning to fight in armour are entirely irrelevant to the possession of *andreia*. As I hope to show, I believe that the irony is only partial: Socrates is not necessarily denying that pursuits and techniques have a role in *andreia*; he could simply be suggesting that they are not the only requirements.

A final point concerns the implications of Socrates' reworking of *aretē* for the translation of *andreia*. The claim that *aretē* is solely a condition of the *psuchē* implies that from now on in the dialogue *andreia* is to be read chiefly as 'courage', a faculty (*dunamis*)[16] of the soul. This, however, does not mean that notions of manliness and efficiency in battle drop out of the picture; Socrates' interlocutors, after all, may still perceive courage both as an innately male virtue, and as displayed paradigmatically in war. Even if *andreia* is now to mean courage, we still need to ask how courage, manliness and efficiency in battle interrelate.

SOCRATES' QUESTIONING OF LACHES (190d–194b)

The point is borne out immediately by Laches' initial response to Socrates' request for a definition of *andreia*. That's easy, says Laches, anyone who is willing to stay at his post and face the enemy is *andreios*. Although Socrates dismisses this as an example rather than a definition, it still tells us a considerable amount about how courage was currently perceived by the average non-philosopher, and raises interesting questions for the dialogue as a

---

[16] 192b1.

whole. Laches simply takes it for granted that the paradigmatic context for courage will be war. While this is hardly surprising given his profession, we may still remember the beginning of the discussion and Lysimachus' assertion that his and Melesias' fathers displayed *kala erga* not just in war, but also in peace. Can *andreia* also exist in peace, or are different virtues required? We may also wonder whether Laches is taking it for granted that courage is the preserve of men: while nothing is said about the innate structure of men's souls, in practice only men would normally have been in a position to live up to his ideal. Finally, it is worth noting that Laches' example is specifically a hoplite one: again, we can see the relevance of contemporary fighting practices for how *andreia* is understood.[17]

Socrates, however, reminds Laches that other types of fighting are still important: the Scythians, for instance, fight the enemy while fleeing, a continuation of an ancient practice celebrated by Homer. Laches concedes the point and admits that his example is too narrow (though the fact remains that the more maverick Homeric methods of doing battle were not his first choice as an illustration of *andreia*, an attitude we shall have cause to remember when we come to consider Plato's treatment of Achilles). What he is seeking, Socrates continues, is a general definition that will apply to all instances of courage. He is concerned not only with courage in war, but with displays of courage in any difficult situation: storms at sea, disease and poverty, public affairs – even in situations where morality requires that one resist desire and pleasure (191c7–e2). Surely Laches will not deny that courage can be shown in these non-martial contexts as well?

This widening of the scope of *andreia* is critical for a number of reasons. Not only does it answer the question of whether *andreia* has a role in peacetime, it also prompts speculation on who may be *andreios*: even within the constraints of historical contingency, some of Socrates' examples apply to women just as much as to men. Also significant is the surprising claim that *andreia* can be displayed in the face of desires and pleasures as well as fears and pains: as in *Republic* 442b,[18] courage seems here to merge with self-

---

[17] See p. 81 above.

[18] See p. 22 above. The relation between courage and self-control or temperance (*sō-phrosunē*) is discussed further on pp. 231–3.

control. This stress on endurance as well as risk will also be important when we come to assess Nicias' definition of courage as knowledge of what is to be feared and what dared; Nicias' definition – at first sight, anyway – does not appear to be broad enough to cover many of the instances Socrates wishes to include. If Socrates intends his remarks here to be taken seriously, then this would seem additional evidence that we are not necessarily supposed to interpret Nicias' position as Plato's final word.

After some further clarification as to what a general definition might look like, Laches attempts one of his own: *andreia*, he claims, is 'a kind of endurance of the soul' (192b9–c1). As befits one who has scant time for subtle distinctions,[19] the definition is, as definitions go, pretty vague: it is not clear, for instance, whether 'a kind of' (*tis*) is supposed to mean 'something like' or 'a subdivision of'. For all its imprecision, however, Laches' statement is important. The most telling feature is that endurance of soul is explicitly portrayed as a natural quality (*pephukos*): does this mean that practices and skills are irrelevant to its possession? Laches certainly makes no mention of them, and although some Greek thinkers held that the true nature of a living thing was something to be achieved over time and through effort, it is doubtful whether a general with limited intellectual aspirations would have been familiar with the concept.[20] It seems far more likely that in speaking of courage as 'natural', Laches means that it is an innate quality which you either possess or you do not; nothing you study or practise can alter the situation.

Socrates, however, remains dissatisfied. Surely not all instances of endurance are courageous? Let it be agreed that *andreia* is one of the 'extremely noble things'. Now, while endurance accompanied by practical wisdom (*phronēsis*) is both noble and good, when it is accompanied by folly (*aphrosunē*), it is harmful and hurtful. But nothing harmful and hurtful can be noble, so foolish endurance cannot be courage. Only wise endurance can count as such.

---

[19] Witness his derision of Nicias at 197c.

[20] Although Aristotle is clearly the chief proponent of this conception of a thing's nature, the idea arguably has some roots in pre-Socratic and sophistic thought, albeit delicate ones. At *E.N.* 1152a30–3, Aristotle quotes Evenus' remarks on practice becoming (τελευτῶσαν) nature. The idea seems to correspond roughly to our notion of 'second nature', and it is reasonable to suppose that second nature must at least have its seeds in 'first nature'.

Although the conclusion is not necessitated by strict logic, it seems a fair explication of Laches' position, and one with which Laches concurs, if a trifle dubiously. Whether we wish to concur is a different matter. All the value terms of the argument require careful scrutiny: 'wise' and 'foolish', 'good' and 'harmful' are all ambiguous. First, however, we need to examine the premise on which the argument is based, for it is absolutely critical that both Socrates and Laches take it as axiomatic that courage is something noble. This immediately rules out certain modern approaches to the problem of misdirected endurance or boldness, such as that of Foot, who holds that while courage is generally a virtue, it does not always operate as such: 'courage is not operating as a virtue when the murderer turns his courage, which is a virtue, to bad ends'.[21] Other thinkers have conceived of courage as a purely executive virtue, which can be put to morally noble or ignoble use; all that matters is that the agent should believe his or her objective to be worthwhile for them.[22] On either count, it can be the bedfellow of criminality, madness or stupidity,[23] and one may wonder whether it would not be more accurate to speak of it as simply an executive capacity. Such a solution, however, raises problems of its own, most notably the apparent divorce between means-related and end-related reasoning;[24] even more importantly for present purposes, there are serious linguistic barriers preventing such an approach being readily available to Greek thinkers. No matter how conceived, the very term *andreia* connotes an ideal of male character and behaviour which cannot be value-neutral. Different city-states, generations and individual thinkers may have drawn different boundaries between blameworthy recklessness or ruthlessness and *andreia* proper, but the word itself suggests that the boundaries exist.

Accepting the premise, however, does not mean that we need

---

[21] Foot 1978: 16. Foot compares courage to arsenic: arsenic is a poison, but does not always act as such.

[22] This is the position taken by Wallace 1978: 76–8. Williams also classes courage as an executive virtue in Williams 1981: 49, though his definition of 'executive virtue' is not the same as that of Wallace: such virtues 'do not themselves yield a characteristic motive, but are necessary for that relation to oneself and the world which enables one to act from desirable motives in desirable ways'.

[23] See also von Wright 1963: 53.

[24] For an account of how the different types of reasoning could be related in courageous actions, see Walton 1986 chs. 7 and 8.

accept the argument as a whole. Why should 'foolish' endurance not sometimes be noble? What does 'foolish' mean here? The conclusion follows because of another vital assumption made by Socrates and Laches, namely that the concepts of the noble and the good are to be bracketed together, and conversely the harmful and ignoble: no tensions are perceived between the two sets of value terms. This, however, surely requires more explanation: we need to know a lot more about what, in particular, 'good' and 'harmful' mean. As 'good' is here contrasted with 'harmful', it presumably means 'beneficial'; the question, however, is: 'beneficial to whom?' Does Socrates wish to suggest that acts of endurance which harm their agent are foolish and therefore ignoble and not courageous? If so, then he seems wilfully to be missing the whole point of courage, for surely it is reasonable to believe that acts of courage are often intended to result in benefit to others, and that, of all the virtues, courage is the most likely to cause the agent harm?

These doubts receive support from ordinary Greek usage, in which the noble and the useful are frequently contrasted. We have already seen this contrast in Aristotle's depiction of the character of young men, who

> would rather perform noble (*kala*) actions than useful ones: for they live according to their habitual character rather than calculation, and calculation aims at the useful, while virtue aims at the noble.[25]

Even more telling in the context of the *Laches* is *Alcibiades I* 115a–c: in this passage the young Alcibiades not only maintains that some *kala* actions are harmful (*kaka*) for their agent; he also agrees to Socrates' suggestion that the distinction he has in mind is best illustrated by a man helping his comrade in battle, and being wounded or killed in the process. It is true that Socrates immediately tries to disassociate himself from this view, arguing unconvincingly that rescuing one's comrades is not harmful and noble in the same respect; but this only implies that he believes the view to be common enough to require addressing.[26] The message is plain:

---

[25] *Ars Rhet.* 1389a3–b13; the *megalopsuchos* is also said to prefer to own beautiful (*kala*) and unprofitable things as a mark of his independence at *E.N.* 1125a11–12. See pp. 39–40 above.

[26] Even if *Alcibiades I* is spurious (as I am inclined to think), it is still a useful source for non-philosophical conceptions of the relation between the *kalon* and the *agathon*.

if in the *Laches* Socrates intends courage to be always beneficial to the agent, then it appears that 'benefit' and 'harm' will have to be radically redefined. In turn, such redefinitions will also compel us to reassess what is meant by 'wise' and 'foolish': the criterion for wisdom will not simply be an ability to protect oneself from physical harm. Finally, given that benefit and wisdom are here linked to the noble, the *kalon* and *aischron* will have to be examined as well.

There is also the question of how Socrates regards a display of endurance which is intended to bring benefit to others but fails to do so. Does the failure of the enterprise preclude the act from having been courageous in the first place? This seems to put courage at the mercy of moral luck, which does not accord well with Socrates' description of *andreia* as a 'faculty' (192b1), and Laches' claim that it is a natural quality of the soul. However, if the unsuccessful act is to count as courageous, then, again, how are benefit and harm, and the noble and ignoble, to be defined? We have seen how Plato employs the *Laches* to explore and perhaps rework the meaning of *andreia*; it now appears that this will entail the scrutiny of the key value terms in the Greek language.

Socrates' next question shows that the scrutiny is to begin straightaway. If courage is now defined as wise endurance, then we need to ask in what (*eis ti*) it is wise: is it wise in all things, whether great or small? Is a financier who persists in spending money wisely courageous? Or a doctor who persists in giving his patient the correct treatment, despite the patient's entreaties? Laches is adamant that such cases are not what he has in mind. Precisely why they are to be rejected he does not say. Although the interchange clearly implies that there are different kinds of wisdom, involving different objects of knowledge, Laches gives no positive indication of which kind, or kinds, are involved in courage, and is probably unable to do so.

In order to help him clarify his views, Socrates now turns to Laches' special field of expertise. Consider the man who 'endures in war, and is willing to fight, on a wise calculation that others will come to his aid, and that the forces against him will be fewer and weaker than those who are with him, and who besides has the advantage of position'. In the opposing army is a man who is also willing to fight and endure, though lacking all the advantages of the first man's resources. Which man, asks Socrates, is the more *andreios*? The man lacking resources, replies Laches. Even though,

Socrates continues, his endurance is the more foolish (*aphronestera*)?
Laches says yes. Socrates now turns his attention to purely technical knowledge: cavalry fighting, stone slinging and archery, and
diving into wells. Again, Laches is invited to consider twin examples of endurance; in each case, one man possesses the relevant
technical knowledge while the other does not. Laches remains firm
that in each instance the man who endures without technical
knowledge is both more courageous and more foolish than the
man who endures with the assistance of such knowledge. But, says
Socrates, did we not agree earlier that foolish boldness and endurance were shameful[27] and harmful, while courage was something noble? Whereas we now appear to be saying that foolish
endurance is courage after all? And Laches agrees to retract the
latter statement, and admits that he and Socrates have failed to
meet his requirement that words and deeds should accord in the
Dorian mode:[28] though their actions at Delium were truly courageous, their current argument has portrayed courage in an illegitimately shameful light. Again, the one premise that he and Socrates wish to retain at all costs is that *andreia* is something *kalon*.

What are we to make of all this? It seems to me that Laches
makes two main errors, and that Plato's chief purpose in writing
this passage is to prompt us to uncover these for ourselves. Both, in
different ways, arise from a failure to perceive distinctions between
different kinds of wisdom and foolishness. Firstly, Laches does not
have to agree that fighting against the odds is necessarily more
foolish than fighting with them: as we have seen, 'wise' and 'foolish'
need not only refer to self-protection. Commentators on the *Laches*
rightly stress that the argument at this point cries out for a distinction between prudential knowledge, narrowly defined in terms
of one's physical and material wellbeing, and a knowledge of
overall objectives and values, the kind of knowledge which Nicias
will make the definition of courage.[29] If the ill-equipped soldier is
fighting to save his city from destruction, he may well not be foolish

---

[27] In fact, this is the first time that boldness has been mentioned in this stretch of the argument. This may be because boldness fits some of the examples (e.g. diving into wells)
better than endurance; nevertheless, its introduction is an implied criticism of the nar-
rowness of Laches' definition.

[28] 188c–e.

[29] See C. C. W. Taylor 1991: 154; Vlastos 1994: 109–17.

at all. Socrates' supposed counter-examples against 'courage is wise endurance' do not necessarily hold.

The key word here, however, is 'necessarily'. While I certainly agree that 193a–d is designed to show the need for a distinction between prudential knowledge and knowledge of ends, it seems to me that this is not all the passage is intended to do. I would suggest that there are various possible scenarios in which the ill-equipped soldier is not courageous, and that these scenarios demonstrate that the interrelation between prudential and end-related knowledge is considerably more complex than has often been supposed. In particular, I wish to argue that technical skill, which in the commentators is simply subsumed under prudential knowledge, also has an important role to play in the knowledge of values and ends.

The nub of the problem lies in the second of Laches' errors, and this is the relation between *andreia* and risk. Surprisingly little critical attention has been paid to Laches' claim that the degree of courage displayed will increase with the degree of risk, particularly since he was earlier at pains to distinguish *andreia* from mere boldness.[30] In all the examples, technical skills and resources reduce the degree of risk, and hence, Laches thinks, reduce the degree of courage displayed. It seems to me that this equation is too simple. I believe that we need to consider very carefully how the actions of the opposing soldiers are to be described.

Firstly, when assessing whether a dangerous act is in fact courageous, it seems a reasonable precondition that the agent be aware of the danger.[31] We need to know whether Laches' technically inexpert but apparently plucky fighter is actually conscious of the risks he is taking; if he has simply run amok and lost all sense of what he is doing, then it is not clear that either he or his acts can be called courageous at all. However, even if he is aware of the risks, there are still a number of other vital questions that need to be answered before courage can be ascribed to him: if courage is to be unambiguously noble as Socrates and Laches want, then it would seem to be just not true that the degree of courage automatically rises in proportion to the degree of risk. We clearly, for

---

[30] 184b. See p. 83 above.
[31] This difficult issue is discussed in Walton 1986: 138–40.

instance, need to know more about the ends for which the risky action is taken: is the ill-equipped soldier in fact trying to protect a corrupt and tyrannical regime? We also need to know more about his perception of the situation: is he aware that the regime is corrupt? If he is not, should he be? And we need to know about his options: does he have any choice?

Even favourable answers to these questions, however, will not be enough. We also, I believe, need to ask whether an action can be termed courageous if it is so risky that it is absolutely hopeless. By this I mean not just that the agent is bound to die, but that he is bound to die without having achieved his objectives. The question is a delicate one, for it is often extremely difficult in these cases to decide what is to count as failure: the dramatic but apparently hopeless gesture against a tyrannical regime may serve as an inspiration to others by reinforcing certain values.[32] Nevertheless, there still appear to be situations where we would want to call such a gesture foolish and irresponsible rather than courageous, and its agent likewise.[33] It seems important, therefore, that the agent not only possesses wisdom concerning overall ends, but also a prudential ability to assess the likelihood of achieving those ends. This is where technical skills become relevant, for it will often be the presence or absence of a technical skill which makes the difference between some hope of success and no hope of success: there seems little moral worth in leaping into a deep river to save a child if both (a) you cannot swim, and (b) an experienced lifeguard is poised for action. In other words, the moral knowledge

---

[32] A good illustration would be the Spartans at Thermopylae. Although they did not prevent the Persians from marching on to take Athens in the short term, their action became the paradigmatic example of heroic resistance in the face of oppression, and may well have helped the Greek cause more generally by encouraging others to make their sacrifices worthwhile. Diodorus Siculus certainly thought so: '... what man of later times might not emulate the valour of those warriors who, finding themselves in the grip of an overwhelming situation, though their bodies were subdued, were not conquered in spirit? ... One would be justified in thinking that it was these men who were more responsible for the common freedom of the Greeks than those who were victorious at a later time in the battles against Xerxes; for when the deeds of these men were called to mind, the Persians were dismayed, whereas the Greeks were incited to perform similar courageous exploits.' (11.11 trans. Oldfather. Compare Pausanias 3.4.7–8.)

[33] The fine distinction between courage and irresponsibility also highlights the point that risk need not only involve physical danger: there is also the risk of cultural condemnation. It might in some circumstances be more courageous for a general to pursue the safer course, if there is strong but misguided public pressure on him to lead his troops into hopeless and futile action. Kutuzov's refusal to engage with Napoleon after Borodino (at least as presented by Tolstoy) would be a case in point.

of ultimate values which true *andreia* undoubtedly requires may in turn involve a number of prudential and technical considerations. The ability to fight in armour could turn out to be a factor in the reasoning process after all.

There is also the possibility that the confidence instilled by the possession of the skill may be the decisive factor in persuading the agent to undertake the action in the first place. Again, there is a very fine line here. On the one hand, Laches is correct that in many cases the possession of the appropriate skill will, by reducing the risks, reduce the degree of courage displayed; and if the risks are reduced to zero, it is not clear that the action is courageous at all. On the other hand, if there is still some risk involved even for the skilled practitioner, and if it is really true that he would not have undertaken the action without the support of the skill, then the skill is a positive aid to the virtue. We shall be returning to this complex issue when we reconsider the training of the Auxiliaries in the *Republic*: the purity of a virtue is not necessarily compromised by providing the right conditions for it to flourish.[34]

In 193a–e, therefore, Plato is I believe setting up a number of critical problems concerning the different kinds of knowledge involved in courage, and inviting us to make the distinctions needed to solve them. The corollary of this strategy is of course that Socrates and Laches must remain at a loss (even if Socrates' *aporia* is ironical); hence Socrates' claim at 193d11 that his and Laches' confused words on courage do not match the clarity of their courageous exploits at Delium. However, not even the ostensible conclusion of the argument is entirely negative, for Socrates goes on to say that he is keen to retain one element of Laches' definition, and that is the part which commands endurance. For the practice of philosophy requires considerable endurance – indeed, this philosophic endurance may be the very courage that they seek.

The implications of this apparently casual exhortation are far-reaching. Many commentators have assumed that both Socrates and Plato wish ultimately to endorse some suitably reworked version of Nicias' intellectualist definition of courage as knowledge of what is to be feared and what dared, a definition in which endur-

---

[34] See p. 111 below and compare *Prt.* 326b–c, where Protagoras emphasizes the importance of sending one's sons to a physical trainer so that, 'they may not be forced to display cowardice through bodily weakness, either in wars or in any other enterprises'.

ance receives no mention. My own view is that Socrates' explicit praise of endurance in 194a makes such an interpretation extremely difficult, unless the 'suitable reworking' is to include the need for psychological stamina. It may be that Laches' contribution to the discussion has been dismissed far too quickly. Secondly, the extension of *andreia* to the field of philosophy is a further, and vital, example of Socrates' general project in the *Laches* of broadening the term's scope beyond the martial arena. It is important not only because it forces us to think about the different contexts in which courage can be displayed, but also because it prompts us again to reconsider *andreia*'s etymology. Socrates is certainly claiming that the practice of philosophy requires courage; is he also proposing that philosophy is a specifically 'manly' occupation? Or, even if he is not making such a claim himself, is it nevertheless reasonable to assume that his audience will think that he is? And is Plato aware of this? The dialogue is, after all, at least ostensibly concerned with the proper education of young men, and at least two young men are actually present. Plato may think that it cannot do any harm if philosophy is cloaked in a manly aura.

This suspicion is intensified by what comes next. Laches assures Socrates that a competitive ardour (*philonikia*) has taken hold of him and he is anxious to grasp what courage is, even though it has currently given him the slip. The hunting metaphor is taken up by Socrates, who agrees, saying that the good huntsman must follow the hounds and not give up the chase. Again, we are in traditionally masculine territory, and some of this 'maleness' must inevitably rub off on philosophy, whether Socrates intends this or not.

At this point, however, a serious difficulty arises. If the talk of hunting and philosophic *andreia* is meant to give the practice of philosophy a masculine appeal, how is this strategy supposed to accord with the view of the historical Socrates that the virtues – presumably including wisdom – are gender-neutral?[35] It is, after all, a view of which Plato would have been well aware from youth; we do not necessarily have to wait until its explicit appearance in the *Meno* and *Republic* 5 before ascribing it to him, though it is true that dialogues written before and after these two watersheds (par-

---

[35] See pp. 72–3 above.

ticularly the latter) will require rather different approaches. Let us assume that the *Laches* is pre-*Meno*. Let us also assume that the Socrates who appears in it is the Socrates who, at least on one level, supports the gender-neutral conception of virtue attributed to him elsewhere – an assumption that receives some support from his pointed use of *anthrōpos* rather than *anēr* at 186d1 and his desire to broaden the field of *andreia* to include hardships and temptation in general as well as the dangers of war (191c–e).[36] If these assumptions are made, what are we to make of the apparent portrayal of philosophy as a 'manly' activity? One possibility, of course, is that at this early stage Plato has not fully realised the implications of the historical Socrates' teaching on virtue for the practice of philosophy and the gender of philosophers. Or he may be simply confused: his rational mind may have accepted Socratic teaching, but at an unconscious level he may still be thinking at times in traditional 'gendered' terms. It seems to me that some degree of confusion on Plato's part is very probable; nevertheless, this could still coexist with a conscious strategy of some kind, and it is worth enquiring what such a strategy might be. There are, I believe, three main interpretations of Plato's depiction of the practice of philosophy in apparently 'manly' terms:[37]

(i) The terms are not in fact meant to be perceived as specifically manly at all; they are simply intended to portray philosophy as a generally assertive and robust occupation. Plato may well be hoping that such a portrayal will appeal to the kind of young men he is hoping to attract, but, if challenged, he could also claim that there is nothing in this depiction which prevents philosophy from being taken up by women in different historical circumstances.

The trouble with this interpretation is that Plato must have been well aware that, whatever his intentions, such a depiction of philosophy would have been perceived as 'masculine' by the majority of his readers, especially before *Republic* 5 was in circulation. It seems to me more likely that he does wish philosophy to possess manly connotations at some level; the difficulty is in deciding precisely what this level might be, if it is also true that he wishes the

---

[36] Pp. 78 and 87–8 above.

[37] In the formulation of my views on this issue, I am indebted to some searching questions posed by Mary-Hannah Jones.

Socrates of the *Laches* to represent the views on virtue of his historical original. I submit that two main options are open to us:

(ii) Plato may be hoping to work on his almost exclusively male audience[38] in two separate chronological stages. He may wish to attract them to philosophy in the first place by portraying it in apparently 'manly' terms, and then, once they are attracted, to persuade them that in fact all the virtues, including the virtuous practice of philosophy, are equally the provenance of both men and women, and that *anēr* must be replaced by *anthrōpos*.

(iii) Plato may want to work on two different parts of his readers' *psuchai*.

The difficulty with option (iii), of course, is that there is no evidence in the *Laches* to suggest that Plato is operating even with a bipartite *psuchē*, let alone the tripartition of the *Republic*. And, as we have seen, it is only in the *Republic* that he even approximates a theory of the conscious and the unconscious.[39] My view is that in the *Laches* Plato is most likely to be hoping to effect some version of (ii), though (i) remains an outside possibility. Whatever the correct interpretation, however, there is no question that the issue of what Plato wishes to achieve through his rhetorical manoeuvres is both central and complex, and we shall be returning to it in our discussion of the *Republic* in chapter 8.[40] The balance of probability between the different interpretations may well shift considerably with the introduction of a tripartite *psuchē*, courageous female Auxiliaries and wise Philosopher-Queens.

Even if we leave the gender issues to one side, however, the hunting metaphor raises a problematic question: what is Socrates doing employing such agonistic language when he standardly criticizes the sophists for their competitive approach to debate? At *Protagoras* 334c, for instance, Socrates asks Protagoras to give him briefer answers, claiming that he cannot follow lengthy speeches. Protagoras, however, has no interest in making concessions: he re-

---

[38] It is important to remember that, whenever the Academy grew up or was founded, Plato was addressing students as well as general readers. When we come to consider apparently 'masculine' imagery in the *Republic*, we shall further have to distinguish between the intended effect on readers/students, and the intended effect (if any) on the young citizens of the ideally just state.

[39] See p. 57 above.

[40] Pp. 244-9.

plies bluntly that he has in his time engaged in many 'contests in words', and if he had succumbed to his opponents' methodological demands, then, 'I should not have shown myself superior to anyone, nor would the name of Protagoras have become famous among the Greeks.' We may remember our first glimpse of Protagoras lecturing as he marches around the cloister, clearly in competition with the other sophists for the attention of the star-struck young Athenians. His combative approach is further exemplified at 339e, where Socrates compares being questioned by him to being hit by a boxer.

There is, however, a decided difference between the way these agonistic images are used. Protagoras sees himself in competition with his interlocutor, and the interlocutor is left in no doubt about the sophist's desire to overthrow him; in the *Laches*, on the other hand, the struggle lies in the joint attempt to track down the truth about *andreia*. A comparable reworking of traditional sporting imagery occurs at *Protagoras* 335e–336a, where Socrates requests that Protagoras slacken his pace to accommodate his own speed: again, the race is not viewed by Socrates as a competition between the runners, but as a joint pursuit of the truth. Protagoras and Socrates may both employ the kind of sporting imagery likely to appeal to young men, but their purposes are not the same.[41]

SOCRATES' QUESTIONING OF NICIAS (194C–199e)

Whatever the truth of such speculations, Laches' and Socrates' philosophic endurance requires new material to test it, and Nicias is invited to join in the hunt. Whereas Laches' initial response was to define courage solely in terms of a non-cognitive psychological quality, Nicias' line is austerely intellectualist throughout. He starts by saying that Socrates and Laches have not been approaching the discussion in the right way, for they have not been making use of Socrates' own dictum that each man is good in those areas in which he is wise (*sophos*), and bad in those areas in which he is ignorant (*amathēs*). Courage, therefore, is a kind of wisdom. It is not, however, a purely technical wisdom or skill, such as the ability to play the flute, but wisdom of a more general kind:

---

[41] The complex issue of Socrates' use of agonistic imagery is also discussed further on p. 244.

namely, the knowledge (*epistēmē*) of what is to be feared and what
dared (*hē tōn deinōn kai tharraleōn*), either in war or in anything
else.

Laches is baffled and tells Nicias that he is simply talking nonsense. His reaction shows just how counter-intuitive the definition
can appear to those who are not Socratic disciples: what has
bloodless knowledge got to do with having the guts to stay at
your post? Before we can assess Nicias' statement, however, we
first need to ask precisely what it is claiming. It is clear that, like
Socrates, he wishes to extend the field in which *andreia* can be displayed (though it is still war that he cites as the most obvious
environment). In all other respects, however, his definition is mysterious. Is it significant, for instance, that *phronēsis* has now been
replaced by *epistēmē*? And what is the connection between *epistēmē*
and *sophia*? Even more critically, do *deina* and *tharralea* refer to
things which inspire the emotions of fear and confidence, or to
things which also provoke certain behavioural responses?

Such questions can only properly be understood in terms of the
referents of *deina* and *tharralea*. At 195c7–d2 and 195e8–196a3
Nicias makes it plain that the kind of knowledge he has in mind
is a knowledge of *overall* goods and bads in a person's life. The
doctor knows what is healthy and what diseased, but he cannot tell
through medical knowledge alone whether health itself should be
welcomed or feared, because it is not true for everyone that it is
better for them to live; for many it is better to die. Again, the
seer's job is only to divine what will happen to someone; he (or
she) cannot tell through the mantic art alone whether it is better
or worse for the person that certain things befall. The seer may be
able to tell if someone is to meet with death or disease, victory or
defeat, but they cannot know whether such outcomes would, overall, be good or bad for the person concerned.

On the face of it, such claims seem deeply strange. Even if we
take care to consider the long-term view, how can it not be better
for someone to be victorious rather than defeated, healthy rather
than sick, alive rather than dead? The counter-intuitive nature of
Nicias' contribution seems to be intensifying. The only possible
explanation is if health, success and life in these cases could only
be purchased at the expense of some value which is perceived as
more important. The text gives no indication of what such a value
might be, but the most obvious candidate is surely the *kalon*, the

morally fine and noble; support for this inference is also provided by the *Protagoras*, where in a similar discussion the *kalon* is referred to explicitly as the goal of the courageous.[42] It seems reasonable, therefore, to reconstruct Nicias' position as follows: if it is always better for someone to pursue the morally noble course, and physical wellbeing and even life itself are always less important, then it makes sense to conclude that the only thing to be truly feared is the morally shameful. To say, therefore, that the courageous person knows what is to be feared and what dared is simply to say that he knows what is morally noble and what shameful. The only mental state that he truly fears is an awareness that he has behaved dishonourably.

The problem, of course, is why Nicias should suppose that it is always better for the individual to pursue the morally noble course. Clearly it may be better for society if certain courageous individuals are prepared to die for their country, but in what sense is it better for the individuals concerned? How can Nicias (or Socrates) show that the tension often thought to exist between benefiting others and benefiting oneself is false? We saw in our discussion of 192 that Socrates and Laches seemed to bracket the fine and the good together too readily: if Socrates really intends courage to be always beneficial to the agent, then he will have to show that 'benefit' and 'harm' do not mean what they are usually taken to mean.[43] If our reading of Nicias' elliptical explanation of his definition is correct, then this same challenge applies to 195c–196a. Nicias needs to redefine benefit in order to show that there is no real tension between the personally beneficial and the morally noble; if he does not, then it is not at all clear why knowledge of the noble alone should be sufficient to ensure courageous action. (Indeed, as we shall see, courageous action may not be guaranteed even if the beneficial and the noble are reconciled; nevertheless, reconciliation is at least a necessary start.)

Such a redefinition, however, is not provided in the *Laches*; the dialogue ends with the problem not only unresolved but largely unexplored. Also unexplored is the question of what the courageous person feels about the kind of physical dangers that most people find fearful. The courageous person may know that the

---

[42] *Protagoras* 359a–360b. See the discussion on pp. 131–2 below.
[43] See pp. 89–91 above.

only truly fearful thing is the shame of having acted ignobly, but does this mean that he can, by definition, feel no fear whatsoever of death, pain and loss? It is at this point that the precise meaning of *deina* becomes relevant. If *deina* means things which inspire a behavioural response as well as an inner emotion, then it would be possible for the courageous person to feel some measure of fear for such things, providing he did not actually shrink from them. If, on the other hand, even the feeling of fear in these circumstances precludes his being courageous, then we need to ask whether he has never feared them, or whether he has, but has managed to stop.[44] In the *Laches* this may seem only an interesting side issue, but we shall find it taking centre stage when we come to explore Plato's critique of Achilles as a role model in chapter 8.[45]

Analysis of Nicias' definition, then, shows that considerable work is required in order to clarify its terms and to make plausible its (probable) underlying assumption that the noble is beneficial. But it is also puzzling when we consider its relation to other claims made in the dialogue. Whatever their precise meaning, *deina* and *tharralea* are explicitly said to be concerned with what is better and worse overall. Where, however, does this leave the other kinds of knowledge that we have seen to be involved in courage, such as knowledge of circumstances and means, calculations of the likelihood of success, and the technical skills on which success may depend? It was Nicias, after all, who was originally in favour of the new technique of fighting in armour, arguing that such a skill would promote *andreia*. If his definition is to stand, then the knowledge of overall ends which the courageous person possesses will somehow have to incorporate these other types of knowledge. Abstract values can only be realized through particular acts, necessarily embedded in complex webs of contingencies: a particular agent saves a particular child from a particular river in a particular set of circumstances requiring specific skills.

Another difficulty concerns the relation of Nicias' definition to that of Laches. Whatever the exact meaning of his terms, the general gist of Nicias' position seems at first sight to be plain

---

[44] To 'overcome' fear is an ambiguous phrase: it can mean either that one continues to fear, for example, death and pain but does not let the emotion interfere with one's actions, or that one manages to stop fearing such things altogether. Depending on which reading we give to *deina*, both types of 'overcoming' are possibilities here.
[45] Pp. 235–9.

enough: the virtue of courage has everything to do with knowledge and, apparently, nothing to do with the kind of quality of character that Laches wanted to press. Yet we have seen how Socrates wishes to retain the notion of endurance in any statement on courage, and even suggests that the philosophic endurance required in the search for courage may turn out to be courage itself.[46] This partial endorsement of Laches' position indicates that Nicias' definition is too limited: knowledge as it is usually conceived may be necessary for courage, but is it sufficient? Even if Nicias can somehow show that the beneficial and the noble are not at odds, what about the temptations of pleasure and the opportunities they provide for weakness of the will? This leads to the third respect in which Nicias' contribution sits uneasily with what has previously been agreed. Though he clearly supports Socrates' assertion at 191c–e that *andreia* can be displayed in non-martial contexts, his definition does not fit Socrates' explicit claim in the same passage that courage can be manifest not only in relation to fear, but also in relation to present pain, and even to desires and pleasures. This close affiliation (to say the least) between courage and self-control now appears to be critical: Nicias needs to show precisely how his knowledge of overall goods and bads can be preserved and acted upon in all circumstances.

It is with such questions in mind, I would suggest, that at 196e Socrates returns to the common notion of *andreia* as a non-cognitive psychological or behavioural trait, though the trait he refers to is not so much Lachean endurance as raw mettle or drive. If courage is knowledge, he says, then this presumably means that no animal can be courageous, not even a lion or a boar? Or is Nicias prepared to admit that such animals are so wise that they know what the vast majority of men do not? Laches adds his support to the critique: everyone calls such animals as the lion courageous, but is Nicias really willing to say that they are wiser than we are?[47] The only solution to the dilemma, Laches implies, is for Nicias to abandon his bizarre definition of courage.

Nicias, however, is resolute. His definition can stand because he

---

[46] 194a1–5; see p. 95 above.
[47] For the attribution of *andreia* to animals, see Aristotle *Hist. An.* 608a–b and 610a. The implications of this attribution for *andreia* as manliness are discussed on pp. 105–6 below.

refuses to describe any animal as courageous; those animals generally termed courageous are simply fearless and foolish.[48] No creature can be called courageous which is merely unaware of the dangers: the fearless and the courageous are not the same thing (197b1–2). A great many men, women, children and animals are bold, daring and fearless through lack of forethought, but very few people possess true courage, which can look ahead and perceive the dangers but still not shrink from them. Only wise (*phronima*) acts can properly be called courageous.

The interchange is important for a number of reasons. Firstly, the apparently casual use of *phronima* provides an answer to our question concerning the relation between *sophia* and *epistēmē* on the one hand, and *phronēsis* on the other: Nicias, at any rate, is happy to employ all three terms more-or-less interchangeably when talking of knowledge of overall ends.[49] This does not mean that the terms cannot refer to purely technical knowledge as well, but it does suggest that we should be wary of constructing interpretations in which the shifts from one term to another play a key role. The chief contribution of the passage, however, is to raise a question rather than answer one. Nicias may be justified in arguing that raw mettle should not be identified with courage proper, but it still seems legitimate to ask whether raw mettle does not play some part in the virtue. Is knowledge really all that is needed to fear only the ignoble, even when confronted by the present reality of pain and the imminent reality of death? Will not such a person require some other psychological quality after all, whether it be the endurance advocated by Laches, or the raw spirit or drive that to some extent we share with animals?[50]

Such questions, of course, do not apply only to *andreia* as courage; they also apply in principle to *andreia* as manliness. The operative term, however, is 'in principle', for it is a moot point whether *andreia* as manliness is in fact an issue in this section of the dialogue. One of the most intriguing aspects of 196e–197c is the evidence it provides for current conceptions of *andreia*. Does not the conventional ascription of *andreia* to animals show that, in some of

---

[48] Contrast *Resp.* 375a11–12, and see p. 9 above.
[49] See p. 100 above.
[50] Though note the important distinction between raw drive in humans and raw drive in animals suggested on p. 26 above.

its uses anyway, the term was in the process of becoming detached from its etymological roots? The answer is surely that while the ascription may indicate this, it is by no means necessary: it is also possible that certain animals, such as the lion and the boar, were consciously or unconsciously perceived as 'manly' by association.[51] The same reply can also be made to the implication that *andreia* is conventionally ascribed to women as well.[52] In short, while the dialogue at this juncture is clearly concerned to define courage, there are no grounds to suppose that the notion of manliness has become irrelevant.

If manliness is still an issue in this passage, then we need to ask what its ascription to certain animals can tell us about it. At this point, however, a complication arises. For although the text only discusses the fact that certain animals are perceived as *andreioi*, the talk of lions and boars may remind us of all the similes in Greek poetry which make the reverse claim, and ascribe the qualities of these animals to men. Whether Plato intends us to make the connection we cannot be sure,[53] but, whether intended or not, two questions follow. Firstly, if Nicias is right to deny full courage to animals, does this mean that we should, for example, question the 'courage' of the Homeric hero who is compared to a lion? Does not the comparison suggest instead that the warrior has lost all sense of what he is doing, and what dangers he faces? Secondly, is it not rather strange simultaneously to conceive of manliness in terms of bestiality, and bestiality in terms of manliness? Is it not rather peculiar to imagine a father saying to his son: 'be a real man; be a *lion*'? Yet this, of course, is precisely the situation we get if we put together two of the key passages concerning the *thumos* in *Republic* 8 and 9. At 549–50 we saw the son of the philosophic man being encouraged by his mother and the servants to be 'more of a man' than his father, and opting as a result for the *thumos*-dominated life; at 588, however, this 'manly' *thumos* is compared to

---

[51] It is significant that although Aristotle is happy to attribute *andreia* to animals in the *Historia Animalium*, he also writes that, 'all female (animals) are less spirited (ἀθυμότερα) than the males, apart from the bear and the leopard: in these the female is considered to be braver (ἀνδρειοτέρα) (608a; *vide* also 610a, where the female elephant is said to be 'much less spirited' than the male).

[52] 197c5.

[53] Though the allusions to Homer we have noticed elsewhere in the *Laches* may suggest that Plato does want us to reflect on the Homeric similes at this point.

a lion. We can now see that this apparent anomaly arises from tensions within the conventional application of *andreia* itself. It is an anomaly that we shall find at the very heart of the *Gorgias*.

Nicias' distinction between *andreia* and raw animal drive, therefore, leads to some highly complex areas which the *Laches* flags but does not explore. Nevertheless, the establishment of the distinction allows Socrates to return to the central issue: what, precisely, is the object of the courageous person's knowledge? Having reminded Nicias that they began by considering courage as just one of the parts of virtue, together with justice, temperance and the like, he turns his attention in 198b to the terms *deina* and *tharralea* themselves. *Deina* are defined as things which cause fear, and fear in turn is defined as expectation of future evil (*kakon*); in contrast, *tharralea* are things which do not cause fear, and these are either future non-evils or future goods (*agatha*). Courage, then, is according to Nicias the knowledge of future evils, non-evils and goods. But the knowledge of future goods and evils is in fact only a branch of the knowledge of goods and evils *simpliciter*, for it is always the same knowledge that deals with the same things, whether they lie in the future, the present or the past: medical knowledge, for instance, deals with all medical processes, past, present and future alike. So if courage is the knowledge of future goods and evils, then it is in fact the knowledge of goods and evils in general; Nicias' definition thus covered only a third of courage. However, if we reformulate the definition to cover goods and evils in general, it will, paradoxically, become too broad. For surely someone who has knowledge of goods and evils in general is wholly virtuous, showing that knowledge of all goods and evils is not a part of virtue but the whole of it? We saw earlier[54] how one of the problems with the popular conception of *andreia* was that it was simultaneously felt to refer to both part of a man's virtue and the whole of it: if you are a man, then what else can you need but manliness? It now seems that Socrates is suggesting that Nicias' decidedly anti-populist definition of courage is open to a similar charge. *Impasse* has been reached and courage itself continues to elude us.

Socrates' line of reasoning here is not without its problems: in particular, it is highly debatable whether one can treat the knowl-

---

[54] Pp. 82–3 above.

edge of a future truth as identical to knowledge of the 'same' truth in the past or the present. If we take Socrates' and Nicias' words at face value here, then the underlying assumption is that the propositions which are the objects of *epistēmē* proper are tenselessly true. *Epistēmē* proper is thus concerned only with general truths; historical contingencies cannot directly be its objects at all.[55] Such a claim clearly requires more philosophical support than the *Laches* provides. For present purposes, however, our chief task is not to critique Socrates' logic, but to work out exactly what he is up to. What is his underlying strategy in this final argument? It is only by attempting to appreciate this that we can hope to reach an interpretation of the dialogue as a whole.

The first point to note is that, whatever the logical rights and wrongs, the alleged identity of 'pieces' of knowledge concerning the same things in past, present and future may have extremely important implications for the dialogue's ethical framework. We have seen how at 187e–188a Nicias claims that each of Socrates' interlocutors is compelled 'to give an account of himself, of the way in which he currently lives, and of the kind of life he has lived until now'.[56] What we now have to consider is whether there is, or could be, a general *epistēmē* of character and accompanying way of life. If there could – and it is clearly a very big 'if' – then there is a sense in which acquaintance with a person's past and present way of life can also tell us something of their future. Although the historical details cannot be the object of the general *epistēmē* to which Socrates is referring, those details may reveal a general pattern of character and life which can. As a result, general predictions concerning the likely shape of the interlocutor's future character and life are possible. At 198e–199a Socrates attacks the pretensions of the seer, arguing that it is the specialist, not the seer, who is in the best position to predict what will happen in his particular field: it is the doctor, farmer or general whose word we should trust. If, therefore, there is a specialist science of character and ways of life, then it will accordingly be the ethical scientist who is best able to predict how an individual's life will take shape, by applying his

---

[55] See Vlastos 1994a: 121. Stokes (1986: 102–6) proposes the qualification that Nicias and Socrates are only interested in knowledge of general truths in this passage, and their remarks apply to such knowledge alone; contingencies may or may not be the objects of a different kind of knowledge.

[56] Pp. 50–1 above.

knowledge of tenseless general truths to the particular historical case. It is perhaps in this light that we should view the probable allusions to Nicias' disastrous reliance on seers in the Sicilian expedition.[57] The suggestion is that, despite his sidelining of prophecy in the dialogue, there is still something about Nicias' character and conduct which permits Socrates to foresee his future downfall. Nicias may say all the right things, but he does not yet fully understand them.

The main challenge that Socrates' final argument presents, however, is the question of how to interpret its formally aporetic conclusion. When Socrates claims that they have not yet discovered courage, does he mean what he says? Perhaps the most common view is that he does not, and that his aporetic stance is purely ironic. On this interpretation Socrates' purpose in the final argument is an unambiguous demonstration of the Unity of Virtue. All the so-called 'virtues' are in fact to be identified with one reference, the knowledge of overall goods and evils, and it consequently makes no sense to talk of virtue as comprised of parts.[58] All that needs to be done is to reject the premise that courage is a part of virtue and the *impasse* can be avoided.

This reading, however, has the drawback of requiring us to believe that all the earlier attempts to define *andreia* are simply an elaborate hoax; yet if they are only set up to be brushed aside as fundamentally misconceived, why does Plato set them up with such care? It seems to me far more plausible that Socrates is being sincere when he says that they have not yet defined *andreia*; the difficulty is to decide on his reason for doing so. One possibility is that he is simply and genuinely puzzled, unsure how to reconcile the apparently conclusive evidence that the virtues are one with the common-sense belief that they are distinct.[59] After all, if the virtues do not differ in any way, then how have they come to be given different names? If this is Socrates' position, then a possible explanation for it is that neither he nor Plato has properly appreciated the distinction between meaning and reference. Had that crucial distinction been made, then Socrates could have maintained without incoherence that the virtues are one in reference

---

[57] 195e; 199a. See Thucydides 7.50.4; 7.86.5.
[58] See Penner 1973: 35–68, especially 60–2 and 1992: 127 n. 21 and 141–2; C. C. W. Taylor 1991: 107; Taylor goes on to discuss the inadequacies of Socrates' account.
[59] See Irwin 1995: 44.

but different in sense as a result of the different contexts in which the reference may operate.[60]

Alternatively (or additionally), Socrates may think that they have failed to define courage because Nicias' definition was inadequate all along. The knowledge of overall values that Nicias identifies with courage is necessary, but not sufficient; also required is the capacity for endurance stipulated by Laches, and endorsed by Socrates at 194a. Does such a reading mean that Socrates is not, in the *Laches*, seriously interested in considering the thesis that the virtues are somehow one? Once more, I believe that this does not follow: Socrates could genuinely be trying to reconcile some version of the Unity of Virtue with the common-sense belief that different virtues involve different psychological and behavioural traits. Were the sense/reference distinction available to him, then he could again argue that all the virtues refer to the same state of soul – say, the knowledge of goods and evils – but that this state will manifest itself in different ways according to what the situation requires. If the situation requires endurance for knowledge of the good to be implemented, then endurance must be shown. He could even allow Nicias' definition of courage to stand, providing Nicias can show that knowledge of the good necessarily implies that one will be willing and able to persevere in whatever way necessary in order to achieve it.

On both the second and the third of these readings, then, Socrates is raising the Unity of Virtue thesis in the *Laches* in a more questioning spirit than has often been assumed. He believes that the argument in its favour is a powerful one, yet he is reluctant to abandon the common-sense notion that the virtues are distinct, and that courage is distinct because it is (at the least) associated with endurance and drive. There is also, of course, yet another possibility, which may be more attractive to those who are determined to see the Socrates of the early dialogues as the forthright and undivided champion of virtue as knowledge. Even if Socrates is clear that, despite the apparent puzzles, virtue is one, it may well be that Plato is more hesitant. However enthusiastic the support of the historical Socrates for the Unity of Virtue,[61] Plato may

---

[60] See Taylor 1991: 107–8.
[61] It still seems hard to imagine the historical Socrates supporting any thesis without submitting it to rigorous questioning.

always have found the view problematic as well as seductive, and there is no reason why he should not employ the *Laches* to present both sides of the picture.

CONCLUSION

In trying to decide which interpretation of the final argument is the most persuasive, we need to consider its function in the dialogue's overall structure. If we consider the three definitions of *andreia* offered in the *Laches*, a clear pattern emerges. In the first, courage is defined simply as a non-cognitive psychological capacity; in the second, as a non-cognitive psychological capacity accompanied by wisdom; finally, it is identified with a cognitive state alone. All three definitions give rise to problems, but all three also bring to light important and complex questions that anyone reflecting on courage needs to face. It seems legitimate to conclude, therefore, that an ultimate definition will either possess the formal structure of the second attempt, in which cognitive and non-cognitive elements are explicitly combined, or will rework the third in the way outlined above, so that the non-cognitive element of endurance is an implicit aspect of the kind of knowledge required.

As we have seen, it is the former option that Plato eventually takes. In the *Republic*, the political *andreia* of the Auxiliaries is defined at 430b as the capacity (*dunamis*)[62] to retain in all circumstances correct belief concerning what is and is not to be feared. The definition is an adroit combination of the second and third positions offered in the *Laches*. Socratic intellectualism is retained to the extent that active correct belief is sufficient for action;[63] however, for correct belief to remain active in the face of danger and difficulty, a non-rational psychological quality is also necessary. This non-rational quality, as 375a makes clear, is *thumos*; belief needs to be supported by the emotional drive of *thumos* for its implementation. In the untutored state in which *thumos* first emerges in *Republic* 2, it replaces, I would suggest, *andreia* in its sense of raw animal drive or mettle, the sense referred to at *Laches*

<hr/>

[62] Compare *Laches* 192b6.
[63] In the Philosopher-Rulers, of course, correct belief has been transformed into *epistēmē* proper; their courage will thus not merely be 'political' (or 'civic'), but true *andreia*. See pp. 242–3 below.

197a; Nicias is right to deny that such raw mettle is courage, but we can now see that it still has an important role to play. However, the reason that *thumos* can later be successfully conjoined with correct beliefs concerning overall values and ends, and its energies harnessed to support those beliefs in time of danger and hardship, lies squarely in the fact that *thumos* in Book 4 is no longer in its raw state. Beliefs and drive cannot just be glued together: their useful alliance is only possible because of the lengthy process of education outlined in Books 2 and 3, in which the valuable aspects of *thumos* are toned up and the more savage aspects softened. It is only through such a training that mettle can be transformed into endurance for a good cause. If correct belief needs to be supported by emotional drive, then emotional drive needs equally to be informed and guided by a wide variety of correct beliefs. *Thumos* also, we may note, requires the assistance of technical skills. The Auxiliaries are to go through a tough and lengthy physical training and education in the arts of war: it is simply assumed that the confidence that such training instils will better enable them to hang on to their correct beliefs. In the *Laches* Plato debates the value of such technical abilities, giving the case for and against (though I have suggested that he never ultimately rejects their value). In the *Republic* he has made up his mind. Technical skills on their own will not make for courage; nor can they provide *thumos* if *thumos* is altogether lacking. They can, however, help bolster *thumos* and make it more effective; so providing *thumos* is also guided by the correct view of what is and is not to be feared, then technical skills can play a positive role in promoting courage. Plato does not confuse technique with virtue, but he is clear-eyed about the need to provide the best possible environment for virtue to develop.

I am not claiming that when Plato wrote the *Laches* he had the psychology of the *Republic* clearly in mind. But I do believe that a careful study of the former shows the need for the *Republic*'s concept of the *thumos*, and I also believe that Plato is at least aware that Nicias' austerely intellectualist definition lacks something. This, however, is not the only respect in which the *Laches* reveals the need for further discussion to resolve the problems it raises: as we have also seen, the assumption that if courage is noble then it will also be beneficial requires considerable exploration of the nature of both values, and the further assumption that if a course of action is beneficial it will naturally be undertaken raises the troubling issue of weakness of the will.[64] Both these issues are of course also tackled in the *Republic*; their exploration, however, begins in depth in the *Protagoras*, which complements the *Laches* so closely that they could almost be written as companion pieces.[65] Not only does it provide the discussion of values which the *Laches* lacks, it also deepens our understanding of the problems surrounding *andreia* and thus helps prepare us for the solutions Plato offers in the *Republic*. Finally, the *Protagoras* is one of the most important dialogues for helping us to appreciate the general ethical framework within which Plato works, and shows how the roots of that framework do not just grow from the teaching of Socrates. It is to the *Protagoras*, then, that we now turn.

---

[64] See pp. 89–91 and 103 above.

[65] For the debate on the relative chronology of the *Laches* and the *Protagoras*, see Vlastos 1994a: 109–26. I am not convinced by his arguments for the *Protagoras* being the earlier (see p. 119 below), but in truth I do not much care either way. It seems to me that each dialogue can help with problems raised in the other, and there is much to be gained from the exercise of taking each as prior in turn. I see no reason why such an exercise should not have been Plato's intention, whatever the actual dates of composition.

CHAPTER 4

Odd virtue out: courage and goodness in the Protagoras

VIRTUE AND THE VIRTUES (328d–334c)

The complexity of the relation between *andreia* and *aretē* as a whole is first raised in the *Protagoras* at 329e. At 328d Protagoras finally brings his Great Speech to a close and Socrates offers his praise; there is, however, just one point he would like clarified. Protagoras made reference to both particular virtues, such as justice, respect and temperance, and also to virtue (*aretē*) in general; does he see the former as parts of virtue, or are they simply different names for the same single thing? Protagoras replies that they are parts. In that case, continues Socrates, are they heterogeneous in the way that eyes, ears and nose are parts of the face, or are they homogeneous like the parts of a lump of gold? Protagoras says that they are like the parts of the face. And do different people possess different virtues, or is it the case (as the analogy would seem to suggest) that if you possess one virtue you must necessarily possess them all? No, says Protagoras, many people are courageous (*andreioi*) but unjust, and many again are just but not wise (329e5–6).

If we leave aside for the moment the issue of what precisely Socrates means when he suggests that the virtues are names of the same thing,[1] the most striking features of this exchange are Protagoras' immediate citation of *andreia* as problematic, and his belief that justice may be divorced from wisdom. While he does not quite say that being just may not be to one's personal advantage,[2] his claim certainly raises the possibility: we at least need to know more, once again, about how wisdom is to be conceived. In any event, Socrates is unhappy with Protagoras' response, and

---

[1] See p. 133 n. 41 below and pp. 108–10 above.
[2] And indeed at 333c1 is reluctant to admit that the unjust could be temperate.

launches into three connected arguments apparently designed to show that the virtues not only coexist, but are unified in some stronger sense. First, he tries to persuade Protagoras to agree that justice and piety are either the same thing or very similar, since justice is holy and holiness just. When Protagoras demurs, saying that he does not take quite so simple a view, Socrates swiftly moves on, attempting to prove that wisdom is identical with temperance, since folly is the opposite of both, and one thing can only possess one opposite. This time Protagoras does not protest, and Socrates again sweeps on, asking Protagoras whether he thinks that a man acts temperately if he acts unjustly. Protagoras says that he would be embarrassed to admit such a thing, though it is true that there are many who proclaim it openly. Socrates takes up the challenge. Do such people think that to be temperate is to be prudent (*eu phronein*), and that to be prudent is to be well advised (*eu bouleuesthai*)? And does this mean that they think people do well (*eu prattein*) out of their injustice? Protagoras says yes, this is what they think.

In an apparent change of tack, Socrates now asks whether good things are those which are profitable to men. If his intention is to try to show that justice must also be profitable because justice is good, then the relevant response would be to ask 'profitable to whom?' The way would then be open for a serious discussion of the relation between morality and personal benefit. Protagoras, however, loses the thread at this point and starts talking about species relativism instead: while some things are good for men, others are good only for cattle or trees. The question of how the various virtues relate to each other and to virtue in general is abandoned, not to be formally resumed until 349b.

Taken together, these three arguments form a curious passage, and the logical complexities and flaws have been well analysed by the commentators.[3] For our purposes, the most important point to note is that, in his attempt to demonstrate that the various virtues are either identical or very similar, Socrates significantly leaves *andreia* till last. If his aim in the inconclusive third argument is to show that temperance is in fact identical to justice, then he could draw the arguments together and infer that if justice is the same as (or very similar to) piety, wisdom the same as temperance and

---

[3] See Stokes 1986: 258–311; Taylor 1991: 103–32.

temperance the same as justice, then these four virtues are either identical or very similar. There is, however, no clue at all to suggest how courage could be incorporated into this general scheme; it appears that Protagoras may have been right to claim that it is a difficult virtue to accommodate.

COURAGE, DARING AND TECHNIQUE (347c–351b)

The ambivalent status of *andreia* in popular thought is picked up again in 347c, following a debate on philosophic method[4] and a partly ironic disquisition by Socrates on a poem of Simonides. Abruptly changing tack, Socrates says that discussing poetry is in fact a vulgar occupation; he and Protagoras ought rather to imitate the kind of men who converse directly, testing each other in turn by means of argument. He accordingly persuades a reluctant Protagoras to resume their debate on the relation of virtue and the virtues. Does Protagoras still agree with his earlier statement that justice, wisdom and so on do not refer to the same thing, but are distinct parts of *aretē*, differing from each other and possessing different functions? Protagoras replies that he still thinks that they are all parts of virtue, though he admits that justice, wisdom, temperance and piety are fairly similar;[5] *andreia*, however, is something 'utterly different from all the rest'.[6] For proof, one need only consider how many people are extremely unjust, impious, dissolute and ignorant, yet outstandingly courageous (349d6–8).

At one level Protagoras may feel that courage is the easiest virtue to single out as it was the only one not tackled by Socrates in his initial attempt to establish the identity of the virtues in 330–3. Nevertheless, there is every reason to suppose that this conception of courage was a common one: it is very close to the view of *andreia* as a raw aggression drive, shared in by animals as well as humans, which Socrates refers to at *Laches* 196d, and which Laches says is held by 'everyone' (apart, of course, from Nicias). Yet, common or not, we may be surprised that Protagoras subscribes to it, since it suggests that courage is unteachable. At 326b–c, however, he was adamant that the physical prerequisites for *andreia* should form a basic part of civic education: children should receive gymnastic

---

[4] See pp. 98–9 above.   [5] ἐπιεικῶς παραπλήσια ἀλλήλοις.
[6] πάνυ πολὺ διαφέρον πάντων τούτων.

training, so that 'they may not be forced to display cowardice through bodily weakness'.[7] And just below the present passage at 351b he insists that *andreia* arises from 'nature or good nurture of the *psuchē*'.[8] In trying to get out of one hole, he seems to have dug himself into a deeper one.

Socrates, however, does not explicitly point out the incoherence of Protagoras' position until the very end of the dialogue. His immediate tactic is to attempt to demonstrate that courage, far from being compatible with ignorance, is actually identical to wisdom. The argument runs as follows:

(1) The courageous are bold (349e2–3).[9]
(2) Virtue is a very fine thing, and its parts are as fine as possible (349e4–8).
(3) Men who are knowledgeable in some technical skill are bold on account of their knowledge, and they are bolder than those who are not knowledgeable in the relevant skill (349e8–350b1).
(4) Yet men who are ignorant of the relevant skills can also sometimes behave boldly – indeed, too boldly (350b2–4).
(5) These men who are bold but ignorant are mad (350b5–6).
(6) So they cannot be courageous, because that would make courage a shameful thing [since madness is a shameful state] (350b5).
(7) The courageous men are the bold men (350b6–7).
(8) The extremely wise are the extremely bold, and being extremely bold are extremely courageous (350c2–4).
(9) So wisdom is courage (350c4–5).

Protagoras' response is indignant, if not particularly lucid. Apparently oblivious of the definite article which Socrates slips in at (7), he protests that he never said that the bold are courageous, only that the courageous are bold. All Socrates has done is show

---

[7] See p. 95 n. 34 above.

[8] Either Protagoras has forgotten his earlier stipulations about physical as well as psychic nurture, or he is taking it for granted that the *psuchē* can best be tended if it receives the support of a well-trained body.

[9] The term translated 'bold', *tharraleos*, can mean both confident in feeling and daring in action. The examples in 350a (diving into wells, going to war on horseback etc.) make it clear that it is chiefly the latter meaning that Socrates and Protagoras have in mind here, though the daring actions are doubtless viewed as both stemming from and accompanied by a confident feeling.

that knowledge/wisdom[10] makes a difference to the degree (and kind?) of boldness people display. If Socrates were to follow through his line of reasoning, he might just as well take strength to be wisdom: the strong are powerful, and those who know how to wrestle are more powerful than those who do not. Yet the truth is that though wisdom again makes a critical difference, it cannot be identified with strength any more than it can be identified with courage, for though all the strong are powerful, not all the powerful are strong. Power and boldness alike arise from skill[11] or from madness or from rage,[12] whereas strength and courage arise from natural constitution (*phusis*) and good nurture of the *psuchē*.

It is an odd passage in a number of ways. Socrates' baroque argument and Protagoras' reply both contain a bewildering variety of ellisions, ambiguities and plain fallacies, and some commentators, such as Vlastos,[13] have taken these as evidence of the dialogue's immaturity. Plato, however, is perfectly capable of making even Socrates utter a fallacy or an equivocation if he thinks that such tactics serve his pedagogical aims; before laying charges, therefore, we should consider how the passage fits in with the dialogue as a whole. Just because it is well suited to the probings of modern logical analysis does not mean that it should be treated as an isolated incident. Apparent inconsistencies and fallacies may be deliberately included by Plato to make us re-think what has gone before and point up the need for what is still to come.

First, however, we need to examine the argument with some care. An immediately striking feature is the fact that two of the examples of technical prowess it cites – cavalry-fighting and diving into wells – are also used at *Laches* 193a–c. There, however, possession of these technical skills was said by Laches to reduce the degree of *andreia* displayed; here, Protagoras claims that their possession will increase boldness. Furthermore, their presence will at the very least constitute the difference between the foolish boldness of the mad and the kind of boldness possessed by the courageous. Whichever dialogue is the earlier, there is no doubt that

---

[10] Protagoras uses both interchangeably: see 350d3–5.
[11] Again, Protagoras uses *epistēmē* and *technē* interchangeably.
[12] 'Rage' translates '*thumos*', a clear instance of how the term may be used in ordinary speech.
[13] 1994a: 116–17 and 125–6.

Plato is deliberately exploring the complex interrelation of *andreia*, boldness, skill and risk from the perspectives of two very different men. In the following analysis of *Protagoras* 349–51, therefore, I shall assume that the discussion of the companion argument in the *Laches* has been read.[14] Issues that have already been discussed need only be briefly recapitulated here.

In one respect, at any rate, the *Protagoras* version appears superior to that of the *Laches*, in that it seems more straightforward to suggest a positive correlation between technical skill and boldness than an inverse correlation between technical skill and courage: the link can be made directly without having to consider the worth of the ends involved. Yet even here the correlation will by no means always hold. Firstly, it is significant that Protagoras does not explicitly mention the issue of risk: if the skill actually reduces the risk to zero, can one call the skilled agent bold at all? Secondly, even in those situations where he faces unarguable risks, it is not necessarily true that possession of the relevant skill will invariably make him prepared to undertake them. There will be occasions when the skilled man will hold back precisely because he is in a position to estimate the full extent of the danger; it is because he is skilled that he declines to be bold.

Protagoras does not appear to have considered this possibility, but he does admit in (4) that the converse situation can hold, and that people without the relevant technical knowledge can after all behave extremely boldly at times. The inconsistency is glaring, but it need not present a serious problem: in (3), Protagoras probably only means that the correlation between knowledge and boldness *usually* holds, and it seems charitable to assume that a 'usually' is to be understood.[15] We can conclude that Protagoras is cavalier in his use of generalizations, but not that his position is thereby untenable. More worrying is his claim that all those who are bold without the relevant knowledge are mad, and therefore not courageous, since courage is a fine thing and madness (it is inferred) is shameful. While we may want to deny that the pointlessly reckless are courageous, we may also wonder whether all actions undertaken without the appropriate skill come under this heading. What exactly does 'mad' mean here? Does it just mean that the agent is likely to come to harm, or that he has absolutely no hope whatso-

---

[14] See pp. 91–5 above.   [15] See Stokes 1986: 333–4.

ever of succeeding in his aim? If the latter, then there could be a good case for calling him mad, or at any rate foolish; but if the term simply implies that the agent is putting himself at great personal risk, then we might not want to call him mad at all. If he is fully aware of the dangers but has decided that the desired end is worth the risk, then we might on the contrary want to call him extremely courageous, as Laches does at *Laches* 193.[16] It would depend on whether we agreed with the agent that the overall objective was worth it.

The chief problem is that both Protagoras and Socrates seem to conceive of knowledge, wisdom and ignorance in this passage solely in terms of the kind of technical skills which provide means to ends; there is no mention of knowledge of the ends themselves. And, while we saw in our discussion of the *Laches* that technical skills do have some part to play in courage,[17] we also saw that they can never be sufficient to account for courage on their own: there always needs to be a reference to the ends and values for which the action is undertaken. It is because of this apparent failure to distinguish ends and means that Vlastos dated the *Protagoras* before the *Laches*, arguing that Plato had not yet come to appreciate the distinction himself.[18] Yet this is to assume that the *Protagoras* argument is simply to be taken as it stands, and in isolation. There is no reason why Socrates should not have included it precisely to demonstrate the need for such a distinction, and more generally to prompt us to consider the many different ways in which a person may be knowledgeable or wise.[19] It is Socrates after all who will in 356 introduce a totally different kind of *technē*, the *technē* concerned with the ultimate goals of life. It is of course possible that he does not in fact appreciate that the 'measuring art', the *metrētikē technē*, is of a fundamentally different kind from the art of diving into wells; but it seems to me far more plausible to assume that the first argument concerning courage is designed to be proleptic. It can hardly be chance that when Protagoras and Socrates return to the

---

[16] The text simply refers to the person who is unskilled (ἀνεπιστήμων); there is no indication whether Protagoras envisages him as aware or unaware of the dangers involved. We do not even know whether he fully appreciates his lack of skill.

[17] Pp. 93–5.

[18] See p. 112 n. 65 above.

[19] This possibility will be underestimated or missed altogether if one concentrates solely on giving a formal analysis of the argument, in which 'knowledgeable' and 'wise' are taken to stand for the same property throughout.

issue of courage in 358, courage is defined solely in terms of values and ends.

Nor is this all. The claim that the *metrētikē technē* of 356–7 is of a very different sort from the *technai* referred to in 349e–350a has implications that reach far beyond the *Protagoras* itself. Much has been written of the analogy Socrates draws between virtue and the technical crafts in a number of early and early-middle dialogues,[20] and *Protagoras* 356–7 is usually cited as a – perhaps the – key text. Yet both supporters and opponents of the craft analogy have assumed too readily that Socrates simply presents it as an established tenet: we may agree or disagree but this is what he believes. Careful consideration of the 349–51 argument on courage, however, and comparison between this and the later passage, show that Socrates is deeply concerned to explore the notion of *technē*, and hence, inevitably, the craft analogy itself. This is not to say that he thinks the analogy should necessarily be rejected; it is simply that his use of the idea is never glib. Virtue may be comparable to a craft, but only if the craft is of the right kind, and properly understood.

Matters become even more complex when we consider Protagoras' distinction between courage and boldness. Taken as a general and isolated statement it is a distinction that will prove very helpful, particularly in its insistence that courage is a settled disposition whereas boldness may be a purely transitory mood or state. In terms of detail and context, however, it is decidedly frustrating. Protagoras makes absolutely no attempt to define either property; and as we have seen, his assertion that courage arises from 'nature and good nurture of the *psuchē*' takes no cognizance of his earlier claim (326b–c) that courage requires in addition appropriate physical training. It is also unclear how courage and (the right kind of) boldness are supposed to connect, as they must if the courageous are to be bold. Protagoras' position, in short, is suggestive but fuzzy, which is perhaps not surprising if he is in some ways a representative – albeit an intelligent one – of conventional thought.

His confusion may help us to understand what most commentators have taken to be the chief difficulty of the passage,

[20] See, particularly, Irwin 1977 and 1995.

namely the undeniable fact that Socrates' procedure is deeply flawed. When Socrates asks Protagoras at 350b6–7 whether the courageous men are the bold men, his insertion of the definite article before 'bold' does not follow from anything previously agreed, and Protagoras only lets it pass here through momentary inadvertence, or a failure to appreciate its implications. As we have seen, he later (350c) protests that he never said that the bold were courageous, only that the courageous were bold. If the article is removed, then the most Socrates can try to argue for is that the courageous are the bold-and-wise, and even this will depend on ignorance and knowledge being both mutually exclusive and mutually exhaustive.[21] He certainly cannot conclude that the set of courageous people is coextensive with the set of wise people, and even if he could, this would still not be sufficient to permit him to argue that courage and wisdom themselves are identical. Coextensive sets do not amount to property identity. Though commentators have differed considerably in their analyses of the precise structure of the argument, all agree that Socrates' conclusions cannot be made to accord with the requirements of logic.

So much may be granted without controversy; the debate centres rather on how the logical inadequacies of Socrates' procedure are to be understood. This is where it is vital to consider the passage in its context. Taken in isolation, one might conclude that Socrates is being wantonly deceitful, or even that he is simply as muddled as Protagoras; if we consider the framework of the argument, however, things look rather different. Stokes has suggested that Socrates is not trying to prove the identity of courage and wisdom so much as disprove Protagoras' reasons for believing that courage is distinct,[22] and I would certainly agree that undermining Protagoras' position forms at least part of Socrates' objective. After all, the only evidence Protagoras has so far offered in support of his thesis is the empirical claim that some outstandingly courageous people are also extremely unjust, ignorant, impious and dissolute. When pressed, however, Protagoras finds that he does not entirely agree with this assertion: he cannot after all bring himself to admit that ignorant people can be genuinely courageous. Even if the kind of technical ignorance he has in mind is at best only

---

[21] See Stokes 1986: 340.   [22] Stokes 1986: 342.

part of the story, his reluctance still provides Socrates with important ammunition. The crucial factor here is Protagoras' determination that *andreia* must be something fine (*kalon*):[23] Socrates has at
least forced him to reconsider whether a property can be both fine
and the bedfellow of ignorance and stupidity, even if considerable
attention needs to be paid to which kinds of ignorance and stupidity are involved. Furthermore, if wisdom is very similar to justice, piety and temperance, as Protagoras has admitted,[24] then he
may be persuaded to agree that ignorance is very similar to injustice, impiety and wantonness. So if courage is incompatible with
ignorance, then it will also be incompatible with these vices as
well. However, even without the supposed close similarity of the
other four virtues and vices, Socrates could still exploit Protagoras'
assumption that courage is fine to expose the improbability of
courage being compatible with any vice. Protagoras' position is
revealed as profoundly incoherent.

Yet even so it seems hard to believe that disclosing Protagoras'
confusion is Socrates' sole intention in this passage. His conclusion
is framed in the positive, not the negative. He does not simply
argue that courage cannot coexist with ignorance, but that wisdom
is courage. Let us for a moment ignore the fact that this claim is
not justified and consider it simply as a statement. Let us further
make the distinctions between different kinds of knowledge and
ignorance which Protagoras fails to address. Finally, let us even
suppose that the claim means no more than that knowledge of
ultimate ends is both necessary and sufficient for courage, and that
it alone automatically leads to the right kind of boldness.[25] Despite
all these concessions, however, some extremely tough questions
still arise. Why should knowing what is fine mean that one necessarily acts on it? Suppose one's desire to do what is morally noble
conflicts with one's desire to be safe and comfortable – a conflict
which appears to be particularly likely if the moral virtue in question is that of courage? And even if one decides that the morally
noble course would irrefutably be best overall, including for oneself, what of the possibility of one's good intentions being sub-

---

[23] Compare Laches' similar determination at *Laches* 193a.
[24] 349d3–4.
[25] I do not mean to suggest that this is the correct interpretation of Socrates' meaning; it
is simply a hypothesis which frees us to consider other problematic features of the
argument.

verted by *akrasia*, weakness of the will? If weakness of the will is
possible, then Protagoras will be at least partly right when he says
that courage arises from nature and good upbringing, rather than
from skill. While we might want to allow that skill is sometimes
necessary for courage (and add that knowledge of ends is always
necessary), we would surely agree that nature and good nurture
play a critical role in preventing moral backsliding.

These are serious challenges. Yet once again we need to view
the 'conclusion' that wisdom is courage in terms of its position
within the dialogue as a whole, for it is precisely to these questions
of conflict and *akrasia* that Socrates now turns. In this respect too
it would seem that the main contribution of the first argument on
courage is the way in which its apparent shortcomings demonstrate the urgency of the issues raised.

THE UNIFICATION OF VALUES (351b–358b)

At 351b Socrates appears to abandon his attempt to prove the
identity of courage and wisdom, and asks Protagoras instead
whether he regards some men as living well, and others as living
badly. Protagoras says that he does. And would someone who had
lived pleasantly have lived well? Again, Protagoras agrees. So,
presumably, living pleasantly is good and living unpleasantly bad?
The smoothness of Socrates' tone makes the inference seem easy
and natural, but this time Protagoras insists on a qualification:
living pleasantly is good, but only if one lives in enjoyment of *kala*,
of fine and honourable things.

Socrates claims to be surprised. Is Protagoras saying that he
agrees with the many, who call some pleasant things bad and some
painful ones good? Are not things good just in so far as they are
pleasant, and bad just in so far as they are painful? Protagoras
wavers a little, but decides that it will be 'safer' for him to say that
not everything pleasant is good, and not everything painful bad;
moreover, there is a third class of pleasurable and painful things
which are simply neutral. He continues to hold out when Socrates
reformulates his question and asks whether pleasure itself is not
agathon. This, says Protagoras firmly, is a matter that requires further discussion.

The most striking feature of this interchange is how Socrates
blithely sweeps aside Protagoras' concerns about possible tensions

between the pleasant and the fine. Indeed, he does not explicitly pick up on Protagoras' mention of *kala* at all, rephrasing the sophist's reservations in terms of perceived tensions between the pleasant and the good. The *kalon*, in short, is simply subsumed under the *agathon*. Such cavalier disregard for its claims is all the more surprising given the vital role the concept of the fine and honourable has just played in the first argument on courage, in which the distinction between courage and boldness depended on Protagoras' conviction that courage must always be something fine, whereas boldness could arise from shameful lunacy as well as admirable skill. What does Socrates think he is doing?

I believe that the key to this puzzle lies in the ambiguous nature of the concept of the *agathon* itself, which can be used in Greek to cover a very wide range of meanings. The same ambiguity also applies to the opposite term, the *kakon*. When used of a thing or action, as here, *agathon* expresses approval for one or more of a number of reasons: the thing or action may be beneficial to me personally; but it may also be good simply because it displays its own specific excellence, which may or may not happen to benefit me, though it is likely to benefit someone. In some cases this specific excellence can reasonably be termed 'moral'. When used of a person, *agathos* denotes both individual excellence (including moral goodness) and high social status, though the personal and social aspects are usually intricately intertwined.[26] In brief, *agathos/on* possesses a range which runs from strict utility to moral virtue, though it is true that its moral dimension will almost always be perceived in terms of the utility the virtue is likely to bring about. As a result, its relation to the concept of the *kalon* will vary greatly depending on which of its aspects is to the fore: though in ordinary Greek the two value terms can easily complement each other (again, as in the notion of the *kalos k'agathos*), they can also stand in decided opposition, as Protagoras' initial demurral shows.[27] By entirely subsuming the *kalon* under the *agathon*, therefore, Socrates is explicitly attacking ordinary assumptions.

What he does not do, however, is justify the attack; nor is it clear at this point that justification could be found. Before such a radical step could be warranted, one would need to address two

[26] As in *kalos k'agathos* for 'a complete gentleman'.
[27] For tensions, see p. 90 above.

vital questions. Firstly, one would need to show that the moral dimension of the general term *agathon* was sufficient to cover all the noble and aesthetic resonances of the general term *kalon*; yet it is far from obvious that this could be done.[28] Secondly, even if one allowed that the *kalon* could, in some contexts, be roughly and inadequately incorporated into the *agathon*, it is plain that even this inadequate incorporation could only occur in passages where the moral dimension of the *agathon* was very much to the fore. Is this the case here?

Protagoras' usage of *agathon* and its cognates is inconsistent; indeed, it is only the ambiguity inherent in the term itself which prevents his replies from being altogether incoherent. He does not deny that the adverb usually linked with *agathon* – *eu* – implies self-benefit: witness his readiness to accept Socrates' claim that to live pleasantly is to live *eu*, to live well. In this context we may remember 333d7–8, where to 'fare well' (*eu prattein*) meant to live in a way that was beneficial to oneself. When Socrates asks whether to live pleasantly is *agathon*, however, Protagoras unconsciously shifts his focus to the moral sense of the term, and inserts the necessary qualification: to live pleasantly is good providing one takes pleasure only in fine and honourable things. The fine and the good must at least go together.[29]

Socrates' position with regard to the *agathon*, however, appears very different. Firstly, by claiming that pleasure is the sole yardstick of goodness, he seems to be limiting the *agathon* to utility alone. This in itself might not be particularly worrying, given the fact that the moral dimension of the *agathon* is, as we have seen, normally presented in terms of benefits bestowed. However, given that Socrates' restriction of goodness to the pleasant is made in the context of how an individual lives his or her life, it seems clear that the notion of utility is here perceived as purely personal utility: something is good if and only if it benefits *me*. Furthermore, it is a concept of personal utility that itself appears to be unduly restricted: is my benefit really to be conceived only in terms of what gives me pleasure? Socrates appears to be moving towards some sort of unification of value terms simply by ignoring many of

---

[28] Relations between the *kalon* and the *agathon* are discussed further in chs. 5, 6, 7 and 8.

[29] For Plato's skill at exploiting the ambiguity inherent in *eu prattein*, see Dodds 1959: 335–6.

the values that those terms usually convey. In disregarding the claims of the *kalon* he is unduly restricting the *agathon* as well.

Whether Socrates' apparent manoeuvres are the whole picture, however, is another question, and one to which we shall return; at this juncture he gives no hint that his words might be open to a different interpretation, but instead opens a debate on the possibility of *akrasia*, weakness of the will.[30] It is at this point that we learn that his apparent abandonment of the topic of courage in 351b was deceptive. For the argument on *akrasia* depends entirely on the immediately preceding identification of the good and the pleasant, and we are clearly told that the purpose of the argument is to show how courage is related to the other parts of virtue (353b). Socrates' apparent change of subject at 351b, in short, was simply an attempt to prove that courage is knowledge by a different route.

The nuances of the *akrasia* passage have received detailed and illuminating attention,[31] and for present purposes we do not need to go through the text in detail, though we shall be considering some of the main problems below. Our immediate concern is with Socrates' conclusion: namely, that if there is only one kind of value, the pleasant/good, then our wellbeing will depend solely on our ability to calculate which course of action will provide the greatest amount of it. And if there is only one kind of value, then there can only be one kind of desire; there can thus be no conflict between competing desires, and hence no possibility of weakness of the will. Once the good has been identified with the pleasant, and the bad with pain, then it is absurd to say that a person does what they know to be bad because they are overcome by the pleasant: this would simply be to say that they do what they know to be bad because they are overcome by the good, which is clearly nonsense. Furthermore, if someone does bad things because they are overcome by the good, then this shows that the good, despite being the overcomer, is not worth the bad, and hence not able to conquer it. But to say that the good is not worth the bad can only mean that in this particular case the good is smaller than the bad.

---

[30] Although the term *akrasia* is not used by Plato, it is much more convenient for our purposes than the periphrases employed.

[31] See Vlastos 1969; Nussbaum 1986: 109–17; Stokes 1986: 370–411; Ferrari 1990; Taylor 1991: 170–200.

Yet why would anyone knowingly choose a course of action which led to more bad than the alternative? In brief, the whole notion of *akrasia* is profoundly incoherent; what is normally termed weakness of the will by the many is in fact simply ignorance of which course of action offers the greatest amount of the pleasant/good, an ignorance which in turn arises from ignorance of the 'measuring art'.

These are inspiring claims. Whereas the *Laches* merely referred to a vague 'knowledge of goods and bads', we are now offered the more refined science of measuring pleasures and pains, and told that it is only by acquiring this science that our lives can be saved. Such an enticing prospect clearly requires the most careful consideration. Can we accept the huge assumptions on which Socrates' argument rests?

The first thing to emphasize is that Socrates is not simply claiming that there is only one kind of value, the pleasant/good. The argument also assumes that all pleasures/goods are themselves qualitatively the same, differing only in amount; it is this qualitative homogeneity of pleasures that provides the commensurability the measuring art requires. Yet as we have already seen, such homogeneity appears to be achieved at an unacceptably high cost. What of the brusquely dismissed claims of the *kalon*? Is it really true that everyone is always motivated by self-interest? Even if it is, why should self-interest be cashed out solely in terms of pleasure? And why should pleasures be indistinguishable except in mass? At 358d1, in the course of the second argument on courage, we shall find Socrates appealing to 'human nature' to support his claims; if we turn to 'human nature' in the present case, however, it seems more plausible to suppose that there is an irreducible multiplicity of types of value, pleasure and desire, and that one's most intense desire may well not be for the course of action that one knows in theory to be best, even for oneself. Socrates' analysis of the phenomenon of *akrasia* ultimately appears to rest on a decidedly impoverished theory of (or, more loosely, assumptions about) human psychology.

Nor do Socrates' problems end here. Even if one accepts his identification of pleasure and the good, and the implied model of the *psuchē* and its desires on which the identification rests, it is still highly doubtful whether the good can simply be substituted for pleasure in the way that he needs. As Taylor notes,[32] the 'indiscernibility of identicals' does not hold in intentional contexts: objects are desired under certain descriptions, so even if x is identical to y in reference, a person may nevertheless desire only y. Socrates' redescription of *akrasia* is inadmissable because it ignores the crucial distinction between reference and sense.

Such serious difficulties prompt one to ask whether Socrates really means what he says: after all, in the *Gorgias* we shall find him vigorously opposing Callicles' ostensible hedonism.[33] The issue is further complicated by Socrates' decidedly ambivalent tone. On the one hand, his repeated challenges to the many to say whether pleasure is their only goal in life may suggest that he himself is sceptical about the identification of pleasure with the good;[34] he certainly confines himself to saying merely that this is the answer he and Protagoras would have given to the world at large (358a1). And his exhortation at 357e that the many should lavish money on Protagoras and the other sophists to cure their ignorance fairly drips with irony. If one considers such jibes in isolation, one may perhaps be tempted to think that Socrates is trying to beat the sophists at their own game: it is a tactic he has already employed in his parodic analysis of the Simonides ode, and would give point to the scene in which he and Hippocrates are initially mistaken for sophists by the porter.[35] Yet if Socrates does not believe what he is saying when he identifies the good with pleasure, why does he explicitly use the identification as the basis for a vital argument? For he certainly seems to be speaking in his own voice when he concludes that all apparent weakness of the will is in fact only ignorance (357b–e), and it seems bizarre if the premise is simply a joke at the many's expense. Furthermore, in other respects the tone of the *akrasia* passage is anything but flippant: Socrates appears genuinely impassioned in his depiction of the measuring art as the saviour of mankind.

Is there any reading of the text available which resolves such apparent contradictions? I believe that there is. Perhaps it is not so much a case of Socrates not meaning what he says, as a case

---

[32] Taylor 1991: 180–1, following a suggestion of M. J. Woods.
[33] See ch. 5. Whether Callicles' version of hedonism is the same as that of the *Protagoras* is discussed below.
[34] *Vide* 353d7–e1; 353e5–354a1; 354b7–c2; 354d1–3; 354d7–e2; 354e8–355a3.
[35] 314d.

of Socrates not saying what the many (who of course may well include ourselves) take him to be saying. It may be that the many have misunderstood what pleasure really is. Gosling and Taylor, for instance, have claimed that the apparent incompatibility between the *Gorgias* and the *Protagoras* regarding pleasure is groundless, in that the *Protagoras* is concerned with a life in which pleasure predominates over pain as a whole, whereas the *Gorgias* is only concerned with immediate gratification.[36] There is certainly some truth in this, but I am doubtful whether such a distinction resolves all the difficulties: as we shall see, Socrates' main charge against hedonism in the *Gorgias* is that not all pleasures are good, and the reason they lack goodness is not simply that they bring more pain than pleasure in the long run. It would seem that if the *Protagoras* and the *Gorgias* are to be brought into line, then more will be needed than a distinction between short-term pleasures and pleasures which contribute towards a predominantly pleasant life.

Nor is it possible to offer a utilitarian reading of the passage, whereby the function of the measuring art is to maximize the pleasure of humanity in general, rather than the purely personal pleasure of the agent. At first sight, this might seem quite an attractive option. It is true that a simple Benthamite equation of the good with undifferentiated pluralistic hedonism would be just as vulnerable to the *Gorgias'* demand that distinctions need to be made between good and bad pleasures; yet it can be replied that the more sophisticated utilitarianism of Mill allows for just such an evaluative hierarchy.[37] The only trouble is that there is absolutely no firm evidence to support a utilitarian interpretation of Socrates' position, either in the *Protagoras* itself or indeed in any other dialogue. In the present passage, the sole possible candidate is Socrates' claim in 354b that the pains of physical training and military service are called good because they result in the deliverance of cities; yet even this example can be viewed in terms of enlightened self-interest. Even if the agent believes that he will be killed in the defence of his community, he could still wish to protect his family and dependants as extensions of himself. And apart

---

[36] Gosling and Taylor 1982: 75–82.
[37] See *Utilitarianism* ch. 2, where Mill argues forcefully that the pleasures of the intellect, feelings and imagination are qualitatively superior to those of the body, claiming that 'it is better to be Socrates dissatisfied than a fool satisfied'. Contrast Bentham *Introduction to the Principles of Morals and Legislation* chs. 3 and 4.

from this one case, all the other examples of pleasure that Socrates mentions very clearly refer to the personal advantage of the agent: we are left in no doubt that it is specifically the notion of *personal* pleasure that the many are supposed to find attractive.[38]

There is, however, a third way in which the notion of pleasure might be reinterpreted. Although we shall find that this reworking is also problematic – not least in regard to its popular appeal – I believe that it nevertheless offers a more promising approach to the puzzle of Socrates' deployment of hedonism in the *Protagoras*. It is a possibility that is suggested by the second argument concerning courage, and it is to this argument that we now turn.

THE PLEASURES OF COURAGE (358b–360e)

By 358b Socrates has persuaded the sophists to agree that the pleasant is good and the painful bad, and he now proceeds to carry out his plan of 353b and put the identification to work in a second attempt to prove that courage is knowledge. Such an attempt will clearly depend in part on how the *kalon* is conceived, and it is no surprise that Socrates' first move is to build on the implicit subsumation of the *kalon* under the *agathon* at 351c. Is it not the case, he asks, that all actions aimed at living painlessly and pleasantly are fine and noble? And is the noble act not good and beneficial? In other words, if the good is to be identical with the pleasant, then it plainly follows that the *kalon* must now be subsumed under the pleasant as well.

Having secured the sophists' agreement to this point, Socrates proceeds to remind us that if the good and the pleasant are identical, then it will also follow that no one will willingly go after bad things, or at least what he or she believes to be bad. It appears that it is simply not in human nature[39] to pursue what one believes to be bad for oneself in preference to what one believes to be good, or to choose the greater bad when one may opt for the lesser. This psychological fact is of particular relevance to our conception of fear. For if dread or fear is to be defined as the expectation of bad, then it is clear that no one willingly pursues what he dreads, when he may pursue what he does not.

---

[38] See also pp. 134–5 below.

[39] ἐν ἀνθρώπου φύσει (358d1). Whether the 'it appears' (ὡς ἔοικεν) is supposed to indicate scepticism on Socrates' part is a moot point.

They are now in a position to tackle Protagoras' assertion that courage is very different from the other virtues, and that a man may be extremely impious, unjust, dissolute and ignorant, and yet outstandingly courageous (349d). Let it be agreed (as Protagoras also claimed) that the courageous are bold (*tharraleoi*) and ready (*ites*). The question is: for what (*epi ti*) are the courageous ready? Are they ready for the same things as cowards? Common opinion has it that cowards go after things which easily allow boldness (*tharralea*), whereas the courageous are willing to go after things which inspire dread (*deina*). Yet according to the present argument, this view cannot be correct: if dread is the expectation of bad, then no one willingly pursues what he believes to be dreadful. In this formal sense, the cowardly and courageous are alike, in that both groups go after things which inspire them with boldness, i.e. things they do not fear.

Protagoras admits this formal point, but is still adamant that in practice the cowardly and the courageous pursue very different activities: the latter, for instance, are willing to go to war, whereas the former are not. Socrates does not dispute this, but simply enquires whether going to war is an honourable (*kalon*) or shameful activity. When Protagoras replies that it is honourable, Socrates has all the evidence he needs. Since it has already been agreed that all honourable actions are good, going to war must also be good; and since the good is identical with the pleasant, going to war must be a pleasant activity as well. So the cowards who are reluctant to go to war must simply fail to understand that such a course of action is not only more honourable, but also better and more pleasant than the craven alternative they misguidedly prefer. Their fear of going to war is shameful because they do not realize that going to war is not in fact to be feared at all. Like *akrasia*, therefore, cowardice is simply ignorance of where one's best interests lie. And as courage is the opposite of cowardice, it follows that courage is neither more nor less than wisdom (*sophia*) concerning what things really are and are not to be feared (360d4–5).

But if death, injury and enslavement are not actually fearful to the right-thinking person, then what things are? For Socrates does not deny that the courageous sometimes fear; it is just that they fear different things from the cowards, and their fears are consequently of a different quality. Whereas the fears of cowards are base, those of the courageous are as honourable as their boldness.

Although the object of these honourable fears is never specified, it can presumably only be the shame of having behaved ignobly.[40] If this is right, then courage, like *thumos* in the *Republic*, appears to be intimately connected with notions of self-image and second-order desires: the courageous person fears not being the person he or she wants to be. Furthermore, the person they want to be is the person they should be: in the courageous person, subjective and objective goods and bads coincide.

If we compare this second argument on courage with the first, we can see that its scope is considerably wider. Whereas the earlier argument dealt with the relations between courage, knowledge and confidence, 358–60 adds to this list the crucial element of fear. It works in two directions. On the one hand, it attempts to show that courage is knowledge by building on the results of the discussion of *akrasia*, namely the agreement that pleasure and the good are identical, and that the fine is (at least) a subset of the pleasant/good. On the other, the argument also seeks to reinforce the claim that *akrasia* is impossible: in 352–8 Socrates tried to demonstrate that knowledge of what is best cannot be overcome by pleasure; he now tries to prove that it cannot be swayed by fear either.

The definition of courage offered here ('wisdom concerning what things are and are not to be feared') also clearly invites comparison with Nicias' definition at *Laches* 194e–195a ('knowledge of what things are to be feared and what dared'). Despite the close similarity of the wording, however, it is important to note that the contexts of the two definitions are very different. In our discussion of the *Laches* passage, we saw that any attempt to define (a) virtue as knowledge requires a supporting theory of the unity of values: without such support, the claims of the good and the fine could conflict, and there would be no reason to suppose that knowledge of the fine on its own would lead to virtuous action. We further saw that one of the main problems of the *Laches* is that no such theory of value is offered. In the *Protagoras*, however, Socrates does attempt to provide the necessary theoretical underpinning. It is a major advance.

Nevertheless, there is no question that 358–60 also raises diffi-

---

[40] Compare Nicias' similarily elliptical definition of *andreia* at *Laches* 194e11–195a1, and see the discussion on pp. 100–1 above.

culties. As a paradigmatic example of courage, Socrates not un-
reasonably selects going to war: he presumably intends to reassure
his audience that he is not trying to persuade us to abandon our
basic intuitions about what are to count as courageous acts; he
simply wants such acts to be redescribed. Yet the example prompts
us to ask once more whether there could be any role for *andreia* in
peacetime, a question to which the *Protagoras* offers no reply.[41]
Furthermore, if the first argument about courage in the *Protagoras*
and its companion argument in the *Laches* have taught us anything, it is that knowledge of general ends also requires knowledge
of particular means and circumstances in order to be properly implemented. Socrates' and Protagoras' over-easy assumption in this
passage that going to war is honourable highlights the point: fighting to save one's country may normally be admirable, but the final
verdict will always depend on the particulars of the case. Suppose
one's country is ruled by a tyrannical regime? Can the definition
'wisdom concerning what things are and are not to be feared' accommodate such exceptions to the general rule? If not, then the
lessons of *Laches* 193a–c and *Protagoras* 349e–350b do not seem to
have been learnt. Common intuitions about courage do not only
need to be redescribed; they also need to be refined.

Even more problematic is the fact that the *Protagoras'* unification
of values relies on such an impoverished model of human psychology and desire, with the result that all the key value terms
receive inadequate treatment. In 351c–d, and in the subsequent
discussion of weakness of the will, we saw the *kalon* and the moral
agathon being given extremely short shrift; the morally fine was
simply assumed to be a subset of the personal good without any
proper debate.[42] In the second argument on courage we now find
this alleged unity deployed in a way which distorts the customary
meaning not only of the fine, but of the personally beneficial and
pleasant as well. Firstly, although the *kalon* is here placed at the
formal centre of the argument, its claims still seem lamentably
neglected. If going to war is only honourable because it is pleas-

---

[41] The issue clearly depends partly on how we are to interpret Socrates' thesis of the Unity
of Virtue, which he refers to again at 361b. Unfortunately the dialogue provides no in-
contestable evidence in this respect, as the continued scholarly dispute shows (see Vlastos
1981: 221–69 and 418–23 and Penner 1973 and 1992: ch. 4 n. 21; *vide* also pp. 108–10
above). For the question of *andreia* in peacetime see *Laches* 191d–e, discussed above pp.
87–8; the issue will reappear in chs. 7 and 8.
[42] Pp. 123–7 above.

ant, then we may wonder whether courage is actually so praise-worthy after all. Equally, we may legitimately have qualms about any argument which concludes that going to war *is* pleasant and personally beneficial: at the very least, such a counter-intuitive position requires a radical reworking of ordinary notions concerning pleasure and personal advantage. Yet if our ordinary notions are so misguided, we may again reasonably ask what business Socrates has in appealing at 358d to an apparently unambiguous 'human nature' (*anthrōpou phusis*), as if it were an obvious concept shared by all.

It is, however, also possible that the purpose of the argument is precisely to invite us to undertake the required reworking of value terms for ourselves. Although its formal premises rely on the sub-sumation of the *kalon* to the *hēdu*,[43] it may be that Socrates (or at any rate Plato) intends us to reject this formal structure, and indeed the structure of the whole of 351–60, and to ask instead whether the notions of pleasure and benefit cannot be brought into line with the morally noble and beautiful. On this reading, the unity of values that Socrates desires would be achieved through a movement in the opposite direction from the one offi-cially adopted: something would only be truly pleasant and good if it were *kalon*. And perhaps the key to such an approach again lies in the notion of a way of life. Perhaps it is not so much argu-ment which can unite pleasure and the good as certain *psuchai* and their modes of living: it is properly formed and educated *psuchai* which can take pleasure in the fine and morally good, and which can enjoy going into battle for a noble cause.[44]

Interpretations which rely on rejecting so much of the surface meaning of a text are, of course, always highly suspect, and I put the suggestion forward as speculation only. It is certainly true that the *Protagoras* does not attempt such a reworking itself, and it plainly lacks the psychological complexity to do so. If Plato wishes to turn our ethical notions upside down, then he must be able to tell us precisely *why* our ordinary conceptions of human nature and human happiness are so profoundly misguided. There is also a problem in that any reformulation of the *hēdu* is perhaps unlikely

---

[43] *Vide* particularly 358b3–5.
[44] For this final speculation I am indebted to some suggestions made to me by Myles Burnyeat.

to be acceptable to the many, whose view of pleasure is portrayed as extremely conservative – not much broader than Prodicus' earlier definition of *hēdesthai* in terms of physical sensation alone (337c1–5). If the criterion of value is what people actually desire, rather than what they should desire – or would desire if their desires were substantially reconstructed – then it appears that this option will be extremely difficult to implement.

Nevertheless, it still seems to me that the interpretation is worth considering: it may be that at this stage Socrates is seeking to convert not the many, but the few. In contrast to the utilitarian reading, it is furthermore a position that Plato explores at length in later dialogues, as the following chapters will show.[45] I do not wish to deny that, in the context of the discussion with the many, the hedonic calculus of the *Protagoras* depends on staunchly traditional conceptions of personal pleasure and benefit; nor do I deny that the formal structure of the argument marginalizes the *kalon*. I am only proposing that Socrates' repeated riders that the argument will only work *if* we agree with the (conservative) beliefs and values of the many indicate that he is at least asking us to consider how pleasure and benefit should really be conceived. The fact that Plato does not yet provide explicit support for a position which defines pleasure and benefit in terms of the morally fine does not mean that he is not inviting us to construct such support.

CONCLUSION

Though tentative, I believe that the above line of thought offers the best hope we have of making sense of Socrates' hedonist stance. Nevertheless, it is undeniable that if we ignore Socrates' hints and confine ourselves to his ostensible arguments, the attempted unification of values does not succeed. As a result, the intellectualist definition of *andreia* remains unconvincing, based on an unacceptably etiolated model of action and desire. It seems, then, that Plato will be right to reject this definition in the *Republic*: one of the main lessons to be learnt from both the *Laches* and the *Protagoras* is that the virtues cannot be properly understood without a more complex account of psychic structure and motivation. In

---

[45] It is also of course the position that Aristotle will take: see *E.N.* 1099a13–25; *E.E.* 1213a1–8; and *Ars Rhet.* 1366a33–4.

particular, it appears that courage cannot be properly understood without appeal to the *thumos* and its especial characteristics and concerns: courage requires both mettle and a due appreciation of the fine as a value which does not necessarily lead to my comfort and pleasure, at any rate when conventionally conceived. It is also notable that the *Protagoras* makes no attempt to relate courage to the presence or absence of *thumos* as anger, despite the reference to *thumos* in the list of alleged enslavers of knowledge in 352b.

This more sophisticated account of desire and the virtues, however, will present Plato with some extremely tough challenges. As we shall see, most of these challenges stem from the fact that although in the *Republic* he does not want the *kalon* to be subsumed under the pleasant/good, he still wishes values to be unified and virtue and happiness to be knowledge. The task he sets himself is to accommodate this hope into a new psychological theory which both does justice to the *kalon* and also allows for weakness of the will and mental conflict.

How Plato tackles this project will be explored in chapter 8. Before we can consider it, however, we need first to understand considerably more about the nature of the problems such a project faces. Above all, we need to see in more detail just how ambivalent a force thumoeidic motivations can be[46], and how, if not carefully directed by reason, they can attach themselves to conceptions of the *kalon* and ideals of *andreia* which are in Plato's eyes profoundly flawed. In short, it is time to return to the conflict with which this book began, the debate between Socrates and Callicles in the *Gorgias*.

---

[46] I shall be arguing that Plato is concerned with 'thumoeidic' characteristics even in dialogues which do not envisage a formally tripartite *psuchē*.

CHAPTER 5

Why should I be good? Callicles, Thrasymachus and the egoist challenge

MAN AND SUPERMAN

At first sight, it may seem rather odd to claim that Callicles is an example of thumoeidic tendencies gone astray; it may seem more plausible to view him as a forerunner, not of the *thumos*, but of the pleasure-seeking *epithumētikon*. After all, from 491e to 492c Plato puts into his mouth what appears to be one of the most forceful exhortations to hedonism ever made. The man who would live rightly, Callicles asserts,

> should let his desires grow as great as possible and not restrain them, and be capable of ministering to them when they are at their height ... and of satisfying each desire in turn with what it wants.

One might imagine that a life devoted to such relentless sybaritic indulgence could hold little time for the thumoeidic pursuit of worldly success and honours. Yet at 484d Callicles makes it plain that a man should aspire to be a well-respected *kalos k'agathos*, and to this end should emulate men who possess wealth and reputation (486c–d) – a remark which is significant not only for the content of its ideal, but also because it shows that he is interested in ideals and role models in the first place. His chosen route, furthermore, is the energy-consuming one of politics: at 515a we are told that he has just embarked on a political career, and at 481d that he is in love with the Athenian *dēmos*.[1] Politicians, of course, are not necessarily averse to a spot of hedonism after hours, but it seems clear that there will always be situations in which they will be forced to choose between immediate gratification and long-term ambition. I believe that a careful study of Callicles' speeches leaves one in no doubt that his apparent espousal of hedonism is superficial. His

[1] Compare Alcibiades' courtship of the *dēmos* at *Symposium* 216b and (perhaps) *Republic* 492c.

real sympathies lie elsewhere, and the real threat that he poses stems from his ungoverned *thumos*.

In order to substantiate these claims, we need to examine the reasons for Callicles' entry into the debate at 481b, and the underlying position from which his ostensible hedonism springs. The crucial point to note is that he is prompted to join the fray because he disagrees with Polus and Socrates on the issue of what is or is not *aischron* and *kalon*, shameful and fine. Initially, Polus had held the conventional view that though it is admittedly more shameful, *aischion*, to wrong than be wronged, receiving wrong is nevertheless worse, *kakion*, than committing it.[2] However, by a dubious analysis of the concept of the fine to be discussed below, Socrates eventually manages to persuade him that if doing wrong is more shameful than suffering it, then it is worse for the agent as well. Indeed, doing wrong is so harmful to the agent's soul that if we do err we should hurry to the law-courts and denounce ourselves as fast as we can, just punishment being the only means of spiritual purification (480b–d).

Callicles, who so far has taken no part in the discussion, is appalled: such conclusions, he protests, rely solely on a cunning manipulation of the antithesis between law or convention (*nomos*) and nature (*phusis*), and are consequently in extremely poor taste (482e3). Polus only got into difficulties because he was fool enough to give in to convention and say that doing wrong was more shameful than suffering it in the first place; in fact it is suffering wrong that is naturally the more shameful, because this shows that one is too weak to stand up for oneself and one's own, and in nature weakness is the mark of the inferior being. Indeed, the man who submits to wrong is not really a proper man at all (483b1), but a mere slave; the real man, by implication, is the man with the natural ability to protect himself and his own and not be wronged in the first place. Laws and customs only say that doing wrong is more shameful than suffering it because they are made by the naturally weak, who are always in the majority, to protect themselves against the naturally strong and few: this craven majority sententiously proclaim that equality of both power and wealth is fine and just because equality is the most they can expect. If we look not to

---

[2] E.g. 474c–d. For potential tensions between the *kalon* and the *agathon* in popular thought, see p. 90 above.

custom but to nature, however, we will see that in fact it is naturally right and fine for the superior to rule the inferior and have more than an equal share of goods; this is the 'law of nature',[3] as both the animal kingdom and interstate relations amply show. Strong men are like lions and the laws are the lions' chains; they should, if they can, break free from such ignoble imprisonment, and 'trample underfoot all our rules and tricks and charms and laws which are all against nature'. Then 'the justice of nature' can finally blaze forth, and we will see in operation Pindar's law of natural force, whereby Heracles is justified in taking the cows of Geryones simply because he is the stronger (484a–c).[4]

Having set up his ideal of the superman, Callicles proceeds to launch into a coruscating attack on philosophers, whom he regards as woefully lacking in leonine qualities. While a little philosophic dabbling is a fine occupation for a boy, to continue such studies as an adult is ridiculous and unmanly (485c): the adult philosopher is utterly ignorant of the ways of the world, and entirely inexperienced in the pleasures, desires and characters of men. If he ever has to engage in any public business, he is thus bound to make a fool of himself; he is equally bound to lack manliness, since he spends his days huddled in a corner with a few callow youths, avoiding the social centres where, as Homer notes, men win glory.[5] Unable to protect himself or his own if wrongfully accused, he is both a boy amongst men and a slave amongst the free. In short, he would be much better off abandoning his fooleries and nonsense (*lērēmata kai phluaria*)[6] and emulating men of substance and repute.

If one is looking for evidence of Callicles' true sympathies, this speech provides the clearest possible proof: it anticipates throughout both the *thumos* of *Republic* 4 and, even more specifically, the degenerate *thumos* of the timocratic man in Book 8. His passionate concern for the concepts of the noble and shameful – albeit on his own terms – and the value he places on success and reputation mark him out as undeniably thumoeidic rather than epithumeitic.

---

[3] κατὰ νόμον γε τὸν τῆς φύσεως, 483e3.

[4] Pindar fr. 169 (Bergk). Callicles also refers to 'natural justice' at 490a7 and 491e7; the phrase is picked up by Socrates at 488b2–3.

[5] Callicles is paraphrasing *Il.* 9.441.

[6] 486c6–7. Callicles directly accuses Socrates of uttering *phluaria* at 489b7; 490c8–d1 and 490e4, while conventional morality is dismissed as worthless *phluaria* at 492c7.

Equally telling is his obsession with manliness,[7] an obsession which calls to mind *Republic* 549–50, where the main reason the son of the philosophic man is persuaded to adopt timocratic values is the insistence of his mother and the servants that he be 'more of a man' than his father when he grows up. Callicles' contemptuous dismissal of the philosopher as unmanly prefigures this scene in some detail, and his rejection of philosophic discussion as *lērēmata kai phluaria* further reminds us of *Republic* 581d, where the honour-loving man is said to regard the pleasures of learning as mere 'vapourings and nonsense' (*kapnos kai phluaria*), unless they bring him prestige. In marked contrast to his depiction of the effete philosopher, Callicles later claims that by 'naturally superior' he means those who are wise and *andreioi* in affairs of state: such men have the strength to carry out their plans to completion, and not falter through softness (*malakia*) of soul.[8] *Andreia*, of course, would be the especial virtue of the *thumos* even if it carried no connotations of manliness; Callicles' earlier and unambiguous appeals to 'manly' behaviour, however, strongly suggest that in his usage of *andreia* the concepts of courage and manliness are inextricably intertwined, and the suggestion appears to be confirmed by the contrast he draws between *andreia* and effeminate *malakia*.[9]

Further evidence of Callicles' essentially thumoeidic nature is provided by his comparison at 483e5–6 of the natural superman to a lion: as we have seen, the *thumos* is specifically likened to a lion at *Republic* 588d. We have also seen that it is an image which calls to mind the many similes comparing heroes to lions in Homer,[10] and its use here is particularly significant because it highlights the aristocratic roots from which Callicles' model springs. In this context, his appeal to *Iliad* 9.441 on the importance of frequenting the public arenas where men are made pre-eminent is also highly telling, since it is a quote from Phoenix' speech to Achilles in which the tutor recounts Peleus' instructions for raising his son in the traditional heroic mould. Callicles has already spoken approvingly

---

[7] References to how 'real men' should or should not behave occur at 483a8–b2; 484a3; 485c2; 485d4.

[8] 491a7–b4. It is interesting to compare *Alcibiades* 1 124e, where the young Alcibiades says he wants to excel in the affairs appropriate to Athenian gentlemen.

[9] For associations between *malakia* and effeminacy see the discussion of *Resp.* 590a–b in ch. 1 p. 27. *Malakia* is there specifically described as the enemy of the *thumos*.

[10] See p. 25 above. The oddity of perceiving a human ideal in animal terms is discussed on pp. 105–6 and 161–2.

of Heracles' exercise of *force majeure*; he now seeks to associate himself with Achilles as well.[11] While we shall find in the following chapters that Achilles' values in fact differ significantly from those of Callicles, there are still sufficient similarities to make Callicles' allusion more than simply the product of vanity. In important respects his political ideal is a modern adaptation of the ancient warrior-kings.[12]

Another more loosely heroic link that the lion image suggests is between Callicles' superman and Alcibiades. At Aristophanes' *Frogs* 1431-2, in a discussion of whether Alcibiades should be re-called to Athens, Aeschylus says that 'it is best by far to rear no lion within your city's walls; but, if one is raised to adulthood, you must humour its ways'.[13] The *Frogs* was first performed in 405, and it is at least possible that Plato intends Callicles' simile to remind his readers of these well-known lines. Again, this is certainly not to claim that Plato thinks the ideals of Callicles and Alcibiades are alike in every respect, or even in most; as in the case of Achilles, however, the similarities are sufficiently striking for us to suspect that Plato believes Achilles, Alcibiades and Callicles to be related character-types. I would also suggest that by the time he writes the *Republic*, Plato realizes that the connection between these types is the Homerically-inclined *thumos*.[14]

THE USE AND ABUSE OF PLEASURE

Callicles, then, possesses firm convictions about the nature of the naturally *kalon* and how 'real men' should in consequence behave. It is these convictions which lead him to deliver his passionate speech in favour of extreme hedonism. As we have seen, at 491c–d

---

[11] This nexus of association is further strengthened when we recall that at *Il.* 18.117 Achilles himself speaks admiringly of Heracles.

[12] Callicles reveals the generally martial tenor of his thought, as well as his agonistic approach to philosophic discussion in particular, in his greeting to Socrates in the dialogue's opening lines: 'To join in a war or a fight, Socrates, as the saying is, you have chosen your time well.' The translation is adapted from that of Lamb (1925).

[13] The translation is an adaptation of Sommerstein (1996). Most of the manuscripts include two variants of 1431 (a and b); the most likely explanation is that Aristophanes revised the line for the production of 404. The version given here is 1431b, which is also the version quoted by Plutarch to describe his volatile hero at *Alcibiades* 16.2. It is probably the original; see Sommerstein 285–6.

[14] See p. 44 above for the Platonic *thumos* being to some extent a living repository of Homeric values.

he asserts that the natural rulers, the tough and energetic men of affairs, should have more than the ruled. Socrates, with seeming irrelevance, asks how this is possible, given that *everyone* is – or should be – both a ruler and a ruled, in that it is the business of one's reason to rule one's desires.

Once more, Callicles is incensed. Those who restrain their desires, he claims, are simply idiots, *ēlithioi*, and like those who allow others to harm them are in their lack of freedom no happier than slaves. The naturally fine and just course of action[15] is to let one's desires grow as great as possible and satisfy each in turn when it reaches its peak. The man who can do this, who has both huge desires and the *andreia* and practical intelligence to satisfy them, is the man who 'lives rightly' (491e8), and true excellence (*aretē*) and happiness consist in the luxury, licentiousness and liberty of such a man's Rabelaisian existence. Most people, however, lack the ability to live like this, and so, as in the political sphere, they invent a code which calls temperance a virtue, and decry as shameful the superb rampageousness of the naturally superior few. The reality is that such conventional systems of 'morality' are simply covers to mask the impotence and unmanliness (*anandria*) of the servile crowd,[16] who willingly submit to the despotism of their invented laws and censures. The craven agreements of these puny creatures are against nature and not worth a jot.

Two things are to be noted here. Firstly, it is vital that Callicles is only talking about the man who can satisfy his desires; he is not concerned with the weaklings who may well have desires – though probably paltry ones in Callicles' view – but are unable to gratify them, and thus live lives of pathetic frustration.[17] Secondly, although Callicles appears to be thinking mainly of the physical

---

[15] τὸ κατὰ φύσιν καλὸν καὶ δίκαιον, 491e7.

[16] Identical charges against temperance are voiced at *Resp.* 560d–561a, in the account of the origin of the democratic character. When the son of an oligarchic man falls into bad company, his mind is invaded by unnecessary desires and false opinions, and he starts to call temperance unmanliness, shamelessness *andreia* and anarchy freedom. As we shall see, however, Callicles' alliance with epithumeitic democracy does not last long; though he is certainly interested in redeploying the notion of *andreia*, his redeployment will turn out to be rather different from that of the dissolute young democrat. What similarities do exist can be accounted for by the fact that Callicles has more in common with the unstable timocratic man of Book 8 than with the steadfast Auxiliaries of Book 4: we should, I think, expect some evidence of degeneracy from thumoeidic towards epithumeitic features. (For a roughly comparable subversion of the conventional meanings of *sōphrosunē* and *andreia*, see Thuc. 3.82.4, discussed on p. 70 above.)

[17] Compare *Ars Rhet.* 1360b15, where Aristotle reports that a common view of *eudaimonia* is that it is 'the most pleasurable life accompanied by security'.

appetites,[18] his claims in this passage apply equally well to *any* desires: the 'real man' is precisely the man who has the ability to satisfy any desire he happens to have, to do just whatsoever he happens to feel like doing at the time. The connection with his political ideals seems clear. His fundamental position is: if one *can* do whatever one wants, it is right and noble that one *should*. It is magnificent to be able to gratify one's desires, so the bigger the desires the better. It is this underlying position which, at first sight, makes his apparent espousal of hedonism so powerful: he is not simply claiming that the superior man can do whatever he likes, and that this would be enjoyable for him; he is claiming that such behaviour is a naturally moral imperative.

Socrates' opening move against this eloquent tirade is to remark drily that Callicles plainly would not agree with the people who say that those who need nothing are happy. When Callicles scornfully rejects any such analysis of *eudaimonia*,[19] Socrates approaches the question from the opposite direction, trying to convince Callicles that the sybaritic life he describes would be nothing but an exhausting and vain attempt to satisfy inherently insatiable desires. It would be as fruitless as constantly trying to fill leaky jars with a leaky sieve, or with foodstuffs that were intrinsically difficult to obtain. Callicles, however, is unimpressed: Socrates may view such a life as one of unceasing effort, but he views it as one consisting of the unceasing and delicious inflow of pleasure. He is equally nonchalant when Socrates reminds him that the outflow will be unceasing too: if his hedonist's desires are insatiable, this is only because when one is gratified, another appears; in the case of the superman, each *individual* desire is perfectly satiable.

Socrates now tries a different tack. If Callicles really believes that a happy and flourishing life consists simply in doing whatever happens to give you pleasure, then this will mean that all sorts of people must be considered to lead happy and fulfilling lives, such as, for instance, the incessant scratcher. Take the argument to its logical conclusion, indeed, and you will have to say that the catamite, the passive homosexual,[20] also leads a flourishing life.

---

[18] 'Luxury and licentiousness', τρυφὴ καὶ ἀκολασία (492c4–5), usually imply sybaritic indulgence.

[19] This interchange is discussed further below pp. 159–61.

[20] According to Winkler (1990: 46), the term *kinaidos* always implied 'promiscuity, payment, and passivity to another man's penetration'. More generally, the Greeks perceived male homosexual sex in terms of an active and a passive partner, whether a *kinaidos* was involved or not. See Dover (1978) index entry 'active and passive roles'.

Yet surely Callicles will admit that the life of catamites is awful,
shameful and wretched? Callicles is discomfited, protesting that it
is Socrates who should be ashamed to lead the discussion to such
topics; he adds, however, that in order to preserve a consistent
position, he will continue to maintain that the pleasant and the
good are the same thing (495a5–6). Nevertheless, there is no doubt
that he is reluctant to allow that the catamite's pleasures can constitute a good and flourishing life, and that his commitment to
unqualified hedonism has been severely shaken. Why? What precisely is Callicles objecting to?

One thing seems plain. It can hardly be homosexuality as such
that troubles Callicles: it is stated clearly in 481d that he is in love
with the beautiful young Demus, son of Pyrilampes, an attachment that would have been routinely accepted by Athenians of his
class and time. What disturbs Callicles, I would suggest, is not the
catamite's homosexuality but his *passivity*, which is not at all in
keeping with his ideal of the energetic and forceful man of affairs.
Being leaped upon, he thinks, is just not very lion-like. Furthermore, it is a passivity which is in Callicles' eyes disastrously associated with effeminacy: the catamite was widely regarded as taking
the 'female' sexual role.

Sensing victory, Socrates presses on. He begins by arguing that
the pleasant and the good cannot be the same, since while one
can, for example, simultaneously feel both the pain of thirst and
the pleasure of quenching it, one cannot simultaneously fare
both well and badly (495e–497a). Similarly, one can simultaneously cease to feel pleasure and pain, but one cannot simultaneously cease to fare well or ill (497a–497d). Both arguments are
contentious: it is true that one cannot concurrently fare both well
overall and badly overall, but one can certainly fare well in some
respects and badly in others. Socrates also illegitimately assumes
that all desire must be painful. Fortunately, the shortcomings of
this stretch of the dialogue need not detain us;[21] far more telling
for our present concerns is Socrates' second main argument
against the identification of the good and the pleasant from 497d–
499b.

Socrates opens by securing Callicles' agreement to the claim

---

[21] For helpful discussions, *vide* Irwin 1979: 201–2; Gosling and Taylor 1982: 71–4; Dodds
1959: 309–10.

that the good are good due to the presence of good things; he then
reminds him of his earlier definition of the 'better and superior'
men as those who are wise (*phronimoi*) and *andreioi* in the affairs of
the state (491d). In other words, Callicles wanted there to be a
clear distinction between the good and the bad man, as he defined
them. Now, when we consider who feels pleasure and pain, we
find many cases of foolish men enjoying themselves just as much
as the wise, and many cases of wise men feeling pain just as much
as the foolish. Similarily, in war both cowards and the *andreioi*
feel pleasure about equally when the enemy retreats; and when
the enemy advances both also feel pain, though in this case the
cowards feel pain to a greater degree. Pleasure and pain, then,
cannot be identical to the good and the bad: if they were, there
would in most cases be no distinction to be drawn between good
and bad men, given that the good are good due to the presence of
good things, and all men feel pleasure about equally.

And at this point, Callicles finally gives in, saying blithely that
of course he regards some pleasures as better and some as worse
(499b6–8). How could Socrates have ever supposed otherwise?

Here too, Socrates' reasoning is certainly open to question: in
particular, given the ambiguity inherent in the terms *agathos* and
agathon,[22] his claim that good people are good by the presence of
good things at the very least requires further clarification. Once
more, however, these possible flaws do not immediately concern
us; what matters is why Callicles should accept that it is this argument that is fatal to his position of unqualified hedonism.

The answer is surely the same as the reason why Callicles was
unhappy about including the pleasures of the catamite in his conception of the good life: he realizes that if he makes no distinction
at all between pleasures, then he will undermine his ideal of the
forceful and effective man of affairs. What he cannot bear is the
thought that the craven pleasures of the coward should make that
coward the equal of the courageous warrior. He thus finds his
position torn by a profound contradiction. He is attracted to hedonism precisely because he feels that it is fine and magnificent to be
able to do whatever one wants: it is this *power* which is the mark of

---

[22] Discussed on p. 124 above. Socrates' exploitation in the *Gorgias* of the ambiguity in '*eu*' is
discussed below p. 154.

the brave new man. But he now realizes that 'doing whatever one wants' may be interpreted by some in ways which he does not like at all, ways which do not at all accord with his image of the superman. The message is clear: the reason Socrates is able to defeat Callicles' espousal of unqualified hedonism with such comparative ease is because Callicles was never an unqualified hedonist in the first place.[23] Like Leontius, he has strong second-order attitudes towards first-order desires: he simply does not want to be the kind of man who wants passive pleasures, and is embarrassed at the very mention of them. In the terminology of the *Republic*, he was always thumoeidic.

It is also plain that Socrates is well aware of this. In turning Callicles' attention to the pleasures of the catamite and the coward, he astutely selects the exact types of 'unmanly' pleasure from which he knows Callicles will recoil; such choices show that he possesses a clear sense of the ideal which informs the whole of Callicles' thinking and responses. Further evidence of this comes in the discussion of the inveterate scratcher: at 494d4 Socrates remarks coolly that surely Callicles will not avoid a frank answer, since he is so *andreios*. And at 512e1 he slyly tries to persuade Callicles to concentrate on the goodness rather than the length of life, as mere length is a thing which any 'real man' ignores.[24] The same sly appeal to Callicles' deepest concerns is also displayed at 509a, where Socrates maintains that not even someone 'more spirited' (*neanikōteros*) than Callicles could disprove the claim that it is worse for the agent to do wrong than to suffer it: anyone who tried to do so would simply make himself ridiculous.

These moves of Socrates, however, raise an urgent problem. By acknowledging and exploiting Callicles' notion of manliness, he may expose his hedonism as superficial, but he also inevitably highlights Callicles' real position, the fundamental belief that might is indeed right and that it is fine and noble that natural force should hold sway. It would seem that Socrates is aware of this too: at any rate, at 508d4 he says that he realizes that for Callicles the failure to retaliate a wrong would be *aischiston*, and at 488e4–5 he asks Callicles to confirm that on his account the ordinances of the superior will be '*kala* according to nature'. Socrates

---

[23] It is, however, perfectly possible to depict Callicles as a *qualified* hedonist: his lion-man takes pleasure in suitably magnificent activities in a suitably magnificent way.
[24] ἀληθῶς ἄνδρα.

may lack the terminology to articulate Callicles' psychology, but he is well aware of the strength of the opposition he faces.

THE CALLICLEAN CHALLENGE

Before considering whether he also possesses the resources to tackle this genuine position of Callicles, it is worth emphasizing just how important and influential a doctrine it is. We saw earlier how in 468–74 Socrates and Polus originally disagree over the relation between virtue and personal benefit: whereas Socrates makes the radical claim that if doing wrong is more shameful for the agent then it is also worse for him,[25] Polus' initial response is to protest that virtue is far from being a guarantee of personal wellbeing. Furthermore, he adds, there is nobody in the world – not even Socrates – who really believes that it is: everyone knows that the fine and the good are not the same. Yet in this assumption at least Polus is immediately proved wrong. The chief threat that Callicles presents is that formally he agrees with Socrates' harmonization of the *agathon* and the *kalon*: he does indeed hold that *aretē* and performing *kala erga* will bring the agent personal benefit. The problem, of course, is that he achieves this harmony by cashing out both concepts in ways which Socrates cannot accept. Wellbeing is conceived solely in terms of the acquisition of power, reputation and material goods, plus the satisfaction of (suitably manly) desires, and the *kalon* and natural *aretē* are conceived solely in terms of the promotion of this conception of wellbeing. Callicles' brand of egoism is thus both psychological and normative.

It is, furthermore, an egoism which finds powerful support in a number of contemporary texts, such as the speeches of Thrasymachus in *Republic* 1, and the Mytilenaean debate and Melian dialogue in Thucydides.[26] Although we shall also find important divergencies between these positions and that of Callicles, it is still plain that Callicles is not a lone and disregarded voice in the ideological wilderness; in his admiration for raw power he is the eloquent spokesman for a view which the strictures of the Peloponnesian War had brought into the mainstream of political

---

[25] Socrates' reasons for making this claim are discussed below pp. 154–6.

[26] *Resp.* 336b–354b (pp. 164–74 below); Thuc. 3.38–48 and 5.85–111. The Thucydides passages make it plain that it was not uncommon for such theoretically anti-democratic sentiments to be expressed – or at least held – by professed democrats.

debate. It is a view which is still under discussion when Plato
comes to write the *Laws*:[27] at 690b, in his list of commonly made
claims regarding who should govern, the Athenian Stranger refers
to the belief that the stronger should rule and the weaker be ruled,
citing in support the same lines from Pindar on natural force that
Callicles quotes at 484b. These lines also appear at *Laws* 714e–
715a in a discussion of the thesis that justice is simply the interest
of the stronger – which is, of course, Thrasymachus' opening
statement in the *Republic*. Whatever the differences between Callicles and Thrasymachus, Plato clearly considers their political
views to be closely allied.

At the level of the individual, Callicles' credo receives even
more extensive support from ordinary Greek thinking. We have
already noted his admiration for Heracles and his links with
Achilles and Alcibiades,[28] and we are now in a position to understand these connections more fully. His conception of *andreia* as
the ruthless promotion of self-interest and desire-satisfaction is in
some respects only a more extreme version of the long-established
(and in practice largely aristocratic) tradition of praising the man[29]
who can look after himself and his own, helping his friends and
harming his enemies; it is a tradition we have already witnessed in
Meno's definition of male *aretē* at *Meno* 71e, and in the scornful attitude shown towards the unassertive philosophic gentleman at *Republic* 549c–550b.[30] Even Socrates subscribes to it at *Republic* 590b,
where he claims that,

we blame flattery and servility of mind (*aneleutheria*) when they subordinate the spirited element in us to the unruly beast, and when, for the
sake of money and greed, they accustom the lion to putting up with
insults and turn it into an ape.

Ample testimony to the view that suffering harm is shameful is
also provided by Aristotle: as we have seen,[31] at *Nicomachean Ethics*
1126a3–8 he reports the belief that it is foolish and servile[32] to put

[27] Plato died in 347 BC. The *Laws* was probably composed in the last decade of his life.
[28] See pp. 137 n. 1 and 140–1 above.
[29] The gender-specificity is vital.
[30] *Meno* 71: pp. 68–9 above; *Resp.* 549–50: pp. 28–9 above.
[31] P. 39.
[32] The same term for 'foolish', *ēlithios*, is also applied by Callicles to the temperate at *Grg.*
491e2. 'Servile', *andrapodōdēs*, indicates the absolute antithesis of the real man: the man in
chains.

up with insults to oneself or one's friends through deficiency in anger. The same view appears at *Ars Rhetorica* 1367a24–5, where it is said to be the mark of the *andreios* not to allow himself to be beaten; while in a key passage at *Posterior Analytics* 97b15–26 he says that of the two basic meanings of *megalopsuchia*, one is a refusal to submit to dishonourable treatment.[33]

Such views in their turn are an expression of an even more widespread Greek assumption, namely that a quality of character does not necessarily have to be directed towards the benefit of others in order to count as a virtue: all or most of the virtues can also be exercised on behalf of oneself. What matters here is that this notion of self-beneficial virtues is of course taken up and transformed by Socrates himself. Firstly, the psychic structure that for him constitutes *aretē* is always and necessarily advantageous to the agent, even when the agent also aims to assist others. Secondly, assisting others does not necessarily have to be involved at all; the inner psychic harmony may sometimes manifest itself outwardly in purely self-directed acts. Plainly, Socrates' substantive conceptions of both virtue and personal wellbeing are very different from those of Callicles,[34] yet the point remains that his and Callicles' general agreement that virtue benefits the agent is of great importance. It may, for instance, account for Socrates' initially puzzling move at 491d. As we have seen, Callicles has just defined his 'natural rulers' as those who are courageous, manly and resourceful in public affairs; we have also seen that Socrates' response is apparently to change the subject, asking whether everyone is not his own ruler, in that reason is the natural ruler of one's desires. Now, however, Socrates' tactics seem clear: if Callicles is interested in promoting those qualities which further self-interest, then he should realize that *sōphrosunē* is at least as important in this regard

---

[33] It is significant that two of the examples Aristotle cites of this kind of *megalopsuchia* are Achilles and Alcibiades; it would seem that Aristotle agrees with Plato that these men represent a basic character type.

[34] Socrates' position is discussed below, pp. 151–8. A similar view to Socrates' is put forward by Aristotle in his perceptive discussion of self-love in *E.N.* 9.4 and 9.8. While he is dismissive of self-love viewed in terms of material and sensual indulgence, he is thoroughly in favour of loving what he depicts as the truest and best part of the self, namely reason. This kind of self-love will manifest itself in a life devoted to the moral and intellectual virtues, and it follows that 'the good man ought to be a lover of self' (1169a11–12). Furthermore, since the best thing is moral nobility and the good man knows this, it also follows that the good man will want good things for himself (1169a28–9).

as *andreia* or *phronēsis*. Yet Socrates also needs to be careful: in recommending his own very different doctrines as a form of 'enlightened' egoism, he will have to think hard about how he opposes
the egoism of Callicles. He cannot simply aim to uproot Callicles'
position in its entirety.

Yet though both Callicles and Socrates are committed to the
belief that virtue benefits the agent, the notion of self-beneficial
virtue is far from easy to analyse. This is because it is extremely
difficult to know precisely how the 'self' is to be defined in this
context, and consequently how relations between self and others
are to be conceived. The *Meno*'s account of male *aretē*, for example, makes it clear that the 'self' involved in the aristocratic cult of
personal honour may be the extended self of family or polis: self-
assertion can be – at least superficially – community-minded. Callicles' position does not seem altogether coherent on this point,[35]
but he certainly subscribes to the notion of the extended self at
times: at 483b, for instance, the 'real man' is said to be able to
look after himself or 'anyone else for whom he cares', and at 486b
the adult philosopher is accused of being unable to save either
himself or anyone else in a court of law. It is also important to remember that Callicles defines the natural rulers as those who are
both manly and 'wise in the city's affairs' (491c6–7). Athough this
does not necessarily imply that the natural ruler sees the city as an
extension of himself – he could just see it as the source of his reputation and wealth – it still shows that Callicles does not regard his
egoistic ideal as incompatible with civic activities; he is, for
instance, quite happy to accept Socrates' ascription of *andreia* to
soldiers in 498a: defending oneself and one's own can sometimes
only be achieved by defending the polis. Whether he would also
be happy to term such civic activities 'duties' or 'service' is a moot
point; nevertheless, his willingness to incorporate them at all
shows that in this respect too Socrates will have to be extremely
careful in how he articulates his opposition to Callicles. Not only
can Socratic morality be viewed as egoistic; Calliclean 'natural
justice' can itself incorporate a number of at least superficially
others-directed acts. Again, the real disagreement between Socrates and Callicles does not lie in formal oppositions between

---

[35] Tensions in Callicles' thought are explored below pp. 162–3.

beneficial and noble, or self and community, but in how these concepts are to be substantively interpreted.[36]

Equally important is the subsequent influence of Callicles. His most significant inheritor is undoubtedly Nietzsche, as Dodds convincingly demonstrates in the appendix to his edition of the *Gorgias*.[37] This is not the place for a detailed study, but it is worth noting that Nietzsche cites Callicles' speeches with approval in his early lectures on Plato,[38] and praises the sophists in general for possessing 'the courage of all strong spirits to *know* their own immorality' (*Will to Power*, 429).[39] Certainly, the similarities are striking: Callicles' scathing dissection of conventional morality is forcefully voiced in, for example, *The Genealogy of Morals*, *Thus Spake Zarathustra* and *Beyond Good and Evil*,[40] while the construction of an alternative ethic based on *phusis* rather than *nomos* forms a central strand in all his writings from the *Birth of Tragedy* to the *Will to Power*.[41] Furthermore, potent expressions of this alternative ethic are provided by the image of the noble as a magnificent and untameable 'blond beast' and the image of the coming superman as a 'laughing lion'.[42] If we accept that the *Gorgias* played a formative role in Nietzsche's thinking on these issues, then Callicles' *nachleben* has been dynamite indeed.

SOCRATES' RESPONSE TO CALLICLES

Does Socrates possess the equipment in the *Gorgias* to dispose of such explosive material? His first use of the term *andreia* is deceptively Calliclean: rhetoric, he claims, is not an art, but a pursuit which requires a '*psuchēs ... stochastikēs kai andreias*', 'a manly spirit with a talent for guesswork'.[43] '*Andreias*' here seems to imply the resourceful determination which Callicles admires at 491b, when he says that the 'superior' are those who are not only wise in public

---

[36] For a radical attempt to break down distinctions between self and other within the state (at least in certain respects), see *Resp.* 462a–464a.

[37] Dodds 1959: 387–91. I am indebted to Dodds for the majority of the following references.

[38] Musarion edition: iv. 422.

[39] Trans. Kaufmann and Hollingdale.

[40] For instance: *Beyond Good and Evil* 260; *Genealogy of Morals* i.10; *Thus Spake Zarathustra* ii.7.

[41] E.g. *Genealogy of Morals* i.17; *Zarathustra* iii.12.29; iv.3.2; *The Will to Power* 933.

[42] See, for example, *The Genealogy of Morals* i.11, and *Thus Spake Zarathustra* iv.11; iv.20.

[43] 463a6–7.

affairs, but also *andreioi*, having the strength to carry out their
plans to completion and not falter through softness of soul.[44] Yet
warning bells are immediately sounded by Socrates' description of
this supposedly 'manly' practice of rhetoric as a branch of flattery,
an activity that Callicles would surely dismiss as unworthy of the
naturally noble and autocratic few. There seems little doubt that
Socrates' appeal to *andreia* here is ironic, and the inference is confirmed when we consider his subsequent deployment of the term.
At 480c, for instance, far from associating *andreia* with a robust
ability to manipulate conventional moral responses, Socrates
argues that it is in fact displayed by those who submit willingly to
a just punishment, knowing that it is only by being punished that
they will be able to purify their souls and achieve true happiness.
The same thought also appears at 522e, where Socrates maintains
that it is irrational and unmanly (*anandros*) to fear dying; the only
genuinely fearful thing is doing wrong.

   These illustrations are of critical importance in helping us interpret Socrates' implied definition of *andreia* at 507b. He has been
arguing that the temperate soul must be pious and just, and he
now adds that such a soul will necessarily be *andreia* as well: it is
the mark of the temperate man to shun and pursue what he ought,
and steadfastly to endure where he ought. By this stage of the discussion Callicles has in effect given up, and is sulkily 'agreeing'
with whatever Socrates says in order to bring the debate to a
speedy conclusion; what matters, therefore, is not whether he
actually protests at this definition of *andreia*, but whether he should
protest on the basis of his earlier speeches.

   If we view the matter in purely formal terms, it is perhaps just
possible to argue that he should not: the emphasis on resolution
and toughness does after all echo his account of the unfaltering
andreioi at 491b. It is admittedly true that the association with
sōphrosunē is hardly in keeping with his advocacy of sybaritic gratification, yet we have seen that indiscriminate hedonism is not his
real position. Though he would probably object to the unglamor-
ous wording in terms of duty, he might nevertheless be prepared
to accept Socrates' account, *providing* the notion of 'doing what
one ought' could be cashed out solely in terms of 'natural justice',

---

[44] The similarity is noted by Irwin 1979:132.

namely the promotion of one's own wealth and power by whatever means. The problem, of course, is that such a proviso is entirely out of the question. Socrates' appeal to the courage of the person who willingly accepts a just punishment shows that his notion of *andreia* is fundamentally different from that of Callicles, and that it differs because it is based on a very different conception of personal obligation. What Socrates intends by *andreia* is the steadfast commitment to an ideal which holds that both the *aretē* and the wellbeing of the individual consist partly in his fair treatment of others (where 'fair' implies not causing harm) and the performance of his civic duties. Though Callicles' ideal can accommodate the notion of civic activity to a certain extent, it emphatically does not embrace this interpretation of fairness.

Socrates and Callicles also appear to disagree over the question of whether virtue is gendered, though the evidence here is admittedly difficult to interpret. While Socrates' jibes at Callicles' 'manliness' plainly do not commit him to a gendered view of *andreia* himself, it is less clear whether irony is in play when he claims at 522e that it is 'unmanly' to fear death; it is also noticeable that at 507b5 Socrates talks explicitly of the courage of the temperate male, though this specificity may only be due to the contemporary conditions of warfare. At 500c, however, he seems to deny that the virtuous philosophic model he is advocating is specifically 'masculine': at any rate, he certainly opposes the philosophic life to the 'manly' pursuits of the Calliclean politician, and he does not suggest that the philosophic model be viewed in terms of an alternative ideal of masculinity.[45] 470e may also be relevant here. In this passage Socrates pointedly claims that the good and honourable man *or woman* is happy, and the unjust and wicked man or woman wretched; though he does not actually say that men and women are good and honourable in the same way, there is nothing to imply that they are not.

Socrates, then, appears to alternate in the *Gorgias* between trying to rework Callicles' notion of manliness, and trying to move towards an ideal of ungendered humanity. Yet if his use of 'manly' terminology is ambivalent, in other respects he is quite prepared to employ the rhetorical devices of his interlocutors. We

---

[45] This passage is discussed further on p. 159 below.

have seen how Callicles accuses the philosopher of being a boy amongst men and a slave amongst the free,[46] and the former charge is also implied by Polus when at 470a he mockingly says that a mere child could refute Socrates' claim that it is more beneficial for the agent to act justly than unjustly. In response, Socrates turns these accusations on their heads: it is the irrational and intemperate man who is 'enforced' (493e8) by his desires constantly to carry out their bidding, and it is the jury members appointed to try the philosopher who are the children (521e); the philosopher cannot win his trial because such adult children will always prefer the sweet flatteries of the cook to the true medicines of the doctor (464d). In their refusal to accept just punishment they are no different from a child fearful of painful surgery (479a).

It is, however, one thing to set up an alternative conception of *aretē*, and another to be able to support it. Socrates' insistence that harming others will necessarily harm the agent is far from obvious, as the initial reactions of Polus and Callicles show. Equally counter-intuitive is his claim that 'the good man does well (*eu prattein*) and finely whatever he does' (507c): in what way, for instance, does the hoplite fare well who holds his position in battle and is killed in the process? His self-sacrifice may benefit his community, but in what way does it benefit him? Socrates supports the claim in 507c by maintaining that he who 'does well' (*eu prattonta*) is blessed and happy, but this seems an illegitimate play on the ambivalence of *eu prattein*, which can mean both 'do well for oneself', 'fare well' and also 'act well', 'act in a praiseworthy manner'.[47] There is, however, a more charitable interpretation, as we shall shortly see: it may be that 507c is not supposed to constitute a proof in itself, but is rather to be read as the conclusion of a much more substantive argument which begins at 503d.[48]

Before turning to this larger argument, however, we first need to consider another key passage (474d–e), where Socrates attempts to counter Polus' belief that though doing wrong is fouler (*aischion*) for the agent than suffering it, suffering wrong is worse (*kakion*). In

---

[46] P. 139.

[47] For the ambiguities inherent in both *agathon* and *eu*, see pp. 123–5 above. See also Dodds 1959: 335–6. For a different interpretation see Irwin 1979: 223, who denies the existence of equivocation here.

[48] So Dodds ibid.; he makes the salient point that the final words of the *Republic*, '*eu prattō-men*', are surely deliberately intended by Plato to convey both meanings.

response, Socrates defines the concept of the *kalon* in terms of either benefit or pleasure. If x is finer (*kallion*) than y, then this must be because x exceeds in its effect of either pleasure or benefit or both; similarily, if x is fouler than y, then it must exceed in its effect of either pain or harm (*kakon*). So if doing wrong is fouler than suffering it, then it must be either more painful or more harmful or both. Since it is clearly not more painful, it must therefore be more harmful. Conversely, we may infer that if self-sacrifice for one's polis is a *kalon* act, then it must produce either pleasure or benefit; since it can scarcely be said to be pleasurable (at least in conventional terms), then it must be beneficial.[49]

It is a bold argument, but it is plainly no reply to Polus. The first problem is that the definition of the *kalon* seems too narrow – a suspicion that we shall find supported by the *Hippias Major*, where Socrates concludes that neither pleasure nor benefit nor a combination of the two is adequate to cover all the connotations of the term.[50] Yet even if one were prepared to accept the definition offered here, Socrates' argument would still be unconvincing because it fails to address the critical question of *to whom* the pleasure or benefit of the *kalon* x is supposed to accrue. Polus has challenged Socrates to demonstrate that immoral behaviour, in the sense of treating others badly, will harm *the agent*; he has by implication also challenged Socrates to prove that treating other people fairly will be to the agent's benefit. To define what is morally *kalon* and *aischron* in terms of effecting benefit and harm in general is no answer to these challenges at all: Socrates still has to show that my virtue will specifically benefit *me*.

Nor is this all. As we have seen, the entry of Callicles into the debate makes it clear that it will not be enough for Socrates to show that *kalon* behaviour formally benefits the agent; he must explicitly show that the agent is benefited by a particular conception of the *kalon*, namely one which includes fair treatment of others. Logical arguments alone will not suffice for this; Socrates must

---

[49] If this is right, then the *Gorgias* takes a different view from the *Protagoras* on the pleasures or otherwise of fighting for one's country: see pp. 130–1 above.

[50] The contrast is noticed by Dodds 1959: 249–50. There may, however, even be an indication in the *Gorgias* itself that Socrates is prepared to question his analysis of the *kalon*: at any rate, when Polus complains that his views concerning the preferability of being wronged are extraordinary, *atopa*, (480e1), Socrates simply replies that either their former findings (i.e. concerning the *kalon*) must be overturned, or this conclusion necessarily follows.

provide a substantive account of *aretē* which both connects it to fair treatment of others and also shows it to be at least the main constituent part of the agent's wellbeing. Is such an account forthcoming?

We are now in a position to turn to the critical passage which begins at 503. In the opening section (503d–505b) Socrates maintains that the key to this question lies in the notion of psychic order. Just as it is the presence of structure (*taxis*) and order (*kosmos*) which distinguishes a good (*chrēstos*) house, ship or body from a bad one, so it is structure and order which differentiate the good *psuchē* from the bad. It is these 'structures and orderings of the *psuchē*' which are termed 'lawful' (*nomima*) and 'law' (*nomos*), and which constitute justice and temperance (504d1–3). Now, to say that a body possesses structure and order is to say that it possesses health and strength (504b9), and it is clear that such qualities are beneficial to the agent. Similarly, we may infer that a well-structured and orderly *psuchē*, that is to say a just and temperate one, will also necessarily be to the agent's advantage.

Such moves clearly anticipate the *Republic*'s doctrine that *aretē* is a 'kind of mental health';[51] they also comprise a brave attempt to combat Callicles' alleged antithesis between *phusis* and conventional *nomos*. Socrates' claim that the order of the *psuchē* is what is called lawfulness and law suggests that conventional *nomos* is simply the external manifestation of a natural inner order; indeed, at 507e–508a we learn that this natural order of the *psuchē* is itself a part of a much greater natural order, the order which constitutes the entire *kosmos*.

And wise men say ... that heaven and earth and gods and men are bound together by communion and friendship and orderliness and temperance and justice; and this is the reason why they call the whole the world-order (*kosmos*), and not disorder or intemperance.

There is more. The term *kosmos* can mean ornament or decoration as well as order, and even when it primarily denotes the latter, there is the implication that the order is fine and beautiful. Its use here provides further evidence of the very close relation in Platonic thought between what we would usually distinguish as ethics and aesthetics: the virtuous and orderly soul is beautiful, and its

---

[51] *Resp.* 444d13–e1.

possessor will live in a state of harmony with himself.[52] The connection between 'ethical' and 'aesthetic' evaluations is the principle of 'geometrical equality' which forms the basis of the universe (508a): it is proportion which accounts for both the goodness and the beauty of all things, and it is proportion which, Socrates claims, Callicles has failed to consider.

Is this fair? How successful is Socrates' theory of psychic order as a response to Callicles? It is certainly true that strategically it is on the right lines: if Socrates can show that Callicles has misconstrued the notion of *phusis*, and hence the relation between *phusis* and conventional *nomos*, then he can dismantle the alleged antithesis on which Callicles' whole position depends. Yet it seems clear that his execution of this strategy fails. Firstly, the *Gorgias* simply does not offer the detailed account of the structure of the *psuchē* which any appeal to psychic order requires. It is plain that the *psuchē* must contain at least two 'parts', if the notion of structure is to be applied to it at all, and the discussion of hedonism and self-control suggests that these parts are reason and the desires; 493a–b also talks of 'that part of the *psuchē* where the desires are'. Beyond this, however, we are told very little. Socrates depicts the desires as limitless, but we are not informed whether they are also supposed to possess some reasoning abilities, nor whether reason possesses desires of its own; in consequence, we have no idea how reason and the desires are supposed to interrelate. Despite Callicles' allegiances, there is no suggestion that there might be a middle part of the *psuchē* to facilitate such interrelation. There are also inconsistencies: at 493c1, '*psuchē*' seems to refer to reason alone, while in 505a–b the desires are divided between those that belong to the soul, and those that belong to the body. Indeed, in a number of passages this relatively crude mind/body dualism is undeniably far more central than the embryonic theory of a divided soul.[53]

Equally important is the question of just why Socrates should suppose that psychic order and harmony should manifest themselves as temperance and (more-or-less) conventional justice and result in the good treatment of others. The question can, I think,

---

[52] 503e8. The notion of living in a state of internal harmony or disharmony is first raised in the *Gorgias* in 482b–c, where Socrates charges Callicles with being in a state of internal discord.

[53] See, for example, 464a; 501c; 512a; 513d–e; 517d.

be divided into two parts, though both stem from Socrates' belief that the underlying structural cause of both temperance and justice is not simply order, but the order that results from the rule of reason. The first issue, therefore, is why Socrates should suppose that psychic harmony can only result when reason is in control: why could not harmony exist in a soul in which reason obediently carried out the whims of the desires? The answer presumably lies in Socrates' portrayal of the desires as grasping and insatiable, entirely lacking in any sense of geometrical proportion. The order that constitutes goodness and beauty can only arise when reason is in control, and if reason is in control then the soul will, according to Socrates' definition, inevitably be temperate and just.

Such an account, however, still does not address the fundamental question of why temperance and justice, so conceived, should lead to good treatment of others. Why could not rational order produce Callicles' ruthless politician, the man with the courage and determination to carry out his plans to completion, and not be deflected by softness of soul? Indeed, why could not rational order produce a certain kind of hedonist, a hedonist dedicated to achieving the greatest amount of pleasure in his life overall, and prepared to forgo some short-term satisfactions if he calculates that they are incompatible with long-term gain? To rebut such suggestions, Socrates must respond that the ruthless politician and the calculating hedonist are not in fact ruled by reason at all, even though they may possess and utilize considerable rational powers. In order to make such a response convincing, however, he will need to say much more than he does in the *Gorgias* about the nature of reason, and what it really means for reason to rule in the soul.

THE PHILOSOPHER AS ROLE MODEL

Socrates' response to Callicles, then, lacks the detailed psychological support necessary to make it fully effective. As a result, and despite the internal inconsistencies of Callicles' position, the ambivalent glamour of the superman remains. Nor should we overlook the fact that, for all his sulkiness and bad temper under Socratic questioning, Callicles is himself allowed to possess some attractive qualities. He has a considerable share of the vigour and honesty of the ideal he admires, and, while he cannot sustain a rational argument, he is certainly no fool. He is also generous and hospitable: it is with him that Gorgias is staying and right at the beginning of the dialogue he invites Socrates to come to his house to hear the rhetorician any time he wants; while ambition doubtless plays a significant part in such hospitality, there is no reason to suppose that this is his only motive. Both in what he says and who he is, Callicles offers genuine opposition.

This opposition is intensified by the undeniable fact that the figure of the philosopher in the *Gorgias* may seem decidedly unappealing as a role model for the young. Part of the problem, as we have seen, is Callicles' portrayal of the adult philosopher as an unmanly wimp, a portrayal that calls to mind the contempt shown towards the philosophic man in *Republic* 549–50.[54] A similar picture of the philosopher's public image also appears in the *Theaetetus* digression, where Socrates himself cheerfully admits that when the philosopher has to take part in legal or business proceedings, his unworldliness makes him seem ridiculous to the crowds.[55] Such apparent indifference to public opinion, however, may be misplaced: the philosopher may well need to attract young male students, and such potential students are likely to be very conscious of the general social standing of their prospective teacher. In this context, Socrates' provocative contrast at 500c between the 'manly' life of the Calliclean politician and the life of the philosopher now appears an over-hasty move: before introducing the notion of a gender-neutral ethics, he must first convince his young male audience that by taking up philosophy they will not be abrogating their manhood.

This, however, may not be possible, for an even more disturbing issue raised by the *Gorgias* is whether the practice of philosophy requires giving up one's humanity altogether; the question is particularly troubling because it arises not just from how others view the philosopher, but from how the philosopher sometimes portrays himself. The key passage occurs at 492e, after Callicles' vigorous endorsement of the life given over to the constant arousal and satisfaction of desire. In that case, says Socrates, it cannot be true to say, as some people do, that those who want nothing are happy. Certainly not, replies Callicles, 'for such a view would mean that stones and corpses are the happiest of all'.

---

[54] *Vide* pp. 139 and 28 above.   [55] See especially 174c and 175b.

Socrates does not comment directly on these charges, concentrating instead on trying to portray the life of desire in the most unattractive terms possible – a portrayal in which the sybarite appears, not as a corpse, but as a tortured soul in Hades. Yet the images of the stone and the corpse need addressing, for they are images which reflect Socrates' depiction of the philosopher elsewhere. The most obvious example is the *Phaedo*, in which he claims that the true objects of the philosopher's search, the Forms, are only fully apprehensible after death, here perceived simply as the separation of the rational and immortal part of the soul from the perishable body. In life, the distractions and deceptions of the body get in the philosopher's way (65b–66d). Yet this does not mean that the regrettably embodied cannot begin the search for knowledge: we can try to anticipate the philosophically favourable conditions of death by attempting to rid ourselves of as many bodily desires as possible. Philosophy is, in short, 'the practice of dying'.[56]

It is a discomforting passage, and scarcely likely to appeal to energetic young men, discovering the delights of the world for the first time. At *Memorabilia* 1.2.16, Xenophon claims that Alcibiades and Critias only associated with the ascetic Socrates in order to promote their own political ambitions; for, 'Had God granted them a choice between living the life they saw Socrates leading in its entirety, or dying, they would have chosen to die.' It is true that Xenophon's Socrates does not actually describe the philosophic life as a preparation for death, but he is still portrayed as austere enough to make the language of the *Phaedo* appropriate. Alcibiades and Critias might well decide that rather than waste a life practising for death, one might just as well get it over with. As the sophist Antiphon puts it in *Mem.* 1.6.3, Socrates' way of life is so severe that if he wants his students to imitate him, then he must consider himself a teacher of unhappiness.

It would seem, therefore, that if Socrates really wants such an ascetic ideal to be the model for the philosopher, then Callicles may be doubly correct in saying that philosophers are demonstrably ignorant of 'human (*anthrōpeiōn*) pleasures and desires' (484d5–6). Not only would philosophers in general lack experience of such pleasures, but Socrates would have shown himself to be profoundly ignorant of human psychology in appealing to such

[56] 66a; 67e.

an ideal in the first place. The operative word here is '*anthrōpeiōn*': the type of asceticism that Socrates is recommending just does not appear to be human. In the *Nicomachean Ethics*, Aristotle will say that while it is certainly possible to indulge in pleasures too much, it is also possible to enjoy them too little, and 'such lack of response does not seem to be that of a human being (*anthrōpikē*)'.[57]

Perhaps the main problem arises from the fact that neither Plato's nor Xenophon's Socrates appears likely to be bothered by the charge of presenting an inhuman model, at any rate as normally conceived. At *Memorabilia* 1.6.10, for instance, Socrates robustly counters Antiphon's criticisms by saying that to have no wants is something divine, while at *Philebus* 33b he maintains that a life devoid of either pleasure or pain is the most divine life of all. It is admittedly unclear precisely how this aspiration is to be understood: does Socrates perceive the task of the philosopher to be the transcendence of humanity – or at any rate what humanity is normally taken to be – or does he perceive the fostering of our 'divine' potential as the ultimate fulfilment of our humanity? In either case, however, there remains the urgent question of how prospective students of philosophy are to be enticed rather than repelled; Socrates the educator ought to be concerned with the general image of the philosopher, whether he likes it or not.[58] He also needs to address the question of whether a divine model of self-sufficiency is in fact desirable for humans at all: what of the alternative Greek tradition which holds that mortals should think mortal thoughts? Nor is it clear in the *Gorgias* or *Phaedo* how such a divine ideal could be even partially attained. How can reason on its own conquer the myriad and insatiable desires of the body, which in the *Phaedo* are said to include all the non-rational desires, including the love of success and honour (68c2)? What kind of apparatus is needed to make transcendence possible?

Underlying all these questions, of course, is the issue of exactly what it is to be a human being; until this fundamental problem is fully addressed, we cannot possibly know what ideals a human should or could reasonably hope to emulate. Callicles may think self-sufficency a bizarre and inhuman model, but it is worth re-

[57] 1119a6–7; see also 1150a22–3.
[58] Plato the educator, on the other hand, is certainly concerned by such issues, as his portrayal of the Calliclean challenge shows.

membering that his own model is not presented in human terms
either: 'be a real man – be a *lion*' is surely almost as strange an
injunction as 'practise for death'.[59] Yet though the *Gorgias* raises
these basic questions and illustrates with great vividness the difficulties they present, there is no escaping the fact that it cannot
properly answer them. For the debate between Callicles and Socrates to be resolved, Plato needs a much more sophisticated psychology and corresponding theory of human flourishing than the
Gorgias can provide.

THE NEED FOR THE *THUMOS*

My contention, then, is that Plato cannot properly respond to
Callicles without the *Republic*'s concept of the tripartite *psuchē* in
general and the *thumos* in particular. Firstly, only a detailed account of the divisions within the soul can give substance to Socrates' claims at 506d–507a that flourishing and virtue are to be
identified with psychic order, and that this psychic order is secured
solely through the rule of reason. We have seen how at 484d Callicles asserts that the philosopher is entirely ignorant of human
nature; if Plato wishes to counter this assertion, he needs to give
chapter and verse.

More particularly, Plato cannot deal with Callicles until he is in
a position to articulate the true nature of the threat that he poses.
If Callicles could be depicted as thumoeidic rather than hedonistic, then his position could easily be revealed as profoundly inconsistent; he provides a telling, if unwitting, example of the inner
tensions that can arise when *thumos* is not guided by reason. On
the one hand, he appeals to a stark antithesis between *nomos* and
phusis to support his claim that the 'real man' will act ruthlessly to
promote his own interests, both in public and in private; yet he
also holds that such interests are to include social success and a
good reputation[60] – both of which are plainly dependent on satisfying the local *nomoi*. Once thumoeidic values are adopted, in
other words, the alleged antithesis between *nomos* and *phusis* breaks
down: it will be part of our nature to adapt to at least some of the
values and requirements of our culture. Indeed, this dependence

---

[59] For further discussion of the image of the lion, see pp. 105–6 above.
[60] E.g 484d; 522c.

of reputation on *nomos* will be especially powerful in the democratic context within which Callicles is obliged to operate and which in public at least he professes to support.[61] Such public endorsement, of course, is hardly borne out by his scathing analysis of 'democratic' morality in the comparatively private setting of the *Gorgias*, and this disparity may account for the hint at 519a that the *dēmos* will later seize on him, as they will also seize on Alcibiades.[62] Neither can afford to be so contemptuous of the source of the *timē* he seeks.

The concept of the *thumos* would also, I believe, allow Plato to make the philosophic ideal itself seem more attractive. As this is an issue which we shall be exploring in some detail in chapter 8, we need only briefly mention two of the main points here. Firstly, the inclusion of properly controlled thumoeidic (and epithumeitic) desires in the philosopher's personality makes that personality seem altogether more human: the philosopher must plan not only for the life of the state but for his or her individual life as well, and this will require some consideration of the needs of all parts of the *psuchē*. More particularly, we have seen that if the figure of the philosopher is to be made more appealing to energetic young men, the whole notion of *andreia* needs to be rethought in a way that allows the philosopher to display it. Yet we have also seen that this operation will require considerable care: the reworked conception of *andreia* must remain mettlesome and gutsy, or the energetic young men will still look elsewhere. Now, while it is certainly true that a reconsideration of *andreia* is well underway by the *Gorgias*, and continues in the *Gorgias* itself, it is also true that an explicit connection between *andreia* and *thumos* would help ensure that this reconsideration remained palatable to Plato's students and readers. Austerely intellectualist definitions, for instance, à la Nicias in the *Laches* and Socrates in the *Protagoras*, are unlikely to do the job.

Finally, the introduction of the *thumos* can make the philosophic

---

[61] At 481d–e Socrates remarks that Callicles is in love with the Athenian *dēmos*, and that he always says what he believes it desires.

[62] It seems to me that the detail Plato bestows on Callicles' portrait strongly suggests that he is a historical figure. The absence of any reference to him outside the *Gorgias* does not contradict this: it would serve Plato's purposes to select a character whose youthful promise was known to have come to nothing as a result of moral and intellectual indiscipline. See Dodds 1959: 12–13.

ideal more attainable. In the *Republic*, reason with its desire for truth no longer has to fight against all the other desires at once: in the properly educated person it will receive the support of the *thumos*. It is the *thumos* which will chiefly constitute the apparatus for transcendence that reason in the *Gorgias* and *Phaedo* so urgently requires.[63]

The tripartite psychology of the *Republic*, therefore, can I believe be read partly as a response to the unanswered questions posed by Callicles' brand of psychological and normative egoism and his corresponding conception of *andreia*. Yet it is also, of course, more directly a response to another proponent of ruthless egoism, a proponent whose position, as we have seen, is sufficiently similar to that of Callicles for Plato to connect them by means of the same Pindar quote.[64] It is time to look more closely at the challenge of Thrasymachus.

THRASYMACHUS AND THE LAW

Thrasymachus' entry into the *Republic* is dramatic. It occurs at a point when the discussion has reached an *impasse*, since both Cephalus' and Polemarchus' attempts to define justice have been shown by Socrates to fail. Justice cannot be telling the truth and returning what one has borrowed, as Cephalus was taken to claim, because this would require one to return a weapon to a friend who has subsequently gone mad. Yet neither can it be Polemarchus' 'giving others their due', if this is to be cashed out in conventional terms as 'helping one's friends and harming one's enemies' (331e–332d): not only does such a definition leave the sphere of justice unspecified, but, crucially, it is not the function of a good man to harm anyone; the function of goodness is always to benefit (335d). Since traditional conceptions of justice have proved unhelpful, therefore, a fresh approach is required. Is there anyone, asks Socrates innocently, who has a new suggestion to offer?

Thrasymachus, who we soon learn has been impatient to speak for some time, takes up the challenge with gusto. In language strongly reminiscent of Callicles, he angrily dismisses Socrates'

---

[63] For difficulties in employing this apparatus in practice, see ch. 9.
[64] P. 148.

debating techniques as simple-minded nonsense, *phluaria*,[65] and demands that Socrates give a positive account of justice, instead of always demolishing the accounts of others. However, since it is patently obvious that he is longing to impress the company with a definition of his own (338a), Socrates suggests that he might prefer to speak first and enlighten them all. Very well, says Thrasymachus, I say that justice is simply the interest of the stronger: in every city it is the stronger party which, by definition, wields political power, and this ruling person or group makes the laws in his or its own interest and calls obedience to these laws 'justice'. Whether the government is tyrannical, aristocratic or democratic, the institution of justice is simply a cynical cover for *force majeure*.

At first sight it appears that what Thrasymachus has in mind is a legalistic conception of justice: 'justice' is simply whatever the laws prescribe. Socrates points out, however, that rulers may be mistaken about where their true interest lies, and misframe the laws accordingly; in such cases, obedience to the laws will plainly not be to their advantage. Faced with a choice between equating justice with the actual or imagined interests of the ruling party, Thrasymachus opts for the former: obedience to the laws will only constitute justice when those laws really are to the rulers' advantage. Indeed, if one is to be precise in one's use of language, one may say that a ruler is only strictly acting as a ruler when he *does* correctly frame the laws to his own advantage; the man may make a mistake, but the ruler never can.

Such a precise definition of 'ruler', however, gives Socrates an opening. Surely the ruler *qua* ruler is a skilled practitioner, and every skill is directed at the good of its physical subject matter? Medicine does not look to the interest of medicine, but to the interest of the body; equestrian training seeks the interest of the horse. The ruler, therefore, will seek the good of his subjects, and the laws that he frames and calls 'justice' will be to their advantage rather than his own.

---

[65] For Callicles' charge that philosophers talk *phluaria*, see p. 139 n. 6 above. For the accusation of simple-mindedness (*euēthizomai*), compare Callicles' portrayal of the philosopher as a child at 484d and 485a–c; see pp. 139 and 153–4 above. Thrasymachus also calls Socrates 'very simple-minded' (*euēthestatos*) at 343d2. For Socrates, however, the term can possess strongly positive connotations: at *Resp.* 400d11–e3, for instance, good literature, good music, beauty of form and good rhythm are all said to depend on *euēthia*, here perhaps best translated as 'goodness of character' (see Lee 1974:162).

Thrasymachus is unimpressed. He does not address Socrates' general claims about the nature of the *technai*, but brusquely repeats that rulers think only of how to exploit their subjects, in the same way that a shepherd thinks only of the profit that his flock will bring; any care that either shepherd or ruler might provide is intended solely as a means to increase this profit. Indeed, as the shepherding analogy suggests, such exploitative behaviour is equally observable in the private as well as the public sphere. What we term injustice is simply the pursuit of self-interest and pays the individual far better than justice (343d–344c); in consequence, injustice can even be regarded as a virtue (*aretē*), the virtue of common sense (348c–d).[66] The unjust are prudent and admirable; the just are naïve fools. Indeed, we partially admit this: though we criticize and punish petty wrong-doers, when injustice is practised on a sufficiently grand scale by, for example, a tyrant, we merely call the tyrant happy and fortunate. Given sufficient scope, there is no doubt that injustice possesses greater strength and freedom and mastery than justice; we would all be tyrants if we could.

This second main speech of Thrasymachus initially appears to be at odds with his opening statement. If justice is simply the interest of the stronger party, then surely the tyrant who supremely promotes his self-interest is supremely just? Yet Thrasymachus clearly states at 344a that the tyrant is supremely *un*just. Some commentators have argued that, like Callicles, Thrasymachus is here operating with two notions of justice and injustice, conventional and natural;[67] as Kerferd demonstrates, however, such an exegesis involves Thrasymachus in utterly baffling switches back and forth between the two pairs, often in a single sentence.[68] While he may well be confused, it seems implausible that he is confused to such a bewildering degree. Nor can the supporters of

[66] This seems to me clearly stated at 348c2–10. It is true that Thrasymachus immediately retracts the statement that justice is a vice (*kakia*), but I do not see that he ever retracts the claim that injustice is an *aretē*, providing that it is given full scope. As will shortly become clear, this whole-hearted admiration for injustice will prove a problem for Thrasymachus, since the practice of injustice will sometimes conflict with his more deeply held admiration for tough-minded common sense. For a rather different interpretation see Chappell (1993), who argues that Thrasymachus does not in fact quite call injustice an excellence, and thus avoids incoherence.

[67] See Oppenheimer in Pauly-Wissowa *Encyclopädie* VI A (1936) s.v. 'Thrasymachos'.

[68] Kerferd 1947.

such a reading explain why there is no reference to 'natural justice' in the text. Kerferd himself offers a simpler reading, according to which a conventional account of justice is in use throughout: injustice is ruthlessly promoting your own desires at the expense of others and taking more than your fair share; justice is giving others their due. In theory, each can be practised by both rulers and ruled; in practice, however, opportunities for injustice will generally only be available to the rulers, whereas the ruled will usually have to accept the imposition of justice. The initial statement that justice is the interest of the stronger is therefore not to be taken as a complete definition, but as a description of how justice operates in the world of *realpolitik*.[69]

It is a bold interpretation, and I believe that it resolves many of the apparent inconsistencies between Thrasymachus' two statements. It does not, however, eradicate all of them. Firstly, there remains considerable disagreement between the two positions regarding the degree to which it is beneficial for the subject to practise injustice. In his second speech, Thrasymachus says blithely that the just man 'always' (*pantachou*) comes off worse than the unjust (343d), in both private and public affairs; yet his first statement, that 'justice is the interest of the stronger', relies on the assumption that the private citizen will rarely be in a position to practise injustice and get away with it. This problem is part of a larger one, namely Thrasymachus' profound ambivalence towards the usefulness of justice as an institution. In his opening statement, the institution of justice is supposed to benefit the rulers alone, providing they are 'true' rulers who really know where their interests lie; yet in his second speech he implies that *all* individuals benefit from the existence of justice, so long as they do not practise it themselves. It is here, I would suggest, that we come up against a genuinely irresolvable tension in Thrasymachus' position. It simply does not make sense to say that the institution of justice will benefit every individual providing he or she does not take part in it: the proviso, if realized, will clearly have the effect of destroying the institution altogether.[70]

---

[69] This operation is chillingly portrayed by Thucydides in the Mytilenaean debate and the Melian dialogue (3.38–48 and 5.85–111).

[70] Glaucon's social contract theory, although he claims it is a revival of Thrasymachus' argument (358b7–c1), arguably avoids this incoherence, in that it allows participation in the institution of justice to be a second-best compromise. See below p. 169.

Thrasymachus himself seems unaware of these tensions, even though at 344b he admits that the practice of injustice may sometimes lead to capture, punishment and disgrace. In such cases, we may suppose, injustice is plainly an unsuccessful means of satisfying one's desires, and the obvious inference is that in some circumstances justice is the more prudent course to take. However, though this admission emphasizes Thrasymachus' inconsistency towards the merits of injustice, he does, I believe, in all other respects maintain a coherent and consistent position on the nature of *aretē*.[71] His implicit and fundamental ideal is simply the man[72] who successfully promotes his own interests, and who possesses above all the excellence of *euboulia*, 'common sense'. The extent to which unjust methods can be efficiently employed to this end will largely, though not entirely, depend on one's political status: rulers can normally practise injustice with impunity, but powerless subjects must consider whether or not they are likely to be detected.

How similar is this position to that of Callicles? In one central respect, of course, they are totally at odds. For Thrasymachus, 'the stronger' refers solely to whichever political party is in power, providing its members know where their true interests lie; whereas for Callicles, 'the stronger' refers to the naturally more courageous, manly and resourceful few, who may or may not hold political sway. Thus for Thrasymachus the stronger may comprise the democratic majority, while Callicles is adamant that supporters of democracy will always consist of the naturally craven and weak. It is this fundamental difference which accounts for the fact that Callicles alone draws a contrast between conventional and natural justice; in Thrasymachus' view, justice can only be a matter of convention. It also explains why Callicles portrays conventional justice as a device of the weak to suppress the (naturally) strong, while Thrasymachus portrays it as a device of the (*de facto*) strong to exploit the weak.

Yet in other respects, Plato is quite right to link their two positions through Pindar's lines on the supremacy of force.[73] The real

---

[71] On this latter point I am mostly in agreement with, and indebted to, the stimulating discussion in Chappell 1993.

[72] Although Thrasymachus does not explicitly eulogize the 'real man' as Callicles does, Glaucon seems right to assume that his ideal is nevertheless intended as specifically masculine. See below p. 169.

[73] *Gorgias* 484b; *Laws* 714e–715a and 690b. See p. 148.

connection lies in their shared admiration for the ruthless and efficient pursuit of one's own interest, and in their assumption that
'interest' is to be conceived in terms of material wealth, negative
freedom[74] and power over others – from the Platonic perspective,
in terms of the two irrational parts of the soul. Furthermore, the
fact that Thrasymachus identifies this ruthless self-promotion with
aretē and common sense shows that though he may not possess
a conception of natural *justice*, he certainly possesses a notion of
natural *virtue*; he may not explicitly frame his position in the language of the *nomos/phusis* debate, but he plainly relies on there
being a sharp antithesis between the two.

This antithesis is brought out into the open by Glaucon, in his
alleged restatement of Thrasymachus' position.[75] Glaucon claims
that conventional justice is merely a compromise. In nature, the
ideal is wronging others without being wronged in return, while
the worst thing is to be wronged without means of redress. However, as the disadvantages of suffering wrong exceed the advantages of inflicting it, people make a compact to avoid both and
agree to institute a system of justice. Yet such a compromise only
serves a purpose if we think that wronging others will in fact bring
us retribution; if the normally 'just' man believes that he can
do wrong and escape detection, then he too will act according
to greed, *pleonexia*, the motive which all men naturally follow if
they are not forcibly restrained by *nomos* and made to respect each
other's claims (359c).

Glaucon's restatement of Thrasymachus' argument also suggests that Thrasymachus and Callicles share similar views on the
nature of manliness and courage. Again, Thrasymachus does not
explicitly articulate his position in such terms, but at 359b Glaucon asserts that no 'real man' (*alēthōs anēr*) would ever enter into
the social compact if he could get away with acting unjustly, while
at 361b he says that the perfectly unjust man can rely on his *andreia*
and natural force (*hrōmē*) to extricate himself from trouble. It
seems clear that *andreia* is here depicted as overtly gendered; it is
also clear that to display it is to favour *phusis* over *nomos*. It is not
simply, as Protagoras claimed, that a man *can* display *andreia* while
being unjust; rather, it is that *andreia* and (conventional) injustice

---

[74] I am here employing the terminology of Berlin 1969, who defines 'negative liberty' as
that area within which no one else may interfere with me.
[75] See p. 167 n. 70 above.

must go hand in hand. We are in the world described by Thucydides in his account of the Corcyran civil war.[76]

If Thrasymachus, then, has more in common with Callicles than at first appears, does this mean that he is also depicted by Plato as a representative of thumoeidic values? I believe that the answer is yes. His first appearance in the dialogue is telling: he does not enter the discussion quietly, but is said to gather himself together and spring on Socrates and the others 'like a wild beast', as if he wants to tear them to pieces. While it is just possible that the image is supposed to anticipate the epithumeitic many-headed monster (588c), the details are far more suggestive of the thumoeidic lion (588d) – a suggestion which is confirmed by 341c2, where Socrates says that he would not dream of bearding a lion such as Thrasymachus. The comparison is amply borne out by other details in the portrayal of Thrasymachus' character. He is, for instance, extremely anxious to win a fine reputation for his account of justice (338a), and can see no point to a debate other than victory over one's opponents; he further assumes that Socrates must be equally competitive (340d; 341a–c). His sullenness and irascibility also anticipate the description in 411b–c of the naturally thumoeidic man whose *thumos* can find no proper outlet:

If he is thumoeidic, the effect is, by weakening his *thumos*, to make him unstable, a man who flies into a rage at a trifle and calms down as quickly. His thumoeidic temperament has degenerated into peevishness and ill-temper and he is subject to constant irritability.

In Thrasymachus, I would suggest, we see what happens when the thumoeidic lion of the *Gorgias* does not manage to break through its social bonds, but remains imprisoned in a society it despises.

SOCRATES' RESPONSE TO THRASYMACHUS

We are now in a position to consider Socrates' handling of Thrasymachus in more detail. As we have seen, in his first counter-argument he claims that, since every skill *qua* skill has no defects of its own to remedy, its concern is simply to serve the interests of its object; the skill of ruling, for example, seeks the interest of the ruled.[77] It is an unconvincing claim, and Thrasymachus has no

---

[76] 3.82.4. See p. 70 above.   [77] 341c–342d.

difficulty in presenting a counter-example in the form of shepherding: while it seems clear that a skill *may* be practised for the
benefit of its subject matter, it seems equally clear that it does not
have to be. Skills may be exercised from a range of motives, and
the 'perfection' of the skill as such is irrelevant: the practitioner
may possess a range of needs which she or he seeks to satisfy.

A similar objection can be raised against Socrates' second argument, which also focuses on the notion of what constitutes a *technē*.
When Thrasymachus asserts that both the shepherd and ruler seek
to benefit themselves rather than their sheep or subjects, Socrates
replies that Thrasymachus is confusing the art of shepherding
with the art of wage-earning. All skills, Socrates argues, are differ-
entiated by their separate capacities; therefore, since wage-earning
is a benefit common to the exercise of many professions, it cannot
be the particular capacity of any skill but its own. Thrasymachus
clearly does not have to accept this: skills could perfectly well aim
at the financial advantage of the practitioner, and be differ-
entiated simply by the various means they employ to achieve this
aim, and the various fields in which they operate.

These first two arguments are directed against Thrasymachus'
belief that the art of ruling seeks to exploit the ruled; the remaining three seek to tackle what Socrates regards as Thrasymachus'
toughest challenge,[78] namely that injustice pays the individual better than justice. In the first of these (349b–350c), Socrates argues
that just men do not compete (*pleonektein*) with each other, but only
with unjust men; unjust men, on the other hand, try to compete
with everyone, just and unjust alike. In this, the just and unjust
resemble skilled and unskilled practitioners, such as musicians or
doctors: an expert musician will never compete with another expert musician, but only with the unmusical layman; whereas the
unmusical person will try to compete with everybody. The skilled
practitioner, however, is incontestably clever (349e) and wise
(350b), and, *qua* wise, he is also good (350b). In so far as the just
resemble expert practitioners, therefore, they too will be wise and
good, and justice will be *aretē*.

Thrasymachus is not capable of dissecting Socrates' moves here,
but his apparent agreement is grudging and blatantly specious.
His scepticism is justified. Firstly, it is profoundly implausible to

[78] 347e.

suggest that skilled practitioners never compete with each other. Secondly, even if that point were granted, it would not establish an analogy between the skilled and the just. As has often been noted, the unjust person is not trying to do better than the just person at justice, as the bad musician is trying to do better than the good musician at music; the unjust person is, rather, trying to *get* the better of the just person.[79] '*Pleonektein*' covers both meanings, but the distinction is plainly vital. It may also seem that the argument illegitimately exploits other verbal ambiguities inherent in '*epistēmōn*', '*sophos*' and '*agathos*' (350b): a person may clearly possess knowledge and be good at implementing it without being a morally good human being. This, however, may be to miss Socrates' point. He may be saying that if justice really were analogous to professional expertise, then to be good at it must necessarily imply being morally good. What else could being good at justice mean? If this is Socrates' position, then the real problem is not the ambiguity inherent in *sophos*, but the fact that he has given us no convincing reason to suppose that justice is in fact analogous to the expertise of, say, the doctor or musician. He thus remains unable to counter Thrasymachus' assertion that the just man is not remotely skilled; he is simply a fool and a dupe. Indeed, Thrasymachus might even take issue with Socrates' implied claims about what it is to be an expert in justice: he might say that if there is a person skilled in justice, it is not the just man but the man who is skilled at exploiting the existence of the institution of justice for his own (conventionally immoral) ends.

Socrates fares rather better when he abandons the analogy with professional expertise and concentrates instead on the effects of injustice, both within the social group and within the *psuchē* of the individual. Thrasymachus has claimed that injustice is a source of strength (344c). On the contrary, replies Socrates, injustice is always a source of weakness: no group of men, whether acting as a state or an army or gang of thieves, can be effective in carrying out their aims if they wrong each other. Wronging each other will simply lead to hatred and disunity and hence ineffectiveness. Similarly, injustice will also cause internal conflict within the individual, so that he too will become incapable of successful action (351e–352a).

[79] See Cross and Woozley 1964: 52 and Annas 1981: 51–2.

It is a suggestive argument, but it is still not entirely convincing. Clearly, all social groups require some agreed code of conduct if communal action is to be possible, but it is less clear whether this code need fulfil the criteria for justice: certainly the motivation for abiding by it could be fear or greed rather than any genuine respect for the claims of others in the group.[80] As for Socrates' assertions concerning the individual, they possess a *prima facie* plausibility but plainly as yet lack the detailed psychology required to support them. To begin with, the appeal to internal conflict assumes that the individual comprises at least two parts which require unifying, and so far Socrates has said nothing about what such 'parts' might be. Secondly, it is far from clear why the unifying principle within the individual should be thought to be justice, at any rate as ordinarily conceived.[81] It is perhaps best to view Socrates' strategy here as proleptic, anticipating the accounts of the *psuchē* and its potential fragmentation in Books 4, 8 and 9.

A proleptic interpretation also makes the best sense of Socrates' final argument in Book 1. Each type of thing, claims Socrates, possesses its own specific function, an activity which either only it can perform or which it can perform best. In addition, each thing also possesses its own characteristic excellence, a quality which enables it to perform its function well (353c6). The function of the *psuchē* is to deliberate and control the body, and, in general, to be the principle of life; its characteristic excellence has been agreed (350d4–5) to be justice. It is justice, therefore, not injustice, which enables the individual to live well, and it is the just man who will have a good life.

As it stands, the argument is plainly highly problematic. The move from the *psuchē* to the individual requires considerable support, and it is unclear whether a single excellence could enable the *psuchē* to perform the range of activities that are ascribed to it. The chief difficulty, however, is Socrates' assumption that justice has been adequately shown to be the soul's particular excellence. Firstly, in 350d he simply claimed that justice is excellence; he did not talk of it as the specific excellence of the *psuchē*. More seriously, we have seen that the argument from expertise which

[80] See Cross and Woozley 1964: 56.
[81] Such as, for instance, Polemarchus' definition of justice as 'giving others their due' (331e).

purports to secure this claim is profoundly flawed; we have also seen that, despite his apparent 'agreement', Thrasymachus remains unconvinced.

Socrates, then, does not succeed in his attempts to counter Thrasymachus in Book 1; indeed he admits himself (354b) that until he and Thrasymachus define justice, they cannot possibly say whether its possession will make a person happy or unhappy. Yet the very failure of his arguments is of the utmost importance, for it shapes the rest of the dialogue. Henceforth, Socrates will abandon the unhelpful analogy between justice and skill or expertise, and concentrate instead on trying to demonstrate, rather than simply assert, that justice is crucial for the unification and effective functioning of the *psuchē*, and hence individual. This attempt, of course, results in the detailed analysis of the parts of the soul and the radical interpretation of justice as internal harmony. The egoistic challenge of the thumoeidic Thrasymachus thus leads Socrates in the same direction as that prompted by the egoistic challenge of the thumoeidic Callicles. It is only fitting that the substantive psychology required to combat both characters makes explicit acknowledgement of that element of the *psuchē* from which their challenges largely spring.

CHAPTER 6

Heroes and role models: the Apology, Hippias Major *and* Hippias Minor

HOMERIC ROLE MODELS AND ALEXANDER THE GREAT

We have seen how the *Gorgias* raises questions concerning the respective appeal of Socrates and Callicles, or the Calliclean superman, for the young men of fourth-century Athens: Plato is well aware that if he wishes to establish Socrates as a new ideal, then he has competition on his hands. Yet the most widely influential role models were neither the ruthless political operators promoted by some of the sophists, nor the sophists themselves; they were, still, the heroes and warrior-kings of the ancient myths and legends, and above all they were those heroes as depicted in Homer.[1] There is abundant evidence that immersion in the Homeric poems formed the major part of a Greek male's education: both Xenophanes and Plato himself, for example, refer to Homer as the teacher of Greece,[2] and in Xenophon's *Symposium* a certain Niceratus recounts how his father, wishing him to become 'a good man', made him learn the entire Homeric corpus; even now, he says, he can still recite the *Iliad* and *Odyssey* by heart.[3] Nor was the point of such close study simply to cultivate one's aesthetic sensibilities: the poems were commonly regarded as repositories of ethical and perhaps even technical wisdom, practical manuals for a gentleman's life. We have already seen Callicles make use of Homer in precisely this way at *Gorgias* 485d, criticizing Socrates for not frequenting those public arenas where, in the words of *Iliad* 9.441, men 'are made pre-eminent'.

---

[1] As we saw on pp. 140–1, the political ideal of Callicles in particular has significant Homeric roots.

[2] Xenoph. fr. 10; Plato *Resp.* 606e.

[3] Xen. *Symp.* 3.5. While Niceratus is an unusual case, most educated Greek males would have been able to recite fairly substantial extracts from Homer.

From our point of view, however, what matters is not so much this general respect for Homer, as the fact that such respect could sometimes focus on a particular character, a hero whom the student would not only admire but actively seek to emulate. For proof, we need only consider Alexander the Great's well-attested obsession with Achilles. The *Iliad* was, by all accounts, Alexander's favourite work – he took it with him on all his campaigns and is alleged to have slept with it beneath his pillow[4] – and by all accounts too his favourite character was Achilles. His mother Olympias claimed descent from the Aeacidae,[5] and every source agrees that the image of his most famous supposed ancestor dominated his life: for once Onesicritus, Arrian, Plutarch, Strabo, Pliny and Athenaeus are all united.[6] When he first disembarked in Asia Minor, for instance, he made a special pilgrimage to the traditional site of Achilles' tomb near Troy and crowned it with a wreath, while his companion Hephaestion crowned the tomb of Patroclus. On returning to Troy, the villagers asked him if he would like to see the lyre of his namesake, Alexander/Paris son of Priam; Alexander declined, saying that for that lyre he cared little, but, 'he sought rather the lyre of Achilles, on which he used to sing the glorious deeds and actions of brave men.'[7]

There seems little doubt that this respect for Achilles took the form of conscious and detailed imitation. His reckless *aristeia* at the battle of the Granicus bears many Achillean marks, as do the tormented self-chastisement and taking to his bed after killing his Hipparch Cleitus in a drunken rage. Most telling of all, perhaps, are his extravagant mourning for the death of Hephaestion, and the elaborate funeral arrangements in Hephaestion's honour:[8] indeed, Arrian says that the chief reason he believes the story that Alexander cut off his hair on Hephaestion's death is that such a gesture would have been entirely in keeping with 'his desire to emulate Achilles, whom he had sought to rival since boyhood'.[9]

---

[4] Plutarch *Alexander* 8.2 and 26.1.
[5] See Lane Fox 1973: 44 and 59; Hammond 1981: 35.
[6] Onesicritus fr. 38; Arrian 1.12; Plutarch 5.8, 8.2, 26.1–2; Strabo 13.1.27; Pliny *HN* 7.108; Athenaeus 537c.
[7] Tombs: Arrian 1.12; lyre: Plutarch 15.9, referring to *Il.* 9.185–91.
[8] Granicus: Arrian 1.13–16; Cleitus: Plutarch 50–2; funeral arrangements for Hephaestion: Arrian 7.14.
[9] 7.14.

Another source claims that in times of deep anxiety he used to call upon Thetis.[10] This need to present himself as the new Achilles was so apparent that it became a subject for jokes: the fiercely anti-Macedonian orator Demosthenes, who had met Alexander twice, apparently took to referring to Athens' new overlord as 'Margites', the buffoon protagonist of a parody of the *Iliad*. Plainly he could not have done this had not Alexander's pretensions been common knowledge; the suggestion is also that Alexander had been possessed of such fantasies since boyhood, when Demosthenes met him.[11] More disturbingly, it also seems clear that Alexander's ambitions did not end simply with the wish to equal his hero: as we shall see in chapter 7, there is persuasive evidence that on occasion he consciously strove to surpass him, to particularly unappealing effect.

Further evidence of Alexander's *leitmotif*, and his belief in the importance of role models in general, comes with a detail Arrian adds to his account of the pilgrimage to Troy: gazing at Achilles' tomb, Alexander laments that Achilles had a Homer to glorify his exploits, whilst he has only a Callisthenes.[12] This not only shows that Alexander was well aware of Achilles' influence on his own development; it also shows how eager he was to exercise a similar influence on young imaginations in the future. And with his customary knack for success, this wish was fulfilled: in varying degrees, Caesar, Augustus, Caligula and Nero all tried to portray themselves in Alexander's image.[13] Perhaps the most interesting case is that of Caracalla, Emperor of Rome and devotee of Alexander almost 550 years after his death. According to the biography of Caracalla in the *Scriptores Historiae Augustae*, in youth the emperor was gentle and charming, not to say somewhat winsome. Later, however, he became reserved and severe, one of the possible reasons being, 'that he thought he should imitate Alexander

---

[10] Praying to Thetis: *P Oxy. FGrH* 148.44 col.2 (even if this last story is not true, it is still telling evidence of how much influence people thought a Homeric role model could have).

[11] Aeschines 3.160; Plutarch *Demosthenes* 23.2.

[12] See also Cicero *Pro Archia* 10.23–4.

[13] Caesar: Plutarch *Caesar* 11.3; Suetonius *Div. Jul.* 7; Dio Cassius 37.52.2. Augustus: Suetonius *Augustus* 18 and 50. Caligula: Suetonius *Gaius* 52; Tacitus *Annals* 6.31; Balsdon 1934: 51–4. Nero: Grant 1970: 200 and 239.

the Great of Macedon ... Alexander the Great and his deeds were
always on his lips.'[14]

Some of the acts that he imitated were relatively innocent, such
as the following of Alexander's itineraries in Thrace, Egypt and
Asia Minor. As with Alexander's emulation of Achilles, however,
not all the deeds he re-enacted were among his role model's
finest;[15] most significantly of all, we shall find that some of the
atrocities which Caracalla copied from Alexander, Alexander
himself copied from Achilles. Both directly and indirectly, the cult
of a particular hero can perpetuate itself over very long stretches
of time indeed.[16]

THE *APOLOGY*

Turning to Plato, we can see an awareness of the Homeric heroes'
cultural importance right from his very earliest dialogues. Furthermore, we can also see that his stance towards them is not simply that of the disinterested cultural observer: as his work matures,
he engages ever more deeply with the values and ways of life they
represent. Above all his imagination is fired, as Alexander's was to
be, by the charismatic figure of Achilles: daring warrior, bloodthirsty rebel, lover and brooding sceptic rolled into one. His first
appearance comes at *Apology* 28b, where Socrates draws a comparison between Achilles' behaviour and his own: his willingness
to die rather than compromise his commitment to philosophy is
comparable to Achilles' willingness to sacrifice his life in order to
avenge his companion Patroclus. The incentive for the comparison is the complaint of a hypothetical critic:

Are you not ashamed, Socrates, of having followed a pursuit which has
placed you in immediate danger of being put to death?

Not at all, replies Socrates, far from it: such a criticism is not
spoken *kalōs*. No one of any worth should consider whether his
acts carry any risk; his only obligation is to consider whether they
are those of a good or a bad man. Achilles, for example, positively

---

[14] It is notable that the Greek employs the indicative mood in this passage, suggesting that
the author (traditionally thought to be Aelius Spartianus) takes responsibility for the
truth of the story.
[15] See p. 206 n. 26 below.
[16] The innately conservative tendencies of a role model culture are discussed in ch. 9.

despised danger in comparison with enduring some disgrace. For when he announces his intention of killing Hector to his mother, Thetis replies that if he does so, then he will himself soon die, 'Since it is decreed your death must come straightway after Hector's.' In that case, says Achilles,

May I die straightway.[17]

The only thing that Achilles feared was to live as a coward (*kakos*); death and danger did not enter his calculations.

What are we to make of this comparison? Articulated in terms of a common rejection of the *aischron*, at first glance it seems innocuous enough. There is certainly ample evidence that later Greeks took Achilles' self-sacrifice as a prime example of the *kalon ergon*: in the *Ars Rhetorica*, for instance, Aristotle says that epideictic orators praise Achilles since for him, 'Such a death was the nobler [choice], though living was expedient';[18] while the orator Aeschines, in his speech *Against Timarchus* 145, praises Achilles for making the 'great-souled' choice of death over personal safety. Such approval is also voiced by Phaedrus in the *Symposium*: extolling the power of love to make one perform noble deeds, Phaedrus claims that the gods honoured Achilles and sent him to the Isles of the Blest because,

having learnt from his mother that he would die if he killed Hector, but would return home and end his days as an old man if he did not kill him, he daringly chose to rescue the body of his lover Patroclus and avenge him, [thereby electing] not only to die for the slain man, but to follow him in death.[19]

The same attitude further appears at *Alcibiades I* 115a–b, where the paradigm of a *kalon ergon* is said to be giving up one's life in battle for a friend: such an act is true *andreia* (b6–7). And in his discussion of the conflicting views concerning self-love in *Nichomachean Ethics* 9.8, Aristotle writes that one of the common *endoxa* on the subject holds that, 'the good man acts from a sense of what is fine ... and for the sake of a friend' (1168a33–4), and he will, if necessary, lay down his life for his friends or country (1169a18–20).

In appealing to the example of Achilles, therefore, Socrates

---

[17] *Il.* 18.96 and 98; quoted *Ap.* 28c7–8 and d2.
[18] *Ars Rhet.* 1359a4–5.
[19] *Symp.* 179e5–180a2. The exact translation of the final clause is disputed (contrast Dover 1980 ad loc.), but this does not affect the general sense of the passage.

would seem at first sight to be making an adroit rhetorical move. Yet on closer inspection this appeal is soon shown to be extremely odd. Before we can fully appreciate this oddness, however, we need to consider more carefully how the comparison is set up. The central point is that Socrates assumes the conflict between him and the imaginary critic arises from a clear-cut antithesis between pragmatism and moral nobility: a willingness to die for the sake of philosophy or a friend is presumed to be uncomplicatedly *kalon*, while concern for one's physical comfort and safety is not regarded as *kalon* at all. In this context, the appeal to Achilles initially seems to make good sense, as the above references indicate. Furthermore, Achilles' heroic choice in Book 18 is deepened by the fact that it is the resolution of a tension which has run throughout the entire poem, and which is articulated most clearly by Achilles himself in his reply to the embassy in Book 9:

> For my mother Thetis the goddess of the silver feet tells me I carry two sorts of destiny towards the day of my death. Either, if I stay here and fight beside the city of the Trojans, my return home is gone, but my glory shall be everlasting; but if I return home to the beloved land of my fathers, the excellence of my glory is gone, but there will be a long life left for me, and my end in death will not come to me quickly.[20]

The complexities of this key passage will concern us shortly; what is important to note here is that it is this choice which Thetis recalls to Achilles in Book 18. When Achilles elects to re-enter the fighting, therefore, he does not simply do so in the knowledge that he will soon be killed: he also does so in the knowledge that, if he had not decided to fight again, he could have returned to his native land and lived to old age. The message seems straightforward. If Socrates wishes to portray his own situation as a choice between noble death or ignoble safety, then one might think that he could not have selected a better example.

Yet this perception of his situation raises two linked problems for Socrates. Firstly, it is an inadequate reply to the hypothetical critic, in that it ignores the explicit wording of the accusation: the critic clearly believes, as Callicles and Thrasymachus believe, that disregard for one's personal safety is not merely imprudent, but positively shameful. As we have seen in chapter 5, this is a serious moral position, and one which Socrates needs to face: he cannot

---

[20] *Il.* 9.410–16, trans. Lattimore.

simply assert without argument that morality is separate from such concerns.[21]

The second difficulty arises from the fact that while Socrates may be indifferent to physical comfort and safety, he is, as we also saw in chapter 5, far from indifferent to personal wellbeing; it is simply that he conceives of such wellbeing in terms of the care of the soul rather than that of the body, since it is the soul which he considers to be the true self.[22] Damage to his body – even its destruction – is therefore not damage to *him*. Furthermore, this is a point which he goes out of his way to emphasize in the *Apology* itself: at 30c–d he claims that Anytus and Meletus cannot harm him, and at 41d he maintains that no *kakon* can befall a good man, either in life or after death. The only real good, in the sense of personal benefit, is purity and integrity of soul, at whatever cost (30a); moral excellence does not come from money, but 'it is moral excellence that makes money and everything else good for men' (30b3–4).[23]

Things such as wealth *become* (n.b. *gignetai* 30b3) good for men through, and only through, their being used virtuously.[24] Plainly, to say that nothing becomes a good for men except through virtue is not logically incompatible with virtue being responsible for things which are not goods at all; nevertheless, when coupled with 30a, Socrates' words here clearly imply that virtue is beneficial to its practitioners. In other words, while we may well have to choose between the *kalon* and bodily safety, we do not have to choose between the *kalon* and the personal *agathon*. Self-sacrifice, conventionally interpreted, may not be true self-sacrifice at all: it all depends on what is identified as 'the self'. On Socrates' understanding, true self-protection may be entirely compatible with conventional self-sacrifice.

It is this conception of the personal *agathon* which raises questions

---

[21] See especially *Grg.* 486a, where Callicles says that Socrates is in the 'disgraceful' (*aischron*) position of being unable to defend himself if wrongly taken to court.

[22] This is certainly the case in the *Apology*. By the time of the *Gorgias*, Socrates appears to conceive of the 'true self' as the rational part of the soul alone: see p. 1 above. For my use of 'self' and 'true self' with regard to Plato in general, see Preface pp. xiii–xiv.

[23] The translation is adapted from that of Burnet's commentary (1924). Burnet's reading has been, to my mind, persuasively argued for by Vlastos (1984: 193) and Burnyeat (in the forthcoming appendix to his 'The impiety of Socrates' (1997)).

[24] The same thought is voiced at *Prt.* 313a7–9, and, with *sophia* taking the place of virtue, at *Euthyd.* 278e3–281e2. As Vlastos stresses (1984), it is important to note that Socrates is not opposed to conventional 'goods' as such.

for Socrates' comparison between himself and Achilles. Admittedly, it is true that Achilles views his choice of heroic death at least partly in egoistic terms: he is quite explicit about his desire to win 'excellent glory' (18.121), and unquestionably wants to perform deeds which actually receive honour as well as deserving it. Indeed, there is a sense in which his intense desire for glory might even lead him to concede that self-protection and bodily self-sacrifice are not entirely opposed: he might well think that his reputation was the aspect of himself most in need of cherishing. Yet despite these qualifications, it is also true that, for Achilles, the degree to which self-sacrifice and self-protection are compatible is strictly limited: it is absolutely clear that he perceives the choice he has to make as a choice between two intrinsically valuable options. Returning to his 'beloved' (*philē*) native land is something for which he longs, and which he is loth to forgo; life has a strongly positive value for him, and death a strongly negative one. Death is final and hateful; Hades is shadowy, chill and frightening.[25] So while his desire for honour means that it would be too simplistic to say that he views his predicament as a straightforward choice between the noble and the beneficial *simpliciter*, it is plain that he does view it as a choice between the noble and a great many benefits.[26] And in this, he and Socrates are radically at odds.

Furthermore, it is plainly Achilles' conception of the choice which would win general agreement.[27] It is all very well for Socrates to assert that the purity of one's soul is the only real *agathon*, but what argument does he offer in the *Apology* to substantiate this counter-intuitive claim? Why should we believe his implied conception of the self to be correct? If Socrates' position is to be made persuasive, then the *psuchē* and corresponding notions of personal benefit will require detailed attention.

So, too, will the notion of the *kalon*. Achilles and Socrates may both display bravery in the face of death, but in other respects

---

25 See *Il.* 9.408–9; 9.416; 23.65–107. This issue is discussed further on pp. 207–8 and 211 below.

26 Indeed, in Achilles' jaundiced mood in Bk 9, he does not merely complain that his spectacular *aretē* has not brought him the honours – such as Briseis – that he deserves; he also suggests at one point that even if he *were* to receive the traditional honours, they would not compensate for the constant risk to life and limb which the hero must daily face (9.400–9).

27 For long life (providing it is made secure by the production of offspring) being a common constituent of the good life, see *Hp. Mai.* 291d11–e1 (see below p. 188), and Aristotle *Ars Rhet.* 1360b20–1.

their conceptions of *aretē* may well be thought to differ markedly. When Socrates says that a man should consider only whether his acts are those of a good or a bad man, he takes this to mean that a man should consider only whether he performs 'just or unjust deeds' (28b8–9). This emphasis on the primacy of justice is also evident in the way in which he substantially alters the wording of Achilles' response to Thetis' warning in Book 18.[28] In the *Iliad*, Achilles proclaims that he is returning to battle, '... to overtake that killer of a dear life' (18.114), adding that now is the time for him to win glory. In the *Apology*, however, Socrates has Achilles cry out, 'May I die straightway, once I have inflicted punishment (*dikēn epitheis*) on the wrongdoer (*tō adikounti*)' (28d2). This focus on *dikē* and *ta dikaia*, however, clearly prompts two questions. Firstly, is it true that Achilles views his actions under such a banner? And secondly, is Socrates' portrayal of Achilles as an agent of justice consistent with his ethical teachings elsewhere?

Achilles himself would probably not object to Socrates' depiction. At a personal level, he clearly possesses a keen sense of justice: he is certainly bitter that Agamemnon has not given him the honour that he feels he deserves. And as for his specific decision to kill Hector, he is in general – *pace* some disquiet concerning the whole enterprise of the war in Book 24[29] – a firm believer in the rightness of revenge. What is baffling, however, is why Socrates should here seem to endorse revenge as an act of justice. It is, after all, hardly his usual stance. In the *Crito* he asserts unequivocally that, 'One must not requite wrong with wrong, nor do harm to any human, no matter what one may have suffered at their hands' (49c10–11); while in *Republic* 1 his rejection of the ethic of revenge forms his chief argument against Polemarchus' interpretation of *dikaiosunē* as 'helping one's friends and harming one's enemies': 'it is not the function of the just man to harm either his friend or anyone else, but of his opposite, the unjust man' (335d11–12).

Killing Hector in requital for Patroclus would seem to be utterly at odds with such statements.[30] Indeed, one could argue that the

---

[28] So far as we can tell. It is, of course, impossible to ascertain precisely what text of the *Iliad* Plato knew. See Labarbe 1949; Lohse 1964: 3–28; 1965: 248–95; 1967: 223–31.

[29] See especially 540–2.

[30] Act-description is critical here. Socrates does permit punishment for wrongdoing, if the intention is to purify the malefactor's soul (see *Grg.* 478d–480b). The purification of Hector, however, is plainly not what Achilles has in mind; nor is it clear that Socrates would regard Hector's attempt to protect his city as wrongdoing in the first place.

majority of Achilles' actions in the *Iliad* are motivated by revenge, whether directed against Trojans or Greeks; and many of them, such as the slaughter of the young Trojans on the pyre or the dragging of Hector's corpse behind his chariot, are castigated by Socrates in the *Republic* as the very antithesis of right conduct.[31] Yet in the *Apology*, Socrates appears to accept Achilles' view of the matter without question, saying approvingly that Achilles, 'was far more afraid of living as a coward by not avenging (*timōrein*) his friends' (28c8–d1).

Things become even stranger when we consider that immediately after drawing the comparison, Socrates continues,

wherever a man stations himself, considering that it is best for him to be there, or wherever he is stationed by his commander, there he must – so it seems to me – remain and take the risks. (28d6–8)

Achilles is renowned for many qualities, but obeying the orders of his commander and remaining at his post are scarcely among them. The problem is intensified in that these lines of Socrates anticipate some of his later descriptions and definitions of *andreia*, such as that of *Gorgias* 507b;[32] again, for those considering the *Apology* in relation to other Platonic dialogues, the appeal to Achilles strikes an uneasy note. Is the bravery and manliness of Socrates and Achilles really of the same sort? It may be helpful to recall here Aristotle's distinction between two basic meanings of *megalopsuchia*.[33] The first we saw to be a refusal to submit to dishonourable treatment, and two of the examples Aristotle cites are Achilles and Alcibiades; the second, however, is 'being unmoved by misfortune', exemplified by Lysander and Socrates. In Aristotle's eyes, at least, Achilles and Socrates are heroes of very different kinds.

Indeed, this passionate desire of Achilles for *timē* makes Socra-

---

[31] *Resp.* 391b; the passage is discussed on pp. 203–4 below. Total and explicit rejection of the *lex talionis* in the *Republic* is, of course, only to be found in Bk 1, where Plato is often thought to be presenting us with views very close to those of the historical Socrates. The Socrates of Bk 5 (469b–471c) arguably approves a modified system of revenge over external enemies defeated in warfare (the argument concerns whether a state-controlled system would be too impersonal to count as revenge at all). However, the Bk 5 passage does not seem to permit the highly personal, uncontrolled and savage actions which Achilles at times undertakes.

[32] Discussed on pp. 152–3 above.

[33] *An. Post.* 97b15–26; see p. 149 above.

tes' comparison even more puzzling. At *Apology* 28d3–4 Socrates
refers to Achilles' honour-loving nature without apparent concern:
Achilles is made to say that he wants to exact 'justice' from the
'unjust' Hector, 'so that I may not remain here, jeered at (*katage-
lastos*) beside the curved ships, a burden of the earth'. The Homeric original (18.104) does not in fact contain the term *katagelas-
tos*, but its use by Plato seems fair enough: we have seen how at
18.121 Achilles announces that now is the time for him to win 'excellent glory'. Such an emphasis on personal *timē*, however, appears at odds with *Apology* 23d9, where Socrates criticizes his ac-
cusers for being 'lovers of honour', and letting this desire for *timē*
override the truth; at 29d8–e3, too, he condemns anyone who puts
thoughts of personal *timē* before the truth and the state of his soul.
The issue here is not simply whether Socrates should be comparing himself to the undeniably timocratic Achilles. There is also the
highly complex question of the connection between love of *timē*
and love of the *kalon*. In the *Apology*, Socrates generally (28d notwithstanding) seems to want to reject the former motivation whilst
retaining the latter; yet the example of Achilles makes us wonder
whether the separation can so easily be made. Is love of honour
really distinct from love of the honourable?[34] At the very least,
Plato will have to explore the heroic notion of what is to count as
a noble or base action.

Socrates' appeal to the example of Achilles, therefore, is by no
means as straightforward as it initially appears. There is, however,
a hint at the very end of the work that Plato is after all aware of
some of the questions the comparison raises: he is at any rate clear
that the proper response to the Homeric heroes in general should
not be one of uncritical adulation. At 41a8–c4 Socrates says that if
Hades exists then he is looking forward to meeting Agamemnon
and Odysseus and all the other heroes:

and the greatest pleasure would be to spend my time examining and
investigating the people there, as I do those here, to find out who among
them is wise, and who thinks that he is, but is not.

For in the end, 'the unexamined life is not worth living' (38a5–6).
Far from being settled by the time of Socrates' death, the debate

---

[34] This issue is discussed further below, p. 191. See also pp. 38–9 above.

on what really matters in life, and what is to count as true heroism, has only just begun.

THE *CRITO*

It continues in the *Crito*.[35] Here too, Socrates makes what initially seems to be an innocent comparison between himself and Achilles at 44a5–b2. In response to Crito's warning that the ship from Delos which presages Socrates' death is very near, Socrates says that he does not believe that the ship will come that day, since he has just woken from a dream in which a beautiful woman clad in white told him that 'on the third day you would come to fertile Phthia'. Her words are a close adaptation of *Iliad* 9.363, where Achilles claims that with Poseidon's help he and the Myrmidons should reach 'fertile Phthia' on the third day after setting off from Troy. At first sight it appears that Plato is simply attempting to cast his situation in a heroic light, but on closer examination the comparison turns out to be considerably more complex: whether intentionally or not, Socrates' adapted quote also suggests a critique of Achilles' speech. Firstly, there is the obvious point that, for Achilles, home is represented by an area of living Greek soil; for Socrates, of course, home can only be achieved in bodily death. More subtly, it is important to remember that Achilles' thoughts in Book 9 are a very long way from the declarations of Book 18 which prompted Socrates to invoke Achilles' example in the *Apology*. In Book 9, Achilles feels no desire to act nobly at whatever personal cost; on the contrary, his decision to abandon the Trojan War and lead his followers back to Phthia is made during a period of bitter disillusion, and stems from his belief that the heroic preference for glorious death over long and inglorious life is no longer an option: Agamemnon's unjust appropriation of Briseis, Achilles' prize for dangers undertaken and battles won, suggests to Achilles that his imminent death will not in fact be accorded its rightful glory. So why not leave and escape early death altogether? Socrates, on the other hand, is in the *Crito* embracing a death which, if not exactly early, is still untimely. He emerges from the implied comparison not as Achilles' equal, but as his superior.

[35] In what follows, I have profited from the treatment of this passage in Callen King 1987: 106–8.

THE *HIPPIAS MAJOR*

If the *Crito* is deliberately critiquing Achilles' views and conduct, that criticism is oblique; for explicit discussion of Homeric characters and values, we must turn to the *Hippias Major* and *Hippias Minor*.[36] Both dialogues provide valuable insights into the question of suitable guides and models for the young, especially with regard to the continuing influence of the Homeric heroes, and traditional heroic values and practices. Of particular relevance to our concerns will be the extent to which the heroes and values under scrutiny embody thumoeidic characteristics.

The *Hippias Major* introduces the topic of educating young men almost immediately, *via* Socrates' ironic admiration of Hippias' skill at extracting money from them (286b6–7); the issue of education is thus seen from the very beginning to centre on the question of who should do the educating, whose advice and example are really worth following. Men hailed as authorities by their societies – and by themselves – parade through Socrates' and Hippias' opening exchange: as well as Hippias himself, we are reminded of the claims to wisdom of Pittacus, Bias, Thales and Anaxagoras, Gorgias, Prodicus and Protagoras. However, as we saw in the *Gorgias* and as Hippias admits in 285b–d, while such 'wise men' and sophists may have much influence as educators and even occasionally as models, young males are likely to be far more attracted to men of action, whether in politics or warfare. In this context it is significant that Hippias' set speech for the young men of Sparta involves the genealogies of traditional action-men heroes, and begins with a question raised by Neoptolemus, Achilles' son.[37] Plato,

---

[36] This is not the place for a discussion of their respective chronology. I have treated the *Hp. Mai.* first simply because I believe it leads on to the *Hp. Mi.* in dramatic setting (see below p. 196 n. 60). As for whether the *Hp. Mai.* is pre- or post-*Republic*, it may be worth noting the similarities between the examples given of *kala* at *Hp. Mai.* 298a–b and those of *Gorgias* 474d–475a; Dodds (1959: 250) takes these similarities to be evidence of a comparable closeness in dates – indeed, he even suggests that the *Hp. Mai.* is the earlier of the two. This, however, is hardly conclusive, particularly as the *Hp. Mai.* on occasion subdivides the *Gorgias*' examples: the μαθήματα of *Gorgias* 475a1–2, for example, arguably becomes the λόγοι καὶ ... μυθολογίαι of *Hp. Mai.* 298a4. I personally still tend towards a pre-*Republic* date, though as my reasons are based precisely on the theory here proposed of a development in Plato's thought concerning the heroic, I can hardly adduce them without circularity. Fortunately for the present argument, justification for discussing the *Republic* after the *Hp. Mai.* need only rely on the fact that the *Republic* is the most *complete* examination of Greek values and the heroic culture from which they arise.

[37] This speech is discussed below pp. 190–1.

I suggest, is well aware of the importance to the youthful imagination of such legendary demigods, and it comes as no surprise when at 292e Socrates brings into the discussion Achilles himself.

As the issues arising from Achilles' appearance here are similar to those stemming from the *Apology* comparison, our discussion need only be brief. As in the *Apology*, Socrates' attitude towards Achilles is positive. At 291d–e Hippias, foiled in his attempts to define the *kalon* as a beautiful maiden or gold, now suggests that it is in fact *eudaimonia*, conventionally interpreted:[38]

I say, then, that always and for every man and everywhere it is most *kalon* to be rich and healthy, and honoured by the Greeks; to reach old age and, after providing a beautiful[39] funeral for his dead parents, to be beautifully and splendidly buried by his children.

Socrates, however, is not happy about this proposal: indeed, the demanding man that he knows, who is 'not refined, but vulgar, thinking of nothing but the truth' (288d), will be profoundly angered at such a definition. And as a counter-example the man will cite Achilles (292e): would it have been *kalon* (e8) for *him* to have lived to old age and been buried by his children? Would it, in other words, have been *kalon* for him to have preferred conventional *eudaimonia* to sacrificing his life to avenge Patroclus?

Again, Socrates' unqualified approval of Achilles is somewhat puzzling. Not only does he thereby appear to condone the *lex talionis*, but he seems to be arguing explicitly that there is a choice to be made between *eudaimonia* and the fine. Yet later in the *Hippias Major* he appears to claim that there is no such choice to be made – or, at any rate, no choice between the *kalon* and the *agathon*. In 296e he and Hippias consider the suggestion that the *kalon* is the beneficial. But, says Socrates, the beneficial is 'that which creates good' (296e7), and thus this new definition would make the *kalon* the (or a) cause of the good (296e9–297a1).[40] However, since the cause is different from the thing created, this would mean that 'the

---

[38] For conventional views of *eudaimonia*, see *Ars Rhet.* 1360b14–30; conventional notions of what constitute goods are referred to by Socrates at *Gorgias* 467e; *Meno* 78c; *Euthyd.* 279a–b.

[39] In the *Hippias Major* it is clearly more than usually difficult to know how to translate *kalon* and its cognates. I have used both 'beautiful' and 'fine', depending on the context. The issue is discussed below pp. 190–1.

[40] The insertion of the definite article before 'good' is problematic, but this is not the place to discuss it.

kalon is not good, nor the good *kalon*' (297c3–4), and this 'pleases me least of all the things we have said' (297c10–d1).

We do not have to agree with the reasoning on which this objection is based to see the importance of the objection itself. Socrates' desire that the *kalon* be good and the good *kalon* is further emphasized at 303e–304a, in a passage where he and Hippias are again debating whether the *kalon* is something beneficial, in this case beneficial pleasure. But such a definition once more invites the criticism that, if it were true, then 'neither could the good be *kalon* nor the *kalon* good, but each of them is different from the other' (303e13–304a2). This and similar statements elsewhere in Plato on the relationship between the good and the *kalon* will be examined further in chapter 8. At this stage we need only note that Socrates' keen desire to bring the two together in the *Hippias Major* may initially seem to conflict with his rejection of Hippias' attempt to define the *kalon* as *eudaimonia*.

There is, however, a possible resolution of this tension; and again, it is very similar to the solution proposed for Socrates' problems in the *Apology*. As we saw, Hippias' notion of *eudaimonia* is decidedly conventional; there is thus in theory ample scope for a reworked conception which could accommodate Achilles' act of self-sacrifice. The challenge, of course, will be to make such a reworking convincing in practice.

The extent of this challenge is revealed by Hippias' response. He grudgingly admits that burying one's parents and being buried by one's children is not necessarily *kalon* for the heroic offspring of gods, such as Achilles;[41] but he holds fast in his view that it is *kalon* for ordinary mortals (293a–b). For Hippias, what is appropriate behaviour for semi-divine heroes is by no means necessarily appropriate for humanity in general; he would not agree with Socrates' exhortation in the *Theaetetus* that humans should seek to assimilate themselves to the divine in so far as they can (176b). His attitude is not unlike that of some modern thinkers who hold that the notion of heroism (even when divested of any connotations of semi-divinity) expresses a purely personal ideal which no one else has any obligation to emulate.[42] Mortals should confine themselves to mortal thoughts, and, in this mortal realm, looking after one's own

---

[41] Hippias also concedes that such behaviour can hardly be *kalon* for the gods either.
[42] See Walton 1986: 27–8.

comfort and safety is a fine thing: rhetoric is beautiful and valuable precisely because it enables us to protect ourselves and our own (304b). In this, Hippias is simply voicing what we have seen to be a common ethical position; he may be unlovably smug, and lacking in any exalted Calliclean notion of 'manliness', but his views cannot simply be dismissed. If Socrates wants to redefine *eudaimonia*, then he has real competition.

The *Hippias Major*'s exploration of the heroic is not merely confined to its discussion of Achilles. The discourse which Hippias has just been delivering to apparently appreciative Spartans concerns 'what fine practices (*kala epitēdeumata*) a young man should pursue', and takes as its starting-point a question posed by Neoptolemus:

> The story goes that, after the fall of Troy, Neoptolemus asked Nestor what *kala epitēdeumata* a young man should pursue in order to become most renowned. (286a8–b2)

The salient point here is that it is in this context, the context of heroic conduct, that the problem of defining the *kalon* is first raised (286c–d); furthermore, it is the notion of *kala epitēdeumata* that is taken throughout the dialogue as the toughest example of the *kalon* to explain. Twice, at 294c8–d4 and 298b1–9, a proposed definition is queried because it does not appear to account for fine practices. At 294c Socrates and Hippias are debating whether the *kalon* is the fitting (*prepon*), the latter being that which, according to Hippias, makes things both appear and actually be *kala* when it is added to them. But if this were the case, says Socrates, then no one would ever disagree about whether certain customs and practices are *kala* or not, whereas in fact they disagree about these particular things all the time. It is partly as a result of this argument that Socrates and Hippias abandon the notion of the fitting and explore other avenues until at 297e–298a Socrates suggests that perhaps the *kalon* is 'the pleasant through hearing and sight'. Here again, however, such a definition does not account for 'fine practices and laws' (298b). Finally, Socrates returns to the question of fine practices right at the end of the dialogue: the difficult man that he knows will ask him whether he is not ashamed to discuss *kala epitēdeumata* when he does not yet know what the *kalon* itself is. There is no doubt, in short, that the problem posed by fine and noble pursuits is central to the work; and if they are central, then so too is the notion of the heroic.

The basic difficulty arises from the fact that the concept of the *kalon* comprises two fundamental (albeit closely connected) strands, the aesthetically beautiful and the morally praiseworthy; yet a number of the proposed definitions of the *kalon* seem to apply only to the former.[43] Under these conditions, the morally noble and its place in the heroic will inevitably prove elusive. Nevertheless, the Neoptolemus passage still helps us to appreciate some of its complexities. It is important that Neoptolemus' stated motivation for wanting to pursue fine practices is his longing for glory: a willingness to perform potentially self-sacrificial actions is intimately linked with an impulse towards self-glorification. Yet it is no simple matter of fine, altruistic feelings being somehow tainted by gross, egoistic ones, since the desire for glory is itself a highly complex motivation. To achieve glory one must first deserve it, and this will mean performing fine deeds at least partly for their own sake; indeed, one could argue that unless the action is so performed then it cannot count as 'fine' at all. In the *Ars Rhetorica* Aristotle says that honour is regarded as fine because it is a mark of superior *aretē*,[44] while in the *Ethics*, as we have seen, he goes so far as to assert that, 'people seek honour in order to convince themselves of their own goodness'.[45] If self-promotion were the only spur, then presumably goodness could not be claimed, or at any rate not to the same degree; in consequence, 'Generally speaking, what is honoured should be classed as *kalon*, since the two seem to be closely related.'[46] In the case of the hero seeking glory, the job of act-description will again be a very delicate matter indeed.

In both these respects, the desire for glory and a sensitivity to the moral *kalon*, the heroic ethos as depicted in the *Hippias Major* is clearly very much in accord with the impulses and motivations of the Platonic *thumos*. It is notable that Hippias' discourse has proved especially popular in Sparta, a state which Plato depicts elsewhere as distinctly, if degenerately, thumoeidic. At *Republic* 544c, for example, he explicitly says that his timocratic state and man are based on the Spartan (and Cretan) model, and the details

---

[43] It is possible, of course, that Plato intends to stimulate his readers into applying to the *kalon* the techniques of division and collection. The first task is to distinguish the sensible from the moral *kalon*; then we have to consider what unites them.

[44] *Ars Rhet.* 1367a23–4.

[45] *E.N.* 1095b26–8 (trans. Thomson), and cf. *E.N.* 1159a22–4. See pp. 38–9, and 185 above.

[46] *Ars Rhet.* 1367b11–12.

of 547b–550c bear this out: witness the references to a ruling class
devoted to war and holding the rest of the population in subjec-
tion as serfs; the abstinence of this soldier-class from farming and
commerce; the dining in common messes and, above all, the emphasis on physical and military training.[47] This accent on the
physical is of particular importance, since it provides a central link
between Plato's conception of the heroic and his account of the
thumos. At *Hippias Major* 285b–d Socrates slyly elicits from Hippias
the subjects on which the heroically-minded young Spartans do *not*
want to hear discourses: astronomy and geometry and harmonics
are not at all to their taste, and in general they cannot abide anything connected with the 'processes of thought'. The thumoeidic
hero would rather attack with a spear than Voltaire's pen; and he
would normally rather live by an established code than by critical
self-examination.

These points of connection become clearer when we consider
the term *epitēdeumata* in more detail, since it is particularly associated not only with Neoptolemus' heroic young man, but also
with the thumoeidic young Auxiliaries: *vide*, for instance, *Republic*
389d4, 424d8–9 and 427a7. Liddell and Scott give for *epitēdeuma*
'pursuit, business, custom' – something that may be performed
every day.[48] The point here is that though such practices may be
undertaken after careful reflection (such as Socrates' *epitēdeuma* of
pursuing the truth at *Apology* 28b4), they may equally well *not* be;
they may have become 'second nature'. This is why it is important
that Neoptolemus asks the wise and reflective Nestor which practices are really worth pursuing. Neoptolemus' youth is also a factor here. Plainly, habitual pursuits can be practised by anybody,
but it is also clear that Plato views them as playing a significant
formative role in the lives of young men,[49] who as we have seen
are especially susceptible to heroic and thumoeidic impulses and
values.

These ties between the heroic and the thumoeidic, however,
suggest a fundamental problem for Socrates. If the kind of people
interested in performing *kala epitēdeumata* have no interest in defin-

---

[47] *Alc.1* 122c6–7 also mentions the ἀνδρείαν, ... φιλονικίαν καὶ φιλοτιμίας of the Spartans.
   Even if the work is not by Plato, it is still significant that the author thought that this
   thumoeidic description of Sparta would be accepted as Platonic.
[48] As in Thuc. 2.37.
[49] See also *Laches* 180c2–4 and *Euthyd.* 275b2–4.

ing the *kalon* itself, then how much appeal will the searcher of such definitions hold for them? It is the action-man who will continue to win their primary allegiance, and the sophist, who professes to help youths become effective players in the affairs of state, who will win second place. When the notion of the heroic is examined more closely, in other words, Socrates' apparently uncritical approval of Achilles does not seem the wisest of moves.

THE *HIPPIAS MINOR*

Plato's exploration of the heroic continues in the *Hippias Minor*.[50] indeed, the chief philosophical *topoi* of the dialogue – truth-telling and lying, knowledge and ignorance, committing wrongs willingly or unwillingly – all stem from Socrates' original query at 363b concerning Achilles and Odysseus. Hippias has just been giving a discourse on Homer, and this reminds Socrates of a claim by a certain Apeimantus, namely that the *Iliad* is a finer (*kallion*) poem than the *Odyssey* in as much as Achilles is finer than Odysseus. What, asks Socrates, is Hippias' opinion on this matter? Which of the two heroes does he think is the better (*ameinō*)?

Hippias' reply is unequivocal. Homer made Achilles the best (*aristos*) of those who went to Troy,[51] Nestor the wisest and Odysseus the wiliest (364c). Socrates claims to be surprised: is not Achilles also devising? Not at all, replies Hippias; on the contrary, Homer made him 'most simple' (*haploustatos* 364e7).[52] For in Book 9 he has Achilles say to Odysseus,

I must speak out my answer without restraint,
the way I think, and the way it shall be accomplished . . .
For as I detest the gates of Hades, I detest that man, who
hides one thing in the depths of his heart and says another.[53]

Achilles is thus represented as true and simple; Odysseus as wily and false (364b).

Again, Socrates is unsatisfied, this time with the terms 'true' and

---

50 'Continues' only in the sense of dramatic setting. See p. 187 n. 36 above.
51 *Aristos* here almost certainly includes its Homeric overtones of 'most courageous'.
52 The same term is also used by Plato in respect of the timocratic state, which at *Resp.* 547e3–4 is said to prefer the 'thumoeidic and simpler (ἁπλουστέρους) types'. This will be important when we consider the evidence that Plato in the *Republic* treats Achilles as the archetypal representative of untrained *thumos*.
53 *Il.* 9.309–13. Translation adapted from Lattimore.

'false'. If Hippias is right, he protests, then this means that Homer believes that the true man is different from the false. Yet we can see time after time in the sciences and arts – in calculation, arithmetic and geometry, astronomy, poetry and music[54] – that the man who has the ability consistently to tell falsehoods concerning a subject, and never accidentally tells the truth, is the man who possesses a really thorough knowledge of that subject, and who therefore also has the ability consistently to tell truths about it. Such a man is the *agathos* in his particular field. And so it cannot be the case that Achilles is true and Odysseus false, because the true and the false man are not different but the same; thus,

if Odysseus was false, he becomes also true, and if Achilles was true, he becomes also false, and the two are not different from one another, nor opposites, but alike. (369b4–7)

Hippias, quite rightly, remains stubbornly sceptical. At 367d3 he is careful to stipulate that Socrates' assertion has so far only been shown regarding the expert in calculation, and at 369a3, in reply to Socrates' challenge that he produce any science or skill of which the assertion does not hold, he says cautiously that he cannot 'offhand'. Whatever Socrates' word-games may suggest, he says bluntly, there is no denying that Homer portrays Achilles as honest and better than Odysseus. Socrates responds by citing two occasions when Achilles says he will sail home to Phthia and then does not, apparently in direct contradiction of his claim that his words are always transformed into deeds. But, says Hippias, such instances are not legitimate evidence, since Achilles never utters falsehoods by design, but against his will, since the army's misfortunes compel him to remain.[55] Achilles may occasionally say one thing and do another, but he does not act in this way intentionally: lying is simply not part of his general disposition. Though Hippias does not say so, it is clear that the same distinction will apply to the earlier discussion of the specialist: the astronomer may well have more power consistently to tell falsehoods about the movements of the stars, but the relevant question is whether he wants to.

---

[54] Socrates is plainly directing some sly fun at Hippias here. Since Hippias claims to be an expert in all these subjects (368c–d), then he will be able to lie about them too. Should we trust him?

[55] 370e5–6 and 371d8–e3.

It is all very strange. Socrates' does not challenge Hippias' point about lying being a matter of intention and disposition; instead, he simply tries to use it to show how it proves that Odysseus is better than Achilles, since it is always better to act voluntarily than involuntarily. While this moot point does not concern us here, it is worth noting that not only is Hippias unconvinced by it (376b7), but Socrates is not even happy with it himself (376b8). Yet if Socrates is so unperturbed about his argument being exposed, and is ready to admit that he does not believe in it anyway, then what is important to him? What is he trying to do?

The answer, I suggest, comes at 370d6–e4:

Now I, Hippias, originally asked my question because I was at a loss as to which of the two men is depicted as better by the poet, since I considered both of them to be excellent; and it was hard to decide which was better ...

Such a view, however, has far-reaching implications. Even if the two are equal in excellence, Hippias is clearly right that Achilles' strengths are, in some respects at least, different from those of Odysseus; and, whatever his word-play, Socrates cannot seriously deny this. We have seen how Aristotle distinguishes two types of *megalopsuchia*,[56] a refusal to submit to dishonourable treatment and being unaffected by misfortune, and how he cites Achilles as a paradigm example of the first; Odysseus is not mentioned by Aristotle, but, though he displays both kinds, it is plain that he is more readily associated with the second. In asserting that Odysseus is the equal in excellence of Achilles, therefore, Socrates appears to be making a substantive claim concerning two different types of heroism and *andreia*.

Plato's motivation here is not hard to find, since the historical Socrates clearly typifies the second kind of *megalopsuchia* as notably as Odysseus (and is cited in this respect by Aristotle). Not only was Socrates willing to endure whatever the state decreed for him rather than compromise his commitment to philosophy, but he was also capable of extreme physical stamina in the state's service: at *Symposium* 219e–220d, for instance, Alcibiades says that on campaign in Potidaea Socrates surpassed them all in his endurance of hardships, while his fortitude during the retreat from Delium is

---

[56] *An. Post.* 97b15–26; see pp. 149 and 184 above.

emphasized at *Symposium* 220e–221a and *Laches* 181a–b. In short, if Socrates is to be compared to a Homeric hero, then Odysseus would be at least as good a choice as Achilles. And indeed at *Protagoras* 315b9 we find Socrates making the comparison for himself, likening his sighting of Hippias amongst the other sophists in Callias' house to Odysseus' sighting of the shade of Heracles in the underworld.[57]

Yet this focus on Odysseus as well as Achilles raises two linked problems. Firstly, there is the question of the extent to which the two types of heroism are in competition. It is true that Achilles and Odysseus are not actually rivals in Greek mythology, but it is manifestly clear that their approaches differ,[58] and it is equally clear that we cannot emulate both men: we cannot simultaneously achieve our homecoming and elect to forgo it. There will be occasions when we, like Achilles, will have to choose. Furthermore, even though Achilles and Odysseus are not rivals themselves, there is certainly tension in the Philoctetes' story between Odysseus and Achilles' son Neoptolemus, as we shall see below.[59]

Secondly, the need sometimes to choose between their different kinds of *andreia* will make it hard for Socrates to succeed in establishing the two heroes as 'similar' in respect of excellence (*Hp. Mi.* 370e4). If, as we have seen, 'similar' cannot plausibly refer to the *kind* of virtue each displays, then it can only indicate a similarity of *degree*. Yet it seems inevitable that choice will imply ranking. In the *Protagoras* comparison, the victor seems to be Odysseus: he is, after all, the only character in Hades who is alive, and the suggestion is that he is the more contemporary hero.

In ordinary thought, however, it is Achilles who is normally awarded superiority: witness Apeimantus' claim that the *Iliad* is finer than the *Odyssey* in so far as Achilles is better than Odysseus. This accords with the common perception of Achilles' act of self-sacrifice as the paradigm example of the *kalon ergon*:[60] his type of

---

[57] *Od.* 11.601. See also pp. 239–40 below.

[58] The embassy passage in *Il.* 9 is a case in point.

[59] P. 197.

[60] See p. 179 above. The reason Socrates is thinking about Achilles and Odysseus at the opening of the *Hp. Mi.* is that Hippias has just been making a speech about them, and it is reasonable to suppose that this is the speech on *kala epitēdeumata* which Hippias is due to give in two days' time at *Hp. Mai.* 286b – particularly as we learn in the *Hp. Mai.* that the speech has been requested by Eudicus, and Eudicus is not only present in the *Hp. Mi.* but actually opens the dialogue. Furthermore, Apeimantus is Eudicus' father. Hippias' discourse, then, has not just been about Achilles and Odysseus; it has specifically concentrated on their performance (or otherwise) of *kala epitēdeumata*.

heroism simply appears to have been regarded as more noble than
Odysseus' heroics of endurance. Pindar *Olympians* 1.82–4 is also
relevant here,[61] in that it shows Pelops specifically opting for a
glorious death rather than a successful homecoming and old age:

... Great risk
does not take hold of the cowardly man.
But since man must die, why would anyone
sit in darkness and coddle a nameless old age to no use
deprived of all noble deeds?[62]

The message is plain: if Socrates wants to convince his audience
that Odysseus is at least Achilles' equal in *aretē* (never mind the
Protagoras' implication that he may even be superior), then he is
going to have his work cut out.

Nor is it just the case that Achilles' type of heroism was often
regarded as more estimable than that of Odysseus; there is plenty
of evidence that some examples of Odysseus' wiliness were not
regarded as estimable at all. The most notorious instance is perhaps his willingness to trick Philoctetes, *via* Neoptolemus, into
handing over the bow required for the capture of Troy. In his
treatment of the myth, Sophocles makes it clear that the deception
is ignoble, and it is significant that the criticism is put into the
mouth of Neoptolemus himself. Although Neoptolemus begins by
agreeing to the trick, he later comes to repent of his shabby role,
saying that his actions and words have been 'not right' and
'shameful' (902–3; 908–9). The same interpretation of the episode
is also made by Aristotle. At *Nicomachean Ethics* 1146a16–21 he
claims that there are times when it is 'praiseworthy' to abandon a
fixed opinion: Neoptolemus, for instance, is right to give up the
resolution to deceive Philoctetes which Odysseus persuaded him to
adopt. All this, of course, is in keeping with Hippias' story about
Neoptolemus asking Nestor which fine practices a young man
should pursue. Clearly, the more Neoptolemus represents the *kalon*, the more Odysseus will not; and the greater the gulf between
Neoptolemus and Odysseus, the greater the gulf between Odysseus and Neoptolemus' father, Achilles.

Odysseus, then, is by no means an unproblematic hero, as Hippias and Apeimantus recognize; if Achilles cannot serve straightforwardly as a role model and for comparison with Socrates, then

[61] Especially as it is a pre-Platonic source.
[62] Trans. Race. The sentiment is echoed, with satisfying irony, by Tennyson's Ulysses.

neither can he.[63] Each hero embodies a particular version of *andreia* which requires considerable purification if it is to be of use to Plato's educational project. As in the *Apology*, however, there may be indications at the end of the *Hippias Minor* that Socrates realizes some of the difficulties – at any rate, he closes with a questioning of accepted authorities which, though explicitly directed at Hippias, could also be intended to apply to Homer:

> In these matters I go astray, up and down, and never hold the same opinion. And it is not surprising if I, or any ordinary person, do stray. But if you wise men also stray, this is a terrible thing for us, if even when we have come to you we are not to cease from our straying. (376c)

In fact, Socrates' inconclusive, if fruitful, speculations on Homeric questions cease quite shortly. The *Apology*, *Hippias Major* and *Hippias Minor* show unequivocally that the old heroes are still powerful influences in Athens; they also show that reflection on the heroes and their codes of conduct raises ethical and psychological issues of the greatest importance. In the *Republic* we shall find Socrates confronting these issues directly.

---

[63] Odysseus of course is not always presented in such a poor light as he is in the *Philoctetes*; indeed, Sophocles himself gives a favourable portrayal of him in the *Ajax* (in 1356–7 he is even shown honestly speaking his mind). For a stimulating account of reactions to Odysseus from Archaic to modern times, *vide* Stanford (1954).

CHAPTER 7

The threat of Achilles

THUMOS AMOK

The importance of Achilles in *Republic* 2 and 3 has gone strangely unremarked.[1] He makes his first appearance at 379d, very near the beginning of the debate on the young Guardians' primary education. Socrates, disapprovingly, quotes Achilles' lines to Priam on Zeus' distribution of good and bad fates: in Socrates' view, God is responsible only for good; Achilles has got God wrong. From here until 391e, a mere twelve Stephanus chapters, there are fifteen more references to Achilles or his speeches, and two references to Patroclus.[2] Furthermore, fourteen of the sixteen references involving Achilles are sharply critical, and the remaining two voice laments by Thetis on the tragic destiny of her son. Far from being worthy of comparison with Socrates, Achilles is presented in the *Republic* as a highly undesirable role model in every way. What has caused this startling fall from grace?

My proposal is simple. I suggest that by the time of the *Republic* and its more sophisticated moral psychology, Plato has come to see Achilles as the archetypal examplar of the *thumos* gone awry: a terrible warning of what can happen to a man when he is not only characterized by his thumoeidic elements – which must of

---

[1] The major exception is Bloom (1968); I am deeply indebted to Bloom's interpretative essay for first bringing the role of Achilles in the *Republic* to my attention. Bloom, however, concentrates chiefly on the political threat that Achilles poses. To the best of my knowledge, no one has yet written extensively on the challenge that Achilles presents to Plato's ethics, psychology and metaphysics (though there is a helpful – if brief – discussion in Callen King 1987: 105–9).

[2] Achilles: 379d (*Il.* 24.527–33); 383b (Aesch. fr.350); 386c (*Od.* 11.489–91); 386d (*Il.* 23.103–4); 388a (*Il.* 24.10–12); 388b (*Il.* 18.23–4); 388c (*Il.* 18.54); 389e (*Il.* 1.225); 390e4–391a1 (3 references: *Il.* 9.515–18; *Il.* 19.279–80 and e.g. *Il.* 24.139); 391a5–c6 (5 references: *Il.* 22.15 and 20; *Il.* 21.129–32, 212–39, 265–6; *Il.* 23.140–51; *Il.* 24.14–18; *Il.* 23.175). Patroclus: 386d (*Il.* 16.856–7); 387a (*Il.* 23.100–1).

course be the case with all the Auxiliary class – but is actually dominated by them, instead of being ruled by his or someone else's reason. It is true, of course, that the tripartite division of the *psuchē* does not take place until Book 4; yet we saw in chapter 1 that the early education programme of Books 2 and 3, although directed to the entire *psuchē*, is particularly designed to train those characteristics that will later appear as the *thumos*. It is also specifically aimed at the future Auxiliaries, the *thumos'* equivalent in the state.[3] In this context, it is natural to suppose that Socrates focuses on Achilles because he understands his appeal to thumoeidic types, and because he wants to argue forcibly that such attraction is misguided. Achilles is the kind of fighter that the young Auxiliaries should definitely not emulate.

It is certainly not difficult to show that Homer's Achilles embodies many of the characteristics of the *thumos* in *Republic* 4 (at least in its untrained state) and of the timocratic state and man in Book 8. His bravery and warlike tendencies are not in question,[4] nor the fact that his aggressiveness is especially roused when he feels he has been wronged:[5] he is clearly the supreme embodiment of anger in Greek literature. He is also, like Leontius, well acquainted with a sense of shame, as his bitter self-recriminations in *Iliad* 18 show.[6] As for *Republic* 8, it is equally plain that honour and success are fundamental to him, and that he is a man who speaks his mind.[7] So much seems clear enough. What is notable, however, is how little use Socrates makes of Achilles' generally thumoeidic nature; he is only concerned with the words and actions which reveal what can happen to such a nature when it does not receive the benefits of his proposed education system. He has no

---

[3] See pp. 11–12 above.

[4] Though it is possible that his loathing of death prevents him from being *andreios* as defined at *Resp.* 429b–c; see below pp. 235–6.

[5] At *Ars Rhet.* 1378b31–5, Aristotle cites Achilles as the primary example of someone who is angry through wounded self-esteem.

[6] 'May I die straightway; since I was not to stand by my companion | when he was killed. And now, far from the land of his fathers, | he has perished, and lacked my fighting strength to defend him. | Now, since I am not going back to the beloved land of my fathers, | since I was no light of safety to Patroclus, nor to my other | companions, who in their numbers went down before glorious Hector, | but sit here beside my ships, a useless weight on the good land ...' (*Il.* 18.98–104; trans. adapted from Lattimore).

[7] At *Resp.* 547e3–4, the timocratic state is said to prefer 'simpler (ἁπλουστέρους), thumoeidic types, who incline to war rather than peace'; we have also seen Hippias describe Achilles as ἁπλούστατος at *Hp. Mi.* 364e7.

interest at all in presenting a fair and well-rounded portrait of Achilles' complex character.

The immediate target is political. Trainee Auxiliaries might well be expected to hero-worship the glamorous Achilles, whose exploits were so much a part of common cultural currency that in the *Ars Rhetorica* Aristotle says that when appealing to him as an example it is enough simply to name him, as 'everyone knows his deeds' (1416b26–8). The problem, of course, is that Achilles is a highly inappropriate role model for the kind of stalwart civic defence-force that Socrates wants. He may be brave and skilful, and motivated by a (highly personal) notion of the *kalon*, but he can also be wild, bloodthirsty and unruly, a supporter of the *lex talionis*[8] and notoriously contemptuous of his commander-in-chief; as a result, he comes perilously close to undoing nine years hard labour on the Achaeans' part single-handed. There is also the question of the extent to which fighting requirements and methods have changed. We have seen how the Athenian general Laches, when asked to define *andreia*, initially cites the example of the man who 'stays at his post and faces the enemy'.[9] It is an image which specifically calls to mind the hoplite resolutely standing in line; yet one may wonder how temperamentally suited Achilles would be to hoplite warfare: his yearning for individual glory might prove too much. All in all, the chances are that he would be a pretty disastrous inhabitant and defender of the ideal – and perhaps any – city-state.[10]

Socrates makes absolutely sure that the point is not lost. At 389e13 he gives us Achilles' pungent attack on Agamemnon as 'You wine-sack, with the eyes of a dog and the courage of a doe',[11] and says firmly that such lines must be censored because they scarcely encourage self-control. Achilles' verbal onslaught

---

[8] See p. 183 above.

[9] *Laches* 190e (p. 86 above). The hoplite ideal is eloquently voiced by the seventh century BC Spartan poet Tyrtaeus; see especially fr. 11, 7–14 and fr.12, 13–20. For changing fighting practices within the Greek world see Lloyd 1996; Dawson 1996; Cartledge 1977 and 1996; Salmon 1977. It is important, however, not to exaggerate the differences between Homeric and classical techniques and military ideals: see van Wees 'Heroes, knights and nutters: warrior mentality in Homer' in Lloyd 1996.

[10] It is true that during the fourth century BC there was a noticeable swing back in favour of more flexible fighting techniques: see Dawson 1996: 62. Yet the point remains that Achilles' intense *amour-propre* and preoccupation with personal glory would always be a potential threat to the safety of his community.

[11] *Il.* 1.225; the translation is adapted from Lee (1974).

on Apollo is also quoted and condemned, as is his refusal to obey the river-god Scamander and his willingness to fight him.[12] The message is plain: Achilles' *thumos* is in a state of complete insubordination to reason and in consequence he displays nothing but arrogance (*huperēphania* 391c5) towards his rightful masters, whether mortal or divine. If the young Auxiliaries want a role model, they had better choose someone else. The state needs obedient soldiers, not overmighty warriors.

Nor does Achilles simply pose a problem for the training of future Auxiliaries. Although he is explicitly contrasted with the ideal soldier within Books 2 and 3, his heroic status also presents difficulties for the emergence of a Philosopher-Ruler. How many young people are likely to be attracted to the philosophic ideal in a culture that heroizes Achilles? And how many philosophically-minded teachers would exist to try to persuade them? Furthermore, even if a philosopher did happen to emerge, she or he is highly unlikely to be accorded power – a point that Socrates emphasizes in *Republic* 487b–497a, where he vividly depicts the marginalization of philosophers in contemporary (and hence Homer-loving) Athens. Indeed, given the connections we saw in chapter 5 between the egoistic Homeric hero and the ruthless Calliclean lion, a state that admires Achilles may even unwittingly provide space for the rise of a tyrant.[13]

The political argument against Achilles, however, is only part of Socrates' case. As we have seen, the primary aim of the *Republic* is not the founding of the ideal state, but the demonstration that it pays the individual to be just.[14] This is the main purpose of the tripartite soul argument in Book 4: if justice in the *psuchē* consists in each element performing its proper function, and if this correct functioning also equals internal harmony and mental health, it is evident that justice benefits its possessor. The difficulty is that

---

[12] Apollo: *Il.* 22.15 and 20 (*Resp.* 391a5–7); Scamander: *Il.* 21.129–32, 212–39, 265–6 (*Resp.* 391b1–2); Scamander's own deception, however, is blatantly ignored by Socrates, as Callen King notes (1987: 109). Socrates also wilfully misrepresents Achilles' decision to dedicate to Patroclus a lock of hair originally promised to the River Spercheius (*Il.* 23.140–53; *Resp.* 391b): Achilles' father Peleus had vowed that if Achilles returned home safely to Phthia, then he would consecrate his hair to Spercheius; since Achilles now knows that he will never return home, he feels able to rededicate his hair to the memory of his companion.

[13] See pp. 140–1.

[14] Pp. 8–9.

Socrates' bold strategy also seems very vulnerable to the charge of equivocation: many have protested that he has only shown that the just soul is a flourishing one by rewriting the meaning of justice; he has not shown that flourishing requires justice in Thrasymachus' sense, the common-or-garden sense of treating others with fairness and decency.[15] It is a tough charge, and if Socrates is to combat it with any hope of success he will ultimately require a grand metaphysical theory in which goodness plays a central role: he will need to show that the person whose soul is ruled by reason can have no motivation to commit traditionally unjust acts, and this will mean showing that the rule of reason is equivalent to the rule of the Good.[16] However, though substantial backing for the Book 4 thesis must wait until the central books, this does not prevent Socrates from indicating earlier that he is aware of the need to connect his reworking of justice with traditional conceptions; nor does it prevent him from employing rhetorical devices to prepare the way for such a connection. Witness a passage in the Book 4 argument itself, in which Socrates is at pains to stress – though without any particular theoretical support – that his 'just' person will not perform any conventionally unjust actions, such as theft, treason or sacrilege.[17]

I suggest that, once armed with the knowledge of the later books, we can see that a similar rhetorical function is performed by Socrates' unashamedly selective portrayal of Achilles in Books 2 and 3. It is highly significant that at 391c Achilles is said to be in a state of 'disorder', *tarachē*: one of the meanings of *tarachē* is political tumult, and its use here – again in the light of the later psychology – vividly conveys a sense of the irrational elements of Achilles' soul rebelling against rational control. And Socrates is explicit that it is this internal disorder which is the cause of some of Achilles' most atrocious acts, such as dragging Hector's corpse round the tomb of Patroclus and slaughtering the young prisoners at his pyre.[18] These acts are expressly condemned by Socrates as further examples of Achilles' overweening arrogance (391c); moreover, it also seems clear that he intends them to be included in his general

---

[15] *Vide*, for example, Sachs 1963: 141–58 and Annas 1981: 167.
[16] These issues are discussed in Kraut 1973.
[17] *Resp.* 442d10–443b3.
[18] *Il.* 24.14 and 23.175, cited at *Resp.* 391b.

denouncement of the 'terrible and impious things which ... sons
of gods and heroes are said to have dared' (391d).

In this context, we might expect to find some detailed links between the depiction of Achilles and that of the timocratic state
and man, beyond the generally thumoeidic love of honour and
success, and penchant for plain-speaking. There would certainly
seem to be some. At 545d, for example, Socrates claims that the
initial cause of all decline from the ideal state is sedition, *stasis*,
amongst the leaders. *Stasis* is clearly one of Achilles' hallmarks,
and it is at any rate possible that Socrates has Achilles in mind
here. He definitely has Homer in mind, because at 545d7–e1 he
asks the Muses to tell him 'how the *stasis* first began'; the invoca-
tion is an adaptation of *Iliad* 16.112–13, where Homer similarily
asks the Muses to relate the origins of the fire amongst the
Achaeans' ships. And Socrates' audience would not have needed
reminding that the chief cause of the fire was Achilles' wrath and
seditious withdrawal from the fighting.

Other details may also be relevant. At 550b7 the timocratic
character is called 'haughty', *hupsēlophrōn*, which reminds us of the
portrayal of Achilles as 'arrogant' at 391c4–6. Perhaps the most
telling connection, however, is the initially puzzling ascription to
both Achilles and the timocratic man of materialism. At *Republic*
390e, Socrates says that we cannot regard Achilles as so grasping
that he accepted Agamemnon's gifts and refused to hand over
Hector's body unless he was paid a ransom; while at 391c Socrates
charges Achilles with an illiberal meanness over money. At first
sight, such criticisms seem manifestly unjust: it is clear that what
Homer's Achilles is really interested in is not so much the gifts
themselves but the honour that they represent;[19] indeed, Socrates'
own term for 'ransom' in 390e is *timē*. Yet Socrates' blatant mis-
representation of Achilles on this point anticipates a key characteristic of the timocratic man, since although the *philotimos* despises
money when he is young, he grows notably more materialistic with
age. His nature has an avaricious streak (*philochrēmatos* 549b3;
compare *philochrēmatia* 391c5). It is this streak which opens the way
for further degeneration from timocracy to oligarchy,[20] and the

---

[19] See, for instance, *Il.* 1.171; 9.648; 16.83–6. At *Ars Rhet.* 1361a37–8, Aristotle says that a
gift is both 'the giving of a thing' and 'a sign of honour'.
[20] *Resp.* 548a5–6; 550d.

reason it is able to develop is because the timocratic man has lost his best safeguard of '*logos* mixed with *mousikē*' (549b3–6).

Achilles and the *philotimos*, then, are both examples of what can happen when thumoeidic values usurp reason's position as the proper ruler of the soul, and it is consequently not surprising that at some points the two portrayals overlap. Yet although such links are revealing, they are still only links; in other respects, the Achilles of Books 2 and 3 differs markedly from the *philotimos*. The type of thumoeidic degeneration that Plato depicts through Achilles is far more extreme than that exemplified by the timocratic man: the latter remains a disciplined soldier, whereas Achilles at times really does go wild. The timocratic man has after all had some training in rational pursuits from his philosophic father; he has simply – and indeed only partially[21] – rebelled against it. Achilles, on the other hand, has had no such grounding in reason. Plato's point would seem to be that without such a grounding an aroused *thumos* has a propensity for rage which is truly savage.

In castigating Achilles' savagery, Socrates is on firm territory: some of Achilles' actions are condemned by various characters in the *Iliad* itself. Patroclus, for example, says that Achilles must be born of the cliffs and grey sea, so harsh and unyielding is his mind; while Apollo delivers a searing indictment of Achilles' treatment of Hector's corpse:

So Achilleus has destroyed pity, and there is not in him
any shame . . .
. . . he does dishonour to the dumb earth in his fury.[22]

It is also interesting how often the *Iliad*'s condemnations of Achilles specifically cite his *thumos* as the source of the problem. Apollo says that Achilles devours men like a lion which has given way to its arrogant *thumos*, while Ajax claims that Achilles has made his *thumos* savage, implacable and even straightforwardly bad. Phoenix, too, describes Achilles' obdurate wrath as having entered his *thumos*, as does Achilles himself.[23] Clearly, we need to

---

[21] *Resp.* 548e4–5; 550a7–b2.

[22] Patroclus: 16.29–35; Apollo: 24.39–54. It is true that Apollo has been biased against the Achaeans ever since Agamemnon abused his priest Chryses; this, however, does not detract from the central point, namely that criticism of Achilles is possible within the *Iliad*'s world as well as without.

[23] Apollo: 24.41–3; Ajax: 9.629–36: Phoenix: 9.436; Achilles: 16.206.

be careful here, as *thumos* in Homer is obviously not the same as
thumos in the *Republic*; nevertheless, as we saw in chapter 1, the distance between the two is not so great as to deprive the point of all
force.[24]

At this juncture, however, a problem arises. On the one hand,
in highlighting the unpalatable results of Achilles' wrath, Socrates
would simply appear to be voicing a commonly expressed view in
the ancient debate on anger: there is certainly no shortage of texts
denouncing the emotion, either in general or in its more extreme
manifestations.[25] Nor is Socrates the only person specifically to
condemn the ethic of revenge: at *Protagoras* 324a–b, for instance,
Protagoras says that,

> no one punishes wrongdoers simply because they have done wrong,
> unless one is to take irrational vengeance like a wild beast.

Furthermore, there is also good evidence that Socrates was right
to fear that young men might emulate the unlovely aspects of
Achilles' character: it is only too clear, for example, that Alexander's hero-worship of Achilles was responsible for some of his
most repulsive acts.[26] In short, the case against anger seems plain
enough. Yet on the other hand we also need to consider whether

---

[24] Pp. 7–8.

[25] The most severe censure of anger is to be found in the Stoics: in Seneca's *de Ira*, for
instance, anger is consistently portrayed as inhuman, destructive, senselessly obdurate
and completely unstoppable. It is never useful, not even in war. Aristotle's attitude is
more complex; but though, as we have seen, he holds that there are times when it is
proper and praiseworthy to be angry (e.g. *E.N.* 1125b31–2; see pp. 39 and 148–9 above),
he is also keenly aware of the dangers. In *E.N.* 1126a13–28 he distinguishes four different
ways in which anger may be excessive, saying that the most damaging is bitterness, which
is harmful both to the agent himself and to his closest friends. Though Achilles is not
specifically mentioned in this passage, it is clear that he would be the obvious example of
such bitterness; and he is explicitly cited by Aristotle as a general examplar of anger
(*orgē*) elsewhere (*Ars Rhet.* 1378b31–5).

[26] Plutarch claims that, when Hephaestion died, Alexander slaughtered young Cossaei as
human sacrifices to his dead companion (*Alexander* 72.3–5), just as Achilles had massacred
twelve young Trojans to be sacrificed on the pyre of Patroclus. Quintus Curtius (4.6.24)
and Hegesias (*FGrH* 142) also allege that during the siege of Gaza in 332, Alexander
not only dragged the enemy commander Batis behind his chariot, but did so while
Batis was still alive – an especially revolting attempt to outdo his idol. Furthermore, it
was an act of emulation which was apparently repeated in most of its sickening detail by
the Alexander-obsessed Caracalla (*Scriptores Historiae Augustae* 4.1–2). Even if these stories
are not true, the fact that their authors can believe or pretend to believe that they are
still shows that Socrates' fears concerning undisciplined thumoeidic role models are at
least partly justified. Directly or indirectly, the wrath of Achilles lived on. See pp. 176–8
above.

there is any necessary relation between anger and *andreia*; more precisely, we need to ask whether Socrates considers there to be such a relation. He is certainly explicit in *Republic* 375a that *thumos* is essential for *andreia*; the question, of course, is how *thumos* is to be translated here. Does it simply mean 'guts', 'mettle', or does it also imply anger? The image of the watchdog strongly suggests the latter (the dog is said to be 'annoyed' whenever it sees a stranger: 376a5), and there is no doubt that a central aspect of *thumos* in Book 4 is fierce indignation. Socrates would presumably reply that the kind of mettle required for *andreia* will usually manifest itself as some form of anger, but that this anger will be suitably controlled by reason. The example of Achilles, however, makes us wonder just how easy this control will be to effect. There is also the problem of ensuring that it is not subdued out of existence, with the result that the Auxiliaries lose their fighting edge.[27]

These difficulties aside, the fact remains that Socrates appears well justified in excoriating some of Achilles' actions,[28] and his further claim that these actions are caused by internal disorder skilfully prepares us for the psychology of the later books. Asserting that Achilles' lack of psychic harmony leads to conventionally unjust acts, however, is still only the first stage of Socrates' rhetorical purpose: to combat Thrasymachus and answer Glaucon's challenge, he must further show that the unjust person is not *eudaimōn*. It is partly with this in mind, I believe, that he also includes quotes which emphasize Achilles' unhappiness, such as his sorrowful lament on seeing the ghost of Patroclus and his terrible grief on hearing of Patroclus' death.[29] We need to take care here. I certainly do not wish to deny Socrates' express intentions in referring to such passages, namely his wish to censor any lines which might foster in the young Auxiliaries an inappropriate fear of death or excessive emotionalism; I simply wish to suggest that, in addition to these aims, Socrates wants to emphasize that Achilles is often wretched as well as unjust, a profoundly disturbed man whom no sensible person would want to emulate. Witness 386c5–7, a quote

---

[27] The intricate relations between *thumos*, anger and *andreia* are also discussed in ch. 1; see especially pp. 26–7 and 39.

[28] Mackenzie (1978) argues that even if Achilles' behaviour is not seen as specifically criminal in the *Iliad*, it clearly does damage and thus has the potential to be viewed as criminal by another society, such as Plato's.

[29] *Resp.* 386d4–5 (*Il.* 23.103–4); *Resp.* 388a5–b4 (*Il.* 24.9–12 and 18.23–4).

from the *Odyssey* in which the dead Achilles passionately expresses his wish that he were still alive:

> I would rather be above ground still and labouring for some poor portionless man, than be lord over all the lifeless dead. (*Odyssey* 11.489–91)[30]

Again, Socrates' overt reason for citing these lines is his belief that they will instil cowardice in the Auxiliaries; yet it is surely no accident that the Achilles they depict is the very opposite of an appealing role model. It is also telling that they will be cited again, to devastating effect, in the Simile of the Cave;[31] Socrates' rhetoric in this passage is unquestionably multi-textured.

In this context, it is notable that the first reference to Achilles in the *Republic*, 383b2–8, quotes a fragment from Aeschylus in which Thetis laments her son's untimely death; her sorrow at the brevity of his life is also the subject of 388c1. It is true, of course, that Socrates may not himself think that an early death is anything very lamentable, but the point is that the Achilles of the *Iliad* certainly does, and Thetis' suffering reminds us of this. Part of Socrates' intention, I submit, is to suggest that Achilles is painfully overattached to life because his *psuchē* is not in order.[32]

In highlighting Achilles' unhappiness, Socrates is once more on firm ground: the *Iliad* is full of passages in which Achilles bitterly deplores both his treatment and his fate, while at 18.86–7 his grief for Patroclus and realization that he was the cause of his death make him wish that he had never been born. Shakespeare calls his embattled Coriolanus a 'lonely dragon';[33] at *Iliad* 11.762, Nestor says of Achilles that he 'will enjoy his own valour in loneliness, though I think he will weep much, too late, when his people are perished from him'. When Patroclus is killed, Achilles is indeed alone, and he does weep much, too late. He certainly exemplifies the risks of the *thumos*-dominated life.

Many of these risks arise from the peculiarly problematic nature of *timē* as an object of desire. In the *Iliad*, *timē* is depicted as a finite commodity, and thus especially vulnerable. In Book 9, for instance, Achilles spurns Phoenix' attempts to persuade him to accept Aga-

---

[30] Trans. Shewring.
[31] See p. 237 below.
[32] The same would appear to be true of Thetis, though in her case the issue is complicated by her divine status.
[33] *Coriolanus* 4.1.30.

memnon's gifts, and suggests instead that Phoenix 'Be king equally
with me; take half of my honour' (9.616); while at 16.87–90, when
sending Patroclus back to battle, Achilles warns him

> When you have driven them from the ships, come back; although later
> the thunderous lord of Hera might grant you the winning of glory,
> you must not set your mind on fighting the Trojans, whose delight
> is in battle, without me. So you will diminish my honour.

If *timē* is in such limited supply, then adherents of the life of honour will often fail to gain or be deprived of their main objective;
in consequence, it is something that may have to be fought over as
well as for. Its fragility is exacerbated by the fact that it is often
symbolized through gifts and rewards which are open to appropriation by another: Agamemnon's secondment of Briseis, and
Achilles' furious response, show clearly that such appropriation of
a rival's symbolic property was thought to diminish the rival's *timē*
and enhance one's own.[34] These problems are part of a more general one, namely the fact that the timocratic life is disturbingly
lacking in self-sufficiency. As Aristotle succinctly observes, honour
'appears to depend more on those who confer it than on the recipient'.[35] Achilles can rage against his treatment all he likes; he
may believe that he has behaved honourably, but his honour is not
his to bestow. There will thus be ample cause both for wretched-
ness and for subversive behaviour: 'beware of the desire for glory',
writes Cicero in the *de Officiis*, 'for it takes away freedom'.[36]

The message is clear. Socrates may deliberately be omitting much
of the *Iliad*'s complexity, but his choice of Achilles as a warning
against an undisciplined thumoeidic life would appear to be highly
apt: Achilles demonstrates all too plainly that an untrained and
wilful *thumos*, bent on elusive *timē*, is always liable to wreak havoc,
both to society and to its possessor. In seeking to eliminate Achilles
as a potential role model for the necessarily thumoeidic Auxiliaries, Socrates undoubtedly has a powerful case.

---

[34] See, for example, *Il.* 1.171 and 6.648.

[35] *E.N.* 1095b24. Aristotle is quite explicit that honour is something to be parcelled out: at
E.N. 1130b31–2, for example, distributive justice is said to be concerned with the disposal
of 'honour, wealth and the other divisible assets of the state'. Such distribution in turn
leads to 1169a20–1, where honours are said to be among the goods which men 'struggle
to win' (περιμάχητα can convey both 'fought for' and 'fought over').

[36] *De Off.* 1.68. Mackenzie (1978) is particularly good on the vulnerability of *timē*.

THE TRAGIC SHADOW

Winning this case, however, may not be so easy. The first obstacle is that of Achilles' undoubted glamour. Socrates may do his best to play down this dangerous quality, but even he is forced into a grudging acceptance of Achilles' widespread appeal: when castigating his verbal attack on Agamemnon as a dog-eyed, doe-hearted winesack, he admits that it is not surprising that such lines give pleasure.[37] It is also significant that at 391a3–5, when referring to Achilles' alleged greed and clear insubordination, Socrates' tactic is to protest that he simply cannot believe that Achilles ever did such things. He knows that Achilles will continue to be hero-worshipped whatever happens; all that can be done is to try to revise the content of the worshipped heroism. And in this he is surely right: if the impetus to seek role models stems principally from the *thumos*, then it is natural that the role models sought will tend to be thumoeidic ones.[38]

Yet the toughest challenge that Socrates faces is the fact that Achilles does not, as it were, come alone. I wish to argue that the thumoeidic characteristics that Achilles embodies, both good and bad, arise directly from the Iliadic world-view that he represents – a world-view that is, furthermore, essentially tragic. If Socrates wishes to combat the untamed *thumos* of Achilles, therefore, he must confront and counter this tragic vision.

On what grounds can the *Iliad*'s vision be portrayed as tragic? Firstly, it depicts a world in which not only *timē*, but all goods are profoundly vulnerable. The beloved Patroclus, for instance, is only too clearly vulnerable, and the strong suggestion of Achilles' lament to Thetis at 18.79–82 is that he is also unique and irreplaceable:

My mother, all these things the Olympian brought to accomplishment.
But what pleasure is this to me, since my dear companion has perished,
Patroklos, whom I loved beyond all other companions,
as well as my own life.

The death of Patroclus, furthermore, is not simply a loss to Achilles: it is also indisputably a bad thing for Patroclus himself.

---

[37] *Resp.* 389e13–390a6, quoting *Il.* 1.225. See p. 201 above.

[38] At *E.N.* 1167a18–21, Aristotle also notes that we especially feel goodwill towards someone who is 'beautiful ... or manly (*andreios*) or the like, as in the case we mentioned (1166b35) of competitors in a contest'.

As we saw in chapter 6,[39] death in the *Iliad* is consistently portrayed as hateful and, to all intents and purposes, final: all that
survives in Hades is an insubstantial and witless wraith. When the
ghost of Patroclus visits Achilles in a dream, Achilles reaches out
to touch it, but,

the spirit went underground, like vapour,
with a thin cry, and Achilleus started awake, staring,
and drove his hands together, and spoke, and his words were sorrowful:
'Oh, wonder! Even in the house of Hades there is left something,
a soul and an image, but there is no real heart of life in it.' (23.99–104)[40]

We also saw in chapter 6 that it is because death is viewed as so
loathsome, and life as so precious, that Achilles' choice can be
viewed as a choice between the noble (plus the benefit of fame)
and the beneficial-in-all-other-respects: the supreme heroic virtue
of *andreia* comes at a very high price. Nor does Achilles feel able to
take much comfort in religion:

Such is the way the gods spun life for unfortunate mortals,
that we live in unhappiness, but the gods themselves have no sorrows.
There are two urns that stand at the door-sill of Zeus. They are unlike
for the gifts they bestow: an urn of evils, an urn of blessings.
If Zeus who delights in thunder mingles these and bestows them
on man, he shifts, and moves now in evil, again in good fortune.
But when Zeus bestows from the urn of sorrows, he makes a
failure of man, and the evil hunger drives him over the shining
earth, and he wanders respected neither of gods nor mortals.[41]

For Achilles, life may be deeply valuable, but the world is also
harsh and arbitrary, ruled over by capricious deities. Of all the
characters in the *Iliad*, it is perhaps his intermittently bleak outlook which most justifies Socrates in calling Homer the 'original

---

[39] P. 182.

[40] Compare the 'perished dead' who so horrify the ghost of Achilles in *Od.* 11.491, the flit-
ting wraiths who possess no real understanding. An extreme version of this Homeric view
of the after-life was still common in Plato's day: at *Phd.* 70a–b Cebes says that many are
afraid that when a man dies, the soul leaves his body and no longer exists anywhere,
scattering 'like breath or smoke'; considerable argument will be required to persuade
such people that the soul continues to exist after death and 'possesses power and intelligence'. This fear of the dispersal of the soul is picked up by Simmias in 77b, where he
says that it is held by 'the many': Socrates' theory of knowledge as recollection has convinced both Cebes and himself that the soul existed before birth; but it does nothing to
dispense with the fear that after death our souls are simply blown away. Once again, in
addressing the problems posed by Achilles, Plato is dealing with current concerns.

[41] *Il.* 24.525–33. Excerpts from this passage are quoted by Socrates at *Resp.* 379d–e; see
p. 199 above.

master and guide of all the great tragic poets' at *Republic* 595b–c, and the 'chief of tragedians' at 598d.[42]

In such a world, it is understandable that thumoeidic characteristics will achieve particular prominence, whether as prized virtues or simply as natural responses. At a general level, it is because this life matters that its victories and prizes matter, and the competitive type of *andreia* required to win them; it is an inevitable irony of the *thumos* that though it may often lead the hero to death, in essence it affirms life. And it is because the people and things that we value are so vulnerable, and in unique or limited supply, that the assertion needed to procure and protect them will often take the form of naked aggression. Self-assertion may also be prompted by a recognition of life's unpredictability: a magnificent gesture of defiance in a seemingly incomprehensible world. Conversely, the aims of the *logistikon* may well not seem appropriate in such a capricious universe; attempts at rational calculation of one's long-term overall good could easily appear futile.

The perception of death is also critical. If death is hateful and effectively final, then glory and a lasting name may be thought to matter hugely as compensation. Again, this link between world-view and thumoeidic ethos applies especially to Achilles, who not only regards death as generally loathsome and grim, but is also acutely conscious that in his own case it is approaching fast. When mourning the body of Patroclus, he laments that,

Thus it is destiny for us both to stain the same soil
here in Troy; since I shall never come home, and my father,
Peleus the aged rider, will not welcome me in his great house,
nor Thetis my mother, but in this place the earth will receive me
(18.329–32)

– a precognition that is repeated with increasing detail in later books.[43] The salient point here is that it is precisely because of this painful awareness of his own mortality that he usually places such importance on *timē*. Witness his anguished cry to Thetis at 1.352:

Since, my mother, you bore me to be a man with a short life,
therefore Zeus of the loud thunder on Olympos should grant me
honour at least. But now he has given me not even a little.

---

[42] Socrates also calls Homer 'the first of tragedians' at *Resp.* 607a, and 'the pinnacle of tragedy' at *Tht.* 152e.

[43] See 19.421–2; 21.103–13; 21.275–8. For the increasing precision of the references to Achilles' imminent death, *vide* Griffin 1980:163.

This strong connection between the acknowledged fact of mortality and the desire for glory is pivotal to the plot of the *Iliad*. At 9.314–45 we see it swinging the balance in Achilles' decision to remain out of the fighting: the Achaeans have not honoured him as he deserves, so why should he fight and risk death?[44] Under Agamemnon's degenerate rule,

Nothing is won for me, now that my heart has gone through its afflictions in forever setting my life on the hazard of battle. (9.321–2)

In Book 18, however, Achilles has recovered his old faith in the link between heroic death and glory. As we have seen, he is perfectly well aware that if he succeeds in killing Hector, as he surely will, then his own death is imminent. It is a fate which he now accepts with equanimity: even Heracles could not escape death, and 'So I likewise, if such is the fate which has been wrought for me, shall lie still, when I am dead' (18.121–2); but, 'Now I must win excellent glory' (18.122). The 'but' is mine; however, the inference is a natural one given the proximity of the thoughts in the text.

The life of the thumoeidic hero is thus grounded in a peculiarly bitter irony. His loathing of death makes him seek glory as a defiant means of compensation; yet the obtaining of glory will usually require risking, or even seeking, the very death that he abhors. The point is succinctly made by Lucretius in *de Rerum Natura* 3.59–82, where he observes that the 'blind desire for honours' is fed not least by the fear of death, while some men's fear of death is so great that they 'die for the sake of statues and a name' (3.78).[45]

There is a still darker side to the connection between death and glory, some of the consequences of which we have already explored. If death is so terrible, then an acute consciousness of one's mortality will mean that to some extent the *thumos* will *have* to go temporarily mad in order to overcome its aversion and perform the dangerous or self-sacrificial acts by which heroic fame is won. Consider, for example, Achilles' chilling exhortation to Agamemnon at 19.148 that 'Now let us remember our joy in warcraft', where the word translated as 'joy' is *charmē*, real blood-lust, the

---

[44] By 9.400–9 Achilles has talked himself into such a state of bitter disillusionment with the heroic ethos that he is not even sure that rewards and honours *could* compensate for the loss of one's life; but this is not his usual view. See p. 182 above.

[45] Cicero, too, in *de Div.* 1.63 writes that, when men see death approaching, 'their desire for fame is strongest'.

undiluted frenzy of war.[46] It is a battle-cry all the more disturbing for its apparent boys'-own simplicity, and is picked up disquietingly in 19.213–14, where Achilles proclaims that

Food and drink mean nothing to my heart
but blood does, and slaughter, and the groaning of men in the hard
work.

Of all the characters in the *Iliad*, it is Achilles whose intermittent lust for blood is fiercest; it is also Achilles whose awareness of death, and perception of death as something hateful, is keenest. I suggest that these facts are not unrelated.

So far we have considered the links between Achilles' tragic outlook and the thumoeidic facets of his character that Socrates wishes either to control or to extirpate completely. Yet equally problematic is the possibility that the world may need to be the way Achilles perceives it for the full flowering of a quality that Socrates very definitely does want to promote, namely courage. The ideal state is ideally just rather than ideal *simpliciter*; its citizens will still require *andreia*. Yet the harsher and more uncertain world of the *Iliad* might seem to provide more opportunities for courage to be developed, and for the raw drives that courage requires to be properly trained. In particular, the *Iliad* may be thought a more fertile breeding ground for courage in that it depicts a world at war in a way that the *Republic* does not.[47]

Such a possibility is disquieting enough in itself; taken to extremes, however, it can lead to the approval or even the active promotion of war as the essential condition for full manliness. Plato would seem to be well aware of this danger: at any rate, it is one of the signs of the degenerate timocratic state that it prefers war to peace,[48] and at *Politicus* 308a the Athenian Stranger says that the fostering of war is one of the distinguishing features of the undiluted *andreios* type. Witness, too, Euripides' *Andromache* 683, where Menelaus – admittedly somewhat defensively – declares

---

[46] The precise translation of *charmē* in any given context ('joy of battle' or just 'battle'?) has long been a matter of controversy: see van Wees (1996: n.14). I believe that Achilles' subsequent rampage indicates that in this passage he has the former meaning in mind.

[47] Although there is not space to discuss his challenging work here, it will be plain from the above that I am not in agreement with the main thrust of Craig 1994. Despite many interesting observations, I find his argument to rely on a dangerously selective reading of the text.

[48] *Resp.* 547e3–548a1.

that Helen has in fact done Greece a favour by causing a war, for the conflict has brought Greek men '*eis t'andreion*', it has made them brave and manly. War, it would seem, is a critical rite of passage to manhood, even if manhood is thereby abruptly curtailed: better to be a dead man than a live boy. While Achilles' stance towards both conflict in general and the Trojan war in particular is highly complex, some of his speeches and actions can certainly be interpreted as war-mongering: he knows that his brand of heroism requires a battlefield (18.105–6). A similar ambivalence runs throughout the entire *Iliad*: although it does not flinch from portraying the suffering and waste of war, it also undeniably exalts martial virtues, and may thus be viewed by some as exalting their context, whether intentionally or not. Nietzsche – at least in certain moods – illustrates the point. Although his attitude to war and militarism is also more complex than is often supposed, he can still praise the ancient heroes as wild and noble beasts, roaming in search of booty and victory,[49] and declare that

I welcome all the signs that a more manly, a more warlike age is beginning, which will, above all, bring valour again into honour!
... For, believe me! – the secret of realizing the greatest fruitfulness and the greatest enjoyment of existence is: *to live dangerously*!
... Live in conflict with your equals and with yourselves! Be robbers and ravagers as long as you cannot be rulers and owners, you men of knowledge.[50]

Such views are not endorsed in the *Republic*. Although the ideally just state certainly accepts the existence of war, it accepts it reluctantly, as an evil necessitated by the introduction of more sophisticated tastes and activities;[51] the preferred state is peace. Military heroes may be well rewarded,[52] but war itself is neither celebrated nor promoted. Yet the question remains: what if the degenerate thumoeidic view is right? What if *andreia* does require a fiercely belligerent outlook and the active advancement of war?

This leads to a further troubling thought. If manly nobility is believed to require conditions of war and tragedy for its full flowering, then the tragic itself may seem to take on an aura of beauty

---

[49] *Genealogy of Morals* 1.11.
[50] *The Gay Science* 4.283. Translation adapted from Kaufmann.
[51] *Resp.* 373d–e. The acquisitive origin of war is said to be the same as the origin of most evils (*kaka*) at 373e6–7.
[52] See pp. 233–4 below.

and nobility. Consider the powerful lines in which Achilles refuses the supplications of Lycaon and reflects on his own approaching end:

Do you not see what a man I am, how huge, how splendid
and born of a great father, and the mother who bore me immortal?
Yet even I have also my death and strong destiny,
and there shall be a dawn or an afternoon or a noontime
when some man in the fighting will take the life from me also
either with a spearcast or an arrow flown from the bowstring. (*Iliad* 21.108–13)

This portrayal of Achilles' death as something both tragic and beautiful is not simply the effect of the haunting poetry; it is also brought about by the heroic emphasis on the critical moment: the moment of death is also the fulfilment of heroic glory. In his funeral speech, Pericles praises the soldiers who risked their lives for Athens, and who, 'in a brief moment of time, the climax of their lives, a culmination of glory, not of fear, were swept away from us'.[53]

Some of the Auxiliaries, of course, will also die on the battlefield in the briefest of moments. Yet such moments of death are not given special prominence in the *Republic*; on the contrary, the emphasis is on the steadfast obedience, endurance and efficiency of the Auxiliaries over a period of time. As for the Philosopher-Rulers, one of the objectives of their lengthy training is to acquire a vision of the whole sweep of time, as 486a8–9 makes clear. In general, the painstaking educational programmes that Auxiliaries and Philosopher-Rulers must undergo both require and foster an appreciation of time as a continuum, a steady amassing of works and days.[54] It is true that in the philosopher's case this training results in a moment of supreme intensity, but this is the moment of the first revelation of the Form of the Good, not the moment of heroic death.

The challenge posed by Achilles, therefore, goes much deeper than may initially appear. If Socrates is to take him on, he will

---

[53] Thuc. 2.42; trans. adapted from Warner.
[54] The philosopher's need to think in terms of slow, steady progress is emphasized at *Sophist* 261b5–6, while *Laws* 643b4–7 stresses the need for constant and prolonged practice in any important pursuit. Intensity in the field of pleasure is denigrated at *Philebus* 45d–e, especially 45e2–4.

need to confront in its entirety the tragic world-view on which Achilles' qualities and values – both good and bad – are based; above all, he must repudiate the belief that one may have to make a tragic choice between the noble and the personally beneficial. In the process he must sever the links between *andreia* and tragedy, and carefully limit the strength of the connection between *andreia* and war, so that war and violence are not at risk of being glorified and engineered.

Now it is certainly true that Socrates attempts to do all these things in the course of the *Republic*, as we shall see in the next chapter; the question we need to ask first, however, is whether he attempts them at least partly in response to Achilles. There is good – though admittedly not incontrovertible – evidence that he does. To begin with, it is plainly the simplest hypothesis: Socrates is strongly critical of both Achilles and tragedy, and as we have seen he explicitly states at 598b that he regards Homer as the 'chief of tragedians'; he is also explicit in castigating Achilles not only for his wildness, but also for his – in Socrates' eyes – excessive displays of grief and misguided view of the human lot. Achilles has not realized that death holds no terrors for Patroclus (387d); indeed, it may hold positive benefits. He is also mistaken in his belief that Zeus is capricious, and that good and bad fortune are distributed at random (379d–e). Moreover, the Achilles of Books 2 and 3 is clearly guilty of what Book 10 will cite as perhaps the most fundamental misjudgement of the tragic outlook: he has entirely failed to understand that human affairs are simply not worthy of great concern (604b–c).[55] If human life is not worth much, then it cannot be tragic: tragedy presupposes above all that what happens to us has some significance, even if it is only the significance of emphasizing our littleness in relation to the cosmos. From the tragic perspective, the realization of mankind's littleness is poignant and keenly felt; from Socrates', it is merely a rational acknowledgement of the proper order of things. Man does not matter much, and the perception that this is so does not matter much either.

Given all this, it would be extraordinarily perverse to say that Socrates wishes to deny the validity of the tragic perspective, but that he does not have Achilles partly in mind when he does this.

---

[55] *Vide* also 486a8–10; *Symp.* 211d8–e3 goes even further in scorning this world of 'mortal trash'.

Furthermore, there is also structural evidence that Achilles is one of the spurs to Socrates' denial. As we shall shortly see, the reworking of the *kalon* and the *agathon* which forms the core of Socrates' rejection of the possibility of tragedy begins in Book 3, immediately after the discussion of suitable role models in which Achilles has figured so prominently;[56] and it culminates with an adroit adaptation of some lines spoken by Achilles' shade in the *Odyssey* – the very same lines, moreover, which appeared in their original form at 386c at the start of the reworking.[57] Again, it seems highly likely that Achilles has been one of the factors in Socrates' mind throughout his exploration and reassessment of the two fundamental value terms.

It may still be argued that although Socrates views Achilles both as a representative of the tragic perspective and as a potent symbol of *thumos* run amok, he does not necessarily connect the latter traits with the former in the way I have suggested above. It is true that there is no direct proof that Socrates (or Plato) has made the connection, but once more I would appeal to the principle of simplicity. The selection of quotes shows that Socrates certainly appreciates that such traits come as a package, and it is reasonable to assume that he is at least to some degree aware of the links.

It is my contention, then, that in the central books of the *Republic* Socrates is not simply taking up the challenges laid down by Thrasymachus and Callicles; he is also deliberately addressing the threat posed by Homer's Achilles. Thrasymachus and Achilles both represent unwelcome responses to the *Republic*'s central question of whether virtue brings happiness to its practitioner,[58] and their combination presents Socrates with a peculiarly delicate task. On the one hand, he must show that Thrasymachus and Callicles were wrong to identify personal excellence with an ideal of flourishing viewed solely in terms of worldly success and material well-being; on the other, he must prove that Achilles is mistaken in thinking that *aretē* and *eudaimonia* can ever be divorced, and that one may sometimes have to choose between the two. The *agathon*

---

[56] See pp. 227–30 below, and compare *Hp. Mai.* 286a–d (p. 190 above), where Socrates' attempt to define the *kalon* is also prompted by an appeal to traditional heroic aspirations. In the *Symposium*, too, Phaedrus' opening account of the *kalon* behaviour which love inspires relies heavily on the notion of heroic self-sacrifice (179b–180b).

[57] See pp. 207–8 above and 237 below.

[58] And note how soon the discussion of Achilles comes after Glaucon's posing of this question.

and the *kalon* must be united, but not as Callicles or Thrasymachus would wish; in the process, a new conception of *andreia* must inevitably be developed.

It is now, finally, time to consider the precise form of Socrates' response, and whether or not it succeeds.

CHAPTER 8

Plato's response: the valuable as one

THE BEAUTIFUL AND THE GOOD

Socrates' reply is, of course, founded on the Forms. The reason that this life is not of great significance is that reality lies elsewhere (500b), and the reason death is to be welcomed rather than feared is that it is simply the sloughing off of the body and the release of the *logistikon* into the purely intellectual realm of Forms which is its true home (611b–612a). Furthermore, if the Forms are the divine (500c9) origin of all the goodness and beauty in the phenomenal world, then it would seem that divinity is not capricious or dangerous. There is also a point which is implicit in the *Republic* and explicit in the *Symposium*: if all beautiful loved ones (and loved objects) participate in the single source of Beauty itself, then they will all, Socrates thinks, be beautiful in the same way.[1] The beloved is therefore not unique and irreplaceable, as Achilles mistakenly believes, but the replaceable token of an enduring type; for this chilling reason, too, the fear of his or her loss or death will be greatly diminished.

Equally important from our present perspective is the fact that the Forms preclude the necessity of making tragic choices between noble and beneficial courses of action. There are two possible ways in which this might be so. The more common, and less controversial, reading is that the ultimate cause of both all good and all beautiful particulars is the same, namely the Form of the Good. In support of such an interpretation we may perhaps attest 505b2–3, where knowledge of the Good is said to enable us to understand not only what is *agathon* in the sensible world, but also what is *kalon*; also relevant is 506a4–6, where Socrates claims that

---

[1] *Symp.* 210a–212a, following on from the argument of 199c–201c. Contrast *Il.* 18.79–82 (discussed on p. 210 above).

the only useful Guardian of 'just and *kala* things' is the person who knows in what way they are *agatha*. And at 517c1–2 the Form of the Good is said to be the inferred cause (*aitia*) of all *kala*. Further evidence is provided during the discussion on whether women should exercise naked like men (452a–e), in which Socrates argues that it is foolish to regard anything as ridiculous except what is bad and harmful (*kakon*): indeed, no one 'can be serious about the *kalon* unless he keeps his eye solely on the mark of the good'[2] – a warning which seems to be repeated at 457b4–5, where he states firmly that 'it is and will be finely said, that the beneficial is *kalon*, and the harmful is *aischron*'.[3] The substitution of 'beneficial' for 'good' is important: Socrates is well aware that it is the alleged tension between the *kalon* and, specifically, the good-*qua*-beneficial that he needs to deny.

Such a reading will, I believe, effectively serve the required purpose of reducing the potential for a tragic split between noble and beneficial options: even if the set of *kala* is not actually coextensive with the set of *agatha*, there is still only one criterion by which all valuables are to be known and judged. Yet I also wish to submit that this purpose will be even better served if we adopt a more radical interpretation of the nature of the relationship between the *agathon* and the *kalon*; and I further believe that this more radical interpretation has good, if not conclusive, textual support.

So far we have concentrated on the relation between the Form of the Good and good and fine particulars. What of the relation between the Forms of the Good and the Beautiful themselves? It is certainly safe to say that they are, at the very least, represented as being entirely harmonious: the realm of the Forms in general is said to be a place where 'everything is in (beautiful) order[4] and

---

[2] *Resp.* 452e1–2. I have translated τοῦ ἀγαθοῦ in the lower case as Forms have not explicitly been introduced into the dialogue at this point.

[3] Taken in isolation, this sentence could be taken to mean that the set of beneficial things is incorporated into the set of *kala*. The context, however, makes it clear that it is *kala* and *aischra* which are to be identified according to the concepts of benefit and harm: no one can regard a woman exercising naked as shameless when they realize that exercising in this manner is the most efficient way for her to become fit, and a fit female Guardian is of benefit to the state. At 601d, too, Socrates claims that the excellence, beauty and correctness of every implement, creature or action lies in its usefulness.

[4] 'Order' translates *kosmos*, which often carries an aesthetic connotation. See, for example, *Resp.* 403a: 'to love rightly is to love what is orderly and beautiful (κοσμίου τε καὶ καλοῦ) in an educated and disciplined way'.

according to reason' (500c4–5), and the Form of the Good is also specifically said to be 'more beautiful' than knowledge and truth at 508e6, and of 'extraordinary beauty' at 509a6–7.[5] It is my contention, however, that we can go further. I believe there is some indication that, although the human *concepts* of goodness and beauty/nobility differ, the 'Form of the Good' itself is actually identical in reference to the 'Form of Beauty';[6] I also believe that such a theory is perfectly compatible with the above quotes about the Good being the ultimate criterion of fine and beautiful things and practices and indeed the cause of beautiful things themselves.

The main textual evidence is arguably the very claim in 517c which could be thought to pose a serious problem for this theory, namely the assertion that the Form of the Good is the inferred cause of all *kala*. For we already know from 475–9 that *kala* things are *kala* through participation in the Form of the *Kalon*. If Socrates is to escape a charge of inconsistency or extreme incompleteness in presenting his thought, then we must assume that he is treating the two Forms interchangeably.

Further evidence arises from a comparison between *Republic* 505d11–e1 and *Symposium* 210e4–6 and 211c2. In the *Republic*, the Form of the Good is said to be 'that which every soul pursues and for the sake of which everything is done';[7] in the *Symposium*, however, it is the Form of *Beauty* which is 'that for the sake of which all previous labours were undertaken', and which is the 'final goal' (*telos*), 'that for the sake of which' the lover 'always strives'.[8] Moreover, such language also recalls *Symposium* 204e–205a, where *eudaimonia*, explicitly said to be achieved through the acquisition of *agatha*, is claimed to be the final goal (*telos*) of all our desires. The Form of Beauty, in other words, also appears to be the final *agathon*, the ultimate dispenser of *eudaimonia*.

Plainly, such parallels will only carry significant weight if there is also evidence that Plato intended the two dialogues to be read in conjunction. I believe that there is. With the partial exception

---

[5] Although Glaucon in 509a is making fun of Socrates' high-flown language, it is a joke which Socrates is perfectly happy to take at face value.

[6] This is not to claim that Plato is operating with a fully articulated sense-reference distinction in the *Republic* (or indeed in any dialogue, though the *Sophist* might be a contender); I do, however, believe that the distinction can helpfully be applied by us to Plato's text.

[7] ὃ δὴ διώκει μὲν ἅπασα ψυχὴ καὶ τούτου ἕνεκα πάντα πράττει (*Resp.* 505d11–e1).

[8] οὗ δὴ ἕνεκεν καὶ οἱ ἔμπροσθεν πάντες πόνοι ἦσαν (*Symp.* 210e5–6); τέλος (210e4); ἐκείνου ἕνεκα ... ἀεὶ ἐπανιέναι (211c2).

of the educational programmes laid out in Books 2–3 and 7,[9] the *Republic* is mostly directed towards the consequences and implications of the Philosopher-Rulers' knowledge of the Forms; the *Symposium*, on the other hand, is concerned to show us how we are motivated to ascend to such knowledge in the first place. These complementary roles are highlighted by a comparison of each dialogue's opening words. In the *Republic*, Socrates tells an unknown interlocutor that 'I went down (*katebēn*) yesterday to the Piraeus'; while in the *Symposium*, Apollodorus recounts to his – also unknown – companions how 'the day before yesterday I happened to be going up to town'. The *Republic* descends from the realm of the Forms to the everyday world: at 516e4 the Philosopher-Ruler 'goes down' (*katabas*) from the sunlit heavens back into the cave. The *Symposium* moves in the opposite direction: it ascends from the everyday world of individual loves and their beautiful flesh to the vision of Beauty itself. In terms of our moral progress, therefore, the *Symposium* is prior. Socrates went down to the Piraeus yesterday; Apollodorus went up to town the day before.

The identity of the two Forms in reference would also make sense of a number of passages in Plato which go considerably further than simply suggesting that the good is the mark or origin of what is to count as fine and beautiful. We have already seen how, in the *Hippias Major*, Socrates rejects two proposed definitions of the *kalon* because they would mean that 'neither could the good be *kalon* nor the *kalon* good, but each of them is different from the other';[10] while at *Alcibiades I* 116c1–2, Socrates concludes an argument based on the double meaning of 'doing well' by saying that 'So it has appeared to us once again that fine and good are the same thing.'[11]

In the *Symposium*, too, Socrates' dialectical interchange with Agathon from 199c–201c only works if the set of *agatha* is coextensive with the set of *kala*. Socrates first persuades Agathon to agree that *erōs* is directed towards things it lacks, and that these things must be *kala*. Then, at 201c2, he asks whether it does not seem to

---

[9] 'Partial' because, while such programmes train future philosophers (and, in the case of Books 2 and 3, Auxiliaries), they are also the product of the Philosopher-Rulers' rule.

[10] *Hp. Mai.* 303e13–304a2; see p. 189 above.

[11] Again, even if *Alc. I* is spurious, it is still significant that its author thought that this conclusion would be accepted as a Platonic thesis.

Agathon that good things are beautiful, and Agathon concurs. Taken on its own, such a claim could of course be compatible with a state of affairs in which some beautiful things were not good, but this possibility is precluded by Socrates' next move: 'Then if *erōs* lacks beautiful things, and good things are beautiful, it must lack good things too' (201c4–5) – to which Agathon again consents. If *agatha* and *kala* were not here conceived as coextensive, then it would clearly be possible for *erōs* to lack only those *kala* which were not good.

The theory that the Forms of the Good and the Beautiful are identical in reference also receives considerable support from Plotinus. Admittedly, Plotinus' exploration of their relation in middle Plato is not conclusive;[12] nevertheless, during a discussion of the *kalon* which draws on the *Republic*, *Symposium* and *Phaedrus*, he suggests at 1.6.9 that the Good may loosely be called 'the primary Beautiful'; another possibility is that the Good and the primary Beautiful exist 'in the same place' (or 'on the same level'). Even more explicit is a passage in 1.6.6 where he writes that

for God, good and beautiful are the same thing, or the Good and Beauty. So beauty and good, ugly and bad, must be sought in the same way. And first we must posit Beauty, which is also the Good.[13]

Equally significant is the issue of how Plotinus treats the *kalon* and the *agathon* in practice. The overall structure of 1.6, for instance, is closely based on the *Symposium* and its ladder of rational erotics ascending towards the Beautiful;[14] yet at *Ennead* 1.6.7 he writes 'So we must ascend again to the Good, which every soul desires', and then proceeds to describe this Form of the Good not only as *kalon*, but also as 'simple, single and pure' (*eilikrines*, *haploun* and *katharon*) – epithets which, with the substitution of 'unmixed' (*amikton*) for 'single', are specifically grouped together at *Symposium* 211e1 to describe the Form of Beauty.[15] It would seem that Plotinus has taken

---

[12] Contrast *Enneads* 1.6 with 5.5.12 and 6.7.22.

[13] Translation mine. Any translator of Plotinus has to make inevitably controversial decisions regarding the use of upper or lower case for such terms as beauty and good.

[14] *Vide* particularly 1.6.1, where physical beauty is called a 'ladder' (ἐπιβάθρᾳ), and compare with the 'steps of the ladder' (ἐπαναβασμοῖς) at *Symp.* 211c3. Plotinus then ascends steadily through the increasingly abstract order of *kala* outlined in *Symp.* 211b7–d1.

[15] These adjectives are of course *separately* ascribed to various Forms in several passages in Plato (e.g. *Phd.* 66a2: εἰλικρινές; 80d6: καθαρόν). The salient point here is their *grouping*.

the thesis he puts forward in 1.6.6 to heart, and is here treating the two Forms interchangeably.

A theory positing identity of reference, therefore, would explain much. Yet it must also face an obvious challenge: if a single referent exists for the Forms of Beauty and the Good, how does one account for the undeniable fact that at 505a2 the 'greatest knowledge' is said to be knowledge of the Form of the Good? Even given Socrates' *caveats* that a complete account of the Good is far beyond the scope of the present discussion,[16] this is clearly a question that must be faced.

I believe that we need to pay careful attention here to Socrates' choice of diction. Nowhere is the 'Form of the Good' said to differ in (what we might term) reference from the 'Form of Beauty'; it is simply that *knowledge* of the Good is superior. And the reason why this is so is because it is knowledge of the Good which is most useful to humans: what is the point of knowing or possessing anything, Socrates asks, if you do not know how to benefit from it?[17] Many people would choose to do or possess things which only appear to be just and fine, but are not so in reality; yet no one is content to possess the mere appearance of goods. When it comes to *agatha*, we all want the real thing (505d5–9). As the passage from *Symposium* 205a quoted above makes clear, it is the possession of good things which constitutes *eudaimonia*, and *eudaimonia* is the ultimate goal of all human desire and endeavour.

If we bear these things in mind, we are in a position to give an alternative reading of most of the texts which have often been assumed to show that the Form of the Good is separate from, and superior to, the Form of Beauty. The reason that we cannot properly understand what is *kalon* without knowledge of the Good (505b2–3) is not that the 'Form of the Good' is necessarily different in reference from the 'Form of Beauty'; it is rather that we can only fully understand *kala* things if we appreciate how they are useful and beneficial, and we can only do this by appreciating how they 'use' the Form of the Good (505a3–4). This is also the reason why the only worthwhile Guardian of 'just and *kala*' things is the person who knows in what way they are *agatha* (506a4–6): it is only this knowledge which will enable him or her successfully to defend fine and just things in argument.

---

[16] 506d–e; 509c.   [17] 505a6–b2. Compare *Euthyd.* 288d–292a.

Such an interpretation would also account for the assertion at 508e5–6 that the Form of the Good is 'other and more beautiful' than knowledge and truth, and even 'beyond' being (*ousia*) in both dignity and power (509b9–10). It is superior to knowledge, truth and being because it is their *cause*, and must therefore, Socrates thinks, be logically separate.[18] Again, we need to pay close attention to Socrates' diction: in this passage the Form of the Good is not said to be the cause of things *simpliciter*, but of things *qua* objects of knowledge.[19] In post-Homeric Greek, we may remember, *alētheia* means both 'truth' and 'reality': the inference is that unless things are intelligible they cannot strictly be said to be real; knowledge and reality imply each other.[20] The upshot is that if intelligibility derives from the Good, then reality does too.[21]

In the *Republic*, therefore, the Form of the Good is privileged because it is the concept of the good which best explains human desire and action. There is nothing which conclusively proves that its reference is not the same as the reference for the 'Form of Beauty', and some evidence that it is. It is at least possible that the difference lies not between the Forms themselves, but between different human conceptions of the same object.

Whatever the truth of such speculations, it is nevertheless clear that the unification of the two Forms – however achieved – is a powerful response to Achilles' assumption that there are painful choices to be made between the noble and the personally beneficial. Furthermore, it is also a cogent reply to Thrasymachus. We saw in chapter 5 that Thrasymachus, too, unifies the fine and the beneficial; the problem for Socrates is that he achieves this by equating *aretē* with an ideal of flourishing viewed solely in terms of worldly success and material gain. The central books of the *Republic* unequivocally rule out such a conception of *eudaimonia*. *Eudaimonia* can now be seen to consist in that inner psychic harmony which can only be brought about by the rule of reason and rea-

---

[18] It must be stressed, however, that Socrates is far from consistent on this point, and often ascribes reality and truth to all the Forms (e.g. at 500b–c and 595–602).

[19] τοῖς γιγνωσκομένοις (509b6).

[20] See, for example, *Resp.* 585c–d, where Socrates states plainly that the reality of the unchanging is as knowable as it is real, while 'a lesser degree of truth means a lesser degree of reality'.

[21] In Plotinus, being and knowledge appear jointly on the level of the second hypostasis: *vide* especially 5.5.1–6.

son's knowledge of, and desire for, the purely rational Forms, particularly of the Beautiful and the Good.[22] Reason, in short, is not simply a means to procuring the ends of the *thumos* and *epithūmētikon*; it possesses its own superior goals of truth and reality, and must rationally give these goals preference. The resultant unification between the *kalon* and the *agathon* at the personal level will thus be quite different from that advocated by Thrasymachus.

BEAUTY, GOODNESS AND EARLY EDUCATION

Socrates' answer to both Thrasymachus and Achilles, however, does not just rest on the relationship between the Forms; it also rests on their individual constitution. What do the Forms of the Beautiful and the Good – indeed all the Forms – comprise? The most plausible answer seems to be that they are proportional structures or ratios. Witness a crucial passage at 486d, in which Socrates highlights one of the most important qualities required in the true philosopher:

– But furthermore we would say that a tasteless and graceless nature inevitably leads to disproportion.
– Absolutely.
– And is truth akin to disproportion or proportion?
– To proportion.
– So, in addition to all the other qualities, let us also seek a mind endowed with proportion and grace, whose nature will allow it to be led to the form of each reality.[23]

It is the notion of proportion which allows for (though it admittedly does not necessitate) the identity in reference of the Forms of Beauty and the Good. Proportion can be conceived as valuable in a number of ways: it may be considered as beneficial and wholesome, morally fine or aesthetically pleasing. Speaking very roughly, when it is perceived to be beneficial or wholesome it will be called *agathon*; when it is perceived as beautiful or fine, it will be termed *kalon*. 'All the *agathon* is *kalon*', we are told at *Timaeus* 87c, 'and the *kalon* is not disproportionate. So every living creature that is to be thus [*agathon* in body and mind] must also be of due proportion.'

---

[22] This will be a true account of the Philosopher-Rulers' *eudaimonia*; in the case of Auxiliaries or Producers, *eudaimonia* will still consist in the rule of (their individual) reason, but this will now entail willingly submitting to the reason of the Rulers.
[23] Translation mine.

The concepts of *agathon* and *kalon* will thus differ, but they might well have a single reference, a single non-sensible proportional structure.

Less contentiously, it is because the realm of the Forms is intrinsically proportionate and graceful[24] that the philosopher who seeks to sculpt society in its image can be termed an artist (500e–501c).[25] Furthermore, it is I believe precisely because proportion can be viewed as beneficial, morally valuable and aesthetically pleasing that the philosopher-artist can attempt to create his just society by first instilling a sense of rhythm and *harmonia*[26] in the souls of his or her subjects. The process is eloquently described in 400c–403c, in which Socrates expounds the theory underlying the Guardians' early education. He begins by making what initially seems a strange claim, namely that beautiful works of art can only arise from goodness of character. At first sight, such an assertion appears to indicate a profound insensitivity to aesthetic considerations; yet closer examination of the text shows that exactly the opposite is true. The word for beauty in this passage is *euschēmosunē*, which literally means 'well-formedness', while good character is described as a habit of mind that is 'well and beautifully arranged' (400e2–3). Sensible beauty, in other words, is the outer expression of inner harmony[27] and grace, and beauty and moral goodness are thus 'akin' (401a8).

This gives Socrates his opportunity. He knows that one cannot rationally persuade very young children to be good, since reason does not develop until later; he also knows that if children do not develop good habits at a pre-rational stage, they may never do so. However, if beauty and good character are indeed akin, then the problem can be solved: good habits can be instilled in young *psuchai* by immersing them in sensible beauty, since

rhythm and mode (*harmonia*) penetrate deeply into the *psuchē* and take a most powerful hold on it, bringing and imparting beauty (*euschēmosunē*) if the education is correct, and imparting the reverse, if it is not. (401d6–e1)[28]

---

[24] Cf. also *Resp.* 500c4–5, quoted above pp. 221–2. Κατὰ λόγον can mean 'proportional' as well as 'according to reason'.

[25] The philosophic legislator is also called an artist at *Laws* 817b.

[26] For the complexities of translating *harmonia*, see p. 62 n. 31 above.

[27] 'Harmony' may seem to be stretching the meaning of 'well and beautifully arranged' (κατεσκευασμένην), but I believe that the account of mode (ἁρμονία) penetrating deeply into the *psuchē* at 401d6–7 makes it legitimate. See p. 62 above.

[28] Translation adapted from Lee.

An initial appreciation of sensible beauty can thus be internalized and transformed into the inner harmony of the soul which is *aretē*, and beautiful in its own non-sensible right. When this occurs, the child will grow into a true *kalos k'agathos* (402a1); for once the conventional phrase takes on real point. With this in mind,

we must look for craftsmen innately capable of tracking the nature of beauty and grace, so that the young males, living as it were in a healthy place, may benefit whenever some effect of the beautiful creations strikes their sight or hearing, like a breeze bearing health from wholesome places, insensibly leading them from earliest childhood to conformity, friendship and concord (*sumphōnia*) with beautiful reason. (401c4–d3)[29]

In his stipulations regarding the role of artists and craftsmen, Socrates treats beauty and moral goodness not simply as akin, but almost as interchangeable: while craftsmen are required to perceive 'the nature of beauty' at 401c5, at 401b2 they are asked to produce 'an image of good character'. It is also important that reason is itself depicted here as something *kalon*: it is because of this that the child who has been brought up to love sensible *kala* will later be able to recognize and welcome reason owing to the similarity between them (402a3–4).

Nor is Socrates' strategy in this passage simply to unite aesthetic beauty with moral beauty and goodness. In a clear anticipation of Book 4, it is plain that the development of a good character through immersion in *kala* is also perceived as *beneficial* to the child: it is the acquisition of psychic health. Again, this notion becomes easier to understand if beauty and moral goodness are conceived as proportions; we are being led to appreciate what it is that connects, firstly, sensible *kala* to the moral *kalos k'agathos*, and, secondly, the moral *agathos* to the *agathon qua* beneficial.

It is, furthermore, a strategy facilitated by the skilful harnessing of the *thumos*. We have already seen that it is to the *thumos* that this early education programme is principally directed, though it was not clear at that stage of the argument just why the *thumos* was supposed to be responsive to sensible *kala*; we have also seen that the *thumos* is content with things which merely seem to be fine and just.[30] The close connection between sensible and moral *kala*, however, is now plain; and it is also plain that if the *thumos* is content

---

[29] Translation mine.   [30] See pp. 12 and 18 above.

with apparent moral *kala*, it will be content with apparent sensible *kala* as well. Given its need for social approval, it will be responsive to generally accepted canons concerning both aesthetic beauty and the moral good. All the Philosopher-Ruler needs to do, therefore, is ensure that only true *kala* form part of this accepted canon: owing to the socially-regarding nature of the faculty that first responds to sensible beauty as beauty,[31] our notion of what is to count as *kalon* will be easier to work on than our notion of what is beneficial. If the *thumos* is directed towards the appropriate aesthetic *kala*, however, it will end up promoting a moral *kalon* which is also the internalization of *logos*. In these circumstances it will indeed be reason's natural ally (440b3): both parts of the *psuchē* will be serving the same objective under different descriptions.

If the above education goes according to plan, the early immersion in sensible beauty will result in the truly just person described by Socrates at 443d3–e2, for whom justice is not simply a matter of external actions, but an internal harmony of soul. Such a man will not allow the three elements in his *psuchē* to interfere with each other's functions, but

by keeping all three in tune, like the notes of a scale (high, middle and low, and any others that may exist), he will truly set his house to rights, attain self-mastery and order and achieve good terms with himself. By binding all these elements together he will genuinely become one instead of many, self-controlled and harmonious.[32]

Self-control (*sōphrosunē*) is also defined at 430e3–4 as 'a kind of concord and harmony', while at 413e and 423e Socrates says that the aim of the primary education system is to produce men who are rhythmic, harmonious and measured.[33] The point is emphatically repeated at 588a, where the just man is said to be infinitely superior to the unjust man in terms of 'grace and beauty of life'; while in 591d we are told that the just man attunes the harmony of his body to the harmony of his *psuchē*, since he is a 'true *mousikos*'. In short, it is fast becoming clear why at 445c5–6 we are told that 'there is only one form (*eidos*) of virtue': it is an internalization of proportional beauty.

---

[31] Rather than as simply pleasurable; see ch. 2 pp. 58–9.
[32] The translation is based on Lee.
[33] *Metrioi* can also mean proportionate.

ANDREIA REVISITED

What are the implications of all this for *andreia*? We are now in a position to return to the definitions proposed in Book 4 and consider them in more detail.[34] At 442b11–c3, Socrates says that an individual is *andreios* when his *thumos* 'holds fast to the orders of reason about what he ought or ought not to fear, in spite of pleasure and pain'; while at 429c–430b 'political' *andreia* is said to be the ability to retain safely in all circumstances correct opinion concerning what things are to be feared, without being distracted by pleasure, pain, fear or desire:

> Assume, then, . . . that this was the sort of result we were doing our best to achieve when we chose our soldiers, and educated them in gymnastic and *mousikē*. Our sole purpose was to engineer it that they, being persuaded by us, might be finely soaked in the laws like a dye, so that their opinion on what things are to be feared and everything else might become fast through their holding on to nature and fit nurture, and the dye not be washed out by those powerful detergents, pleasure, so much more powerful than soap and soda, and pain and fear and desire, the most effective detergent of all. This kind of ability to retain safely in all circumstances an opinion about what is and is not to be feared, which is correct and in accord with law, is what I propose to call *andreia*.[35]

What strikes us immediately is how close *andreia* here appears to self-control: both comprise the power to hang on to correct beliefs in the face of various temptations to abandon them.[36] A similar picture, of course, was presented by Socrates in the *Laches*,[37] but we are now far better placed to understand it. Virtue as a whole is that inner harmony of soul which both arises from and results in knowledge of (or a set of beliefs derived from) the Good. This knowledge, however, manifests itself differently in different circumstances, and virtue will accordingly take different forms and be called by different names. Yet in the case of *andreia* and *sōphrosunē* the background circumstances may be markedly alike, and the two virtues will consequently at times appear to merge. It would seem that the maverick *andreia* of Achilles has been transformed into something altogether calmer and more dependable.

---

[34] See p. 22 above.
[35] 429e7–430b4 (my translation).
[36] This also seems to be the message of 413b–c.
[37] *Laches* 191c7–e2, discussed on pp. 87–8 above.

The implications of this transformation are profound. Firstly, *andreia* is no longer such a mysterious quality. There is no need of the divine parentage or infusion which is at least partly or occasionally responsible for Homeric courage: 'all' that is required is a combination of natural qualities and correct training. Secondly, any association between *andreia* and uncontrolled aggressiveness or violence is broken, since reason and the Philosopher-Rulers must by definition be in control if *andreia* is to exist at all: it is their measured dictates that the *thumos* and the Auxiliaries must obey. Nor is it just that reason would never counsel irrational violence; if the *thumos* gets too worked up it will not be able either to comprehend the orders it receives, or to form correct beliefs as a result of hearing them. It is no accident that in 381a Socrates links *andreia* to *phronēsis* and says that the most *andreia* and wise *psuchē* will be least likely to be disturbed and changed by external events.

Equally important is the fact that there is no longer any need to foster or celebrate war as the only, or even necessarily the best, backdrop for *andreia*. If one can show *andreia* in resisting the seductions of pleasure and desire, and hanging on to the correct belief that self-indulgence would in certain circumstances be shameful and hence fearful, then there is clearly a role for *andreia* in peacetime. This should not surprise us: the Auxiliaries are, after all, an executive and police force as well as soldiers. Yet even if *andreia* still continues to be seen as an excellence primarily associated with the conquering of pain and fear, there will still be no incitement to promote war and danger for it to flourish. Since it is now only one manifestation of knowledge or belief derived from the Good, and no longer the supreme virtue for a man, there will be no need to create opportunities for its exercise at all: a man does not have to be displaying *andreia* to be virtuous. It can be called upon if required, and that is all that is necessary.

This seems to be the import of a passage in 399 in which Socrates takes a rather less radical approach to the relation between *andreia* and *sōphrosunē*. He is discussing what kind of music the young Guardians should hear, and says that he wants a mode,

that would represent the voice and accent of an *andreios* in military action or any enterprise requiring force, who confronts misfortune in all cases with steadfast endurance, whether he faces injury or death or meets with some other calamity. And I want another mode which would represent him in some peaceful and unforced, voluntary action, such as persuading someone to grant what he requests, or praying to God, or teaching or admonishing some person; or in turn submitting himself to the requests or teaching or persuasion of someone else and then acting according to his decision, not displaying arrogance,[38] but acting with moderation and due measure in all such matters and accepting what befalls with good grace. Leave me these two modes, one enforced, one voluntary, which will represent the voices of *sōphrones* and *andreioi* in good fortune and in bad. (399a6–c4)[39]

Although *andreia* is here placed in a context of war and danger, and *sōphrosunē* in a context of peace, it is clear that the two are still regarded as intimately linked: it is the temperate man who will be *andreios* in war, and vice versa. The same basic character will manifest itself in two different but linked ways – according to two linked modes – in two different sets of circumstances.

Perhaps most importantly of all, if *andreia* depends upon knowledge of the Good or correct belief based on others' knowledge,[40] and arises from that inner harmony of soul which constitutes mental health, then it seems to be severed from a tragic outlook. If the Forms of the Good and the Beautiful are unified or even referentially identical, then performing an *andreion* act will not involve choosing the *kalon* over the personal *agathon*. Yet we have also seen that the particular unification of values on which *andreia* depends is substantively different from that of the psychological egoist, and in consequence the *andreia* of the Auxiliary or Philosopher-Ruler will be far from that of a Callicles or Thrasymachus. It is true that Callicles links *andreia* with *phronēsis*, but for him *phronēsis* is displayed in satisfying the desires of the two non-rational parts of the *psuchē*, not in implementing the philosopher's knowledge of the transcendent Good.

Furthermore, a crucial part of this reformulation of *andreia* will be the harnessing of the *thumos* and redirection of its energies onto appropriate goals. In the context of the ideal state, the Philosopher-Rulers can utilize the *thumos'* yearning for glory by ensuring that only the desired civic *andreia* receives social acclaim and rewards: at 460b, for instance, we are told that the state's most successful young male defenders will be honoured in various ways,

---

[38] 'Arrogantly' renders ὑπερηφάνως. Achilles has just been criticized for displaying ὑπερη-φανία towards gods and men at 391c5.

[39] Translation mine.

[40] The *Republic* does not make it clear whether those capable only of correct belief need to be aware that such beliefs must be based on others' knowledge of the Forms.

including being awarded more sexual opportunities at the official mating-festivals.[41] 468b also emphasizes how those who excel on the battlefield will receive a heady cocktail of honours, embraces and food. The framework of the ideal state additionally ensures that while the Auxiliaries are necessarily characterized by thumoeidic impulses, they are not dominated by them: their *thumos* will always remain subordinate to reason, specifically to their reason's acceptance of the rational decrees of the Rulers. Finally, the definition of *andreia* as correct belief concerning what things are to be feared makes it clear that the focus will not simply be on channelling the *thumos*' desire for glory; the Rulers must also harness its converse fear of shame. Indeed, they may wish to go even further. As we saw from the example of Leontius, the *thumos*' concern with self-image involves self-respect as well as the respect of others;[42] and while the latter clearly plays a significant part in helping to establish the former, it is unlikely to be the sole factor. In this light, it seems probable that one of the results the Rulers are trying to achieve through the primary education system is to establish in the young Guardians a sense of self-respect which will stand fast in the face of danger, temptation or ridicule. In any event, it is plain that the *thumos*' involvement in self-respect will be a particularly important tool in the reworking of *andreia*, since it allows for at least partial reworking to be attempted even in non-ideal societies, so long as some early educator or role model is available to instil the correct sense of self-respect in the first place.

Despite such possibilities for utilizing the *thumos*, however, Socrates' remodelling of *andreia* still raises some tough problems. Some of these problems are practical: the point about self-respect notwithstanding, it undoubtedly remains the case that its most effective implementation requires wholesale social reconstruction. Outside the ideal state, the remodelled version of *andreia* and the impersonal Auxiliaries who embody it are not likely to prove compelling ideals to many. Perhaps the most serious problem, however, is not practical but conceptual, and stems from a deep-rooted sense that the virtue of courage should in some way be concerned

---

[41] This particular honour is plainly also designed as a means of breeding more good soldiers for the state; but it is evident that it is in addition part of a general policy of encouraging the required form of *andreia*. It would be interesting to know whether Socrates envisages the best female Auxiliaries being rewarded in the same way.

[42] Pp. 16–17 above.

with a willingness to risk or endure something unpleasant, for the sake of a good at least perceived to be greater. For if Socrates is right that dying is positively to be welcomed, and if physical pain does not matter much because it cannot harm the soul, then what is so noble about being willing to face them? Has Socrates so re-written the notion of courage that it no longer seems to us to be courage at all? We may feel that we have been led to a bizarre scenario in which, whatever Socrates says, courage cannot take place on the battlefield at all.

The answer, I would suggest, is that although we cannot in fact be harmed by pain or death, our irrational bodily desires still re-coil from them and perceive pain as something unpleasant. This has two important consequences. Firstly, the process of becoming a Socratic *andreios* will often be a genuine struggle; secondly, even the person who has become *andreios* will still have to endure things which his bodily desires perceive as unpleasant, and his beliefs concerning what things are and are not to be feared will have to be very deeply dyed in his soul if they are to remain fast. In other words, Socrates' conception of *andreia* is not so completely di-vorced in practice from more widely-held notions of courage as it may at first appear. Furthermore, as we are just about to see, it is even possible that the *andreios* is permitted by Socrates to feel a minimal amount of fear in the face of physical danger, providing he is not actually deflected by it. To consider this question prop-erly, however, we need to return to the issue of role models.

ROLE MODELS FOR A NEW AGE

There is no doubt that Socrates' reworking of *andreia* has profound implications for the question of suitable role models, both within and without the ideal state. The outlook for Achilles seems partic-ularly bleak: indeed, it is not even clear that his form of bravery and manliness could count as *andreia* at all. The first problem arises if he not only loathes death, but also fears it: would such a fear preclude him from being *andreios*? In the world of the *Iliad*, the answer is no. At 13.284–5, the brave man is described (or de-fined) as the man who 'does not fear too much', and there is no doubt that Achilles meets this criterion: he is unequivocally said to feel fear only once in the poem, when he is confronted by Aeneas in 20.261–3. When we turn to the *Republic*, however, the matter becomes considerably more complex. Here Socrates seems positively to emphasize the fact that Achilles finds death fearful as well as hateful: at 386b4–5 he says that no one who believes Hades to be a terrible place can be without fear of death, and he immediately follows this up by citing two of Achilles' lamentations on the horrors of the afterlife; the sly implication is too obvious to ignore. Far less clear, though, is how we are supposed to interpret it. We have seen how, at 386b1–2, Socrates claims that no one who fears death can ever be *andreios*;[43] yet it is hard to decide quite what this claim involves. Does Socrates mean that the presence of fear actually precludes *andreia* by definition, or simply that the person who fears death will not, as a matter of psychological fact, be prepared to risk his or her life in practice? At first sight, it might seem that the introduction of Achilles into the debate at 386c5 settles the issue in favour of the former interpretation, since Socrates can hardly argue that Achilles' fear, if such it is, prevents him from risking his life: if Achilles does fear death, then it is plainly not the kind of fear which leads him to shun it.[44] On this reading, Socrates would be admitting that Achilles can sometimes undertake brave deeds, but denying that Achilles is truly *andreios*. Unfortunately, however, matters are not quite so straightforward. 386b1–2 may only be intended as a rough psychological generalization, a general rule which the exceptional Achilles proves; after all, in 386a6–7 Socrates takes a more lenient line, saying that the state should only permit stories which instil the 'least possible' fear of death.

Nevertheless, even if Achilles' fear of death does not by itself prevent him from counting as *andreios* in the *Republic*'s terms, there are other facets of his situation and character which almost certainly do. To begin with, whatever his precise beliefs about what is and is not to be feared, they are hardly derived, directly or indirectly, from philosophic knowledge of the Form of the Good. The same can be said, of course, of all the traditional heroes, and even presumably of the historical Socrates himself; yet Achilles is plainly particularly bad at both forming and 'safely keeping' (429c5–d2) correct opinions concerning what actions are to be undertaken or avoided: under the pressure of a perceived personal slight, for example, he abandons his normal belief that it is good

[43] Pp. 12–13.   [44] See p. 22 above.   [45] See e.g. *Il.* 18.102–6; 19.61–2.

to defend his fellow Greeks,[45] and his intense grief and guilt over Patroclus' death drive him to unacceptable savagery. His beliefs definitely do not always accord with those of the ideal law-maker, as those of the civic *andreios* must (429b–c), and even his more palatable *doxai* are dangerously unstable; they are certainly not indelibly dyed in the wool (429d–430a).

For the full implications of Achilles' inadequacies, however, we need to turn to the Simile of the Cave. At 516c8–d2, Socrates recounts how the prisoners in the cave compete amongst themselves for honour and praise: there are established prizes, for instance, for those best able to predict the appearances of the shadows that pass before their eyes. Such details clearly anticipate the values of the *thumos*-dominated man of Book 8; yet Socrates already feels able to say that the true philosopher, reluctantly returning to the cave after his dazzling glimpse of the sun, will find these conventional honours of little value. Looking around him at the prisoners and their insubstantial existence, he feels that he would far rather be 'labouring for some poor portionless man'[46] than live the life that they do. Now this quotation, we may remember, has been employed in the *Republic* before: Socrates first cited it at 386c, right in the middle of the debate on early education and the unsuitability of Achilles as a role model. There it was used in its original context, namely that of Achilles' wraith in Hades, lamenting to the live Odysseus that he would do anything to return to the light of the sun. Its repetition here shows us how far Socrates thinks he has come. In the *Odyssey*, and at *Republic* 386, the shadowy halls of Hades are contrasted with the everyday living world; now, the everyday world is contrasted with the realm of the Forms. The life which the wraith of Achilles so covets is in fact nothing short of a living death. At *Odyssey* 11.476 and *Iliad* 23.103–4, Achilles forcibly expresses his horror of the shades (*eidōla*) in Hades; yet in the simile of the Divided Line *eidōla* are the stuff, not of Hades, but of the phenomenal world which Achilles thinks he loves.[47] Indeed, at 586b–c *eidōla* refer even more specifically to the illusory pleasures of the non-rational parts of the *psuchē*, and it is significant that in this passage, too, Socrates makes a point of introducing the heroes of the Trojan War: those dominated by their *thumos* and appetites fight over their illusory shadow-paintings of pleasures

---

[46] *Od.* 11.489.   [47] 510a1.

just as, in Stesichorus' version, the Greek heroes at Troy unwittingly fought over a mere *eidōlon* of Helen, the real article having
been whisked off to Egypt by Hera. In Socrates' eyes, all human
struggles could be said to be waged over *eidōla*.

The defeat of Achilles is perhaps also suggested by 519c5–6 and
its allusion to the Isles of the Blest. In legend, albeit not in Homer,
Achilles was transported there after his death – a tradition of
which Plato was well aware, as *Symposium* 179e shows.[48] In *Republic*
519, however, the Isles do not appear as the final abode of
Achilles; they are instead a metaphor for how intellectuals regard
the life of pure theoretical reason. The point is made even more
clearly in 540b, where the Isles are explicitly stated to be the place
where Philosopher-Rulers go after death. Indeed, dead Rulers
now appear to be awarded divine or heroic status in some quasi-
official sense: apart from their departure to the Isles of the Blest,
they are also to receive public memorials and sacrifices, 'as dai-
mons, or at any rate as blessed with a good daimon and godlike'
(540b6–c2).[49]

Another telling detail is Achilles' pointed exclusion from the
Myth of Er, right at the very end of the dialogue. Er is recount-
ing how the various souls choose the pattern of life for their next
reincarnation, and in his list appear many famous figures from
legend and myth, but not Achilles; what is more, Socrates seems to
go out of his way positively to highlight his absence. At 620b1–2
he says that, according to Er, the twentieth soul to choose was
Ajax, who selected a lion's life. The numerical specificity would be
odd were it not for the fact that, as Bloom notes, Ajax is also the
twentieth soul whom Odysseus encounters in Hades – only there,
he appears in the company of Achilles.[50] By Book 10 of the *Republic*, it seems that Socrates is no longer content simply to rework the
tales of Achilles; Achilles' life is no longer an option at all.

It may be, however, that this radical exclusion was anticipated

---

[48] See, for example, Pindar *Olympians* 2.79–83. From our perspective it may also be significant that, though the story itself does not appear in Homer, Odysseus does without
apparent irony call Achilles 'most blessed' (μακάρτατος) at *Od.* 11.483, a mere six lines
before Socrates' quote from Achilles' lament.

[49] This apparent supplanting of traditional heroes by philosophers raises complex issues,
which will be discussed below.

[50] *Od.* 11.466–9; see Bloom 1968: 436. I agree with Bloom's calculation, though it is admittedly sometimes difficult to know whether souls are to be counted individually or in a
group. Nevertheless, even if others believe Ajax to be, say, the nineteenth or twenty-first
soul whom Odysseus meets, the parallel is still striking enough to make it probable that
Plato has this passage in mind.

by Socrates even in Book 3. At 399e, during the discussion of the young Guardians' musical education, Socrates states firmly that the orderly and restrained music of Apollo is always to be preferred to the wild melodies of Marsyas, the mythical inventor of the flute who challenged Apollo to a musical contest, lost, and was flayed alive for his presumption. At *Iliad* 22.15–20 Achilles, too, challenges the authority of Apollo – an episode which we have seen Socrates quote with disapproval at *Republic* 391a6–7.[51] Again, the inference seems clear: Achilles is not merely to be remodelled; he is to be extirpated altogether.

Yet even though Achilles can no longer be tolerated in any form, there is perhaps another Homeric hero who can.[52] One soul which is included in the Myth of Er, and allowed to select a new life for itself, is that of Odysseus; it is, however, significantly said to be a soul 'recovered from ambition' through the memory of its former hardships (620c5). This is an important qualification. Book 3, although it does not expressly mention his ambition, has nevertheless made it clear that an entirely unreconstructed Odysseus is still problematic: he is, for example, too prone to physical indulgence (390a8–b2).[53] Nevertheless, there is no doubt that in the *Republic* Socrates regards him as much more suitable for emulation than Achilles, calling him 'the wisest of men' and praising his exemplary self-control and endurance in difficult and dangerous situations;[54] suitably purified, he could well be a useful model. In this light, it is worth noting again that in the *Protagoras* Socrates actually compares himself to Odysseus at one point.[55] At 315b9 Socrates likens his sighting of Hippias in Callias' portico to Odysseus' sighting of the shade of Heracles in the underworld;[56] the implication seems to be that Odysseus and Socrates are the more modern – and vital – heroes: it is they who can visit Hades and caves and return alive.[57]

---

[51] Pp. 201–2 above.

[52] Although Ajax is allowed to be *andreios* at *Resp.* 468d4, he is not otherwise explicitly presented as a suitable candidate for imitation.

[53] For other problems regarding Odysseus' suitability as a role model (not explicitly discussed in the *Republic*), see pp. 197–8 above.

[54] *Resp.* 390a8 and 390d1–6.

[55] See p. 196 above.

[56] *Od.* 11.601.

[57] As we have seen, Aristotle also appears to link Odysseus and Socrates in his account at *An. Post.* 97b15–26 of the two kinds of *megalopsuchia*: the clearly Odysseus-inspired second type, that of being unaffected by misfortune, is said to be exemplified by Socrates. See pp. 184 and 195 above.

Yet the *Protagoras* comparison nevertheless invites some difficult questions, for its main purpose is clearly not to promote Odysseus, but Socrates. Returning to the *Republic*, is it not Socrates who is to be viewed as the principal new role model, the prime exponent of reworked *andreia*? At first sight, such a notion seems both obvious and tempting. Socrates has plainly been portrayed as some sort of hero and model in such dialogues as the *Apology*, *Crito* and *Phaedo*, and to some extent this characterization continues in the *Republic*: we certainly see him worsting the petulant and immature Thrasymachus, and stalwartly fending off the 'three waves' of hostility which threaten to engulf his blueprint for the salvation of mankind.[58] Indeed, he seems perfectly to embody the notion that *andreia* is now to be displayed in the field of philosophy as well as the field of war.[59]

Herein, however, lies the rub. For if Socrates is to serve as a model, it is surely not primarily for Auxiliaries, but for philosophers. Yet when we look at the notion of the ideal philosopher in the *Republic* more closely, we shall find that it raises critical questions regarding the continued desirability of any human role model, even Socrates. It is time, therefore, to turn to that ideal and explore it in detail.

THE PHILOSOPHIC IDEAL

In chapter 5 we saw how the image of the philosopher presented in both the *Gorgias* and the *Phaedo* can appear both unattainable and unappealing, particularly to the energetic young men whom Plato is hoping to attract; I also suggested there that both these problems could be considerably alleviated by the introduction of the *thumos*.[60] We are now in a position to see how this works in practice, both within and without the setting of the ideally just state.

In terms of attainability, the importance of the *thumos* in helping to achieve a philosophic way of life is clear: if the *thumos* is educated to take on its natural role of being reason's supporter, then

---

[58] See 457b–d; 472a; 474b–c. The attacks are directed at the proposals for female Auxiliaries and Guardians, the community of (Guardian) wives and children, and the general practicability of Socrates' ideal.

[59] This complex issue is discussed further below.

[60] Pp. 162–4.

reason no longer has to battle on its own against the myriad and grasping appetites. The mettle and endurance of the *thumos* can provide crucial support in reason's struggle for psychic control. Nevertheless, there is no point showing me how I could attain a particular goal if I do not perceive the goal itself as desirable; at least as important, therefore, are the possibilities offered by the *thumos* for making the philosophic ideal attractive in the first place. It is in this light, I believe, that we should view Socrates' emphasis on the honours that are to be bestowed on the Philosopher-Rulers in the ideal state, both during their lifetime and after their death.[61] Such worldly rewards will be of scant interest to fully-fledged philosophers themselves, as the Simile of the Cave makes plain: local prizes can offer little enticement to those who contemplate 'all time and all reality'.[62] The purpose of such a system of honours is surely to attract and encourage *trainee* philosophers, whose *thumoi* may still hanker after earthly acclaim; it will also presumably impress the *thumoi* of the Auxiliaries and Producers, and thus help keep them in line. And Plato may further intend it to raise the standing of philosophy in the minds of both Socrates' interlocutors and, crucially, the *Republic*'s readers: this is how philosophers should and would be treated in a well-run society. Witness, too, Socrates' claims that the Philospher-Rulers will receive many other blessings in life and after death, quite apart from the state's accolades:[63] all have the same purpose of recommending the philosophic life to a number of different groups, both within and without the republic.

Even more significant, however, are the developments in the content of the philosophic ideal itself, and here too the *thumos* has a critical part to play. In the *Republic*, the embodied *psuchē* is no longer viewed as pure reason battling against the appetitive and thumoeidic demands of the *sōma*, as it was in the *Phaedo*, and in consequence the philosopher's task is not usually conceived as the struggle to 'practise dying' and become pure reason alone. Her or his embodied *psuchē* now comprises the appetites and thumoeidic

---

[61] E.g. 503a; 540b–c. All the Guardian class are said to receive honours in 414a and 415a.
[62] Cave: 516d; breadth of vision of the philosopher: 486a.
[63] See, for example, 521b and 540b; the blessings of the life of both Guardian classes are emphasized at 465d and 466a–b. The bounties of the philosophic life in general (not necessarily within the ideal state) are again stressed at 608c and, with moving eloquence, at the dialogue's conclusion (621c–d).

motivations as well as reason, and Socrates' usual line is that it is part of reason's function to acknowledge these non-rational desires and provide them with the 'best and truest' pleasures of which they are capable.[64] The philosopher thus normally appears as a rather more human creature, and the philosophic life – for all its undoubted simplicity – a little less austere.[65]

In addition to this general point, the *thumos'* sensibilities in particular are appealed to and harnessed in the depiction of the philosopher as courageous:[66] courage is expressly mentioned as one of the philosopher's required qualities in 486b, and at 535a we are told that the young Guardians selected for further studies at twenty must be, amongst other things, the 'steadiest and most courageous'.[67] At one level, such a requirement is straightforward enough: the trainee philosopher is after all expected to take some part in military duties between the ages of twenty and thirty (537d), and then again from thirty-five to fifty (539e–540a); indeed, at 521d Socrates emphasizes that all the higher studies must be relevant in war and appropriate for soldiers. We have also seen that the excellent performance of such military duties is one of the main objectives of the early training in *mousikē* and gymnastic that all the young Guardians must undergo, before being separated into potential Philosopher-Rulers and actual Auxiliaries: the aim is to steep their souls in 'civic' courage, in correct beliefs concerning what is and is not to be feared (429e–430b). And when they are eighteen all these young Guardians are to share a further two years of specifically military training. In short, although war is not especially glamorized in the *Republic*, and philosophers are not depicted as warrior-chiefs, they will be able to fight well if necessary; they are certainly not the effete wimps scorned by Callicles in the *Gorgias* and the household of the philosophic man in *Republic* 9 – and indeed by Athenians in general at *Republic* 487a. Moreover, after apprehending the Form of the Good at the age of fifty, the

---

[64] See, for example, 442c5–8; 586d4–587a1.

[65] There is, however, one very important exception to this: in 608–12 Socrates identifies the immortal part of the *psuchē* with the *logistikon* alone, and urges us to disentangle this immortal soul from its earthly trappings. Such an exhortation appears to be at serious odds with the earlier encouragement to harmonize the three parts of the embodied *psuchē*; see pp. 31–3 above. The dilemma is discussed below p. 249.

[66] For the moment I wish to concentrate only on the courage aspect of *andreia*. The possible gender connotations will be explored below.

[67] Cf. also 487a, 490c, 491b, 494b and 536a.

courage of the fully-fledged philosopher will in fact be more complete than that of the more obviously military Auxiliary, since it is
now based not simply on beliefs, but on knowledge.

The most important manifestation of the philosopher's courage
and related qualities, however, will not usually be in war but in
the practice of philosophy itself. Courage and philosophy, of
course, have been linked from the *Apology* onwards,[68] but the fact
that courage is now explicitly said to require *thumos* as well as reason highlights how the philosopher can no longer be perceived,
whether accurately or not, simply as a cool mind. We need to distinguish here between the admired Philosopher-Ruler within the
ideal state and the despised and beleaguered philosopher without.
In both contexts, courage and endurance will be needed to tackle
the sheer difficulty of dialectical investigations (it is, for instance,
significant that Glaucon is called *andreiotatos* for being persistent
in argument at 358a–b);[69] and within the state they will further
be called upon by the long and arduous training.[70] In the imperfect world of Athens and beyond, however, courage will also be
necessary to face the scepticism, ridicule, contempt and hostility
of the non-philosophic masses; one may even have to endure
physical assault and trial.[71] Speaking the truth is thus a matter for
some trepidation (499b): it is a journey into the unknown which
requires one to be bold and take risks.[72] In these circumstances, it

---

[68] See pp. 95, 178 and 182 above.

[69] For effort and endurance being required from Socrates and his interlocutors, see 432c;
435c7–8; 441c4; 450c6; 453d4–11. The quality of *andreia* is applied to endurance in
philosophical argument at *Laches* 194a3–4; *Meno* 81d3–4; *Tht.* 205a1; *Pol.* 262a5; while
giving up a worthwhile argument is called *anandrōs* at *Tht.* 203e8–9. It is, however, vital
that the philosopher knows when to practise such persistence. At *Resp.* 453b–c, Socrates
imagines a critic protesting against the possibility of female Guardians by appealing to
the *Republic*'s founding tenet, namely that people of different natures should be assigned
different jobs. In response, Socrates claims that the biological differences between men
and women are simply not relevant to the issue of who is naturally suited to a particular
job; he complains that to allow the criticism to stick 'too obstinately', πάνυ ἀνδρείως
(454b5), to a form of words without considering sufficiently what kinds of sameness and
difference the formula intended. In this case the normally virtuous quality of holding
one's position is misguided.

[70] E.g. 499a5–6; 503e1–504a1; 504c9–d3; 531d5–8; 535b6–d7; 536b1–2.

[71] Scepticism: 457d, 474b; ridicule: 452a–b, 473c, 517a and d; contempt and disapproval:
473c, 487d, 488e–489a, 494a; hostility: 450b, 472a, 473e, 474a–b, 502d; assault 474a,
517a; trial: 457e, 517d. While the references to assault and trial in 474a and 457e are
wholly or principally jocular, those in 517a and d appear to be entirely serious. In any
case, the actual fate of Socrates clearly gives any banter on these lines a black edge.

[72] 414d; 497e; 498c; 503b.

is fortunate that the pursuit of philosophy itself is alleged to make its practitioner more courageous, since the person who possesses the greatness of mind to contemplate all time and all reality will not regard human life as anything of great significance, and will consequently not be afraid of death (486a–b).[73]

These are appropriately bold moves: qualities formerly associated chiefly with the battlefield are being claimed by the Academy, and are an effective counter to charges of feebleness and impotence. Furthermore, this sense of philosophic vigour is intensified by Socrates' use of martial, hunting and athletic imagery to describe the philosopher's search for truth: the practice of philosophy is variously compared to making an assault, tracking, swimming against huge waves, wrestling and mountain-climbing.[74] Again, such metaphors make the philosopher seem far less vulnerable to the scorn of such as Callicles.

Yet both the imagery and the ascription of *andreia* and related qualities to the philosopher's task also raise some extremely complex issues. Firstly, it is very hard to know precisely how to interpret the agonistic implications of many of these qualities and images. Admittedly, as we saw in chapter 3, we need to be careful here: Socrates is always at pains to stress that the object of the battle or competition is to capture truth, not to defeat one's opponent.[75] Even if this important caveat is granted, however, such terms and metaphors could still cut two ways. From one perspective, Socrates could be seen as taking traditional competitive activities and reworking them in a less aggressive fashion: the new field on which to win one's sword is that of philosophic discourse. Important though athletic and martial prowess is, it is even more important to train and flex one's intellectual muscles. Yet he could also be accused of promoting the old agonistic ways: why does philosophy have to be viewed as a contest at all?

The second question is even more problematic. To what extent are the 'masculine' connotations of *andreia*, war and sport supposed to be in evidence here? It would be radical enough if Soc-

---

[73] See also *Phd.* 63e–64a, where the study of philosophy is said to give confidence to a man who is about to die, since it shows that death is to be welcomed rather than feared. At *Meno* 86b the practice of philosophy is also said to make a person more *andreios* by increasing their capacity for mental endurance.

[74] Battle: 534c; hunting and tracking: 432b–d; swimming, often against mighty waves: 453d, 457b–d, 472a–473c; wrestling: 554b, 583b; mountain-climbing: 445c.

[75] See pp. 98–9 above.

rates were simply claiming that philosophy both requires and bestows courage and guts; is he also claiming that it both requires and helps create 'real men'? Socrates may be setting up the philosopher as a new hero, and Plato may be setting up Socrates as the paradigm of such heroism, but is this new hero to be perceived as specifically male?

The first thing we need to consider is the *Republic*'s stance on women. Its official view is put forward in 451b–457b and is reasonably, but not entirely, clear. Apart from the different roles they play in reproduction, the natures of men and women are said in 456b to be either 'akin' or 'the same' (a particularly frustrating ambiguity). Women as a class are consequently capable of performing the same occupations as men; they are like men too in that the natural abilities of individual women will fit them for one occupation rather than another. The more able women should thus receive the training necessary to enable them to become Guardians. No mention is made in Book 5 of the distinction between Auxiliaries and Rulers, though it appears to be the former role that Plato especially has in mind: he several times refers back to the account of the young Auxiliaries' education in Books 2 and 3 (e.g. 452a2; 456e9–457a1), and it is expressly emphasized that females of the appropriate type should undergo the physical training necessary to enable them to go to war. In 540c, however, we are 'reminded' that women are also to be trained as Philosopher-Rulers.

Nor is there any specific mention in Book 5 of any individual virtue: at 457a, for instance, it is simply said that women exercising naked will be clad in their general *aretē*. Yet the fact that women have the same or closely kindred natures to men, and can perform the same social functions, strongly indicates that they will possess the same virtues, and in the same way. In particular, if they are to be Auxiliaries and go to war, they will have to possess the virtue of *andreia*. The only problem arises from the qualification that though women can perform the same tasks as men, men will usually perform them better (455d); women are said to be weaker than men (e.g. 451e), and while this may just refer to physical weakness, it is possible that it also implies moral and intellectual inferiority. The claim, however, would still seem to be that women possess the same virtues in the same way as men, only not to the same degree.

On this model, neither *andreia* nor sporting and military pursuits are necessarily 'male' at all. This may appear just as well: if *andreia* is perceived as a 'male' excellence, then presumably the *thumos* would have to be perceived as 'male' too – which would clearly present insuperable problems for Plato's psychology. Yet this does not alter the fact that the term *andreia* would have connoted 'manliness' to at least the majority of Plato's audience, and to a lesser extent appeals to boldness and the like would too. The same holds for the imagery: historically, war, hunting, wrestling and athletic activities in general had almost always been the provenance of men, and in Plato's day usually still were; metaphors referring to such pursuits would thus have been *perceived* as 'masculine' by almost all of his readers.[76] In both cases, Plato cannot plausibly claim to be unaware of such probable responses. In describing the practice of philosophy in such terms, therefore, and maintaining that philosophy both requires and bestows *andreia*, he is unavoidably making some kind of comment on traditional conceptions of manliness. The difficulty is understanding precisely what this comment is.

My suggestion is that Plato's position may be deliberately ambivalent, designed to accommodate the fact that his immediate audience is almost entirely male. On the one hand, he genuinely wishes to convince them of the Socratic theory that the virtues are gender-neutral:[77] beyond the respective roles men and women play in biological reproduction, Plato thinks, there are no specifically male or female activities, and hence no specifically male or female excellences. The traditional view which apportions certain activities and excellences to men and others to women is based on inaccurate conceptions of 'different' and 'the same' (454b). Far from aspiring to a false and outmoded ideal of manliness, in other words, they should follow the teaching of the historical Socrates and seek to be good humans. It is not simply the case that *andreia* can manifest itself in the practice of philosophy at least as well as

---

[76] And it is interesting how often commentators still refer to the 'masculinity' of the female Auxiliaries and Philosopher-Queens. *Vide*, for example, Annas 1981: 185, 'In most of Book 5 Plato spends his time claiming, irrelevantly and grotesquely, that women can engage in fighting and other "macho" pursuits nearly as well as men.' The legendary Amazons have of course received the same treatment: the Shorter Oxford English Dictionary (1973) is only reflecting common opinion when it gives 'a strong, tall, or masculine woman' as one of the word's meanings.

[77] See pp. 72–3 above.

on the battlefield; *andreia* is also, in all its manifestations, just as much the provenance of women as of men.

Yet Plato is in addition acutely aware that some of the young males in his audience are deeply suspicious of higher philosophical studies, believing that the pursuit of philosophy in adulthood would be tantamount to abrogating their manhood. He therefore also wishes to portray philosophy in a way that will alleviate such fears; and in this respect, he may be quite happy to exploit the fact that his depiction of philosophy in robustly active terms is likely to be misinterpreted by many. He may want his audience to feel that philosophy is for 'real men' after all.

The question, of course, is whether and how such apparently conflicting aims are supposed to be reconciled. Any answer must inevitably be speculative, but I believe that there are two main possibilities.[78] It may be that Plato is hoping that the 'masculine' rhetoric will work at a non-rational level (and specifically at the level of the *thumos*), even while the rational mind is beginning to appreciate that such activities and qualities are not really masculine at all. Alternatively, it may even be that these two processes are intended to be chronologically separate – though it has to be admitted that there is no such separation of rhetorical and rational techniques employed in the *Republic* itself.

Whichever strategy is in play, however, there are undeniable difficulties. Firstly, the rhetoric seems directed only at a contemporary male audience; yet if Plato really endorses what Socrates says in Book 5, then he should also be envisaging a future readership of aspiring female philosophers. How are they supposed to respond to such 'masculine' terms? Plato does not appear to have reflected on the issue at all. We have seen that a similar problem arises when we consider the early education of the apprentice female Auxiliaries and Philosopher-Queens. At *Republic* 395d, Socrates states baldly that young Guardians should never take the parts of women when acting or reciting, and the reason he gives is not that there is as yet no fiction starring females of the appropriate kind, but simply because 'they are men'.[79] Furthermore, even

---

[78] See the preliminary discussion of these issues on pp. 96–8 above.

[79] When referring back to this passage in Book 5, Socrates makes it abundantly plain that in Books 2 and 3 he had only been considering the education of young *male* Guardians (451c; 456a). See p. 13 above.

when female Auxiliaries and Philosopher-Queens are explicitly introduced, the education system of Books 2 and 3 is not revised in any way. It is hard to escape the conclusion that Plato has not properly thought through the implications of the radical proposals concerning women in Book 5: who, for instance, are to be their early role models?[80] And this makes one wonder whether, in spite of the apparent incompatibility with the consequences of Book 5, Plato *does* sometimes envisage a stage in the education of young male Guardians when even they are to be encouraged to think in terms of becoming 'real men'.

Equally problematic is the question of whether either a split-level or a two-stage strategy is psychologically desirable or even feasible. If it is supposed to work at two levels simultaneously, then this suggests an unwelcome tension between reason and the *thumos*. Yet if it is intended to operate in two separate chronological stages, it is not clear that the *thumos* will easily be able to cope with such a transformation of ideals. How readily can it swap its allegiances from an ideal of manliness to an ideal of humanliness? It must clearly be persuaded that the practice of philosophy will continue to win social recognition even if it is no longer a male preserve; it must feel that fame and success no longer necessarily depend on being perceived as a 'real man'. And this, of course, can only happen if society itself changes, either in whole or in part. If it is too much to expect that all Athens can be induced to honour philosophy, particularly if it is viewed as ungendered, then Plato must at least be able to point to a substantial community within Athens who will. In order to do this, however, he may first have to create such a community himself, both within and by means of the Academy.[81]

There is also the danger that the male recipient of such an ambivalent strategy – again, whether split-level or two-stage – will feel cheated if and when he realizes what has been going on. He may end up hostile to philosophy altogether, not unlike those

---

[80] As far as I am aware, the only occasion in the Platonic corpus where a woman is held up as a worthy model to emulate is *Symp.* 179b–c, where Phaedrus praises Alcestis' willingness to die for her husband Admetus.

[81] Within the strictly controlled environment of the ideal state, the task of making ungendered philosophy seem attractive to the *thumos* should be relatively straightforward: as we have seen, the young Guardians are surrounded by evidence that both male and female philosophers are honoured above all other citizens. This general fact makes the tensions noted above in the early education system all the more puzzling.

referred to at *Phaedo* 89a–90d who put all their faith in unsound arguments and end up hating arguments *in toto*.

Yet even if the move from aspiring to manliness to aspiring to humanliness could easily be achieved, it still may not be enough to satisfy the philosophic ideal. For the final goal of the aspiring philosopher is plainly to apprehend and as far as possible emulate the realm of the Forms, which is not only gender-transcendent but also divine (500c–d). This process of assimilating ourselves as far as possible to the rational divine is also, as we have seen, eloquently recommended near the end of the dialogue, when we are exhorted to shed the barnacles of our incarnation and become, as far as we may, pure and immortal reason (611–12). In short, it appears that at its zenith the philosophic ideal may require that we move beyond the emulation of even the ideal philospher – that even Socrates is finally to be transcended as a model.[82] If this is so, then the question again arises: is such an attempt to assimilate oneself to the divine conceived as an attempt to transcend one's humanity or as its ultimate fulfilment? Plato seems to be unsure: at any rate, in 589e Socrates oscillates between calling the *logistikon* our 'human' and 'humaner' part and our 'divine' part. Again, too, we may wonder whether such a process of assimilation is either possible or desirable. Should we follow Socrates' call in the *Theaetetus* and try to become like god as far as we may (176b), or should we take Pindar's advice and stick to mortal thoughts?

One thing is clear, however. Whether we are supposed to aim for a gender-transcendent ideal of humanity or an ideal of the rational divine, it is plain that the *thumos*' desires for social recognition will mean that neither ideal will seem attractive to most of Plato's prospective audience. On either model, achieving the philosophic ideal outside the context of the just state is going to be far from easy. It is also clear that Plato is painfully aware of this. In the *Symposium*, he presents us with a vivid and ultimately disturbing portrait of just how difficult it is to implement his ideal in the decidedly imperfect environment of contemporary Athens.

---

[82] As well as the divine model that is enjoined upon us, note too that the ideal state is presented as a model for the individual in 592b.

CHAPTER 9

Alcibiades' revenge: thumos *in the* Symposium

SELF-PERPETUATING HEROES

In the *Republic,* Socrates is in no doubt that our non-rational elements can normally only be harnessed when early education is in the hands of Philosopher-Rulers. The trouble, of course, is that this education system must somehow already be in place for Philosopher-Rulers to be created. How is the ideally just state to get off the ground?[1] The problem is exacerbated by the fact that, as we have seen,[2] a role model culture such as Plato's Athens has an in-built tendency to reproduce itself – an innate conservatism that Plato highlights by stressing the *thumos'* desires for social esteem and success. Once the ideal state is up and running, and state-approved heroes well established, such conservative tendencies can be put to good use: properly purified literature and music, which promote the right ideals, must never be altered in any way (424b–c). In imperfect societies, on the other hand, the same tendencies will plainly work against Plato's blueprint.

The obstacles such innate conservatism raises are forcefully depicted in the *Symposium.* Before looking at them, however, we need first to consider the radical project for educating desire that the dialogue proposes, and the role in this erotic training of the conservatively-inclined *thumos.*

THE *SYMPOSIUM*: *THUMOS* AS INTERMEDIARY

The immediate task is clearly to establish that the *thumos* plays any role whatsoever in the *Symposium*: there is after all no explicit ref-

---

[1] Socrates' recommendations for realizing the ideal state all require that Philosopher-Rulers already exist. See, for example, 540d–541a; 415a–d.
[2] Pp. 67–8.

erence to it, or indeed to a divided *psuchē* of any kind. In response, I shall argue that the characters and speeches of Phaedrus and Alcibiades both display and discuss motivations which are in the *Republic*'s terminology undeniably thumoeidic; I shall also argue that these thumoeidic motivations are of great significance in their contributions. Secondly, I believe that Diotima's speech assumes, if not precisely the tripartite psychology of the *Republic*, then at least something very close to it. Having claimed that personal immortality is impossible for humankind, she argues that humans can and do pursue three different kinds of substitute 'immortality': in ascending order of importance, these are biological offspring, fame for noble deeds, and the creation of artistic, legislative, educative and philosophical works. Such aims undeniably overlap with those of the appetites, *thumos* and reason.[3]

Yet if this is so, then why does Diotima not refer openly to a formal tripartite psychology? The answer, I would suggest, lies in the nature of the *Symposium*'s dramatic setting. The *Republic* is a lengthy and detailed argument in reply to a tough practical challenge: show me that it pays to be just. Such an argument plainly requires an analysis of the structure of the human *psuchē*, and it is emphasized in 435c that this will take some time.[4] The *Symposium*'s enterprise, however, is markedly different. It is a relatively short account of a private dinner party, and the style of its discussion of *erōs* is in keeping with the relaxed surroundings: this is not the time for a technical disquisition on the anatomy of the soul. On the other hand, it is very much the time for a non-technical enquiry into human behaviour and motivation, and this is precisely what we get.[5]

If this is accepted, then thumoeidic goals and attributes are not hard to find – indeed, the first example comes in Phaedrus' opening speech (178a–180b). This may initially seem a surprising claim: it may appear that on the contrary Phaedrus rejects thumoeidic

---

[3] Cornford (1950: 68–80) thinks that the *Republic*'s psychology is definitely assumed in the *Symposium*; I prefer the slightly more tentative formulation proposed above. In terms of their respective chronology, I believe that Plato wrote the *Symposium* while working on the *Republic*; for the detailed linguistic connections between their presentations of the Forms, see pp. 222–5 above.

[4] *Phdr.* 246a also makes it clear that explorations of the human soul are necessarily lengthy affairs.

[5] At 189d Aristophanes is explicit that in order to understand *erōs* it is first necessary to understand human nature and its experiences.

aspirations when he argues that what inspired Achilles to sacrifice his life was not a general desire for lasting fame but love for Patroclus. Yet on more careful inspection we find that this love for Patroclus is itself portrayed in recognizably thumoeidic terms: *erōs* inspires a fervent longing to appear in a good light to the beloved or lover, and can thus be described as 'shame for what is shameful, and ambition for what is noble'. In this guise, it is the producer of all *aretē* and all 'great and noble deeds'. What Phaedrus has done, in short, is not so much reject thumoeidic motivations outright as yoke them to personal love; he has replaced desire for the praise of many with desire for the praise of one. The core thumoeidic notion of self-image is still central. And in this yoked form, thumoeidic traits are unequivocally depicted as a force for good.

When we turn to Diotima's explicit reworking of Phaedrus' speech in 208c–e, the thumoeidic nature of heroic behaviour is emphasized even more strongly. Diotima rejects Phaedrus' analysis of *kala erga* in terms of a desire to impress the lover or beloved: Achilles and Alcestis, she sweepingly asserts, were motivated solely by ambition; what they yearned for was not personal love but the acclaim of the many and the immortal glory of a lasting name. This is why they displayed such conspicuous *aretē*. Here too, thumoeidic motivations are portrayed as uncomplicatedly beneficial: not only do they inspire noble deeds, but they also play a key intermediary role in Diotima's overall programme of redirecting the agent away from love of the individual and bodily *kalon* towards love of the abstract Form of the *kalon* itself. Love of non-sensible fame and the *aretē* needed to acquire it is clearly portrayed by Diotima as superior to the physical begetting of children. Equally importantly, the immortality of fame provides an excellent example of the *kalon* merging with the *agathon*, which as we have seen also appears to be one of Diotima's central themes.[6] It is *agathon* because all *erōs*, including love of glory, is defined by Diotima at 205c–d as a desire of good things and flourishing, which in turn is defined as loving the good to be one's own for ever (206a). And it is *kalon* because it is the reward for fine deeds and is depicted by Diotima as taking on some of the nobility of the acts which win it: she deliberately describes it in poetic diction (208c), and at 208d7

---

[6] P. 222.

the notions of deed and reward are explicitly combined in the phrase 'immortal *aretē*'.

Also significant is the function performed in Diotima's programme by *epitēdeumata*, which we saw in our discussion of the *Hippias Major* to be sometimes associated with heroic, and hence thumoeidic, ways of life.[7] In the ladder of rational erotics, the non-sensible beauty of practices and customs plays a critical part in drawing us away from beautiful bodies and souls towards the abstract Form of Beauty itself (210c3–4). The aspirant lover comes to understand that the beauty of bodies and souls is not only connected, but exemplified in a more general way in such practices and customs; he or she is thus well on the way to appreciating that all *kala* are akin, because they possess a single source.

Thumoeidic motivations and associated practices, therefore, can provide an important link between the physical and the abstract, and in particular between the bodily creation of children and the spiritual creation of lasting works. In this respect, they are one of many mediating forces and characters in the *Symposium*, including Diotima, *erōs* in general and, as an embodiment of Eros, Socrates himself.[8] Such intermediaries, we are repeatedly told, are crucial for human welfare since there is no direct intercourse between mortal and divine: 'god with man does not mingle' (203a). Properly guided, thumoeidic desires can thus help lead us upwards; they can prove a useful tool in the service of philosophy. Furthermore, a quick glance at the *Symposium*'s final scene may initially suggest that this service is successful and that philosophy emerges triumphant. An alert Socrates is engaging Agathon and Aristophanes in robust debate; the tragic and comic poets, however, eventually fall asleep and Socrates is left apparently victorious, still with enough energy to return home, bathe, and begin a new day of intellectual endeavour. At 175e, we may recall, Agathon appeals to Dionysus to act as judge between him and Socrates. From the dialogue's closing words, it may appear that the god, despite his usual association with the tragic and comic muses, has rejected the poet in favour of the philosopher.

Yet the operative phrase in respect of the *thumos*' role in this happy scenario is 'properly guided'. For between Socrates' account

---

[7] Pp. 190 and 192.

[8] Like Eros, Socrates is poor, goes barefoot and stands in doorways. He is described as 'daimonic' (219c1) and claims that he knows 'nothing except *ta erotika*' (177d).

of Diotima's teaching and the dialogue's apparently cheerful ending we witness the explosive arrival and departure of a character
whose willingness to be directed by Socrates is intermittent to say
the least. Both the contribution and implied subsequent history of
Alcibiades show all too vividly what can happen when the *thumos*
breaks free from rational guidance and is able to roam at will.

ALCIBIADES AND THE TRAGIC VICTORY

On what grounds can Alcibiades be claimed as a representative of
thumos at all? Before turning to Plato's complex portrayal of him in
the *Symposium*, it will be helpful to look very briefly at some other
depictions of Alcibiades in Greek literature. The general view is of
a man almost entirely ruled by thumoeidic passions, particularly
in youth. In the *Posterior Analytics*, for example, Aristotle cites Alcibiades as an exemplar of one kind of *megalopsuchia*, that of refusing
to submit to dishonourable treatment,[9] and in Plutarch, too, the
basic picture is also thumoeidic;[10] furthermore, since Plutarch was
steeped in Plato and often deliberately adopts his psychological
terminology, this effect is not likely to be accidental. Alcibiades is
said to love victory and pre-eminence (2.1; 33.3), honours and
fame (6.3); he is dangerous as a lion (2.2; 16.2), yet still retains the
equally thumoeidic capacity for shame (6.1). And in a particularly
telling detail, at 23.6 he is called 'not merely the son of Achilles,
but Achilles himself'.

Perhaps the best evidence of all, however, is the portrait of the
nineteen or twenty year-old Alcibiades in *Alcibiades 1*.[11] His ambition for victory, power and honour is, quite simply, depicted as
gargantuan (104e–105e). He is said by Socrates to be more enam-
oured of renown than 'anyone else ever was of anything' (124b);
he openly refers to himself as 'great-hearted' (119d) and quite explicitly wants to be best (104a–c). At 104e–105a, in what is surely a
less elevated version of the choice offered to Achilles, Socrates
says that if some god were to ask him

whether you wished to continue living in possession of what you now
have, or whether you would choose to die straightaway, if it was not
possible for you to obtain more

---

[9] See p. 149 n. 33.

[10] Though there are important nuances, as we shall shortly see.

[11] Again, even if *Alcibiades 1* is not genuine, it is still an invaluable record not only of how
Alcibiades was perceived by its author, but of how Alcibiades was thought to be perceived by Plato.

then,

it seems to me that you would choose to die.

His heroes are, ominously, Cyrus and Xerxes (105c), though he also admires the *kaloi k'agathoi* who are good at managing the city's affairs (124e–125a). The virtue he values most is unquestionably *andreia*: at 115d he is adamant that he would refuse to live if he had to be a coward, and at 119e both he and Socrates assume that he will perform some *kalon ergon* that will be worthy of himself and the city. He is quick to perceive – or imagine – a slight to himself (110b–c), and in a manner very reminiscent of the *thumos* of *Republic* 440b–c, he bases his sense of justice in general on such personal grievances. The youthful Alcibiades, in short, is portrayed as the clearest possible example of tendencies which the *Republic* would class as thumoeidic.

When we turn to the older Alcibiades of the *Symposium*, however, this simple picture becomes considerably more complicated. On the one hand, the dialogue certainly offers indisputable testimony to Alcibiades' thumoeidic characteristics: at 216b, for example, he admits that as soon as he leaves Socrates' company his inclinations towards philosophy are overwhelmed by his desire for the acclaim of the crowd; and his keen awareness of his own image is also revealed by his concern – notwithstanding his protestations to the contrary – that the company is laughing at him because of his drunkenness (212e–213a). The other side of this longing for recognition and respect is a capacity for shame, though it is true that only Socrates can arouse it (216a–b). Add his combative and high-spirited pursuit of Socrates, and his desire that Socrates' favours should be directed only to him (213c–d; 222c–d), and it is hard to deny that thumoeidic passions are still central to Alcibiades' makeup.[12]

Furthermore, some of these thumoeidic traits appear, from Plato's point of view, distinctly promising. Not only can Alcibiades feel shame in the presence of Socrates, but he also seems to have imbibed a pleasingly 'Socratic' view of *andreia*. At 219d he praises Socrates' *andreia* and explicitly links it to his *sōphrosunē* and endur-

---

[12] And see pp. 137 n. 1 and 141 above, where we noted some similarities between Plato's depiction of Alcibiades on the one hand and his portrayals of both Callicles and Callicles' superman on the other (though there are plainly also critical differences, such as Alcibiades' and Callicles' conceptions of *andreia*).

ance – unlike Callicles' superman, Socrates is said to display *andreia* by *refusing* to have sex. These links between *andreia* and *sōphrosunē* are strengthened by Alcibiades' description of Socrates' physical and mental stamina on campaign at Potidaea and during the retreat from Delium; from our point of view, it is particularly significant that at 220c Alcibiades compares Socrates' endurance to that of Odysseus.

Yet the dialogue also makes it absolutely clear that this promise is not being (and is not going to be) fulfilled, and that the overall effect of Alcibiades' thumoeidic tendencies is harmful. The reason that Alcibiades feels shame before Socrates is because he knows that whenever he leaves Socrates' company he is seduced away from philosophy by the flatteries and adulation of the crowd. A potentially helpful thumoeidic response loses out to a damaging one, and so far from being harnessed in the cause of philosophy, his *thumos* ends up enticing him away. Although he yearns for the good opinion of Socrates, in practice the praises of the many count for more.

Nor is this all. For Alcibiades' ultimately unruly *thumos* is, in the *Symposium*, part of a still greater problem. The text makes it plain that, at thirty-four, Alcibiades is not simply governed by his *thumos* as opposed to his reason: he is also clearly depicted as being in the grip of *all* his non-rational elements; in the terms of *Republic* 8, he is a disturbing example of a timocrat sinking into the chaotic existence of the democratic anarchist. His crown of ivy and violets links him to Dionysus and Aphrodite, the divinities of wine, sex and general epithumeitic disorder, and a fragment of Pindar suggests that the violets also symbolize democratic Athens.[13] Another telling detail is the fact that he enters supported by a flute girl: much earlier in the proceedings the other symposiasts pointedly dismissed a flute girl on the grounds that flute music distracted from serious discussion (176e). As we have seen,[14] flute music is also condemned for encouraging loss of control at *Republic* 399d–e, while at 561c intermittent bouts of 'getting drunk to the sound of the flute' are said to be a marked feature of the indulgent democratic character. At *Alcibiades 1* 106e, too, the youthful and thumoeidic Alcibiades is said to have refused to learn the instrument;

---

[13] As Nussbaum notes (1986: 193), violets are associated with Athens at e.g. *Homeric Hymns* 6.18 and Solon 11.4. They appear as a symbol for Athens in Pindar fr. 76, and are part of an Athenian festival in fr. 75.

[14] P. 239.

yet by thirty-four, it would seem, the undisciplined democratic rot has set in.[15]

It is also evident in the *Symposium* that Alcibiades' general submission to the irrational is extremely damaging, both to Alcibiades himself and to his city and associates. For our purposes, the most significant outcome of such submission is that, although his passionate response to Socrates may initially appear a good sign, ultimately he loves him in the wrong way. This is not to deny that his love for Socrates reveals his promise; nor is it to deny that his tribute to Socrates' extraordinary powers is profoundly moving. Indeed, at 221c Alcibiades not only claims that Socrates is unlike anyone else; he also claims that Socrates is the only person about whom you can say this: *even Achilles* can be compared with Brasidas. Once again, we may surmise, Plato wishes us to understand that the *Apology* got it wrong: Socrates is not like Achilles; he is superior to him.[16]

Yet it is this very testimony to Socrates' uniqueness that is problematic. If Alcibiades regards Socrates as unique, he presumably also regards him as inimitable – at any rate, there is certainly no hint that he has ever considered adopting Socrates as a role model. The practical effects of this are that Alcibiades feels a purely personal love for Socrates. Although he has had the right initial response, he has not subjected his emotions to any serious critical scrutiny, and thus even now remains enslaved to their power (215e6–7). While he repeatedly asserts that he has been entranced by Socrates' words (e.g. 215b8–216a4; 218a2–7), it is their speaker to whom he is – or thinks he is – in thrall; he refuses to be entranced – or again, refuses to admit he is entranced – by philosophy itself. Socrates has been applying to Alcibiades the 'fine words' which the educator applies to his or her charge in 210a and c; Alcibiades' soul, however, remains stubbornly resistant. Yet such enslavement to an individual attachment has been forcefully disparaged by Diotima at 210c7–d1 – not that the carousing

---

[15] This mix of thumoeidic and epithumeitic elements in Alcibiades' character is also stressed by Plutarch, though here the mix is depicted as apparent from youth. However, Plutarch also seems to portray Alcibiades as increasingly attracted to the pomp of tyranny (e.g. 16.2). See also Thucydides 6.29, where it is firmly stated that Alcibiades was 'not demotic'.

[16] The comparisons Alcibiades makes between Socrates and Marsyas (215b – to be discussed below) and Socrates and Odysseus (220c) may seem to contradict this, but Alcibiades probably only means that Socrates resembles Marsyas and Odysseus in some respects. Taken as a whole, Socrates is incomparable.

Alcibiades was there to hear it, a telling fact in itself. Such obsession is condemned because it prevents the lover from appreciating the connections between one instance of beauty and another, and thus taking the first steps up the ladder of rational erotics. And Socrates himself makes it absolutely plain that he does not want to be loved by Alcibiades in this way: he rejects his advances at every turn.

It is of course true that Alcibiades is also resentful of his captivity: it is his desire for escape which partly prompts him to yield to the seductive blandishments of the crowd. But this is clearly the wrong response. Instead of attempting to free himself by climbing the ladder of love, he simply pushes the ladder away. He has absolutely no inclination to use his love for Socrates as a step in the ascent from such personal and sensuous passions towards love of the impersonal and non-sensible Form of Beauty itself. He has no desire whatsoever to transcend what Diotima scorns as 'mortal trash' (211e3); and he cannot agree with Socrates that humanity is 'nothing' (216e3). At 213c, Socrates is said to appear to Alcibiades 'suddenly' (*exaiphnēs*). In Diotima's speech, it is the Form of Beauty which is 'suddenly' revealed to the philosopher (210e); the implication may be that Alcibiades prefers a mortal revelation.

Alcibiades' inappropriate response to Socrates is also suggested by the specific images he employs to depict Socrates as an enchanter. Socrates is a Silenus statue (215a–b; 216e–217a) and a flautist (215b;216c), and these images combine in his comparison between Socrates and the flute-playing Marsyas (215b). Yet, as we have seen, the flute is held by the other symposiasts to distract from serious conversation, while in the *Republic* both Marsyas and his wild music are condemned (399d–e). In these details too, Alcibiades shows that he has badly misunderstood the nature and purpose of Socrates' teaching.

The *Symposium*'s verdict on such misunderstanding is harsh: for all the beauty and wit of Alcibiades' speech, the results of his misguided passions are presented as catastrophic – for Athens, for Alcibiades himself, and for Socrates. In this respect, the image of the Silenus statue is particularly important. Plato's readers would have been well aware that within eighteen months of the dramatic date of the party[17] Alcibiades was to be accused of mutilating the

---

[17] The occasion of the symposium is Agathon's first victory as a tragic dramatist at the Lenaea in January 416 (Athenaeus 217b); the attacks on the Hermae took place in the late spring or early summer of 415.

city's treasured Hermae, statues sacred to Hermes which stood near public buildings and the porches of private houses; the comparison that Plato puts into Alcibiades' mouth thus not only serves as a reminder of these allegations, but suggests that Alcibiades' future behaviour will amount to an attack on Socrates as well. At 215b1, too, Plato pointedly has Alcibiades call the statuaries' shops which contain the Silenus figures *hermoglupheia*, places for the carvings of Hermae; it is the only known use of the word and again appears to be an allusion to the pending desecration. The same would also seem to be true of 217a3, where Alcibiades refers to his youthful beauty as his *hermaion*, his gift from Hermes. The overall effect of these allusions is to highlight Alcibiades' ingratitude: even if he was not directly involved in the attack on the Hermae – and Plato does not commit himself – he certainly turned against Athens in other ways, and these verified betrayals could easily be seen as a rejection of both his natural talents – his *hermaion* – and the education he received from his other potential mediator between the mortal and divine, the daimonic Socrates. At 202e3–4 Diotima describes *erōs* as transporting (*hermēneuon*) messages between men and gods; by attacking the Hermae, whether literally or metaphorically, Alcibiades is destroying his chances of moving beyond earthly affairs.

Another disturbing glimpse into Alcibiades' future is provided by 216a7–8, where Alcibiades says that he habitually runs away from Socrates and his challenging words as fast as he can, 'so that I do not grow old sitting beside him'. Again, all Plato's readers would have known that Alcibiades did not grow old anywhere. And many would have known at least some of the rumoured details surrounding his death: angered because the Athenians had ignored his advice at Aegospotami, he left Greece in 405 for Asia Minor and the service of the Persian king; the following year he was murdered by Persian agents, possibly with Spartan connivance, aged perhaps forty-six. Despite this early end, however, there would still have been ample time in his various exiles to 'learn through suffering' – the very thing he warns Agathon against at 222b.[18] Plato can safely assume that his oblique references to this imminent tragedy of waste will not be lost on his audience.

---

[18] Whether Alcibiades did in fact learn anything from his suffering is, of course, another matter.

The shock waves of this tragedy also affected Alcibiades' former associates. There seems little doubt that Socrates' concourse with Alcibiades was one of the factors that brought about his indictment and conviction, as Xenophon emphasizes.[19] In this light, Alcibiades' apparently playful response to Socrates' appeal for a reconciliation between them takes on an ominous resonance:

There is no reconciliation for you and me. But I shall have my revenge on you for these things another time.[20]

A similarly dark irony also imbues 216c1, where Alcibiades says of Socrates that 'on many occasions I would gladly see him departed from this world'; while in 219c5–6 Plato actually has Alcibiades calling the other symposiasts 'jurors', and claiming that their task is to judge between him and Socrates. The double irony on Plato's part, of course, is that Alcibiades himself will not live to see either the results of the judging or of his wish. The message is clear: Alcibiades' wayward and often destructive career shows all too plainly that the irrational in general, and the *thumos* in particular, are extremely difficult to tame. In chapter 1 we saw how *thumos* in Homer represents an essentially limitless life-force. Both Achilles and Alcibiades illustrate that, for all Plato's attempts to modify *thumos*, its origins are never very far away.

In Alcibiades' case, the danger is all the greater in that, in contrast to Achilles in the *Republic*, Plato does not simply portray him as a disturbing figure; he is also allowed to come across as glamorous and engaging. His entrance is explosive (another *exaiphnēs* 212c6): robustly but courteously drunk, full of warmth and energy, with violets and ribbons in his hair – Plato seems to be deliberately marking him out as a potential rival both to the Form of Beauty and to Socrates. He is quick-witted, gifted (218a4–6), bold and beautiful, a blatant challenge to Diotima's contemptuous dismissal of human colour and flesh (211e). Such attractiveness is itself a reason why the *thumos* is so difficult to control: it will naturally be drawn to charismatic and (partly) thumoeidic characters such as Alcibiades. It is worth remembering that the *Symposium* opens with Apollodorus telling his companions how he was stopped by an acquaintance and asked to recount the story of the party that

[19] *Mem.* 1.2.12–48.
[20] 213d7–8. And note how Alcibiades also talks of his praise of Socrates as a means of revenge at 214e2–3.

brought together, specifically, Agathon, Alcibiades and Socrates. Alcibiades is not merely a vivid appendage to the dialogue: he is depicted from the very beginning as absolutely fundamental to its overall structure.

Yet, despite permitting Alcibiades such allure, Plato makes it clear that there is still no question of our rationally adopting him as any kind of model. As well as the hints of his future downfall, there is also the murky confusion surrounding his exit. At 223b2 there is a final *exaiphnēs* as a chaotic crowd of revellers bursts in on the scene; disorder and the irrational, already present in Alcibiades' speech, take over completely. After the crowd departs, there is no further mention of him; he has presumably left with them, his immediate destination unknown. There can be no doubt that Plato does not intend us to follow in his wake; if he is also now acknowledging that a number of us will, then the the outlook is bleak. Such reflections, I suggest, prompt us to reconsider the work's ending. Socrates may be the only main speaker left standing, but the topic he has just been discussing with Aristophanes and Agathon is whether the same man can write both comedy and tragedy. In contrast to the *Republic*,[21] Socrates argues that such a combination is possible; but if this is so, then who might such a man be? The answer is surely Plato himself, who in writing the *Symposium* has consciously constructed a tragedy as well as an entertaining comedy; and the tragedy is not simply that of Alcibiades, but also of Plato's failed hopes for educating and harnessing the irrational in general and the *thumos* in particular outside the context of the ideal state. The dramatic date of the dialogue is 416. By 405 Alcibiades had abandoned Athens for her Persian enemies and by 404 he had been murdered; by 399 Socrates was also dead. At 201d we learn that Diotima did not prevent the plague from reaching Athens; she only delayed its arrival by ten years. In 179 we saw Dionysus set up as arbiter between Socrates and Agathon. It may be that the god has, after all, ultimately elected his own.

---

[21] *Resp.* 394d6.

Epilogue
The weaver's art: andreia in the Politicus and Laws

The *Republic* and the *Symposium* are not, of course, Plato's last words on *andreia*: it reappears as an important theme in both the *Politicus* and the *Laws*. Yet the *Republic* is, I would maintain, his most sustained and consistent attempt to bring *andreia* and *sō-phrosunē* together, chiefly by means of a careful education of *thumos*. And the *Symposium* is perhaps the most vivid demonstration of how difficult it is to effect such an education in practice.

Although the later dialogues fall outside the scope of this book, a very brief glance at the rich treatments of *andreia* in the *Politicus* and *Laws* will help to illustrate the radical nature of the *Republic*'s project, and the importance of its theory of the tripartite *psuchē*.[1] The *Politicus*, in particular, initially appears to adopt a position diametrically opposed to that (or those) of earlier dialogues on the question of the Unity of the Virtues. In 306a–b the Stranger tells Young Socrates that, in order to understand the statesman's art, it is necessary to explain what many will find a 'difficult' and 'extraordinary' doctrine,[2] which asserts that the virtue of *andreia* and the virtue of *sōphrosunē*[3] 'are in a way in a condition of great hostility

---

[1] It needs to be stressed that what follows is not intended to do full justice to the complexity of these later treatments of *andreia*; my aim is simply to highlight certain features which I believe illuminate the earlier discussions. Much has inevitably been left out: for example, as I stated in the Preface, I do not discuss the interesting gender implications of Plato's choice of a weaving metaphor to illustrate the statesman's art in the *Politicus* (and it seems that stateswomen are not envisaged). I intend to discuss such issues more fully in another work.

[2] It is obvious that a doctrine proclaiming a natural disunity between two virtues would be found extraordinary by followers of Socrates, but it is still decidedly puzzling why the Stranger asserts that such a teaching is 'unusual' (b13). If Protagoras in the *Protagoras* can be taken as an intelligent and educated version of common opinion, then it is plain from *Prt.* 349d that *andreia* in particular was often perceived as an anomaly amongst the virtues. See pp. 115 above and 266 below.

[3] In what follows, I have left *andreia* untranslated, and I have generally left *sōphrosunē* untranslated as well. As we shall see, it is by no means clear that *andreia* in the *Politicus* is

and strife in many things'.[4] These two potentially hostile virtues are, in their turn, to be placed in two opposite classes (*eidē*) of qualities, and those who possess such qualities also naturally constitute two opposing groups (307c).

So much seems (roughly) clear enough; in other respects, however, the Stranger's diction in this passage appears somewhat inconsistent. On the one hand, *andreia* is straightforwardly said to belong to the class of such qualities as acuteness, quickness and energy, and it is further stated that when such qualities are manifested to the appropriate degree – or what we perceive as the appropriate degree[5] – we praise them and call them by the one general term, namely *andreia* (306e). We should naturally expect the Stranger to apply the same principles, *mutatis mutandis*, in his analysis of *sōphrosunē*, and it is true that he begins by saying that it belongs to the class of opposing qualities, such as quietness, slowness, gentleness, smoothness and deepness (307a). Yet he then goes on to state that when such qualities are appropriately displayed we praise them by means of the general term 'orderliness' (*kosmiotēs*)[6] – not *sōphrosunē* as we would expect. Almost immediately, however, this whole class of orderly qualities is said to possess a *sōphrōn* nature (307c2–3), in explicit opposition to the *andreia* possessed by the former class (c3), and thereafter *sōphrosunē* and *kosmiotēs* and their adjectives generally seem to be used interchangeably.[7]

More worryingly, it is also far from clear whether the terms *andreia* and *sōphrosunē* are only supposed to apply to each set of qualities when those qualities are fitting and admirable, or whether they can also apply when the relevant qualities are excessive. As we have seen, initially it appears that the qualities are only to be called virtues when they are appropriate and praiseworthy, and

always supposed to connote 'courage' alone: indeed, the difficulty of translating it in the dialogue is one of the main themes I wish to emphasize. In a number of passages, some such term as 'vigour' would be a better rendition. It may also still carry overtones of 'manliness', even though the policy of intermarriage between the two types shows that it can be possessed by women. As for *sōphrosunē*, we shall find that here too it is far from certain that 'temperance' (or a similar virtue-word) is always the best translation.

[4] Or 'in many beings.'

[5] In 307b–d the Stranger emphasizes that the ascription of praise and blame is based on subjective response as well as, or instead of, objective fact: each class of person tends to praise those qualities which they themselves possess.

[6] As we have seen, *kosmiotēs* also carries strong aesthetic connotations of decorousness and elegance; see p. 221 n. 4 above.

[7] Though *vide* 309e5–6, where an 'orderly nature' is said to become 'truly *sōphrōn*' when it partakes of true and assured opinion.

this is certainly what we should expect from earlier dialogues. Yet in 307b–c, when the excessive versions of each set of qualities are discussed, we still seem to find the one class described as possessing a *sōphrōn* nature, and the other as possessing *andreia* (307c2–3). The same holds true of 307d–308b, where the two opposing sets of qualities are said to characterize two classes of people: in 307e–308a those who display excessive and politically disastrous tendencies towards either appeasement or military aggression are still termed 'orderly' on the one hand (e2), and 'inclined towards *andreia*' on the other (a4). It would appear that in each case the Stranger is employing a single term to cover two different things: namely, both the set of raw natural qualities which can be either appropriate and beneficial or excessive and harmful in its effects, and the rationally educated and modified version of those qualities which is always fitting and praiseworthy and which, in earlier dialogues, is properly termed a virtue. And it further seems clear that the set of raw qualities which the Stranger terms *andreia* would in the *Republic* be called, not *andreia*, but *thumos*.[8]

Whichever of these two forms they take, however, the salient point remains that both *andreia* and *sōphrosunē* (or *kosmiotēs*) are naturally opposed in actions, persons, and those persons' perceptions. Furthermore they will, undiluted, lead the polis into grave difficulties: both excessive pacifism and excessive militarism will swiftly result in the state's enslavement (307e–308a), while intermarriage exclusively between persons of one or the other type will, after a few generations, give rise to citizens who are lamentably unable to be of service to the community. Unmixed *andreia* will eventually bring about offspring who are completely mad, and the offspring of unmixed temperance, orderliness and modesty will in time be utterly crippled by weakness and indecision (310d–e). The task of the statesman, therefore, is to interweave both sets of characteristics and classes of person by a twin policy of 'divine' and 'human' bonds. The divine bonds are true and secure beliefs concerning fine, just and good things (309c5–8): when properly educated in such beliefs, the *'andreia psuchē'* is made gentle and the orderly *psuchē* becomes truly temperate and wise; without such a shared education, the former inclines towards brutality and the latter receives the shameful title of simpleton. As for the human

---

[8] At *Resp.* 375c7–8, for instance, Socrates claims that a gentle nature is opposite from a thumoeidic one.

bonds, these are largely formed by a state-controlled policy of eugenics: intermarriage between the two basic types will check the tendency of the one to descend into savagery and madness and of the other to degenerate into sluggish passivity. In these ways, the citizen body will become a well-woven fabric of resolute warp and softer woof, and the statesman will then be able to compose committees from members of both classes, and even award individual posts to those who combine within themselves both sets of qualities.

From our perspective, the key feature of this passage is that interweaving of the different types of thread is the most that even the consummate statesman can achieve: he can create a piece of tapestry, but he cannot blend his raw or even his finished materials into, say, a cake. The drawing-together of *andreia* and *sōphrosunē* that we saw in the *Republic* does not appear to be an option. The reasons for this can only be a matter of speculation – though the increased pragmatism of the dialogue would seem to be significant – but I would suggest that the absence of any theory of a tripartite *psuchē* may well play a part. Firstly, the Stranger lacks the psychological apparatus which would enable him effectively to distinguish raw vigour from *andreia* proper (and natural quietness and gentleness from temperance proper); secondly, the lack of any such apparatus also arguably prevents him from showing in detail how *andreia* and temperance might both comprise knowledge or correct belief concerning the good and a willingness to implement it in the face of an obstacle, whether that obstacle take the form of fear or temptation.[9]

It should be emphasized, however, that the absence of any tripartite psychological theory can at most only be an influence on the *Politicus'* altered view of the relations between *andreia* and *sōphrosunē*. This is shown by the fact that the theme of a particularly close connection between the two reappears in certain passages of the *Laws*, a work which is also devoid of at least any explicit tripartite psychology.[10] At 633c–d, for example, the Stranger and

---

[9] I accept that this argument could be turned around: it could be that Plato's less radical approach in the *Politicus* to the question of the Unity of the Virtues decreases the need for an explicit and sophisticated psychological theory.

[10] In this matter I am in agreement with Robinson (1995: 124–5), though I accept that there are references in the *Laws* to three main types of motivation (e.g. 632c6–d1). But Robinson is surely correct to say that, although there are a number of references to *thumos* in the *Laws* (in contrast to the *Politicus*), Plato seems very unsure as to its status. At 863b, for example, the Stranger is uncertain whether *thumos* is an experience or a part of the soul, and he also seems uncertain whether to class it with pleasure and the appetites (compare 863e with 864b).

Megillus agree that *andreia*[11] is displayed in battling against desires and pleasures as well as fears and pains, a message that is repeated in 634a and b; in 635d, too, only those who are able to resist shameful pleasures as well as fears are allowed to be called wholly *andreioi*. And in 815e7–816a3, cowardice is coupled with a lack of training in *sōphrosunē*.

Yet other passages in the *Laws* present a very different picture of *andreia*. Far from connecting it with *sōphrosunē*, elsewhere the Stranger can speak of *andreia* as able to exist apart from the other virtues, and in these cases it appears as something decidedly problematic. The Spartan poet Tyrtaeus may praise martial valour above all else, but tough fighters include mercenaries who, we are told, are very often also reckless, unjust, arrogant and completely stupid (630b). In 661d–e, as well, the Stranger examines the case of the man who combines unsurpassed strength and *andreia* with injustice and arrogance, while in 696b it is firmly asserted that the virtue of *andreia* can exist without temperance and with licentiousness. In these passages, it seems that the Stranger is in accord with the view of *andreia* as 'odd virtue out' put forward by Protagoras at *Protagoras* 349d, and it is perhaps because of these difficulties that *andreia* is the virtue to which he turns his attention first (632d–e). It is also because of this darker side that *andreia* must in some way be unified not only with *sōphrosunē* but with all the virtues (630a–b). Yet even so it will still only rank fourth in order of importance, as 630c6–d1 makes clear.[12]

What, then, are we to conclude from these apparently conflicting portrayals? Once again Plato seems to be using the term *andreia* to cover (at the least) both courage proper, which can only exist in some kind of unity with the other virtues, and raw mettle or aggressiveness, which can exist in conjunction with various vices. The distinction is perhaps blurred by the fact that the latter type is still usually referred to as a virtue, but, nevertheless, the difference remains. Indeed, at 963e the Stranger says that the virtue of *andreia* is an explicitly pre-rational drive, possessed by very young

---

[11] I have left *andreia* untranslated when discussing the *Laws* for much the same reasons that I left the term untranslated when examining the *Politicus*: although there are certainly passages (such as 633–5) where 'courage' seems appropriate, we shall also find others where 'boldness' or 'mettle' might be better renditions. And at 802e we seem to be back with *andreia* in its root meaning of 'manliness': the Stranger unequivocally declares that whatever tends towards *andreia* is 'masculine'.

[12] A ranking which the Stranger repeats at 630e2, 631a5, 631c8–d1 and 667a3–4.

children and animals; the *Republic*, of course, also discussed such a drive, but there it was termed not *andreia*, but *thumos* (441a–b). As in the *Politicus*, there seems to be a need for the use of two different terms, and the re-introduction of the theory of the tripartite *psuchē*.

Yet I wish to close on a note of uncertainty. For though I believe that the tripartite psychology of the *Republic* could clarify many of the problems concerning *andreia* in the *Politicus* and *Laws*, I am still not convinced that it could dissolve them entirely. It seems to me that the profound ambivalence of the Stranger's treatment of *andreia* in both dialogues suggests that the difficulties go deeper. It may be that, whatever terminology is used and whatever psychological model is adopted, Plato ends his life doubting (at least unconsciously) whether there really is any secure method for transforming raw drive into true *andreia*. This doubt returns us to a troubling issue which emerged at the very beginning of this book. When discussing the *thumos* of the *Republic*, the question was raised as to whether its raw drive and social aspects could ever fully interrelate; the answer offered there was that such interrelation might be possible given the educational programme of the ideal state. When we turned to the unideal world of the *Symposium*, however, we saw that outside the *Republic*'s carefully regulated environment the *thumos* proves to be considerably less docile. I submit that the *Politicus* and *Laws* bear this out: even in the semi-ideal settings that they envisage, *thumos* (or raw *andreia*) can never be entirely tamed.

Bibliography

Adam, J. (ed.) (1963) *The Republic of Plato*, 2nd edition. Cambridge

Adkins, A. W. H. (1960) *Merit and Responsibility*. Oxford
  (1982) 'Values, goals and emotions in the *Iliad*', *Classical Philology* 77: 292–326

Alderman, H. (1987) 'By virtue of a virtue', in Kruschwitz and Roberts (1987), 82–96

Altham, J. E. J. and Harrison, R. (eds.) (1995) *World, Mind and Ethics: Essays on the Ethical Philosophy of Bernard Williams*. Cambridge

Annas, J. (1981) *An Introduction to Plato's Republic*. Oxford
  (1982) 'Plato on the triviality of literature', in Moravcsik and Temko (1982), 1–28
  (1993) *The Morality of Happiness*. Oxford

Ansbacher, H. L. and Ansbacher, R. R. (eds.) (1956) *The Individual Psychology of Alfred Adler*. New York

Anton, J. P. and Kustas, J. L. (eds.) (1971) *Essays in Ancient Greek Philosophy*. Albany

Austin, J. (1968) 'Pleasure and happiness', *Philosophy* 43: 51–62

Baier, K. (1988) 'Radical virtue ethics', in French, Uehling and Wettstein (1988), 126–35

Balsdon, J. (1934) *The Emperor Gaius*. Oxford

Bambrough, R. (ed.) (1967) *Plato, Popper and Politics*. Cambridge

Barker, A. (1984) *Greek Musical Writings 1: the Musician and his Art*. Cambridge
  (1989) *Greek Musical Writings 2: Harmonic and Acoustic Theory*. Cambridge

Barker, A. and Warner, M. (eds.) (1992) *The Language of the Cave* (= *Apeiron* 25.4). Edmonton, Alberta

Bentham, J. (1823) *An Introduction to the Principles of Morals and Legislation*. London

Bergk, T. (1878) *Poetae Lyrici Graeci*. Leipzig.

Berlin, I. (1969) *Four Essays on Liberty*. Oxford

Berman, S. (1991) 'Socrates and Callicles on pleasure', *Phronesis* 36: 117–40

Bloom, A. (1968) *The Republic of Plato* (tr. with notes and an interpretative essay). New York

Bluestone, N. H. (1987) *Women and the Ideal Society*. Oxford: Berg

Blundell, M. W. (1989) *Helping Friends and Harming Enemies: a Study in Sophocles and Greek Ethics*. Cambridge

Brandwood, L. (1976) *A Word Index to Plato*. Leeds

Burkert, W. (1972) *Lore and Science in Ancient Pythagoreanism* (tr. E. L. Minar). Cambridge, Mass.

Burnet, J. (1930) *Early Greek Philosophy* (4th edition). London

Burnyeat M. F (1980) 'Aristotle on learning to be good', in Rorty (1980), 69–92

  (1987) 'Platonism and mathematics: a prelude to discussion', in Graeser (1987), 213–40

  (1990) *The Theaetetus of Plato* (tr. M. J. Levett), with introductory essay. Indianapolis

  (ed.) (1994) *Vlastos: Socratic Studies*. Cambridge

  (forthcoming) appendix to Burnyeat (1997) 'The impiety of Socrates', *Ancient Philosophy* 17: 1–12, to appear in Russian in *Stranitzi*

Bury, R. G. (ed.) (1909) *Plato: Symposium*. Cambridge

  (trans.) (1926) *Plato: Laws*. Cambridge, Mass.

Cairns, D. (1993) *Aidōs: the Psychology and Ethics of Honour and Shame in Ancient Greek Literature*. Oxford

Callen King, K. (1987) *Achilles: Paradigms of the War Hero from Homer to the Middle Ages*. Berkeley, Los Angeles and Oxford

Cameron, A. (1938) *The Pythagorean Background to the Theory of Recollection*. Menasha, Wisconsin

Cartledge, P. (1977) 'Hoplites and heroes', *Journal of Hellenic Studies* 97: 11–27

  (1996) 'La nascita degli opliti e l'organizazzione militare', in Settis (1996), 681–714

Chappell, T. D. J. (1993) 'The virtues of Thrasymachus', *Phronesis* 38: 1–17

Classen, C. J. (ed.) (1976) *Sophistik*. Darmstadt

Conley, S. (1988) 'Flourishing and the failure of the ethics of virtue', in French, Uehling and Wettstein (1988), 83–96

Cooper, J. M. (1984) 'Plato's theory of human motivation', *History of Philosophy Quarterly* 1: 3–21

Cornford F. M. (1912) 'Psychology and social structure in the *Republic*', *Classical Quarterly* 6: 246–65

  (1930) 'The division of the soul', *Hibbert Journal* 1929–30: 206–19

  (1950) 'The doctrine of eros in Plato's *Symposium*', in F. M. Cornford *The Unwritten Philosophy and Other Essays*. Cambridge

Craig, L. H. (1994) *The War Lover: a Study of Plato's Republic*. Toronto

Crisp, R. and Slote, M. (eds.) (1997) *Virtue Ethics*. Oxford

Crombie, I. M. (1962–3) *An Examination of Plato's Doctrines* (2 vols.). London

Cross, R. C. and Woozley, A. D. (1964) *Plato's Republic: a Philosophical Commentary*. London

Dassmann, E. et alii (eds.) (1991) *Reallexicon für Antike und Christentum: Sachwörterbuch zur Auseinandersetzung des Christentums mit der antiken Welt*, Band 15. Stuttgart

Davidson, D. (1969) 'How is weakness of the will possible?' in Feinberg (1969), 93–113

Dawson, D. (1996) *The Origins of Western Warfare: Militarism and Morality in the Ancient World*. Boulder, Colorado

De Lacy, P. (ed.) (1977–84) *Galen: de Placitis Hippocratis et Platonis*, with tr. and comm. (3 vols.). Berlin

Delatte, A. (ed.) (1922) *La Vie de Pythagore de Diogène Laërce*. Brussels

Dent, N. J. H. (1981) 'The value of courage', *Philosophy* 56: 574–7

(1984) *The Moral Psychology of the Virtues*. Cambridge

Dodds, E. R. (1951) *The Greeks and the Irrational*. Berkeley

(ed.) (1959) *Gorgias*. Oxford

Dover, K. J. (1974) *Greek Popular Morality in the Time of Plato and Aristotle*. Oxford

(1978) *Greek Homosexuality*. Cambridge, Mass.

(ed.) (1980) *Symposium*. Cambridge

Ewans, M. (tr.) (1996) *Aeschylus: Suppliants and Other Dramas*. London

Falk, W. D. (1969) 'Prudence, temperance and courage', in Feinberg (1969), 114–19

Feinberg, J. (ed.) (1969) *Moral Concepts*. Oxford

Ferrari, G. R. F. (1987) *Listening to the Cicadas: a Study of Plato's Phaedrus*. Cambridge

(1990) '*Akrasia* as neurosis in Plato's *Protagoras*', *Proceedings of the Boston Colloquium in Ancient Philosophy* 6: 115–40

Festugière, A. (1971) 'Les trois vies', in *Etudes de philosophie greque*, 117–56. Paris

Flanagan, O. and Rorty, A. (eds.) (1990) *Identity, Character and Morality: Essays in Moral Psychology*. Cambridge, Mass.

Foot, P. (ed.) (1967) *Theories of Ethics*. Oxford

(1978) *Virtues and Vices*. Oxford

Foucault, M. (1984) *L'histoire de sexualité* vol. II: *L'usage des plaisirs*. Paris

Foxhall, L. and Salmon, J. (eds.) (1998) *When Men were Men: Masculinity, Power and Identity in Classical Antiquity*. London

Frankfurt, H. G. (1971) 'Freedom of the will and the concept of a person', *Journal of Philosophy* 68: 5–20

French, P. A., Uehling, T. E. and Wettstein, H. K. (eds.) (1988) *Midwest Studies in Philosophy* 13: *Ethical Theory: Character and Virtue*. Notre Dame

Freud, S. (1940–52) *Gesammelte Werke* (17 vols., ed. A. Freud). London

(1984) 'On narcissism: an introduction' (1914), 'Mourning and melancholia' (1917) and 'The Ego and the Id' (1923), in A. Richards (ed.) *The Penguin Freud Library* vol. 11: *On Metapsychology: the Theory of Psychoanalysis*. Harmondsworth

Gibbs, B. (1986) 'Higher and lower pleasures', *Philosophy* 61: 31–59

Gill, C. (ed.) (1990) *The Person and the Human Mind: Issues in Ancient and Modern Philosophy*. Oxford

(1996) *Personality in Greek Epic, Tragedy and Philosophy: the Self in Dialogue*. Oxford

Goffman, E. (1959) *The Presentation of Self in Everyday Life*. New York

(1967) *Interaction Ritual: Essays on Face-to-Face Behavior*. New York

(1969) *Strategic Interaction*. Philadelphia

Gosling, J. C. B. (1973) *Plato*. London

Gosling, J. C. B. and Taylor, C. C. W. (1982) *The Greeks on Pleasure*. Oxford

Gottschalk, H. B. (1980) *Heraclides of Pontus*. Oxford

Graeser, A. (ed.) (1987) *Mathematik und Metaphysik bei Aristoteles*. Berne

Grant, M. (1970) *Nero*. London

Griffin, James (1986) *Well-Being*. Oxford

Griffin, Jasper (1980) *Homer on Life and Death*. Oxford

Guthrie, W. K. C. (1962, 1969 and 1975) *A History of Greek Philosophy* vols. I, III and IV. Cambridge

(1971) *The Sophists* (= Guthrie 1969). Cambridge

Halliwell, S. (1984) 'Plato and Aristotle on the denial of tragedy', *Proceedings of the Cambridge Philological Society*, 30: 49–71

Hammond, N. G. L. (1981) *Alexander the Great: King, Commander and Statesman*. London

(1983) *Three Historians of Alexander the Great: Diodorus, Justine and Curtius*. Cambridge

Hampshire, S. (1983) *Morality and Conflict*. Oxford

Hardie, W. F. R. (1936) *A Study in Plato*. Oxford

Harrison, E. L. (1960) 'Notes on Homeric psychology', *Phoenix* 14: 63–80

Heinimann, F. (1945) *Nomos und Physis*. Basle

Hollis, M. (1995) 'The shape of a life', in Altham and Harrison (1995), 170–84

Hubbard, B. A. F. and Karnofsky, E. S. (eds. and trs.) (1982) *Plato's Protagoras: A Socratic Commentary*. London

Irwin, T. H. (1977) *Plato's Moral Theory*. Oxford

(tr. and ed.) (1979) *Plato: Gorgias*. Oxford

(1988) 'Socrates and the tragic hero', in Pucci (1988), 55–83

(1995) *Plato's Ethics*. Oxford

Jacoby, F. (1923–) *Fragmente der Griechischen Historiker*. Berlin and Leiden

Jaeger, W. (1943) *Paideia: the Ideals of Greek Culture* vol. II tr. G. Highet. Oxford

(1948) 'On the origin and cycle of the philosophic ideal of life', appendix to W. Jaeger *Aristotle* 2nd edition. London

Joly, R. (1956) *Le Thème philosophique des genres de vie dans l'antiquité classique*. Brussels

Joseph, H. W. B. (1935) *Essays in Ancient and Modern Philosophy*. Oxford

Kalin, J. (1977) 'Philosophy needs literature: John Barth and moral nihilism', *Philosophy and Literature* 1: 170–82

Kenny, A. (1973) 'Mental health in Plato's *Republic*', in *The Anatomy of the Soul*, 1–27. Oxford

Kerferd, G. B. (1947) 'The doctrine of Thrasymachus in Plato's *Republic*', *Durham University Journal* 40: 19–27, reprinted in Classen (1976), 545–63

   (1974) 'Plato's treatment of Callicles in the *Gorgias*', *Proceedings of the Cambridge Philological Society* 20: 48–52

   (1981) *The Sophistic Movement*. Cambridge

Kirk, G. S. (1970) *Myth: its Meaning and Functions in Ancient and Other Cultures*. Berkeley and Cambridge

Knox, B. (1964) *The Heroic Temper: Studies in Sophoclean Tragedy*. Berkeley

Kock, T. (ed.) (1880–8) *Comicorum Atticorum Fragmenta* (2 vols.). Leipzig

Kraut, R. (1973) 'Reason and justice in Plato's *Republic*', in Lee, Mourelatos and Rorty (1973), 207–24

   (ed.) (1992) *The Cambridge Companion to Plato*. Cambridge

   (ed.) (1997) *Plato's Republic: Critical Essays*. Lanham, Maryland

Kruschwitz, R. B. and Roberts, R. C. (eds.) (1987) *The Virtues: Contemporary Essays on Moral Character*. Belmont, California

Kupperman, J. (1988) 'Character and ethical theory', in French, Uehling and Wettstein (1988), 115–25

Lamb, W. R. M. (tr.) (1924) *Plato: Laches, Protagoras, Meno, Euthydemus*. Cambridge, Mass.

   (1925) *Plato: Lysis, Symposium, Gorgias*. Cambridge, Mass.

Labarbe, J. (1949) *L'Homère de Platon*. Paris

Lane Fox, R. (1973) *Alexander the Great*. London

Lattimore, R. (1969) *The Iliad of Homer* (tr. with introduction). Chicago

Lear, J. (1992) 'Inside and outside the *Republic*', *Phronesis* 37: 184–215

Lee, D. (1974) *Plato: Republic* (tr. with introduction). Harmondsworth

Lee, E. N., Mourelatos, A. P. D. and Rorty, R. M. (eds.) (1973) *Exegesis and Argument: Studies in Greek Philosophy Presented to Gregory Vlastos* (*Phronesis* Supplement 1). Assen

Liddell, H. G., Scott, R. and Jones, H. S. (1953) *A Greek–English Lexicon* (9th edition). Oxford

Livingstone, E. A. (ed.) (1984) *Studia Patristica* vol. 15. Berlin

Lloyd, A. B. (ed.) (1996) *Battle in Antiquity*. London

Lohse, G. (1964) 'Untersuchungen über Homerzitate bei Platon I', *Helikon* 4: 3–28

   (1965) 'Untersuchungen über Homerzitate bei Platon II', *Helikon* 5: 248–95

   (1967) 'Untersuchungen über Homerzitate bei Platon III', *Helikon* 7: 223–31

Louden, R. B. (1984) 'On some vices of virtue ethics', *American Philosophical Quarterly* 21: 227–36

MacIntyre, A. (1985) *After Virtue: a Study in Moral Theory* (2nd edition). London

Mackenzie, M. M. (1978) 'The tears of Chryses: retaliation in the *Iliad*', *Philosophy and Literature* 2: 3–22

Mackie, J. L. (1977) *Ethics: Inventing Right and Wrong*. Harmondsworth

Magee, B. (1978) *Men of Ideas*. New York

Marrou, G. (1948) *Histoire de l'education dans l'antiquité*. Paris

Mill, J. S. (1863) *Utilitarianism*. London

Moline, J. (1981) *Plato's Theory of Understanding*. Madison, WI.

Moravcsik, J. M. E. (1971) 'Reason and eros in the "ascent"-passage of the *Symposium*', in Anton and Kustas (1971), 285–302

Moravcsik, J. M. E. and Temko, P. (eds.) (1982) *Plato on Beauty, Wisdom and the Arts*. Totowa, New Jersey

Morrison, J. S. (1958) 'The origins of Plato's Philosopher-Statesman', *Classical Quarterly* n.s. 8: 198–218

Murdoch, I. (1970) *The Sovereignty of Good*. London

(1977) *The Fire and the Sun: Why Plato Banished the Artists*. Oxford

Murdoch, I. and Magee, B. (1978) 'Philosophy and literature: dialogue with Iris Murdoch', in Magee (1978), 229–50

Murray, P. (ed.) (1996) *Plato on Poetry*. Cambridge

Nauck, A. (ed.) (1964) *Tragicorum Graecorum Fragmenta* (reprinted with supplement by B. Snell). Hildesheim

Nagy, G. (1979) *The Best of the Achaeans: Concepts of the Hero in Archaic Greek Poetry*. Baltimore

Nehamas, A. (1982) 'Plato on imitation and poetry in *Republic* 10', in Moravcsik and Temko (1982), 47–78

(1985) *Nietzsche: Life as Literature*. Cambridge, Mass.

(1998) *The Art of Living: Socratic Reflections from Plato to Foucault*. Berkeley and Los Angeles

Nettleship, R. L. (1935) *The Theory of Education in Plato's Republic*. Oxford

Nietzsche, F. (1930) *Der Wille zur Macht*. Leipzig

(1961) *Thus Spoke Zarathustra*, tr. R. J. Hollingdale. Harmondsworth

(1967–) *Werke; kritische Gesamtausgabe* (eds. G. Colli and M. Montinari *et alii*). Berlin

(1968a) *On the Genealogy of Morals*, trs. W. Kaufmann and R. J. Hollingdale (in *Basic Writings of Nietzsche*). New York

(1968b) *The Will to Power*, trs. W. Kaufmann and R. J. Hollingdale. New York

(1973) *Beyond Good and Evil*, tr. R. J. Hollingdale. Harmondsworth

(1974) *The Gay Science*, tr. W. Kaufmann. New York

North, H. F. (1966) *Sophrosune: Self-Knowledge and Self-Restraint in Greek Literature*. New York

Nussbaum, M. C. (1986) *The Fragility of Goodness*. Cambridge

(1988) 'Non-relative virtues: an Aristotelian approach', in French, Uehling and Wettstein (1988), 32–53

(1995) 'Aristotle on human nature and the foundations of ethics', in Altham and Harrison (1995), 86–131

Okin, S. M. (1979) *Women in Western Political Thought*. Princeton
Oldfather, C. H. (tr.) (1946) *Diodorus Siculus*: vol. IV. Cambridge, Mass.
Onians, R. (1951) *The Origins of European Thought*. Cambridge
Oppenheimer, K. (1936) 'Thrasymachos', in Pauly–Wissowa (1936), VI. 1: 584–92
Parfit, D. (1984) *Reasons and Persons*. Oxford
Passmore, J. (1970) *The Perfectibility of Man*. London
Pauly–Wissowa (1936) *Encyclopädie*. Stuttgart
Penner, T. (1971) 'Thought and desire in Plato', in Vlastos (1971), 96–118
    (1973) 'The unity of virtue', *Philosophical Review* 82: 35–68
    (1992) 'Socrates and the early dialogues', in Kraut (1992), 121–69
Peristiany, J. (1965) 'Honour and shame in a Cypriot highland village', in Peristiany (1965), 171–90
    (ed.) (1965) *Honour and Shame: the Values of Mediterranean Society*. London
Pitt-Rivers, J. (1965) 'Honour and social status', in Peristiany (1965), 19–78
Popper, K. R. (1966) *The Open Society and its Enemies vol. 1: the Spell of Plato* (5th edition). New York
Price, A. W. (1989) *Love and Friendship in Plato and Aristotle*. Oxford
    (1990) 'Plato and Freud', in Gill (1990), 247–70
Procopé, J. (1984) 'Quiet Christian courage: a topic in Clemens Alexandrinus and its philosophical background', in Livingstone (1984), 489–94
    (1991) 'Hochherzigkeit (μεγαλοψυχία)' in Dassmann et alii (eds.) (1991), 765–95
    (unpublished paper) 'Attitudes to anger: a sinew of the soul'
Pucci, P. (ed.) (1988) *Language and the Tragic Hero*. Atlanta
Race, W. (tr. and ed.) (1997) *Pindar 1: Olympian Odes, Pythian Odes*. Cambridge, Mass.
Rackham, H. (tr.) (1926) *Aristotle: Nicomachean Ethics*. Cambridge, Mass.
Robinson, T. M. (1995) *Plato's Psychology* (2nd edition). Toronto
Rorty, A. (ed.) (1976) *The Identities of Persons*. Berkeley
    (ed.) (1980) *Essays on Aristotle's Ethics*. Berkeley
    (1988) 'Virtues and their vicissitudes', in French, Uehling and Wettstein (1988), 136–48
Rutherford, R. B. (1995) *The Art of Plato*. London
Ryle, G. (1954) 'Pleasure', *Proceedings of the Aristotelian Society* supp. vol. 28: 135–46. Reprinted in Feinberg (1969), 1–28
Sachs, D. (1963) 'A fallacy in Plato's *Republic*', *Philosophical Review* 72: 141–58
Salmon, J. (1977) 'Political hoplites?', *Journal of Hellenic Studies* 97: 84–101
Santas, G. (1988) *Plato and Freud: Two Theories of Love*. Oxford
Saxonhouse, A. W. (1997) 'The philosopher and the female in the political thought of Plato', in Kraut (1997), 95–113
Schofield, M. 'Εὐβουλία in the *Iliad*', *Classical Quarterly* n.s. 36: 6–31

Settis, S. (ed.) (1996) *I Greci II.* Turin

Shewring, W. (trans.) (1980) *Homer: The Odyssey.* Oxford

Sommerstein, A. H. (tr. and ed.) (1996) *Aristophanes: Frogs.* Warminster

Sorabji, R. (1993) *Animal Minds and Human Morals.* London

Sprague, R. K. (tr. and ed.) (1992) *Plato: Laches.* Indianapolis

Stanford, W. (1954) *The Ulysses Theme.* Oxford

Stocker, M. (1976) 'The schizophrenia of modern ethical theories', *Journal of Philosophy* 73: 453–66

Stocks, J. (1915), 'Plato and the tripartite soul', *Mind* 24: 207–21

Stokes, M. C. (1986) *Plato's Socratic Conversations: Drama and Dialectic in Three Dialogues.* London

Taylor, C. (1976) 'Responsibility for self', in Rorty (1976), 281–99
    (1989) *Sources of the Self: the Making of the Modern Identity.* Cambridge

Taylor, C. C. W. (tr. and ed.) (1991) *Plato: Protagoras* (revised edition). Oxford

Tejera, V. (1987) *Nietzsche and Greek Thought.* Dordrecht

Thomson, J. A. K. (tr.) (1976) *Aristotle: Ethics* (revised with notes and appendices by H. Tredennick, with introduction and bibliography by J. Barnes). Harmondsworth

Trianosky, G. (1990) 'What is virtue ethics all about?', *American Philosophical Quarterly* 27: 335–44

Urmson, J. O. (1969) 'Saints and heroes', in Feinberg (1969), 60–73
    (1982) 'Plato and the poets', in Moravcsik and Temko (1982), 125–36

Vlastos, G. (1969) 'Socrates on acrasia', *Phoenix* 23: 71–88
    (ed.) (1971) *Plato* (2 volumes). New York
    (1981a) 'The unity of the virtues in the *Protagoras*', in Vlastos (1981c), 221–69
    (1981b) 'The individual as object of love in Plato', in Vlastos (1981c), 3–42
    (1981c) *Platonic Studies* (2nd edition). Princeton
    (1984) 'Happiness and virtue in Socrates' moral theory', *Proceedings of the Cambridge Philological Society* n.s. 30: 181–213
    (1991) *Socrates: Ironist and Moral Philosopher.* Ithaca
    (1994a) 'The *Protagoras* and the *Laches*', in Vlastos (1994b), 109–126
    (1994b) *Socratic Studies* (ed. M. Burnyeat). Cambridge

Wallace, J. D. (1978) *Virtues and Vices.* Ithaca and London

Walton, D. N. (1986) *Courage: a Philosophical Inquiry.* Berkeley
    (1990) 'Courage, relativism and practical reasoning', *Philosophia* 20: 227–40

Ward Scaltsas, P. (1992) 'Virtue without gender in Socrates', *Hypatia* 7: 126–37

Warner, R. (tr.) (1954) *Thucydides: The Peloponnesian War.* Harmondsworth, Middlesex

Watson, G. (1975) 'Free agency', *Journal of Philosophy* 72: 205–20 (reprinted in Watson 1982)
    (ed.) (1982) *Free Will.* Oxford

Wees, H. van (1992) *Status Warriors: War, Violence, Homer and History*.
    Amsterdam
  (1996) 'Heroes, knights and nutters: warrior mentality in Homer', in
    Lloyd (1996), 1–86
West, M. L. (ed.) (1989–92) *Iambi at Elegi Graeci* (2nd edition). Oxford
Williams, B (1973a) 'The analogy of city and soul in Plato's *Republic*', in
    Lee, Mourelatos and Rorty (1973), 196–206
  (1973b) 'Egoism and altruism', in Williams (1973c), 250–65
  (1973c) *Problems of the Self*. Cambridge
  (1981) *Moral Luck*. Cambridge
  (1985) *Ethics and the Limits of Philosophy*. London
  (1993) *Shame and Necessity*. Berkeley
Winkler, J. (1990) *The Constraints of Desire*. London
Wolf, S. (1982) 'Moral saints', *Journal of Philosophy* 79: 412–39
Woodruff, P. (1982) 'What could go wrong with inspiration? Why Plato's
    poets fail', in Moravcsik and Temko (1982), 137–50
Woods, M. (1987) 'Plato's division of the soul', *Proceedings of the British
    Academy* 73: 23–48
Wright, G. H. von (1963) *The Varieties of Goodness*. London
Zuckert, C. H. (ed.) (1988) *Understanding the Political Spirit: Philosophical
    Investigations from Socrates to Nietzsche*. Yale

Index

The following references are not intended to supply complete coverage of each heading, but simply to act as a guide to the most important discussions and citations. This applies particularly to such ubiquitous and interrelated themes as *andreia*, *thumos*, role models, the *kalon* and *mousikē*. Further assistance can be found in the Contents pages.